KINGFISH U

KINGFISH U

HUEY LONG AND LSU

ROBERT MANN

LOUISIANA STATE UNIVERSITY PRESS

BATON ROUGE

Published with the assistance of the Manship Chair
in Journalism Endowment at Louisiana State University

Published by Louisiana State University Press
lsupress.org

Manufactured in the United States of America
First printing

Designers: Barbara Neely Bourgoyne & Michelle A. Neustrom
Typeface: Sentinel
Printer and binder: Sheridan Books, Inc.

Cover photograph: Huey Long and LSU cadets on October 26, 1934, before their
departure for LSU's football game with Vanderbilt. (LSU Special Collections)

Library of Congress Cataloging-in-Publication Data
Names: Mann, Robert, author.
Title: Kingfish U : Huey Long and LSU / Robert Mann.
Description: Baton Rouge : Louisiana State University Press, [2023] |
    Includes bibliographical references and index.
Identifiers: LCCN 2022045455 (print) | LCCN 2022045456 (ebook) |
    ISBN 978-0-8071-7952-9 (cloth) | ISBN 978-0-8071-8002-0 (pdf) |
    ISBN 978-0-8071-8001-3 (epub)
Subjects: LCSH: Long, Huey Pierce, 1893–1935. | Louisiana State University
    and Agricultural and Mechanical College—History—20th century. |
    Louisiana State University and Agricultural and Mechanical College—
    Football. | LSU Tigers (Football team)—History—20th century. |
    Louisiana—Politics and government—1865–1950.
Classification: LCC LD3113 .M36 2023 (print) | LCC LD3113 (ebook) |
    DDC 378.763/18—dc23/eng/20220930
LC record available at https://lccn.loc.gov/2022045455
LC ebook record available at https://lccn.loc.gov/2022045456

For Stan Tiner

CONTENTS

List of Illustrations | ix

Preface | xi

Acknowledgments | xvii

1 I Want a Band | 1

2 I Am on My Way | 7

3 The Father of LSU | 16

4 This Temple of Vanity | 28

5 We Must Get a President | 37

6 I Don't Fool Around with Losers | 48

7 The *Whangdoodle* | 57

8 I Did My Damndest | 66

9 A Cow College | 79

10 You Have to Dare a Bit | 90

11 *Cane Juice* | 102

12 What Does the Band Think? | 108

13 I Want a Play | 114

14 Sell Them Plugs | 124

15 Who Is That Awful Man? | 136

16 Tell Them They Can Go to Hell | 142

17 A Laughingstock | 151

18 It Was Huey Long's University | 159

19 I. O. Huey | 170

20 Senator Abe Mickal | 183

21 The *Reveille* Seven | 191

22 That Bunch of Buzzards and Varmints | 205

23 Hollywood's Idea of a University | 213

24 Make Them Steal for the Schools | 225

25 Blood on the Polished Marble | 235

26 The Second Louisiana Purchase | 244

27 The Louisiana Scandals | 251

Conclusion: Neither Saint nor Devil | 263

Notes | 271

Bibliography | 311

Index | 321

ILLUSTRATIONS

Fred Frey, dean of LSU's School of Arts and Sciences in the 1930s | 3

Huey Long as a young man | 11

Louisiana governor John M. Parker | 18

Map of the old LSU campus | 18

LSU president Thomas D. Boyd | 32

The LSU campus in the late 1930s | 33

Colonel Campbell B. Hodges | 40

LSU president Thomas Atkinson | 43

LSU assistant football coach Harry Rabenhorst | 45

LSU Law School dean Robert L. Tullis | 55

Front page of the *Whangdoodle* | 59

LSU student Kemble K. Kennedy of Farmerville | 61

LSU head football coach Russell Cohen | 67

Long with referees in Tiger Stadium | 69

Long with LSU president James Monroe Smith | 72

Arthur Vidrine, head of New Orleans Charity Hospital and dean of LSU's
Medical School | 88

LSU's Music and Dramatic Arts Building | 92

LSU English professor John Earle Uhler and Major Troy Middleton | 104

LSU athletic director Skipper Heard and dean of administration James
Broussard | 116

Louisiana governor Oscar K. Allen with Long | 128

Tiger Stadium in the late 1920s | 130

LSU student Elena Carter Percy and LSU president James
    Monroe Smith | 131

LSU's Huey P. Long Field House | 132

The swimming pool of the Huey P. Long Field House | 132

Long with his elder son, Russell | 135

Long leads LSU Band parade in Houston in 1932 | 138

LSU's Smith Hall | 147

Long on sideline at an LSU-Tulane game | 157

LSU Band members and students in the Greek Theatre | 174

Long speaks to LSU students in the Greek Theatre | 175

Long hands out cash to students in the Greek Theatre | 175

Long and the LSU Regimental Band at the band hall | 176

Long and LSU cadets in Baton Rouge | 176

Long leads the LSU Band and Cadet Corps in Nashville | 177

Long directs the LSU Band in Nashville | 177

LSU star halfback Abe Mickal | 188

The staff of the LSU student paper, the *Reveille* | 196

Long and Mississippi governor Sennet "Mike" Conner | 207

LSU student Joe Cawthon of Logansport | 209

Long with LSU head football coach Lawrence "Biff" Jones | 210

LSU head football coach Bernie Moore | 217

LSU Band director Castro Carazo | 219

Louisiana governor Richard Leche | 247

LSU Band spells out "WPA" in Tiger Stadium | 249

PREFACE

I n late 2019, Louisiana governor John Bel Edwards was in a tough runoff against his Republican challenger. Edwards was a conservative Democrat who some believed won his first race because a sex scandal had weakened his opponent. Now, as the incumbent, he was in a stronger position. But Louisiana was a Republican state, and he needed help. So, he turned to the popular LSU football coach, Ed Orgeron.

Edwards and Orgeron first met two years earlier at a duck-hunting camp near the coach's birthplace in Lafourche Parish. The football coach and the governor became fast friends. Edwards invited Orgeron and his wife to functions at the Governor's Mansion. And the former Amite High School quarterback began attending LSU team practices, where he tossed the ball with players and delivered pep talks. He boasted about texting so often with Orgeron that he could predict the quality of LSU's performance by the tone of the coach's pregame messages. The two men were so friendly that, by April 2019, Orgeron introduced Edwards at a political event. Orgeron's praise for Edwards angered Republican Louisiana US senator John N. Kennedy, who denounced the coach's venture into politics.[1]

Those steeped in Louisiana political history noted it was not the first mingling of Louisiana politics and LSU football. Edwards's predecessor, Bobby Jindal, embraced Orgeron's predecessor, Les Miles. In fact, Jindal intervened in 2015 to save Miles's job when LSU's athletic director considered firing the coach. Jindal tweeted that his friend was "a great coach and a better man. He is a fantastic ambassador for our state. I hope he remains our coach." Miles's position was secure for a few more years. Days later, when Jindal held a fundraiser for his presidential campaign, a grateful Miles attended.[2]

Several generations earlier, in 1977, Governor Edwin Edwards had resisted being drawn into the politics of LSU football. He implored fans to stop demanding he fire Coach Charles McClendon. "I don't have the power to hire or fire a coach," Edwards said, "and even if I did, I would not involve myself. So don't call me." In 1983, before he began his third term, however, Edwards finally succumbed to the temptation to meddle with LSU football. He announced an ill-conceived, short-lived plan for a $1 million trust fund to supplement the LSU coach's salary. Some suspected a plot to push out then-coach Jerry Stovall for a higher-profile candidate. Whatever the case, LSU officials rejected Edwards's idea. When the university fired Stovall six years later, his foremost defender was LSU Board member and former governor John McKeithen.[3]

Louisiana governors, before Edwards, trumpeted their love for LSU and its football team in other ways. Governor Jimmie Davis watched LSU football games from the sidelines. Earl Long, Davis, and McKeithen all recruited football prospects. McKeithen, an LSU graduate, enjoyed being called "Coach" for his devotion to the players. The top recruits during his two terms in the 1960s often went to the Governor's Mansion, where "Big John" feted them with a hearty breakfast. "If they ask mah help, I give it fast," McKeithen explained when asked about his role with the team. "If Charlie Mac [McClendon] wants me to talk to a boy, I'm on the phone to his mommy and daddy one minute after the coach hangs up." McKeithen was so upset by the Tigers' 1970 loss to Texas A&M in Tiger Stadium that he reportedly punched out a window in his state car. McKeithen's political mentor, Earl Long, basked in the reflected glory of LSU football by holding his 1948 inauguration in Tiger Stadium. Long assured the crowd he would make LSU "the finest [university] in the country, with the best football team and band." That night, Long hosted his inaugural ball in the LSU Coliseum.[4]

That LSU—particularly LSU football—and Louisiana politics are intertwined is a fact in the Bayou State. It has been thus for almost one hundred years and is unlikely to change. And the tension between academics and athletics on the LSU campus is another established fact that is also likely to persist. Contemporary political and social critics observe that the big money of athletics has corrupted many universities—and they are correct. But this commentary often overlooks a crucial element about sports at large universities like LSU—one that this book addresses: Football has dominated college campuses since the days coaches were paid a relative pittance, and players had no scholarships and worked to pay for room and board. College football is about the money, to be sure, but it was big, overpowering, and attractive to politicians decades before the money flowed. And the conflict between the academic and the athletic sides of campuses is nothing new.

The exploits of LSU's football team have almost always received more attention than the successes of the English or history departments. In December 1950, long before LSU football games were televised and money poured in for athletics, the tension between the two sides exploded. LSU president Harold Stoke relented after a bitter dispute with Athletic Director Thomas "Skipper" Heard, who had overseen LSU athletics since the days of Huey Long. Heard had proposed financing several Tiger Stadium expansions in the 1930s by using state money to build dormitory space under the bleachers. Now, in a conflict with Heard over whether to prioritize construction of a new campus library or a $1.5 million expansion of Tiger Stadium, Stoke stood no chance. Heard favored the stadium and stood his ground. Stoke resigned.[5]

Stoke learned a hard lesson that Stanley Tiner, my former editor at the *Shreveport Journal,* considered in 1983. "You will always hear a great deal of rhetoric about the twin goals of academic and athletic excellence at [LSU]," he wrote in a column. "Make no mistake, dear hearts, the first goal is always likely to be a winning football and basketball team. Then we will talk about academics. You may decry the cross-pollinization [*sic*] of education and politics that exists in Louisiana, but all of the decrying in the world is not likely to change its nature. It is a part of the very character of this state and its people."[6]

As a faculty member at LSU for over seventeen years, I have fulminated often about the excessive influence of football, and to a lesser extent basketball and baseball, on my campus. I hesitate to accept it as a permanent fact, although I concede it probably is. I hope this book helps readers understand the origins of the LSU version of this dichotomy about which Tiner and others have written.

My journey into this history began with a phone call. In the early spring of 2020, Dan Borné, the voice of LSU's Tiger Stadium, asked me if I knew how Huey Long had selected LSU's drum majors. I recalled something about this from reading T. Harry Williams's Pulitzer Prize–winning biography of Long over thirty years earlier. So, I opened Williams's book, *Huey Long,* and reread the chapter on Long and LSU. What Williams described about Long's involvement with the football team and the band was more outrageous than I remembered. My first thought was that someone should write a book that elaborated on the story that Williams and others have told in part. My second thought was that it *must* be me. Soon, I was neck deep in Long-LSU lore.

I knew Long was important to LSU's rapid growth in the 1930s. I recalled he was obsessed with the football team and the band. I knew his emphasis on building a bigger, better LSU resulted in hiring extraordinary faculty members, like Robert Penn Warren and Cleanth Brooks. I remembered that, because of Long's support, the university had the resources in the mid-1930s to create the *Southern Review* and LSU Press. I also knew about dramatic events after Long's death, when LSU became embroiled in a scandal so large that President James Monroe Smith went to prison, as did Governor Richard Leche.

But I did not know the entire story. I now understand better the origins of Louisiana's mania for LSU football and why generations of political leaders have sought to establish a cultural affinity with fans by supporting the team and befriending—and sometimes firing—the coaches. More than anything, I discovered that LSU—the school where I teach, from which my wife graduated, and which my children, Robert and Avery, attended as I wrote this book—would not be the institution it is today, for good or ill, without Long.

Others played a crucial role in LSU's creation and development. Many of them—including Thomas D. Boyd, Thomas Atkinson, Fred Frey, and governors John M. Parker and O. K. Allen—have their names on prominent buildings on campus. Others, most notably Leche, had their names removed from buildings. But no name was more important than Long's. Although he did not attend LSU—and even attacked one of his predecessors, John Parker, for his leadership in establishing the current campus—Long became the school's greatest fan, its leading cheerleader, its most enthusiastic benefactor, and its biggest meddler.

Long's death at forty-two helped secure his mostly positive legacy at LSU. Many of his allies went to prison, but Long's assassination in September 1935 elevated him to near sainthood and protected him from direct association with the criminal behavior that state and federal authorities uncovered at LSU in 1939 and 1940. Long's death also ended several investigations into his undue influence over the university, probes that jeopardized the university's academic standing. But much of the university that stands today exists because of the efforts of Long and the political organization that governed after his death. Simply put, the institution may be called Louisiana State University, but it is also "Kingfish U."

Five notes for readers:

First: I do not tell the complete story of Long's fascinating and momentous life. Other biographers have done this well. I rely on their research, and that of other historians and journalists, but I do not recreate their work. My focus is narrower. I ignore many aspects of Long's life that are irrelevant to his association with LSU. For example, I explain Long's authoritarian impulses and his near-dictatorial control over Louisiana, but I omit details which would detract from my emphasis on LSU. And when I describe Long's assassination, I do so mostly through the eyes of LSU students, faculty, and administrators. I have, however, devoted several chapters to Long's early life and political career, primarily because that period is important to understanding his fraught relationship with LSU—and LSU patron John Parker—in the early 1920s.

Second: Regarding Long's assassination, there has been a vigorous debate for decades about who killed him and why. I do not address this controversy. Instead, I rely on the most widely accepted version of events: Dr. Carl Austin Weiss fired the gun that caused Long's fatal injury, and Long's bodyguards killed Weiss on the spot. I believe Weiss arrived at the Capitol on the night of September 8, 1935, intending to confront Long. Even if events unfolded differently from the official account, there was a meeting of the two men that resulted in their deaths.[7]

Third: The reader should remember that the story of LSU in the 1920s and 1930s is also a story of racism and white supremacy. With one brief exception in the early 1950s, Black undergraduates could not enroll there for its first one hundred years. The school had no Black professor until the early 1970s. I do not remind the reader constantly that I am writing about an all-white student body and faculty. I hope those deplorable facts will be understood.

Fourth: Anyone writing narrative nonfiction, especially about events ninety years in the past, must rely upon the recollections of others to tell the story. I cannot prove that each word in quotes was spoken exactly as represented here. But my rule was not to use a quote unless I believed it was accurate or was a reliable paraphrase from a credible source. Those sources are listed in corresponding footnotes.

Fifth: I never met Long, who died twenty-three years before my birth. But I knew his son, the late Louisiana US senator Russell B. Long. I served as Russell Long's press secretary in the mid-1980s and wrote a book about him. Huey Long's granddaughter, Kay Long, is a friend, as are two of Long's great-grandchildren. My interest in Huey Long emanates partly from my decades-long association with his family. I have labored to keep my affection for his descendants from influencing my portrayal of him. I also acknowledge that I have always found Long among the most fascinating, complex, and confounding political figures in American history. What I write may not be received warmly by the Long family. Others may conclude that I treat Long too favorably. Whatever the case, I have attempted to remain as objective as possible about him.

Beyond my interest in Long, I wrote this book because I wanted to learn more about the history of the institution where I teach and which I love for all the ways it has contributed to the richness of Louisiana life. My research reminded me, however, about the dangers of over-politicizing a state university and the damage that political leaders can inflict on a university when they use it for self-aggrandizement or plunder. That research also reminded me of the good that politicians can do when they decide to create something large and remarkable out of something small and middling. That is the story of LSU, which, during the 1930s, went from mediocrity to near-excellence, and then to near-ruin. I hope this book is a reminder that, if state leaders desire, they can make LSU great again, and quickly. They can also weaken it, which happened during the severe state budget cuts of 2009–14.

My friend and former LSU faculty colleague James Carville has long maintained that no public university is more important to the intellectual and cultural life of its state than LSU. I do not know if he is correct, but I believe that, whatever ails Louisiana, LSU could play a role in the cure. Other Louisiana universities have significant roles to play, but, as the flagship university, LSU is the school best positioned to lead Louisiana into better days. I hope, in some small way, to remind readers of the greatness that is possible at LSU if Louisiana's leaders ever again resolve to make it happen.

ACKNOWLEDGMENTS

I am grateful for all the help, encouragement, and counsel of friends and colleagues during my work on this book. No one deserves more gratitude than Dan Borné, who gave me the idea for this story when he asked a question about Huey Long and LSU. Dan not only encouraged me to write the book but also reviewed the manuscript in its early stages and volunteered many helpful suggestions.

Others who read all or part of the manuscript and offered useful critiques were Ron Garay, Jack McGuire, Jay Shelledy, Christina Georgacopoulos, Bob Ritter, Richard White, Stan Tiner, Michael Desmond, David Ferris, Margaret O'Rourke, Melissa Kim, Chance Townsend, Lamar White, Kacey Buercklin, and Gloria Weaver. I am also grateful to the anonymous reviewers who read the manuscript and made excellent suggestions for improving it.

The amazing professionals who make up the Special Collections staff at the Hill Memorial Library at LSU were especially supportive of my research. They include Zach Tompkins, Germain Bienvenu, Amanda Hawk, Mark Martin, John David Miles, and Leah Wood Jewett. I am also indebted to the Interlibrary Loan staff at the LSU Library, the Louisiana State Library staff, and the Special Collections staff at the Tulane University Library.

Several students at the Manship School of Mass Communication at LSU helped with my research. They were Zach Roubein, Sarah Procopio, Corinne Chandler, Melissa Kim, Chance Townsend, Mia LeJeune, and Margaret O'Rourke. Margaret, Chance, and Kacey Buercklin also spent months fact-checking the manuscript, saving me from many embarrassing errors. Whatever remain are my responsibility alone.

Those who provided personal memories or helpful suggestions about the story of Huey Long and LSU included: Julia Welles Hawkins, Nina Carazo Snapp, Kay Long, Florent "Pon" Hardy, Russell Long Mosely, and Audra Mc-Cardle Snider. Especially helpful was Jack McGuire, who not only offered suggestions regarding several chapters but also shared documents from his personal papers. Jack's remarkable collection of Huey Long papers, donated to the Tulane University Library, were invaluable, as were those of his father, David R. McGuire, also held by Tulane. At LSU Press, I appreciate the support and professionalism of Alisa Plant, James Long, Rand Dotson, Catherine Kadair, James Wilson, and Sunny Rosen. I am also grateful for the eagle eyes of copy editor Stan Ivester.

The title of this book came from a chapter in Thomas F. Ruffin's *Under Stately Oaks: A Pictorial History of LSU,* a fine and entertaining read for anyone who wants to learn more about LSU's history.

Stanley Tiner, to whom I dedicate this book, helped pave the way for my happy and productive professional life. In 1983, Stan took a chance on a young newspaper reporter and gave him the best assignment in Louisiana politics—the governor's race between Edwin Edwards and Dave Treen. His confidence in me, and the opportunities that came with it, changed my life. Although I have not worked for Stan in almost forty years, he and his wife, Vickie, remain treasured friends.

I'm also thankful for the financial support of the Manship family, which endowed the chair I hold at LSU. Every book I have written since joining the LSU faculty in 2006 was made possible by the Manships' generous support.

Finally, I am grateful to my wife, Cindy, for all the ways she loves me and supports my writing and my teaching. For more than a year, during most of our evening walks, she cheerfully listened to my stories about Huey Long and LSU. Every writer should have such a loving and supportive sounding board, partner, and friend.

KINGFISH U

1

I WANT A BAND

When the well-dressed man burst into the LSU president's office in the South Administration Building (now David F. Boyd Hall) one afternoon in early November 1930, the young secretary, Granville Ober, recognized him instantly. He was the state's governor, Huey P. Long. The thirty-seven-year-old chief executive was ending his third year in office and had recently won a seat in the US Senate. His image—a round, pudgy face with a cleft chin, and his head covered with wavy reddish-brown hair or his signature fedora—was often in the local papers. A commerce major from Monroe and president of women students at LSU, Ober worked part-time in President Thomas Atkinson's office. She often greeted prominent visitors. But she was wholly unprepared for the brash, impatient tidal wave that was Huey Long.

Long asked to see Atkinson. Ober informed him the sixty-three-year-old president was home recovering from the flu. Annoyed, Long asked for the university's business manager, Robert L. Himes, a frugal administrator many at LSU called "Tighty." Ober scurried to a nearby building to locate Himes, but learned he was gone, too, visiting the school's "old campus," just north of downtown Baton Rouge. Ober returned to Atkinson's office to find an agitated governor pacing the room and rapping a table with his gold-headed Malacca walking stick.

"Governor," a nervous Ober told Long, "Mr. Himes is on the old campus, and I can't locate him."

"This is a hell of a note," Long sputtered. "The governor comes out here to try to do business and to talk to the president and he is not here, and the business manager is not here. Is there anyone out here I can talk to?"

Panicking, Ober raced back next door to see Fred Frey, a thirty-nine-year-old sociology professor who had become LSU's dean of men that summer. Ober knocked on Frey's open door. "Won't you come over and talk to the governor?" she pleaded through tears. "He came to see the president. He's ill. Then, he wanted Mr. Himes. I can't find him. He is just talking something awful and beating on the table with his walking stick, and I don't know what to do."

When Frey arrived, Ober introduced him to Long, who studied the slender dean for a moment before announcing, "I come out here to talk to the president and I have to talk to a damn kid." A native of nearby Tangipahoa Parish and a former US Army major with a PhD from the University of Minnesota, Frey was not intimidated by powerful men. Eleven years later, he would tell Governor Sam Jones he could "go straight to hell" when that governor tried to force university officials to hire a crony. To Long's insult, Frey shot back, "Why, Governor, you are quite complimentary. I would like to remind the Governor that I am two years older than the Governor, and so there will be two kids talking to each other."

Long chuckled and relaxed. "Let's get down to business. Where can we talk? Come on, let's go in the president's office." Once inside, he surveyed the room. "You know, this is the first time I've ever been in this office," Long said, before noticing a large wardrobe in one corner. "What the hell is that? Does he keep his liquor in there?" Frey told him "no," as Long threw open the mahogany doors to reveal its contents—a lone umbrella—to which Long scoffed, "Well, that looks like a college professor."

Long plopped into Atkinson's chair, leaned back, and crossed his feet on top of the president's desk. "He had a million-dollar grin if ever I saw one," Frey recalled, adding that Long then asked, "How do you think I would look as president of this damn outfit?"

"I think you would look wonderful, Governor," Frey replied. "You look like a college president."

Finished with these trifles, Long was ready to talk business. "Since I can't get hold of the president, I want you to send for Pop Guilbeau."

Sixty-two-year-old Frank T. "Pop" Guilbeau, a Breaux Bridge native, had directed the LSU Regimental Band since 1918. He also served as the school's superintendent of grounds.

"What's your trouble?" Frey asked.

"I'm going to fire the S.O.B."

Fred Frey was LSU's dean of men and dean of the School of Arts and Sciences in the 1930s. He tangled with Long in November 1930. (LSU Photograph Collection, LSU Special Collections)

"What's the matter?"

"I want a band."

"Well, that's the wrong way to get it," Frey shot back. "I have seen in the paper several times in the last few weeks a statement that you have made publicly that you are going to make a great university of this."

"Yes, that's what I'm getting ready to do."

"No," Frey said, "you are getting ready to ruin it. You can't fire anybody and get away with it. You might be a good politician, but you don't know how to run a university. If you don't think I'm right, just take a look at Mississippi."[1]

Long knew about the political firestorm Democratic governor Theodore G. Bilbo had sparked in Mississippi with his ill-conceived attempt to merge several of the state's colleges into a "greater university" in Jackson. After supporters of the institutions—especially at the University of Mississippi in Oxford—attacked the plan, Bilbo answered with wholesale dismissals of college board members, professors, and administrators. In response to Bilbo's interference, about a week before Long appeared on the LSU campus, the American Association of Universities dropped Ole Miss from its list of accepted institutions. By December, students at Ole Miss would burn Bilbo in effigy at the foot of the flagpole on the school's Oxford campus.[2]

"You know about that, don't you?" Frey asked Long.

"Yes, but I want a band. How in the hell can you get a band? I want you to get [Guilbeau]. I'm going to fire him. I have made up my mind."

Long was well acquainted with the school's thirty-seven-member Regimental Band. Its members performed at his 1928 inauguration, and he led them in a parade through the streets of Shreveport in November that year before the annual LSU-Arkansas football game. In May 1930, he also heard Guilbeau's cadets play at a grand-opening gala for the new, luxurious $150,000 Governor's Mansion that Long built, over the legislature's objections, on North Boulevard, three blocks from the Capitol. Long had not commented on the band's performance that night, but he might have been unimpressed by the group's performance.[3]

Long's desire for a new director may have originated with LSU's new cadet commandant, Major Troy Middleton, who mentioned his hope for a better band a few weeks earlier when the governor paid a surprise visit to his office. Middleton later recalled Long's displeasure with the unit. "Hell," Long told him, "I had a band of twelve pieces in my campaign that made more noise than yours." No matter how the idea for a new director arose, Frey understood that Long would not be denied. His job now was to satisfy the governor without undermining the university.[4]

"Governor," Frey said, "I'm in here to talk to you, and if you really want to help the university, I think I can give you some suggestions. Now, you tell us what you think ought to be done out here and go back to the governor's office and help us get the money. But you can't do it."

"Well, the president's sick and can't do anything," Long countered.

"But the president is the man who has to do it. You can't do it."

"Well, I'll get me another president."

"That's your business."

Long upped the ante. "Pop is not the only one I'm going to fire. He's only the first one I'm going to fire," Long said, rattling off a list of names. Most of them, Frey recalled, were "old timers."

Hoping to save Guilbeau from summary dismissal, Frey tried a different argument. "If you fire Pop, you're going to get in trouble. There's another angle to this. You are a good politician. Everybody knows you are. I don't know whether you know it or not, but Pop Guilbeau is one of your ardent supporters. And down where Pop comes from, down on the bayou, they all think that Pop is important. Now, if you fire Pop, you are going to lose a tremendous amount of French [Cajun] patronage."

"Well, I hadn't thought of that."

Frey pressed his case. "One other thing I ought to tell you. This band we have here is a military band. And it is part of our military unit here, and if you start fooling with that, you are going to get mixed up with the US Army."

Frey believed Troy Middleton could point Long in a more helpful direction, so he asked the cadet commandant to join him and Long in Atkinson's office. A forty-one-year-old Georgetown, Mississippi, native, Middleton had moved to Baton Rouge the previous July. A decorated former battalion commander who fought in France in the Second Battle of the Marne during the First World War, at twenty-nine he had been the youngest soldier promoted to the rank of colonel in the American Expeditionary Force.[5]

Shortly after arriving at LSU, Middleton had visited the Capitol for a courtesy call on Long. He waited outside the governor's office for forty-five minutes. "Every so often, I would see a man with no coat rush through the rotunda with long strides," Middleton remembered. "This was Huey, although I didn't know it." Finally, a secretary ushered Middleton into Long's office. Long jumped up, rushed to meet Middleton at the door, and guided him to a chair. Seated alongside four men he did not know, and to whom Long never introduced him, Middleton tried to enter the conversation but "couldn't get a word in edge-wise." Middleton stood up and told Long "if he was busy, I would go."

"Hell, Major, sit down," Long commanded. "These are just four S.O.B.'s who want to get something out of me." Middleton later learned the identity of two of the men: Oscar K. Allen, a state senator from Long's hometown of Winnfield whom the governor would anoint as his successor in 1932, and Robert Maestri, a state conservation commissioner who would become mayor of New Orleans in 1936.[6]

A few months later, when he arrived at President Atkinson's office to meet with Long and Frey, Middleton was armed with a solution to LSU's sudden bandleader dilemma. "Why, Governor, you don't have to fire Pop. He would be happy to give up the band."

"Can you get me a good bandleader?" Long asked.

Middleton had an idea, a retired Army bandleader who lived in New

Orleans. Thus, on December 1, LSU announced its new Regimental Band director, Alfred W. Wickboldt, a Wisconsin native in his mid-fifties who had studied at the Milwaukee Conservatory of Music. Wickboldt was a respected musician and conductor who had served as chief musician and bandleader of the Second US Volunteer Infantry during the Spanish-American War. A skilled trombonist, he played for two New Orleans orchestras from 1908 to 1930. With Long's enthusiastic support, Wickboldt helped usher the school's band into national prominence.[7]

A new and improved band, however, was only the first of many changes Long would introduce at LSU in years to come. Soon, the small, backwater state school would grow beyond anyone's imagination, especially the residents of sleepy Baton Rouge. With the brash young governor leading the way, LSU would emerge as a celebrated institution, known throughout the country. But what Long had in mind was more than invigorating a university. His plans included melding the school's image with his own. Within a few years, in the minds of millions, Huey Long and LSU would be synonymous.

2

I AM ON MY WAY

As a child, Huey Long yearned to escape Winnfield, the hilly, north-central Louisiana logging and salt-mining town where he was born in August 1893. "From my earliest recollection," he wrote near the end of his brief life, "I hated the farm work." At ten, Long made his first of several unsuccessful attempts to run away. In April 1909, at fifteen, he left again, if only for a few days and, this time, with his parents' blessing: He traveled 170 miles to Baton Rouge with a group of classmates who represented Winnfield High School at the state's first High School Rally. The event on LSU's campus drew students from around Louisiana for athletic matches, literary and choral competitions, and a debating contest. It was the first time Long had been more than 50 miles from Winn Parish. At LSU, he took part in several track-and-field events and the debating competition.[1]

First place in the debating and literary contests came with a four-year exemption from LSU fees (worth about fifty dollars a year). Held in the university's Garig Hall, the debate addressed this proposition: "That the United States Navy should be materially increased at once." Long reported, "I fared badly, but was given honorable mention." It is not known if he argued in the affirmative or the negative.[2]

Long returned to LSU the following April for another try at a rally prize, this time in the "declamation," or speech-making, contest. For weeks, he rehearsed his presentation—a speech excerpt by journalist and orator Henry W. Grady—atop a stump in the woods. He also planned to compete in the one-mile run and on the relay team.

From the rally's inaugural session in 1909, dozens of Baton Rouge families had welcomed rally competitors into their homes for the two-day event.

In 1910, Long and some friends stayed at the home of Thomas H. Harris, the state's superintendent of education. Harris later remembered Long as "a perfect portrait" of the adult he would become. "He came swaggering into the house, leaving the baggage for the others to bring in, and introduced himself to Mrs. Harris. He was all over the place in a few minutes and met all members of the family, including Lily, the cook. He was always late for his meals, left his clothes all over the bathroom floor, and had everybody in the house awake by five or six o'clock in the morning." As Long prepared to leave the house the day of his debate, Harris asked him, "Well, Young Sprout, how do you think you will come out in your contest?" Long answered, "If I get justice, I'll win."

But he did not win. First place went to a young woman Long judged undeserving. Afterward, a surly Long wandered into the room where the debate was about to begin. He persuaded the judges to let him enter this contest. The topic was, "Resolved, that women in the United States should be granted suffrage on equal terms with men." Long argued against women's suffrage because, he said, "they got too many rights, right now. That's why no boy ain't gonna win nothing here." Long returned to Harris's home that evening and informed him, "The committee was ignorant, or bought, and gave me *third* place." (He finished fourth in declamation.) This, he later claimed, earned him a modest scholarship. It is doubtful he won anything. LSU awarded scholarships only to first-place finishers in the rally's choral performance and fee exemptions for those who won the academic contests.

Long may not have won a State Rally competition, but he and classmate Harley Bozeman enjoyed everything else about LSU and Baton Rouge. The Harrises' teenage son, Morton Evans, escorted the two wide-eyed country boys around town. "This was the first time either of us had ever ridden on a streetcar," Bozeman recalled.

As the boys prepared to return to Winnfield, Long told Harris's wife, Mary Elizabeth, "Mrs. Harris, you have been mighty good to us, and when I get to be governor, United States senator, and president of the United States, I am going to do something for you. I am on my way and will not be stopped by a committee of ignorant professors." Eighteen years later, in May 1928, Harris and her husband would stand in a reception line at the Governor's Mansion, waiting to congratulate their former house guest on his election as Louisiana's governor. "Do you recall what I told you?" the new governor asked Mary Elizabeth, recalling his 1910 stay in her home. "Well, I am on my way, and I'll make the rest of the journey." And then he asked, "How are Uriah, Tate, Morton, Sadie [Harris's children], and Lily, the cook?"[3]

Despite his disappointments at the High School Rally, Long said he fell in love with LSU in 1909 and 1910. He yearned to enroll at the state university after high school, but college was not in the young man's immediate future. "Conditions were not very good in the Winnfield community," he wrote years later. He explained that his parents sent his siblings to college, but they had no money for his continued education. "I saw no opportunity to attend the Louisiana State University. The scholarship which I had won did not take into account books and living expenses. It would have been difficult to secure enough money." But Long's family was not as poor as he claimed. His father, a farmer and stockman, was prosperous enough in 1907 to build a large, two-story colonial house he financed with proceeds from selling farmland. Left unstated was the most plausible reason Long had not applied to LSU: He had not earned a high school diploma. For admission to LSU without a diploma, he needed to pass an entrance examination.[4]

Why Long did not graduate from high school is unclear. By one account, the school's principal, W. C. Robinson, insisted students at Winnfield High School complete a twelfth year of instruction before earning a diploma. (Many Louisiana high schools then required only an eleventh-grade education.) Long may have dropped out in frustration or anger over the extra-year requirement. "The eleventh grade students were left dangling in the air," classmate Harley Bozeman wrote years later. "We had finished the prescribed course of study for Louisiana high schools. Robinson refused to certify us and we never graduated from high school, just finished at a dead end."[5]

Another story Long told later in life was that his high school expelled him for publishing a circular that attacked the principal and the faculty, perhaps in protest over the required extra year. In retaliation for this, Long claimed he circulated a petition of protest that gained signatures of most of the town's residents, and which resulted in Robinson's dismissal. Whether or not because of Long, the 1910–11 school year opened with a new principal. Two of Long's sisters told a similar story about his conflict with Robinson, although their version of Long's dispute with the principal involved their brother dropping out of school and attending Shreveport's Byrd High School.[6]

Whatever the reason for Long's inability or unwillingness to attend LSU, he might not have been alone among Winn Parish high school students in regarding attendance at LSU an unattainable dream. In 1910, the year he visited the campus for the second time, only five students from Winn Parish attended LSU. By comparison, Puerto Rico and Cuba each had more than twice as many students enrolled at the university. It is possible that Long never knew more than a handful of LSU graduates from Winn Parish. In 1910, according to university records, only three people with an LSU degree called Winnfield home.[7]

He never attended LSU, but Long seemed to always know which vocation he would pursue. His biographer T. Harry Williams believed "there was only one profession for Huey Long, and he knew what it was at an early age. His recognition of it was intuitive rather than intellectual. He was drawn to the great art of politics as if by an irresistible magnet." Long acknowledged later in life, "I was born into politics, a wedded man, with a storm for my bride."[8]

He first dabbled in politics as a teenager. At fourteen, Long persuaded a candidate for Winn Parish stock inspector to pay him five dollars—half in advance—if he generated enough votes to carry the election. Having once worked in a local print shop, Long applied his skills to producing circulars for his client and roamed the town campaigning for him. "If I am elected, I will inspect every cow, male & female, for ticks," Long wrote for his candidate. "Them that's got 'em will get rid of 'em, and them that ain't got none won't git none." The man won by fourteen votes. "Huey had a taste of politics," a biographer wrote of the experience, "and he liked it."[9]

Politics and sales are not unrelated, which may be why Long proved so successful in the work he pursued when he left high school in 1910. Given a job selling a lard substitute, Cottolene, Long took to door-to-door sales with near-immediate skill. He made almost twice as many sales as his trainer on his first day.

The job also helped him find a spouse. He organized a cake-baking contest in Shreveport and award first prize to Rose McConnell, an attractive young woman who became his wife. But he was restless and had no immediate interest in settling down. He bounced around a six-state area selling Cottolene and other products. He landed in Norman, Oklahoma, and took several courses at the University of Oklahoma. (He may have misled university officials to believe he had graduated high school.) Then, he went to Tennessee, where he found a job with the Faultless Starch Company. Mar-

Huey Long as a young man. Before studying law, Louisiana's future governor and US senator was a traveling salesman. (Wikimedia Commons)

ried to Rose in 1913, he worked in Memphis until the company shuttered its operations there.

He and Rose returned to Winnfield and lived with his parents, but he was still desperate to escape his hometown. This time, Long persuaded his older brother Julius, a Winnfield attorney, to subsidize him as he studied law at Tulane University in New Orleans. Instead of spending years in the classroom, however, Long chose an accelerated program. When finished, he would sit for an exam before a panel of lawyers. (Louisiana law did not then require attorneys to have a law degree if they could pass the state's bar examination.) Long took his exam after passing only four courses.[10]

As a new lawyer who never tried a case, the twenty-five-year-old Long had little choice but to return to Winnfield and apprentice under Julius. The two siblings began feuding within months, no doubt a result of the younger Long's impertinence and outsized ambitions. The brothers soon parted ways, and Huey set up shop in an anteroom of the Bank of Winnfield. Attracting few well-paying clients, he found himself back in traveling sales, this time for the Never Fail Company, which produced kerosene. Later, however, he eked out a living by taking workers' compensation cases, helped by a 1914 Louisiana law that allowed industrial employees to sue their employers for workplace injuries.

Long achieved local prominence as an attorney when he accepted the case of a widow with a claim against the Bank of Winnfield—owned by his uncle George Long—for what the woman alleged were stolen savings. He attacked the bank during the trial with such ferocity that the president, B. W. Bailey, implored him, through Harley Bozeman, to soften his rhetoric. Long told Bozeman to "tell Uncle George and Mr. Bailey that they should feel complimented that Huey Long don't take out after topwaters [small fish] but after the big fish." He won the case and, with it, considerable local acclaim. T. Harry Williams wrote that Long internalized a tactic he employed many times in his political career: "If you want to attract popular attention and support, denounce the biggest, closest target at hand."[11]

In 1918, Long applied that philosophy to Burk A. Bridges of Claiborne Parish, who represented northern Louisiana on the state's Railroad Commission (now the Public Service Commission), a three-member body that regulated intrastate railroads, pipelines, and public utilities. Scorning commissioners for defending the state's wealthy interests, Long told a friend, "I can beat that old man." He campaigned throughout his district in a splendid, head-turning secondhand Overland 90 sedan, ignoring the advice of friends who cautioned that country people would be offended by his ostentatious mode of travel. "Hell," he later said, "they told me I'd have to drive around in an old buggy with a horse and wear slouchy clothes and chew tobacco. But not me. . . . I wanted them to think I was something, and they did." Not only did Long drive a shiny car, but he also wore a new suit, a $37.50 white linen outfit purchased from the Biggest Little Store of Shreveport and donated by a state senator he defended in a high-profile court case.[12]

Bridges did not know Long had campaigned quietly for months before his formal announcement in August 1918. In fact, as early as 1916, Long began writing to elected officials throughout northern Louisiana, laying the groundwork to undermine what Bridges regarded as his greatest strength— his alliances with the courthouse crowd in each parish. Long also relied on a lengthy list of former customers from his traveling sales days, sending them copies of his public remarks about various issues. He littered the district with circulars and signs, at one point borrowing $500 from Oscar "O. K." Allen, a close friend, and the Winn Parish tax assessor, to finance another round of printing. (Long did not forget this favor and would make Allen Louisiana's governor in 1932.)

He drove to almost every town in his district—sometimes knocking on farmers' doors at night to ask for a vote—and often promised locals that, if elected, he would force the railroad to extend a line to their community. At one stop in Lincoln Parish, near Choudrant (known to some locals as "Shooter"), Long scheduled his remarks to occur as a passenger train roared through the village. He looked at the gathering in mock surprise after the train passed, and said, "Folks, do you mean to tell me the Cannonball don't stop at Shooter station? Well, you elect me and that'll be changed." Long beat Bridges by 635 votes.[13]

Harley Bozeman remembered Long as "a genius, but a multiple-charactered person." The books Long read during his high school days, Bozeman believed, influenced his unusual approach to politics. "*The Count of Monte Cristo,* from which he got the idea of paying back his enemies," was one example, Bozeman recalled in 1959, adding, "The Old Testament, with emphasis on the retribution and revenge portions of the Mosaic Laws, the autobiography of Benvenuto Cellini, the Bohemian artist of the Renaissance, and every book he could get his hands on concerning dictator Napoleon Bonaparte."[14]

Now on the state Railroad Commission, Long eagerly attacked the status quo that allowed the state's most powerful corporation, Standard Oil of Louisiana, to have its way with state leaders. The company told Louisiana governors, state lawmakers, and railroad commissioners the amount it should be taxed and the extent to which it should be regulated. And elected officials usually went along.

As Long joined the commission in February 1919, the oil-producing giant was threatening to block about one hundred smaller, independent competitors from gaining access to their pipelines. Long was not only predisposed to dislike Standard Oil; he was also inclined to identify with smaller producers. He represented several independents in his law practice and had accepted company stock as payment. The pipeline embargo jeopardized the value of those holdings. Long later said he watched the Standard Oil executives with disdain at that first commission meeting. "About these men there was that undefinable something that betokens freedom from money cares and anxiety in the future. But the faces of the men in the independent group told a different story. Care, and in some cases, desperation, was written in every line."

When the Standard Oil men bullied representatives of the smaller companies, Long exploded. "This is a free country! You've done this before and got by with it, but this time, go do it and see when you hear the last of it." With that, he stormed out of the meeting. Long made good on his word. He engineered a commission ruling that classified the pipelines as common carriers, placing them under the commission's jurisdiction. He then attacked Governor Ruffin Pleasant for refusing to call a special legislative session to enshrine the commission's policy into law.[15]

The 1919–20 governor's race was already underway, and Long hoped to force the candidates' hands over the Standard Oil issue. He chose a 1919 July Fourth political rally at a resort and spa in the central Louisiana town of Hot Wells to declare war on the oil giant and its political supporters. Long waited until the four gubernatorial candidates in attendance finished their dull, rote speeches before he mounted the podium as a last-minute addition to the program. After mouthing obligatory attacks on the New Orleans Old Regular machine, Long fed the sizable crowd a full dose of the pungent political rhetoric that characterized much of his career—attacking with near-reckless abandon the biggest, most powerful person or corporation at hand.

Besides Standard Oil, on this day his prime target was Pleasant, the lame-duck governor, whom he called "a tool of the Standard Oil Company."

But he reserved his harshest language for the company. "This octopus is among the world's greatest criminals," Long told the stunned crowd, as he unloaded on the corporation and its patrons. Acknowledging the gamble he made with this attack, Long added, "I haven't got a dime, but I'm not afraid of my political future and don't care whether I've any or not."

By day's end, much of Louisiana's political class buzzed over this phenom. One observer told *New Orleans States* reporter A. W. Newlin that Long's speech had been "hot as this boiling water that bubbles up from Hot Well at 116 degrees." As Newlin informed his readers, "Not in years, perhaps never in a campaign in this State, have so many vituperative invectives been used in a brief 30-minute speech as were employed by Mr. Long." For many in New Orleans and elsewhere, it was the first time they noticed this political sensation. With his continuing, brutal attacks on the state's establishment, Long ensured it would not be the last.[16]

3

THE FATHER OF LSU

On February 1, 1918, LSU president Thomas D. Boyd dropped by the New Orleans office of John M. Parker, a wealthy, fifty-five-year-old cotton merchant. One of Louisiana's most influential men, Parker was inclined to politics and public service, having volunteered to serve as Louisiana's wartime federal food administrator. But Boyd was not there this day to help Parker win the war against Germany. Instead, he hoped to enlist his friend in a different fight—a mission to expand LSU in size and scope.[1]

With iron-gray hair and a formidable mustache, the dapper Parker "looked like the typical old-fashioned Southern gentleman and politician," historian T. Harry Williams observed. Years after he met him, *New Orleans States* reporter William Wiegand remembered Parker's piercing gaze. "When he looked at you," Wiegand said, "you felt that he was looking into your soul." Parker grew up a son of privilege, dividing time between his parents' plantation near Bethel Church, Mississippi, and their home in New Orleans. His father was rich and well-connected. Parker's first cousin, once removed, was Mary Todd Lincoln. A Democrat, Parker counted former Republican president Theodore Roosevelt among his closest friends. He hunted and fished with Roosevelt often and had accompanied his friend on a celebrated bear hunt in 1902 near Smedes, Mississippi. Legend had it the softhearted Roosevelt refused to kill a black bear cub that his hunting partners captured. The touching tale inspired stuffed versions of the "Teddy Bear." The truth was Roosevelt would not shoot the bear because the 235-pound animal was old and injured, and his guides had tied it to an oak tree. "Put it out of its misery," Roosevelt told Parker before walking away. The future Louisiana governor unsheathed a hunting knife and stabbed the bear under its ribs.[2]

On the morning President Boyd appeared in Parker's office, he persuaded the business leader to join him at the March 4 inaugural meeting of the Louisiana State Agricultural Federation, organized by William R. Dodson, dean of LSU's College of Agriculture. Parker was already sympathetic to the need for better agricultural education in Louisiana, especially at the state school best equipped to conduct research into new farming methods and train students in them. LSU housed the respected Audubon Sugar School and conducted sugarcane experiments at its Audubon Park Sugar Station in New Orleans. The university operated three other experimental stations: crop and dairy farms in Baton Rouge and Ouachita Parish and a rice station at Crowley. But LSU's College of Agriculture was just one part of an institution committed to offering a variety of academic disciplines, including engineering, law, journalism, chemistry, English literature, geology, economics and sociology, teaching, accounting, history, and government. The College of Arts and Sciences was the centerpiece of a university that some administrators and faculty increasingly regarded as a liberal arts institution. Arts and Sciences, the university's catalog declared, "is, in fact, the nucleus from which all of the other schools and colleges of the University have developed."

Parker understood that LSU, founded in Pineville in 1860 as the Louisiana State Seminary of Learning and Military Academy, was proud of its relationship with the US Army. The school's first president, although he was never celebrated by LSU for his role in establishing the institution, was William Tecumseh Sherman, who became a respected Union general during the American Civil War. Most male freshman and sophomores took a required two-year course of military training as part of the school's Reserve Officers' Training Corps. Those ROTC students lived on campus in military-like barracks, wore olive drab woolen cadet uniforms to class, and drilled and trained regularly. Cadets who completed four years in military science and tactics were eligible for Army commissions.[3]

Parker and the state's agricultural leaders were not hostile to LSU's military emphasis (although in the late 1800s, the Louisiana farm lobby opposed teaching almost anything but farming at LSU). But he and his new allies also believed that, as a federal land grant institution, LSU must do more to support Louisiana's farm economy and train young men in the latest techniques of farming, veterinary care, and animal husbandry. Parker's interest in these subjects only grew on March 4 when he heard the agricultural leaders and

John M. Parker served as Louisiana governor from 1920 to 1924. Long attacked and ridiculed Parker's plan to make LSU a "Greater University" that emphasized agricultural education. (LSU *Gumbo* yearbook, 1926)

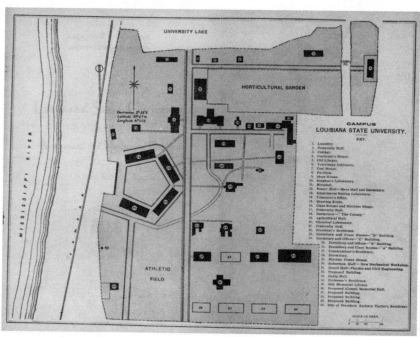

LSU's campus was situated north of town, in and around the current site of Louisiana's Capitol. This 1903 map shows how the Mississippi River, downtown, and Capitol Lake hemmed in the campus and prevented expansion. (LSU Photograph Collection, LSU Special Collections)

LSU officials complain about the dire need for more property for agriculture experiments.

And LSU needed more than simply better agriculture education. Its campus in north Baton Rouge was sufficient for a school of only about nine hundred students, and its buildings were dilapidated and inadequate. One report by the state's Board of Affairs concluded that few buildings at LSU were "comparable to the better class of high school buildings throughout the State." In their conversations with Parker, however, the agricultural leaders focused on the school's deficiencies in training farmers. The university, they insisted, should offer more instruction in practical agriculture. One participant said he knew of an LSU graduate who could not "put a collar on a mule." Boyd reported that this assertion angered Parker so much that he resolved "then and there that if it was humanly possible the University would secure additional land."[4]

Like his good friend Theodore Roosevelt, Parker had been a sickly child. His younger brothers attended Princeton College, while Parker's parents shipped him off to the Texas plains, where he worked as a cowboy and bronco buster. Like Roosevelt, he had developed a robust physique and, although modest in stature, Parker considered himself a vigorous man who enjoyed manual labor. He was fond of farming, one reason he was so disturbed to learn at the meeting that LSU's instruction in this field was deficient.[5]

The delegates applauded Parker when he rose to speak. Unlike the florid, long-winded political orators of his time, Parker was an unconventional speaker. His speeches were often brief. Upon becoming governor in 1920, his inaugural address was under five hundred words. On this day, Parker got to his point. He urged the gathering to embrace the promise of Governor Ruffin Pleasant—also in attendance—to help the state's agricultural interests by asking the legislature to appropriate $1 million to transform LSU into a state agricultural center. He advised the conference to approve a resolution "demanding—not asking—for such a school at Baton Rouge. Go after $1 million. You may not get it all, but I am sure that with Governor Pleasant's support you will get a good, substantial amount—enough to make a mighty good start."[6]

With Parker's powerful, enthusiastic challenge still ringing delegates' ears, Boyd returned to Baton Rouge with a plan to act quickly. But he would not ask Pleasant and lawmakers for $1 million. He made a more modest, but crucial proposal: The state should buy a large parcel of property south of

Baton Rouge where LSU could grow into the greater agricultural center that he, Parker, and others envisioned. Boyd first asked Thomas Atkinson, the university's future president who was then dean of LSU's College of Engineering, to assess the availability of Gartness Plantation, a twelve-hundred-acre former cotton, sugarcane, rice, and sweet potato farm, then blanketed with magnolia trees, along the Mississippi River about two miles south of the Capitol. Atkinson contacted the property's owner and reported that the land could be had for $82,000.

In late May 1918, when the legislature convened for its annual session, lawmakers and other prominent citizens, including Parker and Governor Pleasant, traveled to the property for a barbeque. LSU hosted the gathering, hoping to generate support for legislation by state representative Horace Wilkinson of West Baton Rouge Parish that would fund the land's purchase for the university. Among the speakers that day, on a grandstand erected between the two Indian mounds (across from the present-day Huey P. Long Field House), were Pleasant, Parker, Wilkinson, state education superintendent Thomas H. Harris, and Baton Rouge mayor Alex Grouchy. Pleasant told those gathered that, if the legislature would pass Wilkinson's bill, he would sign it. Meanwhile, a group of nine men, including deans Atkinson and Dodson, borrowed the $82,000 from the Louisiana National Bank to buy the land for subsequent sale to the state at cost. After Wilkinson's bill passed on June 4, the men transferred the property to LSU and the state reimbursed them.[7]

LSU now had the acreage for its expansion, but still needed millions in state appropriations to become the "Greater University" the state's agricultural leaders envisioned. Just as it fell to Parker to inspire university leaders and others to demand funding necessary to expand LSU, it would fall to him as governor in 1920 to find funds to build a new university on the former plantation property. And it would require every ounce of Parker's power and political acumen to make it happen. First, however, he would have to reckon with one of the most vocal and determined opponents of LSU's expansion—Huey P. Long.

Parker may have never held elected office in 1918, but he had been a well-known state and national political leader for years. In 1891, he had risen to prominence after helping lead a mob that stormed the Orleans Parish Prison and lynched eleven Sicilian immigrants. At the time, some civic and religious leaders in Louisiana regarded the murders as a sensible, just response to the growing crime in New Orleans, unfairly attributed to Italian immigrants. A longtime Democrat, Parker bolted his party in 1912 to support Theodore Roosevelt, who was running for another term as president, this time under the Progressive Party banner. Parker ran for governor of Louisiana in 1916 as the state's Progressive Party candidate, losing to Democrat Ruffin Pleasant. The national Progressive Party made Parker its vice-presidential nominee later that year, but the party promptly fell into disarray when Roosevelt refused to accept its nomination. Party leaders grudgingly endorsed Republican Party nominee Charles Evans Hughes while Parker threw his support to the eventual winner, Democrat Woodrow Wilson.[8]

By 1919, as a candidate for governor, Parker had returned to the Democratic Party as a reformer. He promised to rein in the New Orleans Old Regular machine, raise corporate taxes, protect independent oil producers (as Long tried to do), expand the state's highway system, and rewrite the state's 1913 constitution. He also pledged to increase appropriations to Louisiana State University. Parker was just the sort of governor that public service commissioner Long could support. Long campaigned for Parker and attacked his Democratic primary opponent, Col. Frank Stubbs of Monroe, as a tool of Standard Oil and the railroad interests. After beating Stubbs for the party nomination, Parker won an overwhelming victory over token Republican opposition in April 1920.[9]

Long was pleased when Parker asked the legislature to impose a 2 percent severance tax on the extraction of natural resources, including oil, to finance the new governor's ambitious legislative agenda. The independent producers countered with a proposal for a 1.5 percent tax, but Standard Oil agreed to pay only 1 percent. Parker eventually persuaded the oil companies to accept a 2 percent tax, which he labeled a "gentlemen's agreement" and to which he added the promise that he would not increase the tax during his term of office. When Standard Oil officials asked how they could be assured of this, Parker replied, "You write the bill," adding, "If my legal advisers can't find any joker that you might slip into it, it will pass exactly as you wrote it."[10]

Long detested Parker's "gentlemen's agreement" with Standard Oil as a sellout to the company, but he was more disturbed at first by the new governor's refusal to support legislation to codify his pipeline regulations that the Railroad Commission enacted in 1919. The spat over this issue was the beginning of the end of their brief political alliance, doomed from the start by Long's overriding belief that his political future depended on attacking the most powerful politician at hand. In 1920, that was Parker. In a letter to the governor-elect in late April, Long complained that Parker's plan for the pipelines would "afford absolutely no protection of any kind or particular." He grumbled that Parker was "going soft" on his campaign promises. An indignant Parker replied later that summer with a demand for a public hearing on Long's claim that he had not honored his campaign platform.[11]

The animosity between the two men exploded at the 1921 constitutional convention. As delegates convened, Parker worked to head off an effort to set the state severance tax at 3 percent instead of the 2 percent that he and Standard Oil supported. When some of those attending a meeting at the Governor's Mansion suggested a compromise of 2.5 percent, Parker was amenable and summoned the company's treasurer. When the official balked at the proposal, Parker backed down and promised to stick with his "gentlemen's agreement." Eventually, however, public pressure to increase the tax was too great. Parker went along with those who wanted a 3 percent tax. The settlement seemed to satisfy most involved. But not Long, who had no fundamental objection to the tax rate but, rather, sensed political gain in Parker's brief subservience to Standard Oil. In his opposition, Long was also supported by conservatives from oil parishes and former governor Pleasant, who believed the state should divert part of the revenue to the parishes where the taxes were collected.[12]

Lawmakers convened in a special session in September 1921 to consider enabling legislation to implement several provisions of the new constitution, including the severance tax. Even though Parker now supported the 3 percent levy, Long was eager to attack him. In late October, Long distributed the first of three circulars to every member of the legislature, charging that Parker was beholden to Standard Oil. In his first missive, he wrote, "Better to have taken the gold hoarded in the Standard Oil vaults at 26 Broadway [the company's headquarters] and deliberately purchase the votes with which the administration has now ruled this State for nearly two years than to have brow-beaten, bulldozed and intimidated the Legislature for the benefit of the corporate interests through the free use of the peoples' patronage."[13]

Long charged in a second circular that Parker had appointed William Leake, the son of a Standard Oil official, as superintendent of the state's Charity Hospital in New Orleans. He claimed Leake's appointment was evidence of the "open, visible and actual control of our state affairs" by corporations. Long added: "The laws on which you are to vote are written in Broadway; Your candidates are named in the Oil Trust's offices, and your appointments are plunder in the hands of an administration dispensed in such manner as to appease and gratify the corporate lobbyists who have so long been an object of the people's attack."[14]

The circulars stunned lawmakers in the same way Long's fiery speech at Hot Wells scandalized listeners in July 1919. When lawmakers discussed Long on the house floor the next day, one reporter noted, "there was blood on the moon and blood in some of the members' eyes." Lawmakers friendly to Parker reacted with fury. "I think it is about time that we appoint a commission authorized to inquire into this Huey P. Long's sanity," Representative John Dymond of Plaquemines Parish announced during the frenzied house debate. One lawmaker alleged Long wrote the circular while drunk. Other members called for his impeachment.[15]

"If the charges are true," an angry Parker said in response to Long's circular, "I am unfit for governor. If on the contrary, the attacks are wilfully [sic] and maliciously false then the author should be dismissed from office and put in jail." With that, the governor filed a complaint with the East Baton Rouge Parish district attorney, accusing Long of criminal libel. The charges were that Long alleged, falsely, Parker had dispensed state patronage on behalf of Standard Oil, and he gave Leake the Charity Hospital job at Standard Oil's behest.[16]

Long welcomed the tempest because he believed Parker would help make an upstart politician into a martyr. "I haven't begun to fight the administration yet," Long said from his home in Shreveport after the local sheriff served the warrant for his arrest on two counts of libel and ordered him to post bond in Baton Rouge. A few days later, Long drew $5,000 from his pocket as he strolled into the courthouse. "I've brought the cash with me in case you're short of money in Baton Rouge."[17]

Throughout a contentious legislative inquiry in October 1921, and his trial that November, Long remained defiant. His attorneys suggested he should present a conventional defense in court and argue that his words were technically not libelous. Long insisted on a political strategy, saying, "Too much depends upon my standing my ground."[18]

The trial was a statewide sensation, featuring dramatic testimony by Long, Parker, and other state officials. "Without seeming to realize what he was doing," T. Harry Williams wrote, "Parker confirmed the accuracy of

Huey's charges." Parker acknowledged he allowed Standard Oil lawyers to draft the severance tax legislation. When Long testified, he insisted his attacks on Parker were political, not personal. "I ain't interested in saving Governor Parker's personal soul. I've been trying to do something for the people of the state."[19]

There was no jury, and the judge, Harney Brunot, pronounced Long guilty on both charges. On the first charge, Brunot—who ascended to the Louisiana Supreme Court in 1923—sentenced Long to thirty days in parish prison but suspended the sentence if Long exhibited "good behavior" for the next month. For the second charge, he fined Long a dollar or, if he refused to pay, an hour in prison. Long refused. Ever the astute politician, he dared Brunot to toss him in jail. His lawyer paid the fine.[20]

The trial and his other attacks on Parker and Standard Oil, and his battles against other corporations, transformed Long into a poor man's hero. As a so-called "prominent man" from rural southeastern Louisiana told a *New Orleans States* reporter afterward, "You would be surprised how overwhelming this Long sentiment is with the rank and file of our people. They don't know Huey Long. They never saw him and would not know him if he stepped off the train at our station. But, they know him in name and you can't make them believe he is not their defender."[21]

For all his attacks on Parker, Long was truthful when he testified during his libel trial that he had nothing personal against the governor. Long's primary target was Standard Oil, and he aimed to use the oil company's influence over state government as an issue in the governor's race of 1924, when he planned to run. And he would not even have to challenge Parker directly, as Louisiana's constitution did not allow governors to serve consecutive terms.

P arker's administration paved the way for the important work Long accomplished, beginning in 1928, when he became governor. Parker's friendliness to Standard Oil weakened him and played into Long's hands, but his administration would not be without its successes—a foundation upon which Long built his own legacy as governor, including at LSU.

Parker used the proceeds from a two-cent gasoline tax and automobile license fees, along with federal grants, to build farm-to-market roads, the first program of a new state Highway Department. The major deficiency in

Parker's program, however, was that he insisted on a "pay-as-you-go" financing plan. Some critics have observed that Louisiana could have built more highways by borrowing the funds, as Long did when he became governor. Still, Parker's highway program was more aggressive than those in some other states. Nothing, however, attested to his imagination more than championing a new and better Louisiana State University, what he often called a "Greater University" or a "Greater Agricultural College."[22]

Shortly after taking office in 1920, Parker had appointed a Greater Agricultural College Committee to visit five institutions—Clemson College, and the universities of Minnesota, Illinois, Wisconsin, and Tennessee. Its charge was to assess the schools' agricultural programs and prepare a case for replicating their better aspects in Louisiana. Parker also persuaded legislators to purchase an additional 930 acres for the new campus from the adjoining Arlington and Nestledown plantations. The future campus now claimed total acreage of 2,130.[23]

After delegates to the 1921 constitutional convention authorized the oil severance tax, Parker urged them to devote the entire amount generated—an estimated $2 million a year—to LSU for five years. When delegates balked, Parker recruited a group from northern Louisiana to accompany him to the site of the new campus. "We have done less for the farmers than any other class," Parker told the convention delegates. "We have no experts in agriculture lines. We need them. It is either worthwhile making this college one of the finest in the South or sell the land. We have no college in Louisiana that will teach our young men and inspire them to go back to the farm." Parker added: "We are not building for today, but for fifty years to come."[24]

Parker and delegates compromised, agreeing to fund $5 million in building projects at the new campus through January 1, 1925 (the amount raised was about $3.5 million). Then, they guaranteed the school up to $1 million a year from the proceeds of a half-mill state property tax (in actuality, about $700,000). They also dedicated state severance tax funding—the 3 percent levy would not pass the legislature until May 1922—to all the state's colleges, including Baton Rouge's all-Black Southern University, which received $200,000 annually from the fund. And they supported funding the state's School for the Negro Blind and its Deaf and Dumb Asylum.[25]

Despite the revenue he helped produce for these and other state institutions, Parker was prouder of nothing more than what he accomplished for LSU. Near the end of his term, he considered his role in launching the "Greater Agriculture College" his "greatest achievement." Later in life, he delighted in being called "the father of LSU" and its "founder."[26]

But Parker's vision of LSU was limited. He increased funding to the school to build its new campus, but the bulk of the money would flow into the school's coffers only until 1925. Afterward, LSU subsisted on a much smaller appropriation. "Ultimately it may be said that Parker's cautious financing would have prevented dramatic expansion of education opportunity, as would be attributed to [Huey] Long," historian Matthew J. Schott observed. He added that Parker's greatest accomplishment at LSU may not have been "the achievement of miracles in actually teaching the 'three Rs' to the masses, but educating them to the importance of public education itself." Schott believed that Parker "was involved in raising in the public consciousness, the desirability of state support for university education."[27]

Parker supported giving the LSU Board of Supervisors more autonomy by instituting staggered, seven-year terms for its members that limited a new governor's ability to politicize the board. But he did not embrace coeducation for the university, seeing it as a place to train men as farmers and agricultural engineers. LSU officials dreamed of a much larger university, but Parker never envisioned the school with an enrollment greater than three thousand.[28]

Echoing the vision of university leaders for a grand, expanded LSU, Professor W. H. Dalrymple wrote in 1922: "On this newly-acquired site, there is about to be erected an entirely new and very much extended college area, with buildings planned to ultimately accommodate 5,000 students; with a college farm; and the necessary area to be devoted to the various branches of experiment station activities." Noting that the school hired "one of the most famous" landscape architects in the nation—the Brookline, Massachusetts, firm of Frederick Law Olmsted Jr.—Dalrymple wrote, "in a very few years it is hoped that everything will be ready for occupancy, and the University activities in full operation." Although the initial expansion of the new campus only allowed for housing about 1,500 male students—LSU operated two campuses until the early 1930s—"it is the consensus of opinion experts," Dalrymple concluded, "that when completed, this greater institution will be one of the finest and best equipped in the South, if not in the entire country; one of the most valuable assets the State could possibly have; and a lasting credit to the commonwealth as a whole."[29]

By the end of Parker's four-year term in May 1924, the dreams that Dalrymple expressed were still just that—dreams. LSU had about 1,600 students and about 135 faculty members, which made the school eighty-eighth in size among the nation's universities. The Association of State Universities placed LSU among those schools qualifying for only a middling, class-C ranking. Dalrymple's vision for his university's national prominence would wait a few years. Ultimately, it would require the efforts of the most prominent detractor of LSU's expansion to fulfill Dalrymple's dream of a "greater university."[30]

4

THIS TEMPLE OF VANITY

S upport throughout Louisiana for Parker's plan for an expanded LSU was never unanimous. For much of the next century, in fact, supporters of Louisiana's smaller public colleges and universities looked askance at what they regarded as the state's devotion to LSU's growth at the expense of their regional institutions. But among the scattered critics of LSU's move to its new campus, no one during the early 1920s was more prominent or outspoken than Huey Long.[1]

Running for governor in 1923, Long assailed Parker's vision for the "Greater University." Campaigning in Shreveport that September, he declared that, instead of improving LSU, Parker was destroying it. "As a boy . . . I harbored an ambition to attend old Louisiana State University. Every boy in this state loved that college. What has become of it? What are to become of those grounds, beautiful, splendid, and magnificent? Has the governor ever vouchsafed to the people of this state just what he was going to do with all the old university grounds and university buildings that he has abandoned in the reckless waste of nine millions of dollars?" Long added that, "if one-fourth the money spent in the experimental institution [Parker's Greater Agricultural College] had only been spent to enlarge the old university, LSU would have been a standing monument to state pride and there would have been tried-and-proven institutions of learning, organized under perfect operation, perfected with the ages of time and the brain of man."[2]

Long wrote the *New Orleans Times-Picayune* later that month to escalate his attack. He called the new university "this temple of vanity erected to Governor Parker." And he lamented that university officials "now propose to junk Louisiana State University by mixing it up with this Parker experiment.

What money Louisiana State University needed should have been expended for the college where it is rather than that this wonderful institution should be moved down the river and combined with something Parker is experimenting with, and if this experiment is like his others it will end in turmoil and endless confusion."[3]

The same edition of the *Times-Picayune* that carried Long's renewed attacks on Parker and LSU also featured an editorial blasting Long for claiming, falsely, that the state spent $9 million on the new LSU campus. Editors noted that appropriations for LSU were "less than $3,000,000," and the total spent was "less than $2,000,000." The editors also charged that Long failed to appreciate the value of agricultural education to a state's economy. "He does not know that the great state universities and agricultural colleges of the Middle West are the symbols of the agricultural wealth of those communities—and in large measure the creative and directing mind for their agricultural development. He probably does not know that the demagogue or the radical who, in any one of those states, would question the worth of those institutions to the producing 'dirt' farmers of those communities would be laughed off the stump." The lengthy and pungent editorial ended with this jab: "On sober second thought, we are tempted to believe that Huey is merely a singularly uninformed buffoon."[4]

It was not just the press that attacked Long over his position on LSU. One of Long's opponents in that year's governor's race, Henry L. Fuqua of Baton Rouge, suggested Long was attacking not only LSU and Parker but also the state constitution. Fuqua, superintendent of the state penitentiary at Angola who served on the LSU Board of Supervisors from 1904 to 1912, noted that the state's 1921 constitution authorized the funds for a new LSU campus: "We must therefore hear with astonishment that a candidate for governor in some vague way seeks to leave the impression with the people that if he is elected, he will override the constitutional direction by his own unlawful act and junk the buildings and property."[5]

Long persisted. He believed pouring money into the new LSU, in the words of one biographer, "seemed a bit pretentious and far-fetched to the men in overalls, the women in calico, who had come from the hoe and washtub" to hear him speak. "Show me one boy who has been graduated from the agricultural college and went back to the farm and made a living on it," Long said to laughter from a Lake Charles crowd in late November, "and I will quit this race now."[6]

It was not clear why Parker's plan to expand LSU angered Long. Given his eventual role in expanding the university beyond anything Parker might have dreamed, Long likely had no philosophical attachment to a smaller, land-locked LSU. His opposition was probably a product of his antipathy toward Parker and a belief that uneducated rural voters would resent the state spending millions on an institution of higher learning. Whatever the case, Long's attacks on Parker and his vision for LSU were not enough to earn him a spot in the runoff for the Democratic Party's gubernatorial nomination. He missed the February 1924 runoff by three percentage points, finishing third behind Fuqua, who defeated Lieutenant Governor Hewitt L. Bouanchaud for the party's nomination. Running against token Republican opposition in the April general election, Fuqua became governor with 97 percent of the vote.

Long may have worried after his 1924 loss that he had made unnecessary enemies among LSU graduates and other university supporters. And that may explain his odd behavior at an LSU game in Shreveport later that year. One of the state's biggest football contests was the annual LSU–University of Arkansas game, which the schools had played in Shreveport since 1913 (with one exception, because of the world war, in 1918). Louisiana's second-largest city, in the northwestern corner of the state, was a convenient halfway point for fans of both teams. The game also coincided with the Louisiana State Fair, held there each fall. A 4–1 LSU team, led by second-year coach Mike Donahue, had arrived in Shreveport on the morning of Saturday, November 1, for that afternoon's nineteenth State Fair annual game. Four special trains, carrying hundreds of LSU fans, also came from Baton Rouge that morning.[7]

The day was significant in the life of Shreveport. This was the first college game played in the new State Fair Stadium. Governor Fuqua agreed to dedicate the new structure—described by one reporter in attendance as "glistening like an emerald in a setting of old gold"—but he failed to show, as did the Arkansas governor. Although no governor was among the capacity crowd of seventy-five hundred, a future Louisiana governor was: Huey Long, northern Louisiana's Public Service Commission member. Long had no role in the official dedication ceremony held before the game. Even so, he made his presence known to the crowd.[8]

With LSU trailing 10–0 at halftime, Long scampered onto the field. Perhaps he thought he could inspire the team to victory or, more likely, he wanted to draw attention to himself. Whatever the reason for his impulsive action, quarterback Oliver "Ike" Carriere recalled that Long offered unsolicited advice to Coach Donahue and the players. "If you don't win this game, you're cowards," Long added. That remark angered a running back, Walter "Teeter" Chandler of Shreveport. "He started for Huey," Carriere said, "and ran him into the stands." LSU lost the game, 10–7.[9]

Long's strange conduct in Shreveport did not make the newspapers, as his future antics would, but it was only the first of many times he tried to coach the LSU squad to victory. By the early 1930s, Long's outrageous sideline behavior at LSU games would make news regularly—and propel the university to national prominence.

L ong's attacks on LSU and Parker in 1923–24 had not hindered the slow-but-steady growth of the new campus, funded by the influx of state dollars provided by Parker and the 1921 constitutional convention, and now supported by Fuqua. A plan crafted by the Olmsted Brothers landscape firm inspired the campus's layout. The firm had designed dozens of American college campuses, including Stanford University, the University of California at Berkeley, Colorado State University, American University, Northwestern University, and the University of Chicago. Olmsted also designed New Orleans's Audubon Park.[10]

Olmsted Brothers revealed a plan for the LSU campus in late 1921 which the university and the firm shared throughout the state. Frederick "Rick" Olmsted Jr. visited the state senate chamber in December 1921 to present a colorized drawing of his firm's design for the new LSU. As one reporter noted, "he started a procession of interested spectators to the Senate which has not since ended." Olmsted's plan, the *Weekly Town Talk* of Alexandria observed, "combines beauty and utility. Spread over 2,000 acres, including the experimental farms, it presents no inconvenience of crowding classroom or assembling halls or sleeping quarters. There is ample room not only for the requirements of the present, but for those of the future."[11]

Olmsted proposed a parklike campus comprising several quadrangles atop the long, low bluff that paralleled the nearby Mississippi River. Parker, the LSU Board, and a building committee that included former Louisiana US senator Edward Gay and deans Thomas Atkinson and William Dodson, embraced the plan in most aspects. And they hired prominent architect Theodore C. Link of St. Louis to design the buildings that filled in Olmsted's land-

LSU president Thomas D. Boyd speaking in the Greek Theatre during dedication ceremonies for the new LSU campus on April 30, 1926. Seated on the stage, *left to right:* Dr. A. B. Dinwiddie, president of Tulane University; Thomas H. Harris, state superintendent of education; state Senator Charles A. Holcombe of Baton Rouge; Father F. Leon Gassler of St. Joseph's Catholic Church of Baton Rouge; former governor John M. Parker; and former US senator Edward J. Gay, also a member of the LSU Board of Supervisors. (LSU Photograph Collection, LSU Special Collections)

scaping vision. The German-born Link amended and adapted the Olmsted campus layout in various respects, including reducing the cost of the new campus by trimming the number of buildings to accommodate only fifteen hundred students.

Construction work on ancillary structures began in 1922 while Link worked on his plan for the main buildings, which he presented to LSU officials in April 1923. By the fall 1925 semester, the first stage of construction neared completion and many students commenced taking courses on the new campus. A few months later, in early 1926, the new cadet dormitories opened. But there was still no housing for women students. Until such living arrangements could be provided, freshmen and sophomore women attended classes on the old campus. (At first, most male students and faculty rode the 7:25 Yazoo & Mississippi Valley Railroad's shuttle train each morning to the campus. By October 1926, Highland Road was paved all the way to the new LSU, allowing the Baton Rouge Electric Company to offer bus service to and from downtown Baton Rouge.) State officials and three thousand visitors dedicated the campus in April 1926. "The dreamers regard this university the best investment this state has ever made," former governor Parker said at the ceremonies.[12]

Set among the open farmland south of Baton Rouge, the new LSU had twenty-five buildings—many which embodied subtle qualities of Italian Renaissance architecture. Each building was roofed with red terra-cotta tiles and finished in the "Earley process," an architectural concrete technique developed by John Joseph Earley that imbued the material with a beige tint. The main buildings spread in and around the heart of the campus in the shape of a Roman cross: a quadrangle framed on the south by the Engineering Hall (now Atkinson Hall) and Engineering Shops; on the north by the University Dining Hall (soon named Foster Hall); on the northwest by the Teachers College building (then, as now, Peabody Hall); on the west by the Hill Memorial Library and the four buildings of the so-called "agricul-

The rapidly expanding LSU campus in the late 1930s.
(LSU Photograph Collection, LSU Special Collections)

tural group" (now Audubon, Prescott, and Stubbs halls, and Dodson Auditorium); and, on the east, the university's largest building, the Chemistry Building (now Coates Hall).

The campus's distinctive landmark, the 175-foot-tall Soldiers' and Sailors' Memorial Tower—a clock and bell tower known as the "Campanile" and financed by public subscription to honor Louisiana's First World War dead—sat to the east of the quadrangle and flanked by the school's administrative buildings and the Law Building. On the northwestern corner of the campus, outside the quadrangle, were four dormitories for male cadets, built to replicate the Pentagon Barracks, a prominent feature of the school's old campus. Near the barracks was the 3,200-seat Greek Theatre, an outdoor assembly space that accommodated the student body. "There was nothing like it in the South at the time," LSU architectural historian Michael Desmond wrote of the new campus. "The people of Louisiana could hardly have asked for more."[13]

In early 1924, work began on the final piece of the first phase of the new LSU: the football stadium on the west side of campus, a pair of concrete-and-steel grandstands—twenty-five rows on each side—that stretched from end zone to end zone on both sides of the gridiron. The stadium provided spectators with sixteen toilets under the bleachers, something the palatial Yale Bowl, with its seating capacity of 64,000, could not offer. It also featured a sophisticated, twelve-by-fifteen-foot Grid-graph Co. scoreboard (large for the 1920s) which contained dozens of lightbulbs, controlled by operators behind the board, that gave fans the score and other information about the game. The board even shared the type of play, the jersey numbers of the players involved in key actions and, by virtue of a replica of the field that took up most of the scoreboard, a light signifying the progress of the ball.[14]

Built for $73,950 and designed to hold 10,000 fans, the stadium accommodated the larger crowds expected to attend games on the new campus. (For years, LSU had played football games at the smaller, poorly maintained State Field on the old campus, which, despite its humble condition, also featured a Grid-graph scoreboard.) But LSU also hoped its new stadium would help the football program become financially competitive in the Southern Conference (a precursor to today's Southeastern Conference), as well as earn the school membership in the National Collegiate Athletic Association (NCAA), which happened in January 1924, based on the promise of a new stadium.[15]

Finished by fall 1924, the unnamed stadium broke the record for the largest football crowd in Louisiana history on Thanksgiving Day, November 27. On a sunny afternoon, over 18,500 fans—almost twice the stadium's official capacity—gathered to watch the LSU Tigers play the Tulane Green Wave, the last game of LSU's mediocre 5–4 season. Four special trains brought fans from New Orleans to Baton Rouge that morning for the contest, while thousands more flocked to campus from all directions in their automobiles, many decorated with purple or olive and blue streamers. "Every available seat was filled and many [were] sitting on the ground in front of the grandstand," the *Baton Rouge State-Times* reported.[16]

Former governor Parker and his wife, Cecile, were present, along with thirty-seven-year-old Col. Theodore "Ted" Roosevelt III, son of Parker's close friend the late Theodore Roosevelt. The former assistant Navy secretary and US Army brigadier general and future hero of the 1944 Normandy Invasion was among the first to arrive at the stadium before kickoff. After a brief appearance, Roosevelt and his wife, Eleanor, left with the Parkers for a tour of the campus—much of it still under construction—before returning for the game. Among other dignitaries was former governor Ruffin Pleasant. Not in his special box that day, however, was Governor Fuqua, who was too ill to attend. Despite the beauty and joy of the occasion for every LSU fan in attendance, the day was not quite perfect: Tulane won the first game, 13–0, in what would become "Tiger Stadium."[17]

So popular was the stadium that, by year's end, LSU announced it would add three new sections, expanding its seating capacity to 12,500 at a cost of $30,000, raised by the LSU Athletic Association. "Just a few years ago," one university official told the *New Orleans States,* "the athletic association was begging for money, and now it is able to secure $30,000 without any trouble."[18]

With its splendid new campus and a football stadium filled beyond capacity and already expanding, LSU was becoming the pride of Louisiana. Typical of the praise the campus earned was an Associated Press story about its dedication, which ran in dozens of papers across Louisiana in early May 1926:

Set in the broad acres of the new campus, lined with neatly trimmed shrubbery, and shaded by gigantic live oaks, the buildings comprising the physical plant of this great institution present a sight which should prove an inspiration to these visitors as well as to the students who will come here with the solemn purpose of securing an education. The fulfillment of a great architect's vision[,] this plant represents the last word in modern university architecture. It is probably unique among the universities and colleges of the country, being Italian renaissance in design and harmonizing perfectly with its magnificent setting.[19]

By the time Long ran again for governor in 1928, there was no point opposing the new LSU. It was not only a fact; it was also popular with the public. As he campaigned around the state, the crusading public service commissioner promised not only to increase funding to education; he also pledged to give children free textbooks, and vowed to deliver more public hospitals, better roads, and toll-free bridges. And, when he appeared in Baton Rouge in September 1927, he paid homage to the university. "There is no man in this state that holds dearer sentiments than I toward Louisiana State University," Long told a crowd of about 2,500 at the city's Community Club Pavilion. "I was the only one of nine children who didn't go to college. No man ever went to the annual LSU-Arkansas game at Shreveport with more Louisiana pride. When I am governor, LSU will be governed . . . by men as well qualified as those at present in Tulane University."[20]

Voters elected the thirty-four-year-old Long governor by an overwhelming margin in April 1928. He took office on May 21 on the steps of the Capitol, pledging, "Every dollar wrung from the taxpayers of this state forms a part of a sacred fund that is pledged by the people for their own care and to provide for their children and the generations that are to come." Later, he added, "I have been employed to lead the work of charity, of education, of the upbuilding of our general institutions, the promotion of justice, and the like." Long did not mention LSU in his address. The school and its impressive and growing new campus, just two miles south of where he spoke, were not among his priorities on the day he became governor, and LSU would not become central to him and his political future until midway through his term of office. But when Long turned his full attention to the university he once longed to attend—and to the campus he had spurned and ridiculed—life at LSU would never be the same.[21]

5

WE MUST GET A PRESIDENT

In his Pulitzer Prize–winning 1969 biography, *Huey Long*, T. Harry Williams claimed Long "displayed only a cursory interest in LSU during the first two years of his governorship." As evidence of ambivalence toward the university, Williams wrote, Long supported a minor increase in the school's 1929 appropriation. And, he added, "When he discussed his far-ranging plans for Louisiana, he did not mention the university. He did not attend any of its functions, such as the graduation exercises, to which, as governor, he was invited and, apparently, he did not even visit the campus. He seemed anxious to avoid giving the impression that he meant to interfere with the operation of the institution."[1]

The legend that Williams and other biographers accepted about Long's early indifference toward LSU was incorrect in several respects. Long's first visit to the new LSU campus as governor happened on May 25, 1928, four days after his inauguration. He attended the Cadet Regiment's last parade of the school year. Later that day, he spoke to the cadets and pledged to "leave nothing undone to help the Louisiana State University to thrive and progress."[2]

Long returned to campus on the morning of Monday, June 11, for a meeting of the LSU Board of Supervisors. Because of his new office, he was now the board's ex officio chair. He affirmed from his first meeting with acting president Thomas Atkinson and board members that he would be active in the school's affairs. And, unlike those who wanted to consolidate LSU on its new campus, Long told the board he favored maintaining two campuses. "I think it is to the interest of the university that the old grounds should be put in good shape," he said. "The university should look toward the concentration of the ladies at the old campus." Long noted that some legislators hoped to use several buildings on the old campus for legislative offices. "I am discouraging that. I don't think the old university should ever be sold. It should be put back in as good condition as possible."

At this meeting, the thirty-four-year-old Long was also bold in critiquing the sixty-year-old Atkinson and the elders on the board for their management of student conduct. "This school has tightened up some in the past two years, but not half enough. There has got to be a good deal more chaperoning at parties and dances," he said. Looking to Atkinson, he added, "You are not going to make any of us mad in going as far as you like in that direction. You can't be too tight on discipline. I want to tell you I am going to back you to the limit." It was a promise Long did not always keep. Still, he left no doubt about his support for LSU. "If we don't have some unexpected complications, there will be more money for LSU and all the other institutions than there has been in the past." That night, to further show his interest in the university, Long attended the school's commencement ceremony at the Greek Theatre.[3]

Despite his budding concern for LSU, Long's ambitious legislative agenda occupied much of his first two years as governor. That program included raising severance taxes to buy schoolbooks for elementary and secondary students, addressing adult literacy, and building roads and bridges. In December 1928, lawmakers approved his plan to finance $30 million in road construction with state bonds. But some lawmakers and the courts opposed raising even more revenue for his program. That prompted Long to call a six-day special legislative session in March 1929. Among his proposals was a new, five-cent-per-barrel tax on the processing of refined oil, a direct attack on Standard Oil. "Huey had lit the fuse of a political bombshell," biographer Richard D. White Jr. observed. "Every legislator from oil-producing parishes knew that voting for a processing tax meant suicide in their next election."[4]

Long's efforts to tax Standard Oil drew him into a series of explosive confrontations with opposition lawmakers and industry representatives. In a radio speech, he alleged that house and senate members who voted against his tax were "bought" by the oil giant. Four days into the special session, Standard Oil and its allies struck back by trying to remove Long from office. After days of raucous debate and confrontation, the house charged Long with eight impeachable offenses, including bribing lawmakers to pass legislation, carrying a concealed weapon, and razing the governor's mansion without legislative approval. Some charges were valid, others not, but the sum of his opponents' arguments was that Long had been ruthless in pushing to raise taxes on Standard Oil and corrupt in lobbying for his legislative program. In April, Long and his allies halted his senate trial when fifteen senators—one more than necessary for acquittal—signed a so-called "Round Robin" document in which they vowed to exonerate Long "regardless of the evidence."[5]

Long later acknowledged the impeachment transformed his governing style. "I used to try to get things done by saying 'please.' That didn't work and now I'm a dynamiter. I dynamite 'em out of my path." Long's older brother Julius summed up Long's approach to politics, post-impeachment: "He politicized everything in the State that could be politicized. He holds every State office." Those politicized state institutions soon included Louisiana State University.[6]

F red Frey, then LSU's dean of men, was not wrong when he recalled that Long was far from obsessed with LSU during the first half of his term. "He had been having his troubles with the legislature," Frey said years later, when asked why Long did not involve himself more in LSU's affairs in those early years. Although his larger political battles often distracted Long, this did not mean that he was uninterested in LSU or that he ignored the state's other colleges and universities. The State Board of Education (or, at LSU, the Board of Supervisors) appointed university presidents, and Long's involvement in those decisions would weaken the authority of these boards.

In March 1929, for example, the governor demanded the resignation of Victor L. Roy, president of the Louisiana State Normal College (now Northwestern State University) in Natchitoches. Long's sister Olive Long Cooper, an art instructor at the school, sparked the controversy when she alleged that a faculty member, M. E. Downs, had disparaged the governor to his students during a class. Cooper, who sometimes invoked her brother's name to get her way around campus, also allegedly threatened to have a student expelled for unspecified statements he made at a student body meeting. Long placated his sister and exploited the hubbub to persuade the Board of Education to appoint his third cousin, W. W. Tison, as college president. Tison fired Downs.[7]

Although Long spent most of his first two years pushing his agenda through a sometimes-recalcitrant legislature, he found time to intervene at

Colonel Campbell B. Hodges, the LSU Board's choice to serve as university president-elect after the retirement of Thomas D. Boyd in 1926. (US Military Academy, West Point, *Howitzer* yearbook, 1928)

other state institutions, especially when it involved deposing political opponents. This was the case at LSU. In spring and summer 1929, Long took a keen interest in who would become the university's permanent president after he realized that Campbell Hodges, a US Army lieutenant colonel and the brother of a political adversary, was about to get the job. That adversary was W. H. "Will" Hodges, a prominent Bossier Parish planter and former state legislator. In 1928, Hodges had served as northern Louisiana campaign manager for US representative Riley J. Wilson, one of Long's opponents in the Democratic Party's gubernatorial primary. So intense was Will Hodges's dislike of Long that, in summer 1929, he accepted the chairmanship of the Bossier Parish committee of the anti-Long Constitutional League of Louisiana.[8]

Despite his brother's political activism, the forty-eight-year-old Campbell Hodges was apolitical, and his qualifications for the LSU president's job were considerable, at least by 1929 standards, when the school emphasized military training. A Bossier Parish native and graduate of the US Military Academy at West Point, Hodges taught military science and tactics at LSU from 1910 to 1921 and served as commandant of cadets from 1911 to 1913. He was so admired by students that the editors of LSU's yearbook, the *Gumbo*, dedicated their 1913 edition to him. Hodges later served with distinction in France during the First World War.

In 1926, after longtime LSU president Thomas D. Boyd announced he would retire the following year, the LSU Board of Supervisors offered Hodges, then the commandant of cadets at West Point, the president's job. Hodges wanted the position, but the Army still had a claim on him until his scheduled retirement in 1929. When the War Department denied his request to complete his Army career at LSU, the LSU Board voted to hold the job for him until 1929. In June 1927, after Boyd's retirement, the LSU Board named the School of Engineering dean, Thomas Atkinson, acting president until Hodges's arrival.[9]

In early 1929, not long after Long engineered the appointment of his cousin to the presidency of Louisiana State Normal College, he learned that Hodges was poised to retire from the Army and would soon return to Baton Rouge to run LSU. But Long was not about to allow the brother of a political enemy to take a plum state position. Besides knowing of Will Hodges's enmity for him, Long almost certainly knew that Campbell Hodges had appeared in Shreveport in December 1926 (where Long then lived), shortly after the LSU Board named him president-in-waiting. In a speech to the LSU Alumni Association of North Louisiana, Hodges praised one of Long's adversaries, former governor John Parker, for his role in creating the new LSU campus. Although he had been at West Point for most of the previous three years, Hodges told his audience, "I knew about Governor Parker and his plans for a new university and Greater A&M College. It must be a great satisfaction to him to see his dreams come true, and the state owes Governor Parker much gratitude for having the vision to dream those dreams and the energy and executive ability to turn them into reality."[10]

Long's first move was to lobby—and sometimes intimidate—LSU Board members to reverse their 1926 decision to give Hodges the job. On the evening of March 20, 1929, Dr. Roy O. Young, an LSU Board member from Lafayette Parish, encountered Long in the lobby of the Heidelberg Hotel in Baton Rouge. Long was eager to assert that Hodges would not be the LSU president.

"We have got to choose a president for the state university," Long told Young.

Still under the impression that the board, and not the governor, ran LSU, Young replied, "I am willing to discuss the presidency of the university with you."

"Hodges is not coming," Long said, "so we must get a president."

"Why is Hodges not coming?"

"Because I am not going to let him come. He is a military man and unfit for the position."

"And I say that Hodges is going to come."

"If he comes, it will be for two or three months only."

"Unless you get enough votes on the board, you cannot get rid of him."

Long, confident of getting his way, told Young, "I get control of any board I want and do as I please."

Informing Young that he hoped to install state education superintendent Thomas H. Harris as LSU president, Long explained, "I will give it to him. I have six members of the board and my vote makes seven." Long pounded his chest, adding, "*I* will give it to him." He ended the conversation with this taunt: "When you get back to Lafayette, let them know we made it too hot for you."[11]

Although he hoped to install Harris as LSU president, his belief that he could name the university's leader was not as unusual as some of Long's opponents suggested. Harris claimed in his memoir that governors Luther Hall and John Parker both offered him the LSU presidency before Long suggested the same in 1929. Harris turned them all down.[12]

The potential showdown over Hodges evaporated a few days after Long's contentious conversation with Young. President Herbert Hoover, who took office earlier that month, made Hodges his military aide. In June 1929, with Long present and voting, the LSU Board gave the president's job to Atkinson. Hodges would serve Hoover for his entire term, and three months into that of his successor, Franklin D. Roosevelt. He would become LSU president in 1941, six years after Long's death.[13]

Around the same time, Long meddled in the business of another Louisiana university. He made an aborted attempt in May to depose longtime president Edwin L. Stephens from his position at the Southwestern Industrial Institute at Lafayette (now the University of Louisiana). Long did not disclose his complaint about Stephens, although he probably wanted to install a political ally. He mustered five votes to fire Stephens, but several Long allies in the region backed the beleaguered president. Long failed to dismiss Stephens only because he would not oust Tulane University's president, a Stephens supporter, from the State Board of Education. That move, following Long's role in hiring the presidents of two other universities, alarmed the editors of the *Shreveport Times*. "Although not an integral part of that system, and merely chairman of the State Board of Education by virtue of

President Thomas Atkinson led LSU from 1927 to 1930, when Long hired
his replacement, James Monroe Smith. (LSU *Gumbo* yearbook, 1928)

his office," the paper said, "Governor Long has undertaken to politicize the
State's educational institutions—root, branch, twig and leaf."[14]

If anti-Long newspaper editors and other Long opponents were concerned about his meddling with the state's colleges, he soon provided them
more reason to worry: He was also injecting himself into LSU's football program. The *Shreveport Times* reported in March 1929 that Long was encouraging a celebrated player from Centenary College, Joe Almokary, to bolt for
LSU. Long reportedly tried to entice the young man with a $125-a-month
position at the state laboratory in Baton Rouge, as well as an $80-a-month
campus job. Almokary was a former star player for Shreveport's Byrd High
School who worked the night shift as a Shreveport firefighter while attending Centenary. He admitted he was interested in transferring to LSU. He also
acknowledged speaking to Long but swore the governor never offered him a
job. "If I enroll at LSU," he assured the *Shreveport Journal,* "it will not be on
the influence of Governor Huey P. Long or anyone else." Despite Almokary's
denials, Long was courting him. "I hope you'll come to LSU," Long said when
they met, adding that he considered Centenary's faculty deficient. "All they
got there is old [George] Sexton [the college president] who teaches the

Bible. I know a hell of a lot more about the Bible than he does. You come to LSU, and I'll teach you the Bible."[15]

Long was persuaded that, in Almokary, he had found a player of exceptional quality. "I've got you an All-American player," he had told LSU's new football coach, Henry Russell "Russ" Cohen. "This Almokary is the greatest player the world ever saw. He will win plenty of games for LSU." Cohen was not so sure. "Joe is a big boy, and he might develop into a fine back," he told Long, "but he isn't an All-American." Despite Cohen's reservations, Almokary was at LSU that fall, starring on the freshman football squad. And in some vindication for Long, he became one of the team's celebrated players by the 1930 season (although, as Cohen predicted, he was never an All-American). Despite Almokary's assurances to the contrary, the anti-Long *Shreveport Journal* suspected Long had tried to steal a local player. "If it is true that Governor Long has plunged his fingers into the football pie and has attempted to coerce Joe Almokary into leaving Centenary in order to enter Louisiana State University," a *Journal* sportswriter wrote in late March, "he has been guilty of proselyting in its basest form. There is a code of ethics among colleges that forbids any such interference."[16]

It was not the first time Long, as governor, revealed his interest in the LSU football team. The previous year, during the 1928 season, he began appearing at team practices led by Cohen, the school's new thirty-five-year-old coach and athletic director. A stocky, cerebral man, Cohen sported owlish-round eyeglasses and seemed always to wear a brown suit with a matching brown ball cap over his grey hair. An Augusta, Georgia, native and a First World War US Army veteran, Cohen had played football for Vanderbilt. He was the team captain in 1915 when his squad won the Southern Intercollegiate Athletic Association championship. He came to LSU from the University of Alabama, where he had been the top assistant to one of the game's most respected coaches, Wallace Wade. Cohen brought with him one assistant, Ben Enis, a former Alabama player. His other assistant coach was a holdover from former coach Mike Donahue's staff, Harry Rabenhorst, also LSU's basketball and baseball coach. A Baton Rouge native, the affable Rabenhorst had been a player/coach at Wake Forest, serving as team captain from 1917 to 1920, and as head coach for the 1918 and 1919 seasons. A former fullback, he held the record for the longest punt in college football history (115 yards, 75 in the air, on Thanksgiving Day 1919 against North Carolina State).[17]

Part of Long's sudden enthusiasm for LSU football was almost certainly

LSU assistant football coach Harry Rabenhorst.
(LSU *Gumbo* yearbook, 1934)

related to Cohen's relationship with Wade, who had coached the 1925 Alabama squad to a fabled, undefeated season and capped it with a dramatic, one-point come-from-behind victory in the January 1926 Rose Bowl over the University of Washington Huskies. Until Alabama's unlikely trip to Pasadena, California, for the nation's highest-profile and only postseason college football game, many national sportswriters treated southern college football with disdain or derision. In fact, the team from Tuscaloosa earned its spot only after four northern teams rejected bids from the bowl committee. Alabama's improbable win sparked a wave of euphoria and southern pride from Virginia to Texas. LSU fans in Baton Rouge gathered around radios for an Atlanta-based broadcast of the Associated Press's play-by-play of the game and pulled for the Crimson Tide. "If the Louisiana Tigers had been playing there couldn't have been more interest shown [in Baton Rouge]," a *State-Times* reporter wrote. Governor Henry Fuqua sent a telegram to the team captain before the game: "Go to it boys, we're with you." The night of the game, Baton Rouge residents flooded the *Morning Advocate* with phone calls, inquiring about the score. Often, the response to the news that Alabama had prevailed was, "Hooray for Dixie!"

"Alabama was our representative in fighting for us against the world," Vanderbilt coach Dan McGugin said after the game, capturing the jubilant mood of the South. "I fought, bled, died, and was resurrected with the Crimson

Tide." As the *State-Times* observed: "The South, for the first time in history, was being given her chance to show her prowess before the nation and those gallant Dixie boys came through with colors flying. It was Dixie's battle and the South shouted encouragement, even though 'Bama could not hear them."[18]

Alabama repeated the feat the following year, finishing the season undefeated and earning a bid to play Stanford in the Rose Bowl. As it had previous year, Wade's team exceeded low expectations and battled the Cardinal to an upset, 7–7 tie. Across the South, Alabama's second triumph in as many years was added vindication for an entire region. Georgia Tech's dramatic 8–7 win over the University of California in the 1928 Rose Bowl further stoked college football fever in the South, as had the University of Georgia's 14–10 victory in 1927 over Yale in the Yale Bowl. (Georgia had trekked to New Haven the previous four seasons and lost each time.) In the words of historian Andrew Doyle, the wins were "a sublime tonic for a people buffeted by a historical legacy of military defeat, poverty, and alienation from the American political and cultural mainstream."

Long could not have ignored the national acclaim that successful football programs brought to those and other southern teams that performed well against non-southern opponents. So, it was only natural that he might dream of the same success and national renown for LSU and hope that, when it happened, he could bask in the reflected glory. And no wonder that Long may have seen in Wade's former assistant the elements necessary to build something in Baton Rouge to propel LSU into the same college football stratosphere as Alabama and Georgia Tech.[19]

As for Long's aggressive and unorthodox recruiting on LSU's behalf, one college football historian, John Sayle Watterson, has observed that Long's behavior, while excessive, was not unique in the South of that era. "One might attribute all of this quaint boosterism to vintage Huey Long had it not reflected trends in southern and, to a lesser extent, in northern athletics," he wrote. "Outdone by some schools in Pennsylvania, college teams in the deep South went after football talent far more openly than most northern institutions."[20]

Cohen may have brought with him some of the glamor and prestige associated with the highly regarded Wallace Wade and his Crimson Tide, but he was not Wade. Cohen knew football, but some around the team worried he did not understand how to motivate the young men he led. "He was the goddamndest coach," Baton Rouge banker Lewis Gottlieb recalled, adding, "He didn't know men." Said Rabenhorst: "Cohen was a product of Wade's system, a sound system. He knew the game, but [had] no zip or imagination." Sidney Bowman, then a freshman member of the squad, remembered that Cohen had a disconcerting, nervous habit of clearing his throat and pacing as he spoke to his team. "A good coach, solid," Bowman said, "but couldn't handle boys."[21]

Cohen, however, could handle Huey Long. And the new governor liked Cohen, as the coach tolerated the governor's sudden interest in his team. But as Cohen and Rabenhorst soon learned, Long knew little about the intricacies of football. At a team practice before the annual LSU-Arkansas game in 1928, Long surprised Rabenhorst when he mentioned, "I guess they'll kick off to us first?" Puzzled, Rabenhorst asked why. "Well," Long replied, "we kicked off to them last year." At the same practice, a nervous Long pulled Cohen aside and insisted, "Coach, we must beat Arkansas." Cohen asked Long why he cared so much about this game. Long probably had no time to explain his bitter feud earlier that year with Caddo and Bossier parish officials after leaders there rejected the free textbooks that were part of the new governor's education program. To bend the two parishes to his will, Long threatened to kill legislation that would enable the state to compete for an Army Air Corps base (now Barksdale Air Force Base). Instead of describing the textbook saga and the fact that Shreveport counted among its residents many Arkansas fans, Long explained, "Because everybody in Shreveport hates me and I hate everybody in Shreveport."[22]

6

I DON'T FOOL AROUND
WITH LOSERS

Long was not the first Louisiana governor beguiled by LSU's football program. Baton Rouge native Henry L. Fuqua was a frequent visitor to team practices during his brief tenure as governor in the mid-1920s. Said to have been the youngest student in the school's history, Fuqua persuaded LSU to admit him at age ten in the mid-1870s when LSU opened its doors to prep-school students from Baton Rouge. Near the end of his five years on campus, the precocious, athletic young man became the baseball team's star pitcher. Although he never earned a degree from the school, Fuqua loved LSU. His father, James Fuqua, had served on the LSU Board in the 1880s. Governor Jared "J. Y." Sanders appointed the younger Fuqua to the university's Board of Supervisors, and he was its vice chairman in 1909–10. And Fuqua's sister, Annie, was the wife of LSU's longtime president, Thomas D. Boyd.

Friends recalled that Fuqua's passion for LSU baseball was exceeded only by his enthusiasm for the school's football program. Before he was governor, according to an observer, he grew so emotional at one LSU-Tulane game, "it became necessary for him to leave his seat and go out on the back of the stands, away from the game, and recuperate." As governor, Fuqua often left his Capitol office on fall afternoons for a short walk to nearby State Field to watch the squad's practice. And he was a fixture at LSU home games, where the university built a special sideline box for him and his guests. "He never missed a game played on State Field," the *Baton Rouge Morning Advocate* wrote after he died in October 1926. "With a black cigar clinched between his teeth and his hat pulled down far on his head he watched every play made—cheered the Tigers when they won and only the harder when they lost."[1]

During the 1925 season, when the team's fortunes flagged after an embarrassing 42–0 loss to Alabama, Fuqua summoned the players to his office. "Around the executive table they sat, and he questioned them one by one, called them by name, seemed to know them as if he, too, were among their number," the *LSU Alumni News* reported. "And he talked to them—kindly, confidently, jestingly." The result of Fuqua's pep talk, the publication concluded, "was the beginning of a new team. A fighting, plunging, machinelike team that played real football and played it well."[2]

That a Louisiana governor cared deeply about LSU football and would give the team an occasional motivational speech was not peculiar, as Fuqua proved. But a governor, like Long, traveling with the squad and comporting himself as an extension of its coaching staff? This was new, and a sign that Long saw the opportunity for reflected glory from LSU's success on the gridiron.

During his first football season as governor, in fall 1928, Long volunteered to accompany the LSU players to Shreveport for the Arkansas game, possibly the first time a Louisiana governor did so. On Thursday, November 1, he joined the players, the Regimental Band, and fans for the overnight train trip. Somewhere along the way, Long learned that Coach Cohen planned to take the players to a hotel in Marshall, Texas, just across the Texas-Louisiana border, so they could sleep and practice away from the hubbub that always surrounded the State Fair game. Long, who wanted to stay with the team, knew he could not leave Louisiana without his gubernatorial powers devolving temporarily to the lieutenant governor. So, he ordered the players housed at Shreveport's Youree Hotel. "I thought you'd rather stay here and leave some of your money in Louisiana," he explained as he directed Cohen and the players off the train.[3]

Before the game, Long conjured a subtle dig at the Shreveport crowd, many of whom he regarded as Ku Klux Klan sympathizers. (Although KKK influence had declined in Shreveport by 1928, the city had been the informal headquarters of Louisiana's Klan early in the decade.) When the LSU band led a parade down Texas Street from the First Methodist Church toward the team's hotel, the unit stopped at the Caddo Parish Courthouse. With the Klan's strong anti-Catholic sentiments apparently in mind, Long asked the band director, Pop Guilbeau, to lead the cadets in a rendition of the popular song "Streets of New York." The better informed in the crowd recognized the tune as the campaign song of Democratic presidential nominee, New York governor Al Smith, the first Catholic nominated for president by a major American political party.[4]

Long visited Russ Cohen later that day in his hotel room, only to find the first-year coach pacing in an anxious fit. "Sit down," Long ordered, "you're nervous as a cat." Discovering that Cohen worried about the size of the Arkansas players, Long sent one of his bodyguards, Joe Messina, to the lobby to assess the opposing squad. Messina reported that the Razorbacks he saw were not unusually large. "There's nothing to worry about," Long assured Cohen. "They're not too tough. Messina says so."[5]

As the team ate in the hotel's dining room that night, Long breezed in, accompanied by his elder son, nine-year-old Russell. (The next day would be his tenth birthday.) The governor gave the team a pep talk—among the first of many such speeches he delivered to LSU players over the next five years. "Hell, you ought to beat 'em. We got better roads in Louisiana, free schoolbooks, and better everything." It was not clear how better roads and textbooks translated into superior play on the gridiron. But Long had an even stronger argument in his arsenal: the relative size of the Arkansas players. As Long spoke, he noticed some Razorbacks walking by the restaurant's door. "See that, fellows? They ain't got a thing. Joe Messina just scouted them in the lobby."[6]

Dressed in a suit, wearing a light-colored fedora, and swinging his familiar walking stick, Long paced the sidelines during the afternoon game the next day. "No box for the governor when the 'Old War Skule' is battling," the *Shreveport Times* reported. LSU lost, 7–0.[7]

Besides the Arkansas contest, no game was more important to LSU fans than the school's annual showdown with Tulane University. Established in 1834 as the publicly funded Medical College of Louisiana, Tulane was the South's second-oldest medical school. In 1847, the legislature renamed it the University of Louisiana. It earned its current name in 1884, two years after a wealthy New Orleans merchant, Paul Tulane, bequeathed $1 million to the school. The school, which moved to its present campus on St. Charles Avenue in 1894, was rare among the nation's private universities in that it had first been a public institution. For decades, as LSU had struggled to find its footing as a prominent university in Louisiana, the more sophisticated, urban Tulane loomed large and almost always overshadowed the smaller, quasi-rural school to its north. Its enrollment, budget, scope, and ambition had always outpaced LSU. For the 1929–30 school year, for example, Tulane's total enrollment was 3,578, compared to 2,171 for LSU. And Tulane boasted Louisiana's only medical school.[8]

For decades, the two schools had enjoyed an intense athletic rivalry. LSU's first football game, in New Orleans in 1893, was against Tulane. (LSU lost, 34–0.) The teams, eighty miles apart, played each other most of the ensuing years and every year since 1911, except the season lost to the First World War in 1918. LSU's opponent for its first game in Tiger Stadium, in November 1924, had been Tulane.

For Long's first LSU-Tulane game as governor, a 6–1 LSU team traveled by train to New Orleans to play the 6–3 Green Wave. Before a crowd of 30,000 in two-year-old Tulane Stadium, Long staged a show of neutrality. He wore LSU-colored ribbons on one coat lapel, and Tulane-colored ribbons on the other. He started the game on the Tulane side. At halftime, he crossed the field to cheers from LSU fans, who he joined for the second half. The game disappointed both sides, however, as neither squad scored. The contest ended in a 0–0 tie.[9]

To this point in his governorship, Long had encouraged the idea he was not favoring LSU. No one around LSU's football program believed that. He never appeared at Tulane football practices or traveled with the team. But he still wanted Tulane fans and New Orleans voters to think he supported each school equally. Even as late as January 1930, at the Roosevelt Hotel's Tip-Top Room, Long attended the annual banquet of Tulane's Side Lines Club, devoted that year to celebrating the Green Wave's perfect 9–0 season, including its defeat of LSU. "I want to announce my appreciation of a great team," said Long, an ex officio member of Tulane's governing board, "and I did not care to see anything happen Thanksgiving Day [the day of the LSU-Tulane game] to take the championship away from Tulane." Although he assured Tulane fans he had no special fondness for LSU, he soon proved that his affection for the Baton Rouge school was unique.[10]

Beyond keeping Campbell Hodges out of the president's office and cheering on the football team, Long may not have had the time or interest to dive into other affairs at LSU during the first two years of his term. (His active, near-daily involvement would not begin until late 1930.) But it was wrong to assume that Long was ignoring LSU or that he did not view the school's success, academically and athletically, as a result of his influence and support. In October 1929, speaking at a rally at the South Louisiana State Fair at Donaldsonville, on the Mississippi River forty miles south of Baton Rouge, Long defended his education agenda. To most citizens, that meant providing free schoolbooks to students and increasing adult literacy. Long, however, expanded his education reforms to include a vast (and wholly imagined) improvement of the quality of instruction at LSU. "Louisiana State University is under [the] control of Huey P. Long," he bragged to an audience of about fifteen thousand, "and if you don't believe so, let some of them up there start something and I'll clean them out damn quick." It was not clear what the "something" was that Long had in mind. He added, "When I took office, the university was a third-rate school and now the university ranks with Harvard and Yale." No one familiar with the situation at LSU in 1929 believed such a boast. Much of Long's speech that day was a pungent attack on former governor John Parker, whose anti-Long organization, the Constitutional League, Long derided as "the Constipated League." His assertion about LSU's vast improvement was probably a backhanded rebuke of his predecessor, who considered himself the architect of LSU's recent success.[11]

Despite bragging about having transformed LSU into an academic powerhouse, Long was still interested primarily in the school's popular football team and how its statewide renown—and potential for national glory—might reflect on him. Like everything else Long participated in, LSU football soon became an extension of himself and a part of his political success. "I don't fool around with losers," Oliver "Ike" Carriere, a former LSU quarterback, recalled hearing Long tell the team. "LSU can't have a losing team because that'll mean I'm associated with a loser." Long's thinking about LSU football, Carriere believed, was, "it had to be great because he was with it."[12]

Long's acute interest in LSU was consistent with his growing desire to control it. When Long affiliated with an organization or institution, he was not inclined to be a follower. "He was intensely and solely interested in himself," T. Harry Williams wrote. "He had to dominate every scene he was in and every person around him. He craved attention and would go to almost any length to get it. He knew that an audacious action, although it was harsh and even barbarous, could shock people into a state where they could be manipulated." Lewis Gottlieb, a Baton Rouge banker who knew Long well, saw him as "a great seducer of men." After watching and interviewing Long in the mid-1930s, journalist Forrest Davis wrote, "In twenty years of active journalism I never have met a man so confident of his powers, so cocksure of his private destiny. Nor, with the exception of two or three grownups and a couple of badly spoiled children, have I ever encountered an individual so naturally oblivious to the petty graces of human intercourse, so independent of, and indifferent to, persons around him." Davis concluded, "I never met a man so seemingly frank."[13]

When Long started showing up at team practices again in 1929, Russ Cohen seemed not to care—or, at least, he was savvy enough to pretend that he did not mind. "He'd drive right out in the middle of the practice field, get out and watch a while, and then leave," Harry Rabenhorst recalled.[14]

A year earlier, Long had poached standout Centenary player Joe Almokary. Now, before the 1929 season, he suggested a similar raid on another prospect—Don Zimmerman, a star football and track-and-field athlete from Lake Charles, who had enrolled at Tulane. "Tulane is beating us," Long told Cohen and his assistants, raising the idea of luring Zimmerman from the rival school. "I'll give his dad a job with the state and get him up here and we'll put the boy in at LSU." Ike Carriere recalled: "It had to be explained to him you couldn't do it that way, that to build up a team, you started with the high schools and recruited the material."[15]

When it came time for the 1929 LSU-Arkansas game, Long again went along, riding the overnight train to Shreveport with the team, band, and fans. "He played the Jew's harp with the band all night," Rabenhorst recalled. Three weeks later, Long watched from the front row of the LSU side as the season ended with a 21–0 loss to Tulane at Tiger Stadium. Unlike the previous year, he did not split his time between the two teams, a subtle signal of his shifting alliances. Long was already growing more interested in the academic and administrative sides of LSU. And a few weeks later, he would overstep and receive a valuable lesson about what it took to have his way with the university.[16]

L ong made his first move to influence the academic life of LSU in December 1929. He tried to depose the aging founding dean of the LSU Law School, Robert Lee Tullis. An institution in Baton Rouge, Tullis had ruled the Law School since 1908. His colleagues regarded him as a brilliant lawyer, while some students saw him more as a harsh taskmaster. "He was a pretty hard . . . Simon Legree type," one student recalled. Behind his back, students called the Tensas Parish native the "Tensas Terror." Adding to Tullis's problems in late 1929 was his deteriorating eyesight, a consequence of worsening cataracts in both eyes.[17]

Long got much of his information about Tullis from Kemble K. Kennedy, a brash, ambitious twenty-six-year-old LSU law student from Farmerville, a Union Parish town about seventy miles north of Long's hometown of Winnfield. Long first met Kennedy years earlier when he represented him in a personal injury case. Kennedy's father died when he was ten, and the precocious young man, in search of a father figure, attached himself to the charismatic future governor. Kennedy campaigned for Long in Union Parish during the 1928 governor's race. Long encouraged the friendship and treated Kennedy as a protégé. No student on the LSU campus was closer to Long. Some suits Kennedy wore around campus were hand-me-downs from the governor's closet.[18]

"K.K.," as classmates called him, served as student body president before he entered law school. He was now president of the school's new Law Club and vice president of the LSU Student Council. And Kennedy was not shy about challenging university officials. The Law Club he helped create declared in October 1929 that its purpose was to "function as a union" to make "the law student body more of a unit in seeking what they term as 'justifiable concessions' from the faculty and the university."[19]

That fall, Kennedy led a successful student revolt against the school's Athletic Council when it tried to raise the admission price to the LSU-Tulane game by a dollar. Only after Kennedy and others threatened a campus-wide strike did President Atkinson revoke the surcharge. In early November 1929, Kennedy wrote to Long with a complaint about the deportment of a law professor, James B. Smith. He asked the governor to intervene to stop LSU from renewing the professor's contract. Among other alleged offenses, Kennedy complained that "Smith does not conduct himself as a gentleman in the presence of his classes [and] that his general attitude towards students is not friendly."[20]

When Kennedy and nine members of the Law Club asked to meet with Long in early December 1929, the governor was happy to receive them. Whatever Kennedy told Long about Tullis, it was enough to persuade him that the dean must go. It could not have hurt Kennedy's case that Tullis was a vocal Long opponent. Soon, Long made it clear he wanted Tullis out, say-

LSU Law School dean Robert L. Tullis, called by some students the "Tensas Terror." (LSU *Gumbo* yearbook, 1933)

ing he relied on the advice of many students in asking the LSU Board to force Tullis's retirement at its January 1930 meeting.[21]

That prompted a brief-but-fierce protest among the law students who had joined Kennedy in the meeting with Long. These students now complained that Kennedy did not speak for them. Rather, they understood they were meeting with the governor to discuss students' concerns about Professor Smith, not Tullis. And some claimed Long seemed determined to seek Tullis's dismissal before the meeting began. "It seems perfectly clear that Governor Long desired something to use as justification for his meddling with the state university when he obtains control of the board of supervisors in January, which, as members of the Law School, we heartily resent," three students from the meeting said in a statement. On the heels of the students' protest came an open letter signed by twenty-one LSU Law School alumni from New Orleans. They opposed Tullis's forced retirement, urging Long to "spare the people of the state, and the Louisiana State university, from the great and irreparable loss which would be the result if Dean Robert L. Tullis were removed."[22]

Long remained undaunted. "In recognition of Dean Tullis' long service," the governor announced in late December, "I believe, and feel that the university's board of administrators will agree with me, that Mr. Tullis should be made dean emeritus. I believe it is generally agreed that the wearing administrative routine of the school should be turned over to a younger and more active man."[23]

Such meddling by a governor in its internal affairs, one former LSU law professor told the *Baton Rouge Morning Advocate* in early January, might cost the school its membership in the Association of American Law Schools. In a front-page story headlined "Rating of Law School and L.S.U. Threatened by Long's Dickerings," Clarence Updegraff of the University of Iowa Law School opined: "It is greatly to be regretted that the irregularity of a student conference with the governor took place; it is still more to be deplored that the governor has been led to take seriously any suggestion made in such a conference."[24]

Despite his stated desire to see Tullis retired, Long could not yet count on all his orders being obeyed by LSU Board members. Most were men appointed by his predecessor. For that reason and, perhaps, because of the vocal opposition from various allies of Tullis and the school, Long dropped the matter in January. Tullis would remain Law School dean for another three and a half years.

Beyond objecting that Kennedy misrepresented their views about Tullis to Long, some law students also complained that he worked as a campus spy for the governor. This was likely the case. Kennedy came close to admitting the charge in an interview with the *New Orleans Item*. "They stamp me as a 'representative' of Governor Long and intimate that I'm being used as a 'tool' whereby the governor can find out the inside workings at the university. Such is false, but if Governor Long ever feels disposed to call on me for such information, I can give assurances that my services will go at the asking."

Kennedy made it clear, however, that he did not believe all was well at LSU, a message he, no doubt, conveyed to Long. "All the troubles at LSU are not confined to the law school by any means. I'm not attempting to run the university or any part of it because I'm just a student, but I can foresee changes that will be welcomed by the student body." Although he insisted he was not prodding Long to intervene in the daily affairs of LSU, it was not long before the ambitious law student from Farmerville precipitated an incident that prompted Long to do just that.[25]

7

THE *WHANGDOODLE*

I n spring 1930, a mysterious, pink, four-page broadsheet appeared on the LSU campus and around Baton Rouge. Produced by a group of LSU students, the *Whangdoodle* resembled other humorous, rump college newspapers of the era. It ridiculed what its editors and writers regarded as the stuffy administrators and professors who ran the university. Under the headline "The Doodle Dares Suggest," an anonymous writer offered various proposals, including: "That the fossils in our administrative and faculty bodies be cleared out for more progressive blood"; "That our dairy barns and maternity wards for pigs be converted into dormitories for coeds"; and, "That all due credit be given those university authorities who have worked for our school, but that those who have served out their terms be retired on a pension. This is not an asylum for dependents—it is a modern state institution."

Beyond the *Whangdoodle*'s mild attacks on the faculty and the Law School—described as the "prize joke of [the] L.S.U. campus"—there was little to alarm university officials. Perhaps most bothersome was a front-page story detailing "groundless rumors" about the arrest of an unnamed faculty member said to have assaulted a coed with an ink bottle after she expressed doubts about Darwin's theory of evolution.[1]

Those who recalled the *Whangdoodle*'s original 1925 incarnation may have worried about how far another edition of the paper might go. Five years earlier, horrified LSU administrators had persuaded local authorities to arrest three men, including an LSU sophomore, and charge them with criminal libel for writing that police had arrested a faculty member in a local brothel. University officials and some Louisiana newspapers denounced the 1925 paper which some suspected was produced by the LSU chapter of Theta Nu

Epsilon. TNE's national organization did not recognize LSU's chapter, and the university considered it an "outlaw" society. "Theta Nu Epsilon is a national 'sub-rosa' fraternity, operating wherever it exists in defiance of college regulations forbidding its existence," the twice-weekly student newspaper, the *Reveille,* explained in March 1925. The paper added that it had no "definite proof" that a TNE chapter even existed at LSU. Despite the arrests and a lengthy investigation, a Baton Rouge grand jury declined to indict the students and others involved in its publication. Three years later, in May 1928, a variation of the *Whangdoodle*—its editors called this one the *Tattler*—attacked some LSU administrators. One story featured the alliterative headline, "The Asinine Actors of Atkinson's Administration."[2]

When a new *Whangdoodle* turned up in spring of 1930, editors announced its reappearance in a brief story headlined, "The Doodle Returns." The editors wrote:

> Like a thief in the night this scurrilous pink sheet once more invades the sacred precincts of our dear old campus. Unheralded, unwanted, yet undaunted, hiding under the shameful cloak of anonymity, it dares to thrust itself upon our unsuspecting student body and [Baton Rouge police] Chief [King A.] Strenzke. It makes no excuse for its existence. It asks no quarter—it expects none. If it is pressed for a defense of its publication it has but one argument to advance—a feeble attempt to awaken the dumbest of student-bodies [*sic*] in the whole United States.[3]

Despite its efforts to arouse students, the *Whangdoodle*'s first 1930 edition attracted little attention. The same would not be said for what followed.

On Thursday, April 24, a second edition of the paper appeared with a banner headline guaranteed to provoke LSU leaders: "Himes Steals $21,000 Law Library Money Missing." The story claimed that the school's business manager, Robert L. "Tighty" Himes, and Law School dean Robert L. Tullis had embezzled student fee revenue intended for the law library's operation. "Himes has stolen the money, just as he has fraudulently escaped with the other thousands of dollars during his regime," the paper alleged, adding, "'Tensas Terror' Tullis demanded $6,122.50 for his share three years ago to help his disinherited son from going to the Federal penitentiary, when the latter embezzled a large sum from [the] U.S. post office."

Elsewhere in the paper, editors wrote that LSU fired an employee for

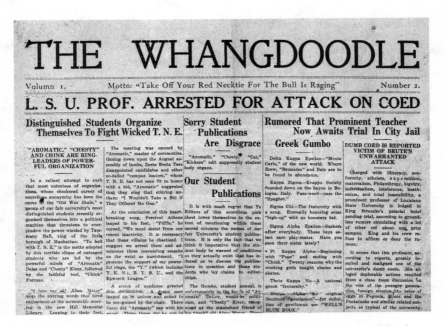

The front page of the *Whangdoodle*, a rogue, satirical newspaper that scandalized the LSU community in spring 1930. (LSU Special Collections)

having intimate relations with her boss, a sergeant in the school's military unit. The editors also claimed a prominent English professor, John Earle Uhler, "acknowledged to two plain clothes officers in Istrouma Hotel that he was hopelessly addicted" to "the excessive use of drugs." Finally, the paper said a law professor, James B. Smith (the faculty member about whom Kemble K. Kennedy and others complained to Long the previous year), had been "indicted and convicted of sodomy, a crime against nature."[4]

The paper scandalized the campus. The *Reveille* condemned it as "libelous." LSU's cadet colonel, Claude Fernandez, issued a statement on behalf of the Cadet Corps, denouncing it as "an insult and disgrace to society." Fernandez said cadets would "render all available initiative and unrestrained assistance" to help the school determine the identity of "the offenders." In a May 7 mass meeting in the Greek Theatre, the student body adopted a resolution condemning the publication as "vulgar and malicious" and demanded the school and local authorities arrest those responsible for the *Whangdoodle*.[5]

"You may be assured that no effort will be spared to discover and punish the authors of this crime," President Atkinson told the LSU Law Club.

Kennedy, who chaired the club and worked part-time as a clerk on the state senate's Agriculture Committee during the 1930 legislative session, also helped prepare a statement on behalf of his club that condemned the paper and called for "a thorough investigation" to "disclose and apprehend . . . the perpetrators of this revolting offense." Atkinson was furious about the *Whangdoodle*. "The assault upon the character of the student body," he wrote to Kennedy and the secretary of the Law Club on May 5, "is the worst thing in the sheet and your just indignation impels you to do everything in your power to punish the perpetrators."[6]

Anyone with passing knowledge of the *Whangdoodle*'s lineage suspected the school's renegade Theta Nu Epsilon chapter was involved in its 1930 iteration. One obvious clue was that the paper listed the fraternity's membership on the front page of the second edition. TNE members were, in fact, responsible. Among the fraternity's thirty-five members who signed a secret oath pledging to protect the identities of those behind the *Whangdoodle* was Kennedy, who was also featured on the front page. It soon became clear to LSU leaders that Kennedy was the paper's editor.[7]

An East Baton Rouge Parish grand jury indicted Kennedy in early June for circulating obscene and indecent matter and for libeling Himes. Just days before he hoped to graduate law school, LSU suspended Kennedy, meaning he would not receive his degree. At first, Long sympathized with his young friend, regarding the paper as a harmless prank. "If they don't give Kennedy his degree," he was overheard saying, "there is going to be a hot time down at the university." Long phoned Atkinson about Kennedy. "I want him kept in his examinations," the governor said, according to an LSU faculty member who listened to the conversation on an extension in Atkinson's office. Atkinson, who some LSU students had nicknamed "Guts" for his fearless demeanor, balked. "I don't intend to keep him in his examination," the president told the governor. Long kept pushing, but Atkinson stood firm. "All right, my friend," Long said, ominously, "I'll see you later." Long did not deny advocating for Kennedy when details of the phone call leaked, but he insisted he had not threatened Atkinson. And Atkinson backed up Long on that point when he spoke to reporters.[8]

When Atkinson went to the governor's office a few days later, he made sure Long had read the *Whangdoodle*. Speaking with reporters afterward, Atkinson acknowledged his brief disagreement with the governor, but also credited him with having seen the light. "He told me that he had, since our

Kemble K. Kennedy, a law student and close ally of Long, was editor of the *Whangdoodle*.
(LSU *Gumbo* yearbook, 1929)

talk over the phone on Monday, secured a copy of the *Whangdoodle,* and he now understood my position and he approved of it. He denounced the villainous publication, as people have done universally after reading it." Of the paper, Long told the *New Orleans States,* "I cannot condone the publication of such a sheet as the *Whangdoodle,* a copy of which I examined only yesterday." The LSU Board, with Long absent, ratified Kennedy's suspension shortly thereafter.[9]

Among those who testified against Kennedy at his criminal trial in Baton Rouge in November 1930 was J. J. Stovall of Winn Parish, a former LSU student who said he helped distribute the papers. Stovall said the Theta Nu Epsilon fraternity, of which Kennedy was president, was responsible for the *Whangdoodle.* Several TNE members who took the stand supported Stovall's testimony. They each insisted they knew little about the paper's production, despite having signed a pledge of secrecy in which they acknowledged their roles. Also testifying was John Earle Uhler, the English professor whose imaginary drug addiction was described in the *Whangdoodle*'s second edition. Uhler denied all the deviant and illegal behavior ascribed to him by the paper. "They are not only indecent but disgraceful and brutal to the person attacked," he said, after being asked by the prosecutor to read aloud from the paper. Tullis and Himes also testified against Kennedy, denouncing as false the charges of embezzlement alleged by the newspaper.

The testimony was overwhelming and damning. Most harmful to Kennedy was that his TNE brothers lied about their part in the paper's production or downplayed their knowledge of its contents. Kennedy's attorney, W. T. Bennett, called only one witness in his client's defense, Harvey G. Fields of Farmerville, Kennedy's hometown. The public service commissioner for northern Louisiana, Fields praised Kennedy's "good character and reputation." In his closing argument, Bennett told the judge that his client, who did not testify, was "taking the rap" for "forty or fifty other members of TNE, who had just as much to do with the *Whangdoodle* as Kennedy had." Bennett also said Kennedy refused to submit the pledge signed by other TNE members in which they affirmed their participation in the paper's publication because Kennedy "will not squeal." Bennett argued that, despite other students having helped publish the paper, Kennedy was singled out and "persecuted." Unpersuaded, the judge declared Kennedy guilty on all counts. "I have no words to express the contempt the court has for the outrageous assassination of character contained in this sheet," he said before sentencing Kennedy to a year in prison, three months for each of the four counts.[10]

In applying to the LSU Board for reinstatement in 1931, Kennedy acknowledged he "made a very serious mistake" by participating in the *Whangdoodle*'s publication. "However, I most emphatically [deny] being the instigator, as charged. There were to my personal knowledge 76 students, 63 boys and 13 girls, equally guilty, implicated, and responsible for the appearance of the said paper." Kennedy said that, because he refused to disclose the names of those involved, "I bore the brunt of criticism and punishment, shouldered the entire load, and was the 'goat' for all concerned."[11]

After Kennedy's conviction, his friends in northern Louisiana urged Long to grant the former law student a one-year reprieve. If Long did so, it was all the mercy he could command until he gained control of the state's Board of Pardons. A majority of that panel were men appointed by Long's predecessors. Louisiana's constitution allowed the governor to issue a pardon only after the board recommended it. Still, a gubernatorial reprieve would keep Kennedy out of prison until Long could engineer a pardon. The Union Parish state representative, its clerk of court, its sheriff, and the mayor of Farmerville organized a petition, signed by hundreds of Union Parish residents, asking Long to sign the reprieve, and argued that Kennedy was "largely a victim of political prejudice and partisanship." Kennedy, whose trial had been delayed after he was injured in a car accident in the summer, was also in poor health, the petitioners claimed. Furthermore, they said, dozens who helped Kennedy publish the paper were never charged.[12]

Long was amenable to Kennedy's request for leniency, likely for several reasons. First, he was fond of Kennedy, who treated him as a surrogate father. Second, the Baton Rouge district attorney who prosecuted Kennedy, John Fred Odom, was the same official who prosecuted Long in 1920 for criminal libel, one of the charges brought against Kennedy. Finally, Long knew well that the secret Theta Nu Epsilon society was not only a rogue group of LSU students; it was also the unofficial Huey Long student organization. In its early years on the campus, TNE had not been especially political. But Kennedy's involvement with the group, according to some of his classmates, transformed it into a pro-Long society. (To counter the Long-supporting students, the LSU chapter of the Cavalier Society became the campus anti-Long organization.) TNE members not only helped turn out voters for Long and his candidates in state elections; they also were an unofficial employment agency, helping pro-Long LSU students find state jobs.[13]

In producing the *Whangdoodle*, however, Kennedy and TNE members went too far. Long could not defend such a profane and scurrilous publication, but he found a way to justify giving Kennedy a break. "I'd like to see the whole fifty or sixty that were in on getting out these sheets have about thirty or sixty days each in jail, and then they would all learn the lesson they need," Long told a reporter a week after Kennedy's conviction. "I don't think it does near the good to pick out one for a year and the balance go free, particularly when the one picked out happens to be a poor down-and-out orphan boy, however, wrong he may have acted." Further defending Kennedy, Long added, "There's no such thing as a ringleader in these kinds of college debacles. All of them were mean as the dickens or they couldn't have been in it." After Kennedy spent a week in the East Baton Rouge Parish Prison, Long signed his reprieve.[14]

Nothing appeared to have sparked Long's desire to apply a firmer hand over affairs at LSU than his frustrating experience with the *Whangdoodle* case. He had no interest in defending the publication, but he believed Atkinson should have acceded to his wishes and awarded Kennedy his law degree. In his phone conversation with Atkinson in early June, Long told the LSU president he had no right to judge the young man's case prior to his criminal trial. "I am not doing that," Atkinson had replied. "He is charged with a grave offense which comes within the rules of this university and as its president, I do not intend to graduate him." Long backed off because of the paper's scurrilous nature, but more so, perhaps, because he did not have full control of the LSU Board of Supervisors. Any credible threat to fire Atkinson over the incident meant persuading board members appointed by his predecessor. In July, Long took the first of several steps that year to dominate the university. He filled six vacancies on the board with his political allies. In August, when he filled an additional vacancy, he controlled a majority of the board.[15]

Atkinson and others at LSU no doubt sensed their time running the university was short. The *New Orleans States* first reported that Long was scrutinizing the school. "A first class political explosion is expected to occur next Monday when the board of supervisors of the Louisiana State University is scheduled to meet in annual session on the university grounds," the paper reported in early June. It explained that Atkinson and Tullis "are said to be slated for official decapitation because of their refusal to give a diploma to K. K. Kennedy." The paper claimed that LSU officials were alarmed enough to have alerted alumni about the threat. "An SOS signal is being sent to alumni of the Louisiana State University all over the state. Those who are really interested in the future of the university are urged to come to Baton Rouge and bring what pressure they can to prevent the catastrophe threatened by Gov. Long." The paper even reported Long would soon name Atkinson's successor: "A member of the faculty who came to Louisiana from Texas about two years ago. The faculty member is reported to be a Russian by birth with decidedly radical tendencies." Long had not chosen a new LSU president, but Atkinson must have known his job was in jeopardy.[16]

O ther, more urgent concerns occupied Long for most of summer 1930. After failing to persuade state lawmakers to pass his plan for selling $60 million in state bonds to continue his ambitious highway construction program, he took his case to the voters. His new statewide newspaper, the *Louisiana Progress,* announced on July 17 that Long would run for the US Senate against longtime incumbent Joseph E. Ransdell, an anti-Long Democrat from East Carroll Parish. Throughout the campaign, Long attacked the seventy-two-year-old Ransdell as senile and ineffective, and mocked him as "old Feather Duster."

"Is there a single person in this audience who can tell me the name of my opponent?" Long asked as he stood on a cotton bale one day in the northern Louisiana town of Plain Dealing. No one responded. "I'll tell you. It's Old Feather Duster Ransdell. When I get to Washington, you'll always know the name of your US senator." As he stumped the state, Long clarified he was not so much running for the Senate as sending a message to recalcitrant state lawmakers. If he were elected, Long pledged, he would return to the Capitol with a mandate and demand that legislators approve his program. He promised not to leave for Washington until his gubernatorial term ended in May 1932, which he hoped would give him time to enact his legislative agenda.

Long also wanted to prevent the office from falling into the hands of Lieutenant Governor Paul Cyr, a former political ally from whom he was estranged. As for leaving the Senate seat empty for as long as a year, Long scoffed that, with Ransdell, the position "has been vacant for thirty-two years." The charge was unfair. Ransdell was an effective senator who devoted his career to improving public health. Among his accomplishments were securing funding for the federal leprosarium at Carville, Louisiana, and authoring legislation in May 1930 to create the National Institute of Health. Despite Ransdell's admirable record, Democrats gave the party's Senate nomination to Long by a large margin on September 9. It was tantamount to election. He won the November general election without opposition. (Although Ransdell was elderly, he was not frail. He lived another twenty-three years, dying in 1953 at age ninety-five. In 1941, five years after Long's 1935 death, Governor Sam Jones appointed the former senator to the LSU Board of Supervisors.)[17]

As governor and US senator-elect, Long now ruled Louisiana supreme. The anti-Long Constitutional League, headed by former governor Parker, disbanded. And another anti-Long group, the New Orleans faction known as "the Choctaws," was ready to deal with Long, agreeing to support his highway bond bill, a one-cent gasoline tax increase, and a bond issue to finance building a new Capitol. In return, Long agreed to spend a sizable portion of the new revenue on infrastructure construction and improvements in New Orleans. "By the close of 1930," Louisiana political historian Allan P. Sindler wrote, "the dominance of the Huey Long faction [in the legislature] was quite evident." Now that Long had conquered the Louisiana Capitol, it was time to turn his attention toward the state university just two miles downriver.[18]

8

I DID MY DAMNDEST

oach Russ Cohen and his LSU Tigers began the 1930 season in spectacular fashion. On September 20, LSU decimated Dakota Wesleyan, 76–0, before a middling-sized gathering in Tiger Stadium, which included a delighted Huey Long. A promising—perhaps, epic—season lay ahead. "Russ Cohen showed Governor Long and the other members of the 6,000-plus crowd in Tiger Stadium yesterday afternoon that his three years of laboring has not been in vain," a *Baton Rouge Morning Advocate* sportswriter gushed, judging LSU's performance "the most brilliant broken field running ever seen at Tiger stadium."[1]

LSU hosted Louisiana Polytechnic Institute the next week and crushed the team from Ruston, 71–0. They were so impressive, an Associated Press reporter commented, that the game "was merely a good workout." LSU next hosted Southwestern Louisiana Institute, running up the score even more than the previous two weeks—85–0. In that game, sophomore halfback Joe Almokary—the standout player Long lured from Centenary College the year before—scored five touchdowns and four extra points. Cohen's squad allowed not a single point in its first three games, while putting 232 points on the board.[2]

"The Tigers haven't as strong a conference schedule as some teams," sports columnist Fred Digby observed in the *New Orleans Item* after LSU's third win, "but the program is sufficient to give them a claim to the honor [of the Southern Conference title] if they go through the season undefeated." One sportswriter advised a smidgen of caution about the Tigers' relative strength. "They haven't played against a real tough line as yet," Harry Martinez wrote in the *New Orleans States,* "but Saturday's game [against South

LSU head football coach Russell Cohen, the first of three head coaches to work under Long's influence. (LSU *Gumbo* yearbook, 1932)

Carolina] will put them to the test. But we don't think the Tigers will be found wanting." Martinez told readers in another column: "The game offers a great chance for L.S.U. to prove to her supporters that the team can hold its own with conference foes of some class. We look for the Tigers to make a fine showing."[3]

As sportswriters raised hopes for his team, Cohen tamped them down. "It's a toss-up," he said about LSU's first away game of the season. "We've got a good chance to beat Carolina and they've got a good chance of beating us." With the team hampered by injuries, Cohen was concerned. "If I had my full strength, I wouldn't worry so much, but I think we're in for a hot battle." The coach was wise to lower expectations. The Tigers left Columbia, South Carolina, the loser by a painful 7–6 score. LSU fell short of a tie when Almokary missed an extra-point kick. Even so, the sportswriters praised the Tigers' pluck. "Seldom did any losing team so clearly outplay a winner as the Tigers outplayed the Gamecocks," Digby wrote in the *Item*. As he and others noted, LSU earned eleven first downs, while South Carolina managed two. "It is hard to lose by the narrow margin of one point," the *State-Times* said in an editorial. "Yet the game with South Carolina was an excellent one, and should help inspire confidence in battles yet to come."[4]

The following week's game against rival Mississippi State in Jackson ended no better. LSU lost another close contest, 8–6. The Tigers came up short after team captain Dobie Reeves stepped back into the end zone while punting. His mistake gave Mississippi State a 2-point safety for the win.[5]

Long was anxious as the Tigers' homecoming game against Sewanee the following week approached. It was Cohen who sometimes confessed his fears to Long, but now the roles were reversed. Long told the coach he worried about the team's chances, despite Sewanee's mediocre 3–2 record. Cohen devised a special play to placate Long: "1099." It would be LSU's reserve call whenever the team was in trouble. Before the game, the coach ordered his signal caller, fullback Tom Smith, to look to him if unsure about when to run the play. "If I have my hat off," he told Smith, "call 1099."

Such subterfuge was necessary because of the rules and culture of college football in the first half of the century that forbade coaches from instructing or exhorting players from the sidelines, and that barred them from calling plays. "Coaching from the side lines is prohibited in the rules because it is considered an unfair practise [sic]," one sportswriter observed in 1934, adding, "The game is to be played by the players using their own muscles and their brains." Although not a coach, Long was probably often in violation of the same football rules mandating that "all coaches and players and trainers, etc. [must] remain upon the bench, seated and that they do not offer comment from the bench in tones audible upon the field, of plays, decision, etc." Referees likely tolerated or overlooked Long's behavior because he was not, officially, part of the team. The fact of his powerful position was almost certainly another reason for their forbearance.[6]

As the game clock ticked down and the Tigers appeared listless, Long went to Cohen to inquire about why he had not called for "1099." Perhaps it was that LSU was ahead by two touchdowns and no such gambit was necessary. Whatever the case, Cohen told Long that he had signaled the special play, but that Smith would not look his way. That was all Long needed to hear. He dashed down the sidelines, shouting to Smith, "Call 1099! Call 1099!" The team ran the play, to no apparent result. Whether "1099" was an actual play or some hocus-pocus to mollify Long, it did not matter. LSU beat Sewanee, 12–0. The victory seemed to right the ship. Winning by twelve points, in the words of a *New Orleans Item* sportswriter, was enough to persuade "the 8,000 homecoming alumni and supporters that the team is now out of the doldrums."[7]

Some Tiger fans worried about the rest of the team's schedule, despite the win. "This year's Louisiana State team has played below par all season

Long with referees in Tiger Stadium in the early 1930s.
(Huey P. Long Photograph Album, LSU Special Collections)

and there is no argument there," sports columnist M. G. McCann wrote in the *State-Times* in late October. "It's time they snap out of it and play over their heads." Among those watching with growing concern as the team's once-promising season faltered was Long, who believed he knew what the players needed as they prepared for the all-important Louisiana State Fair game against Arkansas. Long attended the team's last practice before they departed for Shreveport and gave the twenty-eight-member squad a pep talk. "You've got to win," he told them as he finished.[8]

Long delivered another inspirational speech in Shreveport before the game. And he prowled the sidelines like an assistant coach during the contest. LSU won, 27–12, but Long was angry about a penalty against the Tigers in the fourth quarter. An official had ejected an LSU player for excessive roughness after the Tigers moved the ball to the Arkansas thirteen-yard line. The penalty pushed the team back to the Razorbacks' forty-five-yard line. As the players and fans left the stadium, Long directed an Athletic Department employee to summon the referee, Jim Perry, to meet him under the grandstands. Perry walked up to Long with a football in his hand.

"Do you know who I am?" Long asked.

"Yes, sir, you're Governor Long."

"That's correct. If you want to penalize my boys, do it out in the middle of the field, not near the goal line."

Stunned by Long's brashness, Perry smiled, said nothing, and walked away.[9]

No doubt more pleasing to Long was the *Morning Advocate* sports columnist, who gave the governor some credit for the win. "There was plenty behind the Bengals yesterday," W. I. Spencer wrote. "Law of averages, pent-up steam, Governor Long—laugh if you will, but the knowledge that the chief executive is banking on you makes you fight that much harder."[10]

Despite Long's hopes that the team was back in top fighting form, Cohen and his squad did not help their cause with the mixed results of the next two games. The Tigers beat Ole Miss, 6–0, on November 8. But they lost, 33–0, the next week to Alabama, Cohen's former team, led by his former boss, Wallace Wade. The team that started the season with three of the most overpowering performances in the school's history was now a mediocre 5–3 heading into its season finale at Tulane.[11]

It was at this moment that Long moved to take over the state's top public university. Long convened the LSU Board of Supervisors in his office at the Governor's Mansion on the Monday morning after the Alabama game. To the board, most of whom he appointed that summer, Long revealed that since November 5 he had held a resignation letter from President Thomas Atkinson. It was no surprise to anyone in Baton Rouge that the ailing president's tenure was short. Bowing to the inevitable, Atkinson wrote to Long that "my health is not equal to the burden of work required." Long also announced he had identified a candidate to replace Atkinson: Dr. James Monroe Smith, a forty-two-year-old native of Jackson Parish (just north of Long's Winn Parish). An LSU graduate, Smith had been a public school teacher and principal in northern Louisiana. He taught education at LSU before moving to Southwestern Louisiana Institute (SLI) in Lafayette. He earned a PhD in educational administration from New York's Columbia University in 1927 and had served as dean of SLI's Teacher's College since 1922. Smith may not have been well known to university leaders around the country, but he proved a competent, respected administrator at SLI. He was, some contemporaries recalled, an inspiring figure. "Of above average height and heavy set," T. Harry Williams wrote, "he was friendly and even effusive in manner—'democratic,' thought the students, with whom he was extremely popular."[12]

Smith had entered Long's orbit thanks to a new LSU Board member from Baton Rouge, George Everett. Owner of a stationery and office supply business, Everett had known Smith since childhood. Everett mentioned Smith as a possible candidate for LSU president to one of Long's close friends, state representative Harley Bozeman of Winnfield. Bozeman and another Long intimate from Winnfield, state senator Oscar K. Allen, arranged a lunch meeting with Smith during the first week of November to size him up. They came away impressed. "We thought George Everett had found the ideal man to be president of LSU," Bozeman wrote later. When told about Smith, Long said it was preposterous to appoint an unknown dean as LSU president. However, when Bozeman informed Long that Smith grew up near the village of Sikes, the governor was intrigued. "Reckon Dr. Smith is kin to my Smith kinfolks up around Sikes?" Long asked. Bozeman said he did not know but urged Long to meet Smith to find out. Accompanied by Everett, Smith met Long that evening at the Governor's Mansion. Long discovered no apparent close kinship but was sold on Smith after interviewing him for about fifteen minutes. Most likely—and most importantly—Long judged Smith as someone who would not challenge his authority but adopt the governor's vision for LSU.[13]

Everett, the board's vice president, nominated Smith after Long introduced his candidate to board members during their November 17 meeting at the Governor's Mansion. The board agreed. LSU had a new president. "We want you to run the Louisiana State University yourself," Long told Smith. "Run it until you are called and the only way you can be called is by the Board of Supervisors sitting as a board. If any member of the board has any complaint, he will lay it before the board. You are to be the president of the university. If you don't succeed, it is your own fault."[14]

Smith might have been forgiven if he took Long at his word that he would have free rein to run LSU. But if he paid attention to the newspapers, as he almost certainly did, he was wise enough to take Long's words seriously, but not literally. He soon learned that Long had strong ideas about the university's affairs and its future.

At this meeting, the first gathering of the LSU Board controlled by Long, members also took steps to open the university to more students from underprivileged backgrounds. LSU created ninety-two scholarships for needy students, exempting them from the school's sixty-dollar general fees. Each

Long with LSU president James Monroe Smith.
(LSU Libraries, LSU Special Collections)

of the board's fourteen members was given three scholarships to dispense. Twenty-five went to the LSU president and another twenty-five to the governor.[15]

That Long replaced Atkinson was not unexpected. Sixty-two and suffering from heart disease, he was ill for much of fall 1930. And rumors about his impending departure had been discussed in the press. What the board did next, however, was surprising and controversial, and consumed half of the two-hour meeting. After the board hired Smith, board member and state senator Harvey Peltier of Lafourche Parish—one of Long's new appointees—sought to relieve Russ Cohen of his coaching duties. Cohen's three-year contract was about to expire, Peltier noted, as he proposed demoting the coach to athletic director. Peltier also suggested allowing Long and Smith to hire the new football coach. (The board also voted to rehire a former football trainer and track coach, Francis Thomas "Tad" Gormley, fired by LSU three years earlier.)

Long opposed the motion—the vote was ten to three, with the governor, George Everett, and Bolivar Kemp of Amite in the minority—but he did not insist on keeping Cohen. Any governor with Long's power, who had just appointed a majority of the board, would have prevailed if he demanded LSU keep the football coach. It is clear Long did not. And few board members were closer to Long than Peltier, who likely offered the motion at Long's behest (or with his permission) to give the governor plausible deniability if the move backfired. Long could also have declined to accept the duty of finding another coach, but he did not. Whatever the reason for Long's vote, LSU seemed destined to replace Cohen.[16]

Only the student newspaper, the *Reveille,* noted an additional personnel change: Frank "Pop" Guilbeau, the longtime Regimental Band director, also resigned that day. (He would remain the university's superintendent of grounds.) In two hours' time, Long named a new president and was on his way to hiring a new football coach and band director. His control of LSU was sudden and nearly total.[17]

This gathering in the Governor's Mansion may have been one of the more important meetings of the LSU Board of Supervisors during Long's career. Besides hiring the president, the board authorized Long and Smith to proceed with construction of a $125,000 student center (the future Huey P. Long Field House), if funds for the building could be raised. Where that money would come from was an open question that was soon answered by another decision Long and his board made that day. Although he had once ridiculed suggestions that the university sell the land occupied by its old campus north of downtown Baton Rouge, Long now proposed a surprising reversal. Earlier that year, he had unveiled plans to build a massive $5 million Capitol. Now it became clear where he would find the money for LSU's next phase of expansion: Long and the board voted to allow the new Capitol to be built on the old LSU property and authorized the governor to sell the university's land to the state.[18]

News of the new LSU president and the sale of land from the old campus were prominent stories in newspapers around Louisiana in mid-November 1930. The future of LSU's football coach, however, was even bigger news, especially as the Tigers headed toward their final game of the season against archrival Tulane. With a 7–1 record, Tulane was among the best teams in the South. Whereas LSU lost to Mississippi State by two points, Tulane crushed the Bulldogs, 53–0. Tulane also had victories over Auburn and was coming off a decisive 25–0 win over Georgia the previous week. The LSU-Tulane game was always one of the most eagerly anticipated of the year. And it would take on added significance this season, as it would also save Coach Russ Cohen's job.

N ot everyone had applauded the LSU Board's decision to fire Cohen and search for a new coach. "History repeats itself at Louisiana State," the *New Orleans Item*'s Fred Digby wrote on November 18. "Another change is about to be made in the football coaching staff. The career of a coach at L.S.U. is much less than three years. Even Knute Rockne would need more time or material to get a winner." Noting that Long voted against dismissing Cohen, Digby observed, "I don't think the governor could have done otherwise." He explained that LSU's big win over Arkansas should have settled the matter of Cohen's future. "I judged the governor was convinced that afternoon that he and the Alumni had been dead wrong on Cohen and his aides." Digby argued that Cohen "is a first-class coach," adding, "I might even go further and say he is the best coach L.S.U. has ever had." Firing Cohen, Digby concluded, would be "a serious mistake."[19]

With the Tulane game on the horizon, the LSU Board had not officially notified Cohen of his dismissal. This, *Morning Advocate* sportswriter W. I. Spencer noted, "leaves a loophole for Cohen's remaining at L.S.U." Like Digby,

Spencer made it clear where he stood. "There is no doubt about two facts concerning L.S.U., regardless of contrary report—the Tigers can play football, and Russ Cohen is a plenty smart student of football." An upset against Tulane, Spencer suggested, just might save Cohen's job. Focused on beating Tulane, Cohen said nothing to reporters about his future. "We have a game with Tulane on our hands right now that we'd like mighty much to win," he told the sportswriters when informed about the LSU Board's decision. "And I won't have anything to say until that game is played."[20]

Few thought LSU could beat Tulane. The bookies set a point spread of twenty-five in the days before the contest. The odds of a Tulane win, based on gamblers placing bets on the game, were five to one. Long also expected an LSU loss, but he also hoped he could exhort his team—and their coach—to victory. Before the team left for New Orleans, Long appeared at a practice with Smith in tow. "Boys," he announced, "this is your new president." In New Orleans, the governor stayed near Cohen at the team's headquarters, the aging Bienville Hotel. He paced the locker room before the game with his ever-present walking stick. Long offered the squad a motivational talk, the kind that Cohen always seemed unable to muster. "Do you know that Arkansas beat the Texas Aggies by a bigger margin than Tulane did, and that we beat Arkansas? Keep that in mind."

Long boasted—falsely—to a reporter before the game that he had spoken to the team for ninety minutes. "I told them they could lick Tulane if they weren't quitters. I told them to get out there and fight. I talked to them in groups of three and four—the whole squad. Now, you just watch that team of mine." A reporter noted Long was a Tulane alumnus (he took four law courses) and asked him, "Are you really rooting for the Tigers?" The governor beamed. "Hell, yes. This half, anyway."[21]

As the game began, Long showed up in a brown, double-breasted suit, matching fedora, and a heavy gray overcoat, to which he had pinned a large football with purple and gold ribbons. He sat in his box among the LSU crowd on Tulane Stadium's west side. He planned to cross the field during the second half and watch the rest of the game with the Tulane fans. From the Tiger's first possession—when a fake punt put them on the Tulane seven-yard line—Long was out of his seat. He shed his coat after that big play, tossed his walking stick aside, leaped over the rail, and rushed onto the field. As LSU tried to score, Long dropped to his knees in distress, pulled up handfuls of grass, and flung them into the air. He jumped and shouted. "Come on, boys.

Fight 'em! Fight 'em! You can hold 'em!" His dramatic urging of the team went unrewarded, so Long went to Cohen, and sat next to him on the bench. "Next time one of those Tigers tries to pass and finds his receivers covered," he told the coach, "have him run with the ball the way Don Zimmerman of Tulane did against Georgia." Cohen nodded. Throughout the first half, Long was all over the sidelines, shouting to players. "Come on, boys. Fight 'em! You can hold 'em." When Joe Almokary took a hard hit and limped off the field, Long threw his arms around him. "Boy, you're playing a wonderful game! We're going to lick 'em. You're going to help us lick 'em this last half, boy!"[22]

Long summoned a freshman messenger when he noticed the young man's wounded eye. "Son, run out to the nearest drug store and get some 2 percent solution of Argyrol and a bottle of Murine. I want 'em for Almokary's eye." For the rest of the half, Long alternated between caring for Almokary and watching the game.

LSU had not scored as the half ended, and the team trundled into the locker room, down 12–0. Inside, Long slapped players on the back and handed them towels. And he remained on the LSU sidelines when the third quarter began. "I've got to stay with my team," he told a reporter. For now, there was no show of neutrality by sitting among the Tulane fans.

Early in the third quarter, the messenger returned with the medication Long ordered for Almokary's eye. Long applied the drops.

"I think that'll ease it, boy," he assured Almokary, and then to the rest of the team, "Just let him alone for a little while."

Later, Long turned to the injured player. "How's it feeling, Joe?"

"Fine, Governor."

"I've got to get Almokary's eye right," Long told the players. "We'll have him out there in a minute. How's it feeling now, Joe?" Before Almokary could answer, for good measure, Long squirted more drops.

Only at the start of the fourth quarter, with LSU still down 12–0, did Long cross the field to sit among the Tulane crowd, but not before checking on Almokary one more time. "Can you see now, son?"

"Okay, Governor. I hope I'll be in again in a few minutes."

"Give 'em hell, boy," Long said as he headed for the Tulane side, where he sat with Tulane president A. B. Dinwiddie and his guests, some of whom ribbed the governor about his support for LSU. The Tigers came to life not long thereafter, scoring a touchdown after an LSU player blocked a Tulane punt and recovered the ball.

"It looks as if I was the Tiger jinx instead of the Tiger coach," Long joked to Dinwiddie.

"You're right," the Tulane president said. "I think you had better go back over there where you came from, Huey. LSU could never score with you on their side of the field."

When LSU recovered a Tulane fumble, another guest of Dinwiddie's teased Long. "You'd better get back over there quick, Governor."

But Long remained on the Tulane side, watching the last few plays in silence, as Tulane held off LSU to record a 12–7 win. As he returned to the LSU side of the field, Long recognized that a near miss for LSU was a moral victory for Cohen. Long turned to the *New Orleans States* reporter who had shadowed him the entire game and shouted, "Cohen stays at LSU!"[23]

Long, Cohen, and the team were jubilant in the game's immediate aftermath. Fred Digby, the *New Orleans Item* sportswriter who defended Cohen in his columns, went to Long and grabbed him by the lapels and said, "You're going to fire that man?" Other reporters joined in. Long protested, "He stays. He stays." Digby left Long and went straight to Cohen to break the news. "You're not fired. You still got your job." But Cohen was not sure he wanted to remain Long's assistant coach. "I don't want it," he told Digby. "In the meantime, I've gotten a job with Vanderbilt as assistant coach." In the locker room, Cohen's players pleaded with him to stay. "I want more time to think it over," he told them, "but I sure do appreciate the fight you boys made. I'm proud of you."[24]

An out-of-state visitor to the stadium unfamiliar with Louisiana politics and college football might have mistaken Long for LSU's head coach. "He ran up and down the sideline and got a lot of attention," player W. E. "Billy" Butler later recalled. (The *Morning Advocate* failed to capture Long's enthusiasm for the Tigers. "Every Tiger gain," a reporter wrote, "would elicit spontaneous approbation from the state's chief executive.") Long spoke to the press afterward as if he had coached the team, which, in a way, he had. "Well, I did my damndest, anyhow."[25]

Everyone associated with LSU, including Long, recognized that Cohen had been the game's real winner. One story about the game in the *Morning Advocate* led thus: "The Louisiana State University Tigers were triumphant in defeat." The delighted writer ended his piece by declaring, "The game played today will go down in the history of Louisiana State university as one of the greatest ever played by a Tiger team."[26]

By Monday night, Long and Smith persuaded Cohen to stay. At the Governor's Mansion, the coach signed a $7,000, three-year contract, which included a $500 raise. "Cohen is now head coach and sole boss of athletics at LSU," Long said. "President Smith and I are now through with this coach situation, and all other details of assistants, trainers, and so on are up to Cohen." Cohen, who did not believe Long would give him a free hand to run his team as he wished, said little beyond promising "we will continue to turn out a winning team for Louisiana State."[27]

Keeping Cohen not only appeared to be sound football; it was also good politics. The entire LSU football squad signed a resolution of support for their coach days before the Tulane game. "In our opinion, he is an exceptionally good coach and nothing would please us better than to have him retained here as head football coach." Most of the state's sportswriters were behind Cohen, as was the student newspaper. "No university can ever have a good football team," the *Reveille* said in an editorial, "if it continues to change coaches every time the team loses a game."[28]

At a banquet honoring the team in the University Dining Hall (now Foster Hall) a few days later, Long was among about three hundred fans, business owners, coaches, and players who praised the leadership of the man he was willing to see fired less than two weeks earlier. To his credit, Long backed up his renewed enthusiasm for Cohen and LSU football with new funding, enough to hire a graduate manager to schedule games and expand the coaching staff. Louisiana's governor was optimistic about the 1931 season, as well as the role he would play in the team's success. As for the students, they enjoyed the attention their team was getting from the governor. "If the governor backs the other athletic teams of the university as the football eleven, and makes a regular appearance at the university athletic meets," the *Reveille*'s editors wrote, "he will no doubt soon be popular with the student body. You simply can't dislike a man that fights for the welfare of the Tiger."[29]

Despite what he told Cohen about being free to coach his team as he wished, Long had no plans to leave LSU football and its future to its coach. "I intend to put Louisiana State on the football map," Long told an out-of-state reporter who covered the Tulane game. "What it takes to get good players and develop them—of course, in a legitimate manner—I've got. Don't be surprised to see L.S.U. on top of the map in the next two or three years."[30]

9

A COW COLLEGE

Despite what Long and some others claimed in the late 1920s, LSU was no educational juggernaut. "The university's first sixty years were scarcely more than a prolonged adolescence," journalist Don Wharton wrote in *Scribner's* magazine in 1937. "It would probably be as well off today if its life had begun in 1920 rather than in 1860. For half a century it was a Peter Pan university, threatening never to grow up, and for decades it seemed to exist simply because states had universities and Louisiana was a state." LSU "was a cow college 'til [Long] took over," former LSU football star and New Orleans state judge Oliver "Ike" Carriere insisted. For years, even under Governor John Parker, state leaders harbored modest ambitions for LSU, reflecting the constraints of their imagination but also their refusal to raise the revenue necessary for the school's advancement. "The state simply did not yet have a political leader with the dedication and ability to overcome these obstacles and, therefore, state services were provided half-heartedly and incompletely," historian Jerry P. Sanson observed.[1]

In Louisiana, as across the South, most rural schools of the era lacked the funding available to those in the cities. Schools in rural parishes were usually underfunded, makeshift structures staffed by poorly trained teachers. State funding to those schools was negligible, and local support was almost nonexistent. As bad as support was for white schools, funding for Black schools was abysmal. During the 1929–30 Louisiana school year, white students received an average of 175 days of instruction; Black students, only 106. The state had 353 approved, four-year high schools for white students; only 4 for Black students.

Some have argued that Louisiana's education system at the time was worse than those in other southern states. T. Harry Williams, for example, believed that LSU's "skimpy" education spending in the 1920s was a consequence of Louisianans' "resigned" attitude toward education. Southern historian V. O. Key Jr. observed in the late 1940s that Louisiana during this era was "a case of arrested political development. Its Populism was repressed with a violence unparalleled in the South, and its neo-Populism was smothered by a potent ruling oligarchy." Key added, "If the status of the people's education is an index to the strength of the economic elite, the Louisiana governing class excelled in exploiting of its position." Louisiana residents, Williams wrote, "had a kind of pride in their university and state colleges and lower schools. But at the same time, they knew these institutions were not very good, and they did not think much could be done to improve them." An LSU professor and renowned Civil War historian, Williams concluded Louisiana citizens "were victims of the psychological retrogression into which the South lapsed after the Civil War: the South was poor, and in certain areas, such as education, Southerners simply had to be content with second or third best." In the first half to the century, as one history of the state observed, "most Louisianians either could not afford to send their children to college or cared little whether or not their children pursued a higher education."[2]

In the late 1920s, LSU still suffered from the modest ambitions about which Williams and others wrote. As much as he supported a "Greater University," John Parker never imagined LSU's enrollment would exceed 3,000. Indeed, the student body for the 1930–31 school year totaled 2,317, not many more than when Long took office in 1928. After a spurt of state appropriations in the early 1920s to build the new campus, state funding for the university dwindled. By 1926, Governor Henry Fuqua and LSU's supporters in the legislature struggled to secure a meager $250,000 appropriation for the university's cash-strapped building program.[3]

Notwithstanding its move three miles south to a new and expanding campus, the university was still a small-time operation in the early 1930s. Fred Frey recalled that when he became dean of the College of Arts and Sciences in 1931, he asked his predecessor, Arthur Prescott, about the salaries of faculty members in his college. "Young man," the retiring dean told him, "that is none of my business. I do not know how much money any man in my college is making." Frey went to the university's treasurer to get the numbers. The man bristled at Frey's request and replied, "I have no budgets by departments." He refused to share what little data he had. Only after President Smith intervened did Frey receive what he needed. "The names were not arranged in alphabetical order," Frey remembered, "or any order of rank, but apparently had been written in at the time the individual was appointed to the university." Frey copied the information and discovered that some instructors made more than full professors and that no department had a budget for travel or supplies.[4]

Tuition at LSU was free for Louisiana residents, but it could still cost a student as much as $690 a year to attend the school (about $11,500 in 2022 dollars), a sum out of reach for many young people, especially as the worst effects of the Great Depression spread throughout the state. Long understood the constraints poor families experienced, as well as the tough choices that tight finances forced on them. At least by his telling, he was among those whose parents could not afford to send him to LSU almost two decades earlier. In 1930, some students applied for scholarships from their parish police jury, the Louisiana equivalent of a county commission. Recognizing the difficulties many students had paying for room, board, and other fees, in 1931 LSU began accepting cotton bales as payment. Even football players did not receive scholarships and sought jobs to earn money for room and board, although it is unclear how much work the boosters who hired them required. (In 1935, the Southeastern Conference became the first university athletic conference to offer its athletes scholarships. Before that, most universities with football programs used furtive methods to subsidize players.)

Long and others often found jobs for students in state government or with Baton Rouge businesses to help them stay in school. "I tell you it's hard to turn some of them away when they want to come there and can't pay the tuition we charged students from outside Louisiana [$60 a year beginning in September 1931]," Long later told a journalist. "Some of 'em show up in Baton Rouge with sixty dollars [for general fees], just enough to get in as students from Louisiana. They sure are pitiful when told it costs more if they come from Mississippi or Arkansas or some other state." According to a survey by the *Reveille* in April 1929, about a third of LSU students were working to pay for school. "The janitor jobs, taken from the numerical standpoint[,] seems to be the most popular" campus work, the paper reported. "Many students work in town garages and machine shops, at the local Y.M.C.A., various dry goods firms, and organizations in town. Some wait on tables in the [school] cafeteria."[5]

U nlike earlier governors, Long was willing to increase corporate taxes and government borrowing to provide services like roads, bridges, and better public schools. Two years before he resolved to make LSU one of the nation's top state universities, Long articulated a vision for government and its role in the lives of the people that was far different from some of his timid, less-imaginative predecessors. "On principle, nothing is farther from right than to extort money through taxation and then to use these funds for causes and purposes opposed to the public interest or to spend such trust funds in causes of political pilfer and private or public squander," he said in his May 1928 inaugural address. Three weeks later, he had visited the LSU campus to promise school officials there "more money" for their university. Those new funds did not materialize for another two years, but when Long turned his full attention to LSU, the results would be remarkable.[6]

Long's sudden, active role in running LSU appeared at first to be a product of his pique over the school's expulsion of his protégé Kemble K. Kennedy. Then, as he discovered fully the joys of LSU football, he fell under the school's spell and, perhaps, realized that associating himself with the football team was not only fun, but also good politics. But none of that explains why, beginning in November 1930, Long immersed himself in the university's business. "Others have thought that Huey's interest in LSU was sinister," T. Harry Williams wrote, "that he viewed the school as a personal plaything, a glittering toy that he could toss around for his amusement. Some people who watched him at the time, including football players, decided he had political motives." Football player Sidney Bowman recalled that Long often spoke to the players about politics. "He was thinking of the future in all this. He was getting people who would be for him when he'd follow the ball up and down the field and wave to students."[7]

But he also had other, more personal reasons for attaching himself to the team. Long could not help but notice that his antics on the football field landed him on the sports pages, allowing voters—in Louisiana and beyond—to see him not just as a political figure but as a cultural icon. The explosion of newspaper stories about college and professional athletics during the 1920s—the space devoted to baseball, football, and other games in some large daily papers quadrupled during the decade—made appearing in the sports sections irresistible. By 1929, as many Louisiana newspapers grew hostile toward him—or ignored him—Long knew he needed alternatives for positive press coverage. The sportswriters provided him a convenient vehicle. To their readers, his support of LSU appeared innocent and nonpartisan. After all, this was not Long arguing on behalf of raising taxes on Standard Oil or attacking a political opponent; it was his good-natured, patriotic promotion of the Ole War Skule's football squad.[8]

As one study of Long's obsession with the newspapers concluded, "He demonstrated more concern for public opinion and for how he appeared in the press than ordinary politicians, especially in comparison to the Southern gentlemen of his time, many of whom frowned upon his press agentry and constant desire for attention." In mid-December 1930, for example, a lengthy syndicated feature about Long's LSU football mania, written by a reporter for the Newspaper Enterprise Association, ran in papers across the country. The story, headlined in many papers, "Hey, Rockne—Watch Your Step! Huey Long Is on Your Trail," featured pictures of Long waving his arms on the sidelines of the 1930 Tulane game. "Knute Rockne of Notre Dame and all the other big-time football mentors [coaches] had best look to their laurels," the reporter began, "for Governor Huey P. Long is on their trail. Louisiana's picturesque chief executive and senator-elect—who emerged triumphant from an attempt to impeach him . . . has a new ambition. Now he's out to make Louisiana State University's football team one of the greatest gridiron aggregations in the country."[9]

Long had enjoyed a taste of national renown in February 1930 after he insulted the German consul and the commander of a German naval cruiser which docked at the port of New Orleans. The governor offended the two men by receiving them in his hotel room wearing pajamas under a blue lounging robe. "What's the matter with 'em?" newspapers across the country quoted Long asking afterward, when he learned about the Germans' displeasure. "I had on the green silk pajamas, took time to put on a pair of bedroom slippers and wore the $35 lounging robe given to me by the State Banking Department for Christmas. What more do they want?" Long generated more headlines across Louisiana and throughout the country when he made amends by visiting the German cruiser in formal morning wear. "By the next day," biographer Forrest Davis wrote, "all Americans had learned from their favorite journals of a madcap Governor's transgression and amende-honorable." Long noted the wide acclaim the incident brought him. "Apt at all lessons touching his own fortunes," Davis concluded, "Huey pondered the conclusion that clowning, deliberate or accidental, as in this case, would be treated hospitably by a normally hostile press."[10]

Long "clowned his way into national prominence," historian William E. Leuchtenburg wrote. "A tousled redhead with a cherubic face, a dimpled chin, and a pug nose, he had the physiognomy of a Punchinello. He wore pongee suits with orchid-colored shirts and sported striped straw hats, watermelon-pink ties, and brown and white sport shoes." Leuchtenburg judged Long "a shrewd, intelligent lawyer [who] cultivated the impression he was an ignoramus." Wrote historian Arthur Schlesinger: "He had always been a jocose figure, given to ribald language and homely anecdotes. From this time forward he began to cultivate a public reputation as a buffoon." Harry Gamble, the New Orleans city manager in the early 1930s who knew Long well, said, "I have always said that if Huey was out in front of the band leading it, he would not be willing to walk with the drum major; he would have to be in front of the drum major." Gamble called Long "the greatest extrovert of his generation."[11]

Long's buffoonery reached new heights in early 1931. He joined a good-natured "dispute" with the *Atlanta Constitution* over whether cornpone should be dunked or crumbled into the liquid left behind after cooking a pot of greens and ham hocks or salt pork. It was known as "potlikker." Long first drew attention to the arcane culinary matter in August 1930 when he launched his US Senate campaign in St. Martinville. "When I get to the United States Senate, I am going to tell the people of the nation how to cook potlikker from turnip greens and fat meat. That's the dish that will make you strong and healthy." When the Atlanta paper chided him the following February for saying he had dunked cornpone for the benefit of some visiting bond buyers, Long recognized another issue about which he could play national jester. "I will stand for your questioning my political sagacity and legal capacity," he wrote the paper, "but my recipe for potlikker is given out from a source that cannot be questioned. I do not want anybody misled in the state of Georgia about this matter, so I demand immediate correction." Long jokingly called his special recipe "potlikker a le dictator."

In response, the *Constitution*'s "Cornpone and Potlikker editor"—actually, the paper's news director, Julian L. Harris—reiterated his publication's support for crumbling, adding, "the battle line is drawn between these two points. . . . Unless you telegraph us within two hours that you recede from your untenable position, The *Constitution* will appeal to the people of the South to rise and crush the heresy with which you are seeking to stigmatize this fair section." A day later, the paper persuaded New York governor

Franklin D. Roosevelt, a part-time Georgia resident, to join the fray. "I must admit," FDR wrote, "that I crumble mine." Over three weeks, dozens of politicians and newspapers across the country joined the "debate" with humorous declarations about the controversy. Typical was a statement by Florida governor Doyle E. Carlton, who defended crumbling: "Down here most of us are Baptists and we maintain that dunking does not go deep enough—that the immersion must be an absolute and a complete submerging."

Even the characters of radio's most popular comedy show chimed in. "We are divided over cornpone and potlikker debate," Amos 'n' Andy told the *Constitution*. "Amos will take cornpone any way he can get it as long as he can have potlikker with it. Andy will take potlikker provided he can get cornpone. Andy will eat it either crumbled in potlikker or potlikker with cornpone crumbled in it. That almost leaves Governor Long out. . . . We asked Kingfish how he liked his potlikker and he said 'with gin'erale [ginger ale].'"[12]

It was about this time that Long began referring to himself as "the Kingfish," a humorous nickname taken from "Amos 'n' Andy." One of the show's characters, George "Kingfish" Stevens, was a self-important Harlem business owner who often persuaded the show's two principal characters to invest in shady business deals or lured them into comedic trouble. Long loved the program and appropriated the nickname. "This is the Kingfish," he announced when calling someone by phone. By 1932, upon hearing the moniker, many people were as likely to think of Long as they were of the show's character.[13]

Long understood the value of humor, self-deprecation, and spectacle for expanding his reach and appeal. That partly explains his affinity for LSU football, but it does not mean he was uninterested in bolstering the university's academic credentials and opening the school's doors to thousands more of Louisiana's (white) young men and women. "I think his interest in LSU was sincere," football player W. E. "Billy" Butler said later. "Of course, he got a bang out of it. He wanted the biggest and best band and football team." Butler, however, did not always see the same passion in Long for the university's academic side. "He thought that would take care of itself as LSU developed." T. Harry Williams marveled that "hardly anyone has considered that Huey might have been seriously interested in education or in building up the university—or that he might have exploited such activities as football or the band to get public support for more serious endeavors—a technique that countless college administrators have resorted to." Carleton Beals was among contemporary biographers of Long who judged his motives as completely self-serving. The funding and attention Long showered on LSU, he wrote in 1935, "were for the purpose of show, political power, and to provide a basis for a nation-wide conquest of student and professorial support. With this false glitter he was laying plans to seduce higher education everywhere." If Beals was correct in his assessment of Long's aims, Long would not be the last governor who viewed improving his state's education environment as a qualification for the US Senate or the White House.[14]

President Smith, current and future LSU students, and the school's faculty likely wondered little why Long cared so much—and so suddenly—in their university's well-being. They were simply happy to have the governor's attention and the potential of increased state resources that came with it. If indulging the governor's involvement with the football team—encouraging him to deliver halftime pep talks or prowl the sidelines during a game—was the price for more state support for LSU, everyone in and around LSU was eager to pay. "College for all the boys and girls that want it," as Harnett T. Kane, a reporter for the *New Orleans Item,* described Long's platform. Kane was no fan of Long, and questioned the sincerity of his motives regarding LSU, but he could not deny the results. "Huey adopted this platform early, and used it all his life, eventually as a phase of share-the-wealth [Long's national platform once he went to the US Senate]. He made good on it at L.S.U. Thousands showed up on the campus—many from outside the state—to take him up. They were given a place. Work was found for them, or made for them, if they did not have the resources. Louisiana State University was, in the dictatorship's own words, its 'baby.' It saw that Baby got everything; and by that, it meant every little thing."[15]

A mong everything Long believed LSU needed was a school to train the state's physicians. He announced in late December 1930 that LSU would have a functioning medical school by fall 1931. "Louisiana State University was so organized as to be a complete college," he said in a statement from Shreveport. "That is so that it might complete a medical school along with its other general studies."[16]

Some of Long's detractors believed he launched the school at LSU because Tulane University—which operated the state's only medical school—once refused him an honorary degree. "He said Tulane was a social club for sons of the rich," Joe Cawthon, an LSU student from Logansport who was close to Long, recalled. There is little evidence to support the theory that Long created LSU Medical School out of spite. If Long was looking to harm Tulane, he hid his animosity well. For example, in 1929 he supported allowing Tulane School of Medicine students to train at Charity Hospital. Approved by the Charity Hospital board, the arrangement assigned five hundred beds at Charity for Tulane's use. Long may have sometimes disparaged the school for what he considered the "aristocratic" bearing of its faculty and administration, but the university gave him whatever formal legal training he had. Not a Tulane graduate, he was a product of the school.[17]

The idea for the new medical school came from Charity Hospital's superintendent, Dr. Arthur Vidrine, a twenty-nine-year-old Long ally and Tulane Medical School graduate from Ville Platte. Long appointed Vidrine, a respected surgeon and former Rhodes Scholar, to the position in 1928 after he gained control of the Charity Hospital board and deposed the hospital's superintendent, Dr. William Leake, the son of a prominent Standard Oil attorney. Among those at Tulane who resented what they considered the growing politicization of the hospital was Alton Ochsner, Tulane's head of surgery. Ochsner wrote a letter in 1930 to an out-of-state colleague in which he complained about undue political influence at Charity Hospital. In September of that year, the letter fell into Vidrine's hands and, then, Long's. In response, the Charity board, with Long presiding, revoked the hospital privileges of Ochsner and an associate.[18]

It is not clear why—or if—Long was angry at Tulane, but it was hard to deny that Louisiana needed another school to train its physicians. Although Tulane Medical School was respected, especially for its tropical diseases department, many young Louisianans could not afford its tuition. "Tulane catered to the middle and upper classes," Charity Hospital historian John Salvaggio wrote, "and with its national reputation many of its students were not Louisiana residents."[19]

Long seized on the idea for the school when Vidrine informed him that LSU's charter specified it should have a medical school. "I am sure all other medical schools would welcome the state university going into the field to train the boys that cannot train themselves, particularly those of Louisiana," Long said in a statement on December 22, 1930. "So long as the other schools cannot accommodate our boys, I am sure that their officials, along with the general public, would lend every help possible to seeing Louisiana State Uni-

A young Ville Platte physician, Arthur Vidrine, was Long's head of Charity Hospital in New Orleans and later served as the first dean of the LSU Medical School. (LSU *Gumbo* yearbook, 1933)

versity getting its medical department under way." Long even pitched the plan as beneficial to Tulane. "I believe that the cost of our training to your young physicians might be somewhat lessened at the state university medical department, and consequently that it would serve to lessen the difficulties and cost at Tulane by the natural help which one school would be to the other."[20]

Tulane officials did not welcome this development and insisted that their university had never rejected qualified applicants from Louisiana. Those denials were "positively absurd," Long replied, asserting, "There are so many that have been turned away and had their ambitions blighted that it is not necessary for me to publish the names." If Tulane persisted in its opposition, however, Long threatened to list those he said the Medical School rejected and said he would investigate the school for misusing its state funding.[21]

Long immersed himself in planning the school. Isidore Cohn, then a Tulane Medical School faculty member, recalled seeing the governor in the restaurant of the Roosevelt Hotel in New Orleans one day after the announcement of the Medical School. Eating lunch at a nearby table, Long summoned Cohn and a companion to join him. "I was upset because I was not in politics and had no idea what to talk about," Cohn said. "But the conversation soon turned to the Medical School and medical training. I was utterly astonished by Huey's knowledge of medical history and what was needed to make a good medical school."[22]

Despite their consternation over a rival, state-subsidized medical school, there was nothing Tulane officials could do to stop Long. After the New Year, on January 4, 1931, he convened the boards of LSU and Charity Hospital in his suite at the Roosevelt Hotel. Both boards approved a new $350,000 Medical School building on the property donated by Charity Hospital and appointed Vidrine to serve as dean while he continued to run Charity Hospital. Besides the construction expense, the board estimated the new school would cost LSU an additional $80,000 to $100,000 a year to operate. Long and LSU planned to conduct the first two years of students' medical education in Baton Rouge, but LSU soon consolidated all coursework in New Orleans. And the Medical School was just the beginning. As LSU officials learned, Long had even bigger plans for the school's Baton Rouge campus.[23]

10

YOU HAVE TO DARE A BIT

When Long informed James Monroe Smith about the new Medical School, it was the first of many initiatives he pressed on the new LSU president over the next five years. Despite Long's assurances to the contrary, Smith realized he was running the university only as much as Long allowed. "I had come to the conclusion," Smith wrote years later, "that if I were to accomplish anything of significance, I must always show a willingness to work with him and at his pace." Smith studied his boss's nature better than many individuals who worked with Long. He subordinated his ego and relinquished much of his authority to get funding for what he and Long desired. Smith understood Long "prided himself upon his ability to accomplish the impossible and the possible within half the time ordinarily required." So, he said, he matched Long's passion for LSU "with zest and enthusiasm."[1]

It was a roller-coaster ride for Smith. When he first mentioned a building program for the new campus, Long urged him to begin planning. "Go ahead with your buildings," Long told him. Early on, Long asked what it would take to provide adequate facilities for women. Smith said he needed a women's dormitory. Long did not hesitate. "Get your architect and start on what you need." When Smith asked where LSU would find the funding, Long replied, "That will be my part of the job." Long also advised him, "You have to dare a bit if you build this school. Start ahead. Let the people see what we propose, and we will find a way to do it."[2]

Smith added the cost of the Medical School facility to other projects Long announced for the university, still unsure what funding would materialize. But Long had already identified a source for part of the money: In mid-

December 1930, he had discarded his previous position on the matter and declared LSU would abandon its old campus and sell a portion of its land to the state for construction of the new Capitol. He told reporters that enough revenue would be generated by the sale to build a women's dormitory (first named Smith Hall but now Ruffin G. Pleasant Hall), a student center, and other buildings on the new campus. Long said the land would be sold "as fast as business conditions warrant." (This property, granted to Louisiana by the federal government in 1886 for use as a university, had been recently deeded outright to Louisiana by Congress.)[3]

At least one member of the LSU Board, George Everett of Baton Rouge, also fretted about how Long would fund his other ambitious plans for the school. Noting that the half-mill statewide tax generated about $850,000 a year for LSU, Everett worried, "The university needs every penny of this money and if we are to establish a medical department, additional revenues for the maintenance must be found." Everett, however, expressed "great confidence" that Long would find a way. At the board meeting to create the new Medical School, Long assured members that LSU had "a $3 million reservoir" upon which to draw, suggesting the sale of LSU land to the state would help finance the other building projects. "We are going to need more ground for the new Capitol than we expected," Long told Everett and his colleagues, "and we will purchase it from the university for $350,000." Long said that after the sale, LSU would still own 248 acres, each worth between $1,000 and $2,000. "This land can be sold as needed," he said, "and this will mean $2.5 million to $3 million more." Long added that he had a plan "to get another $1 million for the university," which he discussed with Smith. He said he would soon call the board back into session to ratify it.[4]

By the end of January 1931, Long and Smith unveiled their formal plans for $1 million in construction on the new LSU Baton Rouge campus. It included the previously announced women's dormitory and field house–student center (now the Huey P. Long Field House), as well as a fine arts building (now the Music and Dramatic Arts Building), a home economics cottage, and "buildings to house other departments which may be added to the university."[5]

In early March 1931, Long summoned Smith to the Governor's Mansion to reveal his plan to fund the building program. "Why not sell a portion of the remaining buildings to the [state] Highway Commission for its offices, laboratories, and shops?" Long asked, adding he believed the LSU property

The LSU Music and Dramatic Arts Building.
(LSU Photograph Collection, LSU Special Collections)

was "easily" worth $2 million. "The Highway Commission has $2 million, the university needs $2 million and does not need these old buildings, but the Highway Commission can use them." Long told Smith that LSU would get the better part of this deal, "but they are both agencies of the state and I see no reason why the sale should not be made."

When Smith questioned the plan's legality, Long said that matter "could be tested later, but that in the meantime, the money would be received by the university and spent." What Long proposed was fait accompli. "He was, in reality, not only the Highway Commission, but all other commissions and boards in the state government," Smith said. "So, when he said that if the Highway Commission could be prevailed upon to buy the property, he only meant that he *himself* had determined that this was the procedure to be followed."[6]

A few days later, Long called a meeting with Highway Commission chairman O. K. Allen—his good friend from Winnfield who also served in the state senate—and commission member J. M. "Jess" Nugent. He wanted to discuss the resolution he hoped the commission would adopt. Nugent told him it was illegal. "Here is where we all go to the penitentiary," Nugent, a Winnfield native and childhood friend of Long, said. "This is illegal, using highway money to buy property from LSU." Nugent said he would support the resolution only if Long signed it. "Is that what you want?" Long asked. "Hand me that resolution." On it, Long scrawled, "Approved by Huey P. Long, Governor of Louisiana."[7]

When Long and the LSU Board awarded contracts totaling almost $808,000 for construction of the Medical School buildings in late March, it was still unclear—to the public, at least—how he would finance the work. "Governor Long is attending to that," Smith said when asked about the funding source. After LSU advertised bids for the new Baton Rouge campus buildings a few weeks later—almost $1.2 million in potential construction—the public still did not know how LSU would pay for it. "Just how the $2,000,000 construction work is to be paid has not been definitely announced," the *Rayne Tribune* told readers on April 10, "but the governor has given assurance that the money will be there."[8]

In late April, LSU sold twenty-two acres and five buildings to the Highway Commission for $1.8 million and authorized the sale of the new Capitol site to the state for as much as $350,000. The commission agreed to pay LSU for the land and buildings in twelve increments of $150,000. Even after selling a substantial portion of the old campus, LSU kept most of its property in north Baton Rouge—150 acres, which Smith and the board said would be sold when it needed additional revenue. (Into the 1950s, LSU still owned the Pentagon Barracks and several other small tracts of land in and around downtown Baton Rouge.) "With the exception of the School of Medicine," Smith announced, "all departments and all divisions of the university will be centralized on what is now known as the new LSU campus." In June, the LSU Board gave Smith permission to borrow money to begin the projects before the Highway Commission funds became available.[9]

Long's idea to finance LSU's growth by selling the school's property to the Louisiana Highway Commission won unanimous support from the LSU Board. But two northern Louisiana attorneys sued the university in Baton Rouge state court to stop the plan. They argued the property sale was illegal and "grossly out of proportion to the value of the land," as well as "fraudulently agreed to for the purpose of diverting state funds entrusted to the Louisiana Highway Commission to an unlawful purpose."[10]

Unbowed, a few days later Long went before the annual meeting of the LSU Alumni Federation to declare himself the "official thief" for LSU and vowed to fight the lawsuit. It was the most vigorous public defense of his vision for LSU to date. To the five hundred alumni in attendance in the LSU cafeteria, he said:

> I never have believed that the state of Louisiana should be secondary to a private institution [Tulane University]. . . . The time has come that LSU is rising. The Louisiana State University is the leading university in the state and bids fair to be the leading university in the South. There are certain interests that don't want the school to go forward. There are certain interests which will do all in their power to oppose it, and if there's anybody on the board now who doesn't want to fight for the university, now is the time to get off. Because we're going to have a fight. . . .
>
> This will be no kind of a corncob-and-lightning-bug fight. I didn't put the free schoolbooks in until I had five lawsuits. I haven't done anything without a fight and lawsuits. I haven't known from one year to another that I would be back the next year. But here I am. . . .
>
> Unfortunately, we are prone to think that the Louisiana State University and the other state institutions have a great deal of money. When I became governor, I began to see the problems of the school leaders. They were all fighting for funds. The public schools and the colleges. Well, those school men were pretty clever, and before I knew it, they had the rope around my neck with the bell, and I was the bell cow, leading the procession for money. The fight of this state is to get money for education. There is great opposition. If the Louisiana State University completes its present [building] program, it will require considerable fighting. I am glad to make every fight I can.[11]

Long and the LSU Board plunged ahead with their construction program, despite the legal ambiguity of the funding. They accepted bids of almost $800,000 in August for the Fine Arts Building and the Field House. Work also proceeded on the women's dormitory, expected to house up to four hundred students and scheduled to open in December. Among the buildings for which he was responsible, Long took special pride in the Field House, which would bear his name. The building would serve as the school's student union and recreation center, offering students handball courts, gymnasium, barber shop, beauty parlor, post office, and bookstore. The Field House would also feature a large L-shaped ballroom that extended from the building's entrance to the back of its main section. Its most prominent aspect, however, would be the large, 180-by-48-foot swimming pool at the building's rear. The pool, in fact, sparked the idea for the large building that would surround it.

Cadet Corps commandant Major Troy Middleton recalled that, when LSU Board member George Everett showed the governor the plans for a swimming pool, which he estimated might cost about $75,000, Long asked, "Who done this?" Everett told him Middleton drafted it. "Hell, he don't know nothing about pools, but I do." Long took a pencil and sketched out the rough design for what became the Huey P. Long Field House, to be built around a large swimming pool. Long appeared in Middleton's office one day near the end of construction. "Major, let's go over and see that swimmin' hole of yours," he said. When they arrived, Long asked the construction foreman if the pool would be the longest in the world. The foreman did not know; neither did Middleton. "But I wasn't going to let him [stump] me," Middleton said. "I said the longest was at the Naval Academy, though I had never seen it." (The Naval Academy's pool was 150 feet long.) Long then turned to the foreman and said, "Put ten more feet on this pool." Middleton never knew why Long decided on ten feet. "Anyway," he said, "they dug out the far end to lengthen it."[12]

As work proceeded on the new buildings at LSU, Long defended his funding scheme. "My opponents have charged that I diverted money to Louisiana State University improperly," Long said in Hammond in November as he campaigned for his handpicked gubernatorial replacement, state senator O. K. Allen. "It is true that I had the university sell a piece of land [23 acres] and a building [it was five] to the Highway Commission for $1,800,000, and that the cash was used for improvements at LSU." But Long insisted he broke no law. "I simply used state funds from another department. I kept the money in the family. Probably my opponents, who saw nothing objectionable when the state purchased a $350,000 tract from the university for the new Capitol site, think it's a crime because the money didn't go to a stranger, instead of going back to the state."[13]

For the state university," one historian of the school wrote, "1931 was a year of miracles." As construction continued, and the lawsuit over Long's funding scheme wound its way through the courts, the mood at LSU was exhilaration. "The psychological effect [of Long's attention to LSU] was tremendous," Middleton said. "We were no longer a little college stuck off down here, but a first-class school, or on the way to it." It was not simply buildings that heralded the emergence of a larger, more substantial university; LSU was expanding on the academic side, too. Expecting its first incoming class in October, LSU Medical School was hiring faculty members. In Baton Rouge, the university established a College of Pure and Applied Science in February 1931, and promoted three departments—Journalism, Music, and Geology—to full-fledged, free-standing schools. "I think the time has come," Smith told the LSU Alumni Federation in June, "that Louisiana may say she can produce not only good roads, among the best in the country, not only good public schools, among the best in the country, but also a good university, one of the best in the whole country."[14]

Smith was managing not just LSU's rapid growth, but an energetic governor concerned with every aspect of the school and its growth. To some students in 1931, it appeared that Long was at LSU every day. "I used to enjoy watching him on campus," journalism student Dave McGuire recalled. "He was very popular with the students. After all, the students—a lot of them— were very impressionable. Here is a prominent figure who comes out and spends his time with them."[15] Long bragged—and exaggerated—about his attention to detail at LSU. "I prescribed a uniform for every student so that no one could look better than the others," he would later say in a US Senate speech. "I prescribed a daily menu for them. I prescribed exactly the size of bed each student should have. I let him change sheets twice a week, and no more."[16]

"The governor's interest now had become thoroughly alive to the university," Smith wrote later. He added that Long "was more interested in the extracurricular activities than the academic functions of the university." He did not view Long's obsession with LSU's building projects, the football team, and the Regimental Band so much as a detriment but a challenge. Smith regarded his job as "an attempt to keep up [Long's] interest in the university as a whole by giving his pet projects a sympathetic endorsement." In other words, Smith gave Long whatever shiny objects he wanted to persuade him to support his academic priorities. "A man possessed of such fervor as he wielded could easily make or break the university. I considered it the part of wisdom to hold his interest and for the good of the young men and women of the state to work with him."[17]

Early on, Long urged Smith to fire a group of faculty and staff members, likely those he regarded as political opponents. "I saw immediately that it would be necessary to work cautiously with him," Smith said, adding that he did not reject Long's order out of hand, but asked for time to investigate the "training, efficiency, and loyalty" of the faculty members in question. "I felt then and still feel," Smith wrote years later, "that such drastic action was unwarranted, but I had to have time to convince him of this fact." Smith later assured Long "that the faculty was both loyal and efficient." Further, he advised Long that firing faculty members would jeopardize the university's standing and "that it would ultimately [reflect] unfavorably upon him politically." Long dropped the matter.

During his early months as president, Smith met or spoke with Long almost every day. In their conversations, Smith "discovered the key by which his actions toward the university might be controlled." He realized that Long "was very anxious to be thought of in the role of a builder and a statesman. I had, therefore, only to convince him that his political prestige would be enhanced, and his power increased if he would throw the full weight of his influence back of a program to popularize the institution and to broaden its scope of service." Smith reminded Long that the "schoolboys of today were the voters of tomorrow." He said that he and Long "entered upon a more-or-less unstated gentleman's agreement wherein the educational policies of the institution and all the matters dealing with its academic development, [including] the retention and selection of faculty, should be left to my judgment and that he should devote his energies toward providing funds for the enlargement of the physical plant and for increase in the maintenance funds." Smith, who served as LSU president until 1939, insisted that Long, "with few exceptions," honored this arrangement. Fred Frey, dean of the College of Arts and Sciences during this period, agreed that Long meddled little in LSU's academic affairs. "My own feeling [was] we had less political interference during Huey's time than we ever did."[18]

Smith's recollection of his working relationship with Long was not inaccurate, but it was not the entire story. Over the next four years, Long was Smith's most valuable patron—and his biggest headache. In their near-daily phone calls or visits, Long viewed himself not as an adviser or major supporter of the university, but as something of a co-president. He issued commands and expected Smith to obey them. "Huey exploded at Smith often," T. Harry Williams wrote. "In dealing with all official subordinates, he was blunt and could be harsh. He was especially rough on a man who he judged would take an affront. He had measured Smith, just as the president had measured him. He saw that this genial servant would submit to much to get what he wanted, and he callously exploited the relationship."[19]

As a member of the LSU Board and its ex officio chair, Long believed he had a legitimate role in running the university. As governor, he knew he did, and never hesitated to give Smith and others detailed instructions, expecting they would follow them as issued. Smith saw himself as a buffer between Long and his faculty and administration. He could not stop Long from dropping by Troy Middleton's office to talk about the construction of the Field House. Smith welcomed Long's support of the Regimental Band. And he was probably amused by Long's fanatical loyalty to the football team. But, as a savvy individual, Smith recognized that, if LSU gained a reputation as a school controlled by the governor, and not by its president or its governing board, its standing would decline and its relationships with national accrediting bodies might suffer. When taking the job, Smith must have known there would be days when he would have to choose between fealty to Long and fidelity to LSU. He thought he could manage the tension. Smith understood, journalist Don Wharton wrote, "that Huey had boundless energy, ambition, egotism, and power. He knew that here were springs to tap, not dam, and that part of the secret was letting Huey talk, encouraging his expansive moods, feeding his vanity."[20]

One example of Smith's management of Long's whims came early in his presidency, when the governor told him LSU should stop admitting women. Smith did not share Long's vision of LSU as an all-male institution, but he did not challenge the governor directly. Instead, he reminded Long that co-education in the United States "had become rather thoroughly established" and that he might incur a negative political reaction from such a move. Smith said he believed there were two movements in American politics that were irrevocable. "One was woman's suffrage, and the other was co-education," Smith said, adding, "I suggested, however, that if he were thoroughly convinced that it would be best to segregate the men from the women, it would be necessary to provide a first-class woman's college on the old campus which would entail considerable expense." Long listened and then, Smith said, "seemed suddenly to change his mind." T. Harry Williams observed that Smith "would take the unimportant to get the important. He might argue an issue on occasion, but if Huey exploded and issued a command, he obeyed it." As former LSU football player W. E. "Billy" Butler put it, "[Smith] took his orders running."[21]

Long could be brutal with Smith and others, which was not so much a matter of showing his displeasure or reprimanding them but dominating them. Richard Leche, a Long ally and appeals court judge who became Louisiana governor after Long's death, observed Long's response to a friend and supporter who entered the governor's office one day. When Long saw the man, Leche recalled, "Huey's face just clouded over, and Huey just gave him down the country. The fellow was completely crushed and finally left with his shoulders sagging." When the man left Long's office, Leche said, "Huey's face became wreathed in smiles again." Long turned to Leche and explained, "Did you ever see a [man] driving a mule down a country road? The old mule will just be going down the road and all of a sudden, the [man] will say, 'Whoa.' And the mule will stop and the [man] will get off and go over to a fence and pull a picket off, and he'll just whale the daylights out of the mule. And then he gets up and off they go. Now, that mule wasn't doing anything, but the [man] knows the mule and knows the mule might do something if he don't teach him a lesson. Now, that fellow hasn't done anything, but I got to do that to keep him a pretty good guy, which he is." Leche concluded, "That's how [Long's] mind worked."[22]

For all his meddling in LSU's affairs, Long found, in Smith, an able administrator and competent university leader. "In my humble opinion," Fred Frey later asserted, "the best all-around and most effective president during all that time [Frey's forty years at LSU] was James Monroe Smith." Frey and others remembered Smith as a consummate politician, who knew how to manage Long and the legislature, who enjoyed great rapport with faculty, staff, and students, and who cared about research and graduate education. "His office door was always open to everyone," Frey recalled, "from the top people to the bottom people, including the janitors. He was always glad to see anyone and to try and help them." As further evidence of Smith's capabilities, Frey submitted Smith's personnel decisions, which included hiring three successive, respected deans of administration—James Broussard, Paul

Hebert, and Troy Middleton. (The latter two served as LSU's acting president and president, respectively.) Smith further burnished his reputation for accessibility by becoming the first LSU president to live on campus.[23]

Students and others would one day mock Smith, giving him the nickname "Jingle Money." And some of Long's opponents derided him as "Jimmy Moron." But in his early years at LSU, Smith was as popular a president as the school ever had. This was partly a consequence of his close association with Long. At ceremonies marking Smith's formal inauguration as president in November 1931, Long lavished praise on the LSU leader. He called him "the Lord's elect," a man so destined for greatness that Smith would soon think "Huey Long was only an incident in his life." Long devoted most of his remarks, however, to defending his support of LSU by praising the state's other universities. "Only friendly rivalry exists between the schools of Louisiana." (Long was not delivering new funding for only LSU; in a speech to Louisiana teachers the same day, he proposed eliminating all fees at state colleges and universities, saying he supported legislation in the next session of the legislature to fund his proposal. Such legislation was never approved.) Long also mocked those who were suing to reverse his plan for funding LSU's expansion by selling land to the state's Highway Commission. "I never expected to see the day when prominent citizens of the state would go into court to enjoin and obstruct the progress of our universities."

Long must have been pleased with the praise he received at the event, particularly from his old friend Thomas H. Harris, the state's education superintendent. Harris described Long as "the man who has opened up new avenues of expansion for LSU and is arranging for a service to the people of the state through the university hitherto undreamed of by the institution's friends."[24]

Harris's praise was no exaggeration. The LSU of 1931 was a different institution. New buildings—including the Field House, the Fine Arts Building, the women's dormitory—were springing up around the campus and beyond. The new Medical School would soon open in New Orleans. The university established a new School of Library Science. (It would be nationally accredited by 1934.) Two miles of sidewalks were about to be poured. Registration for the fall semester reached an all-time high of 2,875, an increase of 40 percent over the previous year, including students from thirty other states. Smith reported that LSU now held the record for the percentage of enrollment growth among state universities. The school explored adding PhD programs to its graduate school. "Students coming to the campus for the first time," the *Morning Advocate* reported in September, "will find a greater university than that viewed by former first-year groups."[25]

It was not just the academic side of LSU that was growing. Thomas "Skipper" Heard, the Athletic Department's graduate manager, had an idea that would transform the university's football program: Install $7,500 in new arc lighting on fifty-foot poles to allow games to be played at night. Heard argued that night games would permit more fans for its contests against archrivals, like Tulane, and "make it possible for many of our fans, busy on a Saturday afternoon, to attend our games. For example, we had many well-to-do fans whose duties running nearby plantations made it impossible to get away on a Saturday afternoon." It was the first of several stadium expansions in the early 1930s, including additional dorm rooms under the bleachers in 1932. LSU played its first night game in Tiger Stadium on Saturday, October 3, 1931, against Alabama's Spring Hill College.[26]

LSU students were among those who noticed the rapid changes happening on their campus, and they were aware of Long's role in the school's transformation. "The dynamic young Governor and U.S. Senator-elect of Louisiana is destined to go down in University history as one of its staunchest friends and strongest supporters," the editors of the school's yearbook, the *Gumbo,* wrote about Long on a page they dedicated to him in their 1931 edition. "Since his assumption of the gubernatorial office, he has, with characteristic verve and vigor consistently labored to promote the highest interests of the institution."[27]

As popular as Smith proved to be with his faculty, and despite the autonomy Long gave him and others to conduct the academic affairs of the university as they wished, LSU officials soon discovered there were limits to their freedom from political influence.

11

CANE JUICE

In September 1931, a Baton Rouge Catholic priest, Monsignor F. Leon Gassler, learned about a new novel published by an LSU associate professor of English, John Earle Uhler. *Cane Juice: A Story of Southern Louisiana* was set on the LSU campus. Its protagonist was a brilliant-but-uncouth Cajun boy from rural south Louisiana who struggled to navigate the fast-paced, carefree LSU campus environment. It is not clear how Gassler heard about the book, but its portrayals of uninhibited LSU coeds scandalized the priest. He resolved to defend the young women's honor by attacking *Cane Juice* and what he regarded as its libertine author.

A lean, balding man with a thin mustache, Uhler had become one of the faculty's more prominent members since his arrival from Baltimore in 1928. A native of Media, Pennsylvania, the forty-year-old Uhler taught courses in Shakespeare and American drama at Johns Hopkins University for eleven years. At LSU, he appeared often in the *Reveille* for his plays, books, and even an LSU song, "To the Purple and Gold." Before earning his PhD, Uhler spent a decade as a stage actor, working in stock companies in New York and throughout New England. His theatrical skills made him an entertaining and popular teacher of freshman English, although some younger members of the English faculty were said to regard him as a self-promoter. Uhler had been embroiled in another controversy since arriving at LSU. He was the faculty member portrayed as a drug fiend in the *Whangdoodle,* edited by Long protégé Kemble K. Kennedy. After Uhler testified against Kennedy in the 1930 criminal libel trial, he returned to his teaching and writing. But the way LSU officials and Long responded to Gassler's ferocious criticism of the novel would propel the English professor to brief national prominence and cost him his job.[1]

Uhler awaited publication of the novel and informed his editor that he might next attempt a work of fiction based on Long. "He is an uneducated man, ruthless, unscrupulous, vindictive, but very likable in personality, generous, dynamic, progressive," Uhler told his New York editor, Hewitt Howland of the Century Company. "He's more spellbinding than any demagog I've read of in history." Uhler proposed disguising Long by placing him in an imaginary country, which Howland considered a mistake. Just put the Long-like character in another state, the editor advised. A few months later, however, Howland had second thoughts. If Uhler wrote a book on Long, the editor asked, "I wonder if you have thought of the effect it might have on the University and its relations to the state government?" Howland's concerns about how Uhler's writing could run afoul of LSU and Long were prescient, which became apparent to the author by October.[2]

Several decades later, *Cane Juice*'s portrayal of LSU students' hijinks, drunkenness, and coed promiscuity would not have caused most readers to raise an eyebrow. Even by 1931 standards, the story was tame. The book was a well-paced tale with interesting characters, even if the protagonist— Bernard Couvillon of Lafourche Parish—was a caricature of an uncultured Cajun boy who became a star football player and whose undergraduate research at the Audubon Sugar School revolutionized sugarcane science. After Uhler shipped his manuscript to Howland, the editor averred that his novel was "the best college story I have read in a long, long time." In a story about Uhler and the book in October, *Time* magazine deemed *Cane Juice* "earnestly, sometimes ably written. Like many another contemporary novel of student life, it introduces toping and lechery."[3]

Gassler, whose St. Joseph's Catholic Church was two blocks south of where the new Capitol was being built, did not share any of that enthusiasm for the novel. "The author assails the unsullied reputation of our Creole maidens," the priest fulminated in a two-sheet flier that he passed around Baton Rouge and which the *Morning Advocate* published on October 6. "The students become unclean beasts too drunk to be responsible for their bestial behavior." Gassler demanded answers to several questions: "Will the students at the LSU stand for such an imputation? Will the fathers and mothers of families still entrust their daughters to an institution where their daughters' chastity has to be safeguarded by locked doors?"[4]

LSU English professor John Earle Uhler, *left,* and Major Troy Middleton. Fallout from Uhler's 1931 novel, *Cane Juice,* resulted in his temporary dismissal from LSU. (LSU Photograph Collection, LSU Special Collections)

Uhler defended himself in the *Morning Advocate,* noting in a statement printed alongside the text of Gassler's broadside that he had consulted a Catholic priest "to make certain religious passages of 'Cane Juice' [were] both accurate and entirely agreeable to Catholics." Furthermore, Uhler said scenes involving sexual escapades by LSU students were implied, not implicit. "I have the greatest respect for the women students of our fine state university."[5]

Gassler's attacks on Uhler hit their mark. President Smith fired the professor a week after the priest's screed hit the streets. The LSU Board's executive committee upheld the decision, asserting that Uhler's novel reflected poorly on the university "as a whole" and that it was "impossible to condone the insult." Smith later claimed that he sacked Uhler on his own, bowing to no outside pressure. But some local journalists suspected Long's hidden hand, perhaps because of Uhler's testimony against Kemble Kennedy in his 1930 criminal libel trial. While it was unclear if Long played any role, he supported Smith's and the executive committee's decision. "It's a thoroughly routine case," the governor told reporters, adding it was "just as if the committee were buying a crate of eggs or a couple of chickens. Dr. Smith is president of LSU, and he is running things."[6]

Uhler's friends and others rushed to his defense. A group of LSU coeds said the book did not offend them. "It is not a reflection on LSU co-eds or on women in general, in spite of the few episodes in which women of a certain kind figure," the students said in a petition shared with the *Morning Advocate.* "It is very clear that those episodes do not apply to us." The wife of the rector of St. James Episcopal Church, a few blocks from Gassler's church, and to which Uhler belonged, also vouched for the professor. "Great men, great movements, great books, all meet attack and opposition, but they live on forever," she said. Punishing Uhler for his book, she added, would make LSU a national "laughingstock."[7]

Most helpful to Uhler was the American Civil Liberties Union (ACLU) in New York. The organization sent telegrams to influential associates throughout the country, urging them to support Uhler. "A university so sensitive to criticism on such trivial grounds," ACLU official Forrest Bailey wrote to ACLU members in Louisiana on October 9, "cannot lay claim to fostering higher education." The ACLU's national director, Roger Baldwin, declared in a letter to members, "This is so clear an issue of academic freedom that we are asking all interested friends to *write or wire at once to Dr. James*

Monroe Smith." Letters and telegrams poured into Baton Rouge. "Don't let those cane cracking Bible beating morons get your goat," one correspondent from New York wrote to Uhler on October 12. The president of the American Federation of Teachers told Smith in a letter, "We hope very profoundly that Professor Uhler will receive every consideration due to a teacher of the young men and women of Louisiana and that whatever hearing is given to the case will be given publicly."[8]

Uhler's firing also made national news. Newspapers in at least thirty states carried stories about LSU's response to his novel. The professor's treatment was a public relations problem for LSU. There had been no public outcry about his book. Most who read it were untroubled by its depiction of LSU students.

Uhler mused about suing Gassler and LSU for libel, as the ACLU stirred up national outrage about the case. "[Gassler] has damaged my character and my reputation and has been the actual cause, or one of the greatest causes, why I have lost my position with Louisiana State University," Uhler told a reporter the day that Smith dismissed him. Uhler did not name Long, but it was clear he suspected the priest and Smith were not the only destructive forces in his life. "I realize that behind my dismissal there are sinister and powerful influences, difficult to combat."[9]

It was Uhler's threat to sue LSU, as well as the ACLU's enthusiastic offer of legal help, that persuaded university officials to pay him his full $4,000 annual salary in late November. "My legal efforts were solely on behalf of the principles of freedom of speech and academic tenure," Uhler told the *Reveille*, "and in their at least partial recognition [of that,] the whole teaching profession has been benefited."[10]

Despite being paid through the spring semester, Uhler was out of work. He promoted his novel in the early months of 1932 and sent letters to university English departments around the country, hoping to find another teaching position. He also encouraged newspaper columnists in other states to tell their readers about his cause, which several did. Writing in the *Chicago Evening Post* in January, Llewellyn Jones—the paper's literary editor—observed that, "familiar as we are with the timidity of university presidents, it seems incredible that on the basis of [Gassler's attack] a university professor should be dismissed from his post. If we take the word of the president of the Louisiana State University that the attack had nothing to do with the discharge—which would mean simply that he did not like the book—the thing becomes more incredible still." Jones, perhaps at Uhler's suggestion, said he suspected Long was behind his dismissal. "One of the features of this case was the fact that although the governor of Louisiana was appealed to by both sides of the controversy, he did not raise a finger in Dr. Uhler's defense." Uhler made what appeared to be his only public comment about Long as a possible source of his woes in an interview with the *Shreveport Times* in late February. "Had Long not been catering to votes on a religious issue, I still would be on the LSU faculty," he said of the governor who was campaigning for O. K. Allen, his eventual successor, in that fall's gubernatorial election. Still, Uhler had no hard evidence that Smith fired him on Long's orders.[11]

Whether it was fear of legal action by Uhler, bad press for the university, or that cooler heads prevailed, in early April, LSU restored Uhler to the faculty. In a terse, three-sentence letter, Smith referred to a "recent conversation" with the professor. He formalized the decision to rehire Uhler and characterized his firing as a suspension. Smith told the *Reveille* the following week that "the period of suspension has been sufficient and that Dr. Uhler's conduct during that period has been such as to justify his reinstatement." Many students rallied to Uhler's cause, so it must have disappointed him on April 15 when the student editors of the *Reveille* published an editorial taking LSU's side in the controversy. The paper said LSU "acted wisely," arguing Uhler's dismissal "was its own protest against the author's interpretation of the university, its background and traditions. The dismissal was not an expression of contempt against the guaranty of freedom of speech or the press."[12]

By 1934, a new crop of *Reveille* editors would have reason to wish their predecessors had made a stronger, more principled stand for academic and press freedom. Smith backed down this time, but he would not always do so, with grave consequences for student journalists who incurred Long's wrath a few years later. Although Uhler's saga ended with Smith's and LSU's surrender, the episode should have raised troubling questions about just how much Smith, the LSU Board, and Long believed in free speech and academic freedom. It would be another three years before their actions answered those questions again, but anyone watching closely knew that faculty members and students at LSU were not as free as some might have thought or hoped.

12

WHAT DOES THE BAND THINK?

L
ong devoted as much attention as possible to LSU, but the deepening Great Depression in Louisiana consumed most of his time in 1931 and 1932. As residents of an already poverty-stricken state, many in Louisiana had not immediately experienced the full effects of the Depression. In most cases, their lives were about as miserable as they could be. Still, the state's government, as designed by Long's predecessors, was ill-equipped to manage the expanding economic crisis. Like most other southern states, Louisiana had few programs to help jobless individuals. By 1932, the Depression would spread, as the state's financial institutions began failing. By 1935, almost a third of Louisiana banks went out of business. Income from agricultural products, especially cotton and sugar, fell in Louisiana by 40 percent from 1929 to 1933. Wages for those in manufacturing plummeted, and hundreds of the factories that employed them went under. By 1933, declining state revenue and increased enrollment at LSU compelled the university to briefly defer paying faculty and staff. In his 1934 report to the governor and the legislature, President Smith asserted that only during the Civil War and Reconstruction "has the University been confronted with graver financial problems than those of the last three years."

The same could have been said for the rest of Louisiana. And there was little that Long and the state government could, or would, do. Long's critics have noted, correctly, that during his time in power he did not attempt to institute old-age pensions, unemployment insurance, a minimum wage, or child-labor laws. In fact, Long derided proposals for old-age and unemployment benefits. In the 1932 governor's race, he attacked anti-Long candidate Dudley LeBlanc and his proposal for $30 monthly pensions for the elderly, saying the plan was too expensive. "It will cost $20 million a year to pay the negroes' pensions alone," he said, "and you white people will be working the year around to pay pensions to negroes."

Two areas where the state tried to help were in education and road building. Under Long's direction—and funded by increases in the severance tax passed in 1928—Louisiana had assumed an increasing percentage of the cost of running local schools. Before Long's administration, parish schools subsisted almost entirely on local revenue. By 1936, however, the state provided 60 percent of the funding.

And the same transformation occurred in the construction and maintenance of highways and bridges, largely a local responsibly until the late 1920s. While the state road system had expanded during Governor John Parker's administration—Parker had established the Louisiana Highway Commission and pushed to build hundreds of miles of new highways, financed mainly with federal funds—Long's plan was more ambitious. Under Long, the state began building and maintaining the state's roads and highways with revenue from the $68 million bond issue Long muscled through the legislature, the debt serviced by proceeds from a gasoline tax. Thousands of Louisiana's unemployed found work building roads. During Long's tenure as governor, Louisiana went from 331 miles of paved highways to 2,301. The state also built a hundred new bridges. "All these projects helped to make the Great Depression less stressful in Louisiana by employing thousands who otherwise would have swelled the ranks of those desperately seeking any kind of work," Long biographer William Ivy Hair wrote.

And, as with education, state highway funding came with increasing state control of these once-locally controlled entities. With that came more patronage for Long and his political organization. Whether by design or necessity, Long's administration was centralizing and consolidating its domination of Louisiana and its local governments—a trend that only accelerated as the Kingfish reached for more power.[1]

L ong could argue that he was not involved in the day-to-day personnel decisions at LSU, such as when to suspend or fire a faculty member. But he made no such pretense about his involvement with the football team or the band. He fancied himself an assistant coach to Russ Cohen, although his more formal roles were as the team's chief booster, motivational speaker, and sidelines cheerleader. His relationship with LSU's Regimental Band, meanwhile, was similar, with several basic differences: Long did not play a proper instrument (he enjoyed plucking his Jew's harp) or have any training in music, but he knew a bit more about music than football. He understood the band's vital role in entertaining the Tiger Stadium crowds and in increasing the excitement and spectacle of an LSU home game. And he believed the band could project LSU's image beyond the confines of campus.

That had not been the case before Long became governor. LSU's band performed at halftime for the first time in 1924, when the school's cheerleaders persuaded band members to entertain the crowd with music as they marched up and down the field. However, the small military band—it had about forty members in 1930—did not generate the excitement Long envisioned when he thought about the unit's potential.[2]

Besides replacing the longtime band director, Frank "Pop" Guilbeau, in late 1930, Long put his imprint on the organization in other ways. Among the first changes he encouraged was a new uniform. The band was a unit of the Cadet Corps, and members wore military-style outfits. Long pushed the school to toss this tradition as he supervised the uniform's design to incorporate the school's purple and gold colors.

John T. Hood, a senior from Jefferson Davis Parish who captained the unit in 1930–31, was the band member assigned to call on Long at the Governor's Mansion in late 1930 and show him drawings of several styles for new uniforms. Long pored over the sketches. "What does the band think?" he asked. Hood pointed to a flashier design that band members preferred. "Tell 'em to make one up as a sample and bring it for me to see." When Hood returned to present the prototype to Long, an aide told him the governor was in bed, sick. But Long summoned the student to his bedroom when he learned Hood was downstairs. "There were various officials in the room doing business," Hood recalled, "but he stopped to look at the uniform and to approve it. He made decisions quickly."[3]

In January 1931, LSU announced new band uniforms that maintained the unit's military bearing while introducing additional elements, including aiguillettes—a braided, gold cord resembling the French decoration for valor—which looped over the players' left shoulders. The military-style caps were now made of purple cloth and trimmed with gold braid. Around their coats, members wore a gold belt.[4]

Regimental Band members were not the only ones sporting new uniforms. Football players suited up for LSU's first game of the 1931 season, against Texas Christian University, in what one newspaper reporter called "the spiffiest ever manufactured for an L.S.U. team." The players' new outfits included gold pants with a purple stripe down the back of the legs and a purple jersey with a white leather design on the front and large gold numbers on the rear. It is not known what, if any, influence Long had on the creation of these uniforms.[5]

The band, decked out in its new, flashy garb, also saw its numbers swell to almost eighty members (including a twenty-four-piece Drum and Bugle Corps), thanks to a governor who desired a bigger unit with more instruments to create a larger sound and a greater spectacle. Long also began recruiting the band's drum majors, insisting that they be among the tallest members of the unit. "His unofficial agents scoured the state and went even into neighboring states to get such boys," T. Harry Williams wrote. "Huey equipped them with huge shakos that made them look gigantic."[6]

"He wanted new instruments, oboes, and bassoons," Louis "Lew" Williams, the unit's drum major in 1931, remembered. "Boys who got them didn't know how to play too well." A saxophone player, Williams recalled one concert at the Governor's Mansion when Long asked for a bassoon solo by a student not yet proficient in the instrument. Williams leaned in close behind the nervous young man, who pretended to play. Long, who did not notice it was Williams blowing the melody on his tenor sax, told the student it was the finest bassoon solo he ever heard.[7]

In appreciation for Long's support of the team, the new band director, A. W. Wickboldt, composed "The Governor Long March" in early 1931 and led his band in a performance of the new song for Long during one of the unit's weekly parades in March. Wickboldt flattered Long by telling him he adapted the melody from a tune he once heard the governor hum. The march also contained the chorus of "Just a Memory," which the *Reveille* reported was one of Long's favorite tunes. "Governor Long of Louisiana has a band," LSU bragged in a 1931 promotional piece. "Governor Long reminds Mr. Wickboldt that the band is really his but that he's willing to turn them over to the official bandmaster for training occasionally."[8]

Long persuaded the LSU Board of Supervisors to authorize hiring several assistants for Wickboldt in June 1931. The board also created special band scholarships that President Smith could award to as many students as he desired, exempting them from tuition and other fees, and increased Wickboldt's annual salary from $2,700 to $3,600. By November, the band grew to 105 members, more than double its size when Long became governor. "The band is scarcely recognizable as the unit of last year," the *Reveille* observed, noting the addition of several new $200 French horns and a bass clarinet "costing about the same."[9]

Long was a frequent visitor to the late-afternoon band practices, held in a wood-frame building behind the Pentagon Barracks. On those occasions, band members often entertained him with some of his favorite tunes, including "Alexander's Rag Time Band," "Lindy Lou," and "Shine On, Harvest Moon." John Hood recalled that Long sometimes sat near Wickboldt and interrupted the playing. "Try 'Harvest Moon' again, a little softer," he might say. "Play that soft part again." Other times, Long insisted on directing. "He was popular with the band," Hood said, adding that listening to the unit's music "was his relaxation."[10]

From the beginning of his immersion in the band's life, Long recognized its usefulness in attracting attention for LSU and himself. And the easiest way to draw that attention was with a parade. Long began taking the unit on the road for showy processions in April 1931. Six hundred LSU cadets traveled by train to New Orleans that month for the annual national convention of the Reserve Officers' Association. Along for the ride were Long and the expanded band in its flashy new attire. When the cadets marched down Canal Street, a proud governor and the band led them to the applause of hundreds lined along both sides of the street. When a streetcar threatened to halt the procession by crossing in front of the marching column, Long played traffic cop and rushed to stop the car. The following February, Long led the band on another parade in the city, this time for the parade of Rex during Mardi Gras. When a group of police officers stopped the unit at a red light, Long shouted, "Stand back! This is the Kingfish." The officers retreated.[11]

A few days after Long's April 1931 parade in New Orleans, LSU said the governor would "accompany the 1931 varsity football team on all trips" that season. The occasions for these journeys were football games, but the LSU news release emphasized the band's travel and new uniforms. And the highlight of the 1931 travel schedule would be the November 7 game in New York State against the US Military Academy at West Point. "The flashy purple and gold [band] uniforms will make the unit stand out as they go thru special formations and drills to be practiced for the event," LSU announced in a release, adding that Long and the band would also attend games in Fort Worth, Shreveport, New Orleans, and Jackson, Mississippi.[12]

Long was eager to show off the bigger, better band, and while he would accompany the team, the band, and LSU fans to away games in Shreveport and New Orleans, Louisiana politics would undermine his other travel plans that year. His years-long feud with Lieutenant Governor Paul Cyr meant Long could not risk leaving the state, as much as he yearned to lead "his" band in parades in New York, Oxford, and Fort Worth. To do so would make Cyr the acting governor during his absence. Long loved LSU, its football team, and its band, but he valued even more his powers as governor.[13]

13

I WANT A PLAY

L ong loved LSU football for several reasons. Like many men of his time, he enjoyed sports. Attending LSU games was a way to associate himself with one of the state's more popular pastimes and an excuse to highlight the cultural common ground he shared with Louisiana residents, even those who opposed him. He knew that many football players would become community leaders. Bonding with these young men was good politics in Louisiana.

It was also, as Long knew, good politics beyond the state. "There have been some ignorant and supercilious snickers at Huey's collegiate antics, his liking to lead the college band (he does it well) and his attempts to function as football coach," journalist John Franklin Carter wrote in 1935. "Yet this particular device landed Huey on the sporting-page, the one section of journalism which has been inadequately exploited by political propaganda and has also helped him to organize a specific appeal to youth, by identifying the Kingfish with college life and campus high-jinks." LSU football player Sidney Bowman agreed. "I think he did it all to get the young people on his side. When they saw him on the bench, running up and down the side of the field, they got a love for him that endured." Assistant LSU football coach Harry Rabenhorst believed Long's motivation was less complicated. "He loved the publicity, the attention connected with every part of it."[1]

Long took his obsession with LSU football to a new level in fall 1931 after injuries sidelined three of the team's top players just four games into the season. The first was the team captain, left tackle Ed Khoury, who broke his right arm in the September 26 season opener against Texas Christian University. Weeks later, in the October 17 game against Mississippi State, injuries claimed two additional star players, Billy Butler and Sid Bowman. On the Monday after the Mississippi State game, Butler was called out of class and ordered to report to Tiger Stadium. There, he found Long, who informed him that he and the other injured players would live at the Governor's Mansion while they healed. "I'm a better doctor than those doctors at LSU," he bragged. Next, Long located Bowman at the Paramount Theater on Third Street in downtown Baton Rouge. He sent Khoury inside to fetch his teammate. "I thought it was all a joke," Bowman said. "But, sure enough, the governor was outside in front of the movie [theater], eating peanuts." Long told him, "We got pretty good grub [at the mansion], better than you get out at school."[2]

Butler remembered that "Huey's idea of doctoring was to feed us steaks twice a day, with turnip greens, corn bread, pineapple upside-down cake, and sour milk." The menu was the same every day. "Huey served us," Bowman said. "If you ate one steak, he put another on your plate, thinking you hadn't had enough. We soon learned to eat slowly, chew food well, or we'd have to take that second helping." Khoury said when he was well enough to return to the team, he had gained too much weight to play for more than two or three plays. Bowman believed one reason Long wanted the young men to live at the mansion was "to learn about football from us, so he could talk about it, so he wouldn't be like a lost ball in the high weeds." Over dinner and during informal visits, Long grilled the players about the game's finer points. "He had read about things like the single wing, scouting, wingback," Bowman recalled. "He would ask us about all these things and remember it."[3]

Another player briefly joined the original three at the mansion—Arthur Foley, a halfback from Eufaula, Oklahoma. Long learned of him from the 1930 edition of *Spalding's Official Foot Ball Guide,* which mentioned the young man's exploits for New Mexico Military Institute, including a ninety-yard kickoff return for a touchdown against the University of Mexico. After the 1930 season, Long sent LSU's graduate athletic manager, Skipper Heard, to Oklahoma to recruit him. "This boy may be the finest football player in the country, and I want him to play for LSU," Long told Heard. "I'm not leaving anything to chance. I want you to find out where that boy lives and go out and get him. And I want you to leave right away."

Heard left Baton Rouge by train that evening for Oklahoma. When he arrived, however, he learned that Foley was vacationing with his family in Mineral Wells, Texas. Heard boarded a southbound bus. In Texas, he found

LSU athletic director Thomas "Skipper" Heard, *left*, and dean of administration James Broussard. (LSU *Gumbo* yearbook, 1936)

a young man of uncertain football prowess, but with an obvious passion for golf. He and Heard played golf together every day for a week. "All the time, I was reporting back to Huey," Heard said. "Although I knew nothing about the boy's football ability, other than what I had read, on the golf course he looked like a great athlete." By the time Foley returned home to Eufaula, Long had shipped him a new set of golf clubs. Flattered by all the attention, Foley transferred to LSU. In September 1931, Long sent Heard back to Oklahoma to retrieve the young man.

Long arrived for the team's first scrimmage with Foley in tow, but the recruit had a tooth infection that kept him out of the season's first game against Texas Christian. Foley started in Tiger Stadium the next week against Alabama's Spring Hill College. The back from Oklahoma dazzled the crowd, running fifty-six yards for a touchdown and returning a punt for sixty-two yards to score another six points. LSU won 35–0. (Suffering from influenza, Long missed the game.) As sportswriter and LSU football historian Peter Finney observed, "Foley made Huey Long look like a shrewd judge of talent." But there was a problem: A few days after his splendid LSU debut, Foley fell sick. Doctors discovered tuberculosis. "It hadn't been so noticeable in the dry Western country, but in damp Louisiana, on the banks of the Mississippi River, Foley began to suffer," *New Orleans Item* sportswriter Fred Digby recalled a few years later. "Time and again, exertion on the football field brought on a hemorrhage." Foley played briefly in the October 10 game against South Carolina, but never entered another game for LSU. He returned to Oklahoma, and died from his disease in May 1935.[4]

Long may have known little about football but, as Harry Rabenhorst recalled, "he knew the name of every boy on the squad." And he listened to them and considered their views about the team's direction. This was especially true of the players who lived at the Governor's Mansion in fall 1931. "If any one of us boys at the mansion had said anything against any coach," Sidney Bowman said, "[that coach would have] been fired." Long appeared often at football practices. "He'd drive right out in the middle of the practice field, get out and watch a while, and then leave," Rabenhorst remembered.[5]

Perhaps most annoying to Cohen was that Long fancied himself a shrewd creator of football plays. "He started giving Cohen plays," Billy Butler recalled. "Often, at night, he would discuss these plays with me." Long occasionally lifted plays from *Collier's* magazine, revised them, and showed them to players, asking if they would work. Butler insisted Long had learned to diagram plays. "Later, when I had left school and was doing some coaching, I drew on some of his plays." Rabenhorst, next to whom Long often sat during games, was not so impressed with the governor's play-designing skills. "We forgot about the plays and so did he."[6]

Long was so desperate to provide usable plays to the LSU coaches that he persuaded an assistant coach for Tulane, Lester Lautenschlaeger, to share a few with him. "Every time I show these fellows a play," Long complained, "they think I don't know what I'm talking about. I want a play from an expert, and I want to show them a play that an expert has drawn, and then I want to see what they will say." Lautenschlaeger, Tulane's quarterback from 1922 to 1925 and a third-team All-American in 1925, was also a state representative who voted for some of the 1929 impeachment charges against Long but remained on friendly terms with the governor. He scribbled down several plays. "Huey drew them in his own handwriting," recalled Lautenschlaeger, a 1975 College Football Hall of Fame inductee, "and showed them to Coach [Cohen] and the coach agreed with Huey that they were good plays." Long also enlisted his friend Dan McGugin, the respected Vanderbilt football coach, to draw up "a sure-fire touchdown play" that he could give to Cohen.

Abe Mickal, a halfback who joined the team in 1932, remembered Long approaching him one day during a drill and asking "all sort of questions about passing." He then took Mickal's answers to quarterback Bert Yates; Mickal said, "and gave him the instructions that I had given him and strutted away proud of himself."[7]

At halftime during games, Long often insisted on speaking to the team, judging Cohen as an ineffective motivator of young men. He was not wrong. One player described Cohen as "an ideal assistant coach because of his knowledge." Cohen, however, was often distant and uninspiring. "His pep talks were like a record," Sid Bowman recalled. "He couldn't get you up. He was very nervous, had a habit of clearing his throat and walking around when talking. It made you nervous." Bowman said Long's appearances "relaxed us."[8]

Long not only thought he understood how to coach the team; he also believed he knew better than the LSU cheerleaders how to fire up the crowd. Before the Tigers' game against South Carolina in early October, the governor called a nighttime student body pep rally in Tiger Stadium where he showed students the proper cheering method.[9]

At every home game throughout the 1931 season, Long reveled in his image as the team's top cheerleader. When LSU beat South Carolina, 19–12, on October 10, the *Morning Advocate* gave Long some credit for the win. "After an evenly fought first half," sportswriter W. I. Spencer wrote, "the Tigers came back responding to wild cheers led by Huey Long . . . and played the visitors off their feet." LSU manhandled Mississippi State the following week, defeating the team, 31–0. Clad in a purple sweater with a large gold "L" on the front, Long made his presence known. And Spencer continued to regard him as a crucial factor in the team's success. "In the final period, with Governor Long leading the LSU cheering section," he wrote, "the Tigers opened up their offense and scored two touchdowns in short order." Bowman also praised Long for the Mississippi State win. "In the dressing room, Cohen was making one of his long speeches. 'Go out there and play your hearts out' theme. The sophomores were crying, and the seniors were going to sleep. Then, we heard a bellowing out in the hall: 'Here come the best damn football players in America!'" It was Long, twirling a walking stick. "They ain't got a thing," he assured the squad. "You oughta beat 'em forty to nothing." After Long's brief talk, Bowman said, "We got to laughing and relaxed."[10]

In Shreveport the next week for the annual State Fair game against Arkansas, Long grabbed a baton and led the Regimental Band in a parade throughout downtown. "He marched down the street as people ran to roofs, fire escapes and on top of autos to watch the 'Guv,'" the *Times-Picayune* reported. "He brought the 'house' down with his interpretation of the gubernatorial 'snatch-back' as the band played a ratty number." The paper also noted that Long appeared to lose his energy after a few blocks. "The governor's wind went bad and he had to get in the rumble seat of a car and do his stuff." The weather was unusually hot and humid for late October. At halftime, with the overheated, lethargic Tigers up just 7–6, Long played trainer as he sponged off players and distributed towels filled with ice. LSU won, 13–6. The following week, *Times-Picayune* sports columnist William McG. Keefe praised the governor as "the most spirited cheerleader LSU has ever had."[11]

For months, nothing had excited Long more than his plan to lead the team, the band, hundreds of students, and more than a thousand LSU fans on a train trip to West Point, New York, for LSU's November 7 game against Army. Long hoped LSU could play and defeat a non-southern opponent on the national stage, much like Alabama, Georgia, and Georgia Tech had done in recent years. "Louisiana State needs more advertising," Long said, "and it's going to get it!" The cost of the trip, covering all expenses, would be $150 per individual, he announced. (Long overestimated the eventual cost, which was $96.15 per traveler.) "The magnificence of the project caught the popular imagination," T. Harry Williams wrote. "Louisiana was going 'big time' at last. Significantly, nobody doubted that Huey would bring it off; the state was finally growing up to him. Especially enthused were the students at LSU." The *Louisiana Progress,* the Long organization newspaper, said the game might be "the greatest intersectional gridiron contest of the forthcoming season."[12]

There was one problem: Long could not leave the state because he was estranged from Lieutenant Governor Paul Cyr. A dentist from the Iberia Parish town of Jeanerette, the Catholic Cyr had provided Long's 1928 gubernatorial ticket geographic and religious balance. But Long and Cyr never became friends. Fifteen years Long's senior, Cyr assumed a paternal attitude toward the younger man, sometimes presuming to advise him on political issues. The two men's tenuous political alliance fell apart in 1929 after Long refused to commute the death sentence of a Morgan City physician and his paramour, both convicted of having the doctor's wife murdered. A friend of the doctor, Cyr persuaded the state Board of Pardons to reduce the couple's sentences to life in prison, but Long rejected it. An outraged Cyr attacked Long in the press. The men's partnership was destined for dissolution regardless of the criminal case's outcome, as Long had already made clear Cyr would not be the organization's candidate for governor in 1932 when the term-limited governor vacated the office.[13]

The two men became bitter enemies, a career-ending development for Cyr and a severe inconvenience for Long. If Long left Louisiana, Cyr became acting governor until he returned. Long worried his adversary might also replace his appointees to various boards and commissions. He believed, at first, he and Cyr had reached an understanding about the West Point game: Both would make the trip. In fact, just to be safe, Long planned to take along the entire line of constitutional successors: besides Cyr, the president pro tempore of the senate and the secretary of state. While Long and the others were away, Louisiana would have no governor. "We are all going to see Louisiana play the Army," an enthusiastic Long announced in mid-August.

Long and Cyr never planned to travel together. According to the arrangement, described in a brochure distributed by the LSU alumni secretary, Long would captain a "Blue Train" from Baton Rouge to New York (with stops in Saint Louis, Cleveland, and Niagara Falls). Cyr, meanwhile, would lead a "Red Train" from New Orleans; Secretary of State James J. Bailey, a "White Train" from Shreveport; senate president pro tempore Alvin O. King, a "Green Train" from Lake Charles; and LSU president James Monroe Smith, a "Purple Train" from Baton Rouge.[14]

The deal collapsed not long after Long secured Cyr's promise to attend the game. Cyr backed out, but Long planned to make the trip, anyway. "I will tie his hands so he can't move a foot," he boasted. "I can tie Mr. Cyr's hands and leave the state whenever I please, and he cannot move." But Long soon realized leaving Cyr in charge of Louisiana's government was risky and unwise. Distraught about his inability to travel with the team, Long went to the LSU campus on September 29 to break the news to students at the Greek Theatre. In response, 2,600 disappointed students signed a petition, begging Cyr to reverse his decision. Cyr promised not to undermine Long if he left the state, but he blamed the governor for creating the controversy and suggested Long would not go because of difficulties in organizing the trip. "This governor must assign some reason for his failure to organize several trains to accompany him to West Point," Cyr said in a letter to students, "and any old reason will answer, in his opinion."[15]

Long did not trust Cyr to keep his word. Instead of leading the trip, he announced a few days later that his wife, Rose, and their three children would travel with Smith and others to West Point. On Wednesday, November 4, thirty players, 105 band members, Long's wife and children, about a dozen dignitaries, and hundreds of fans boarded a seventeen-car "West Point Special" train bound for the military academy, via New York City. The trip was a spectacle, even without Long. LSU's caravan generated considerable press attention in Louisiana, although it was not the national sensation that Long first envisioned, a consequence of the headline-making, antic-producing governor's absence. The game was also the first time that a Louisiana university team had trekked to the East Coast to play a military academy in a football game. Long was no doubt happy that "his" band played for fans at the game, but LSU did not make the splash in New York City he expected. During a two-night layover in the city before heading to West Point, the band marched down Fifth Avenue after Long called Band Director Wickboldt and ordered a parade. "We did, but got little attention," the band captain, John Hood, recalled. Afterward, Long phoned and insisted on another parade the next morning. New Yorkers' apathy for his band was bad enough. Long could not have been pleased by the game's result: LSU lost, 20–0. "Aside from the first five minutes of play when the LSU offense clicked, the far south team was outplayed in every department of the game," the *Morning Advocate* reported.[16]

The Tigers returned home with a 4–3 record heading into the season's final two games—both away games—against Ole Miss and the all-important season finale against Tulane. LSU beat Ole Miss, 26–3, but Cohen knew the Tulane contest would determine whether Long considered a coaching change, as he had the previous season. It was no secret to Cohen that Long did not admire his coaching skills. A governor so eager to play the role of coach—including delivering motivational talks to players and designing plays, not to mention his sideline antics—could not have given Cohen much confidence. Cohen also knew that LSU fans cared more about beating Tulane than any other team. "Baton Rouge is being aroused by the game as never before," W. I. Spencer wrote in the *Morning Advocate* the Wednesday before the game, "and knowing the potential power of the Bengals and remembering the great scrap the Tigers put up against overpowering odds in 1930, a great crowd of LSU supporters will throng down to the game."[17]

For this LSU-Tulane game, Long did not divide his time between fans of both teams. He stuck to the LSU sideline. With LSU trailing 14–7 at the half, Long marched into the Tigers' dressing room and delivered a rousing speech to players. Then, he led his team back onto the field, waving his light gray fedora and his walking stick to cheers from LSU fans and boos from the Tulane side. Some Tulane fans shouted, "We want a new governor!" But the Tigers' best play and Long's best "coaching" were not enough. LSU lost, 34–7. Adding to LSU's humiliation was an undefeated Tulane's triumph as the Southern Conference champion and an invitation to the nation's only post-season game, the prestigious Rose Bowl. (Tulane fell, 21–12, to the University of Southern California in the January 1, 1932, game.)[18]

It was clear by Monday that Cohen's tenure was over. President Smith announced that Cohen—who had two years left on his contract as athletic director, head coach, and team trainer—was relieved of the last two of those duties. With Long's constant meddling, Cohen knew he would be unhappy at LSU, even if he were not coaching. Word leaked within days that the coach was negotiating with Vanderbilt, his alma mater, to become an assistant coach under Dan McGugin. It was official by late December: Cohen was leaving. The divorce was amicable. LSU agreed to pay Cohen one year's salary of $7,500. Long and LSU had solved one problem, but now they had another: Where to find a new coach who could deliver the winning program for which fans and the governor longed?[19]

I n the meantime, Long's feud with Lieutenant Governor Cyr moved toward its chaotic conclusion. In early October, Cyr went to Shreveport to announce he would sue Long in state court, asking the judge to declare Long a US senator and, therefore, the former governor. Long had declined to take his Senate seat until he could install his handpicked successor, O. K. Allen, after the 1932 governor's election. But Cyr argued that, when Louisiana sent the US Senate the certification of election after Long's 1930 victory, he had technically vacated the governor's office.

Cyr's impatience proved his undoing. His impetuous actions not only enabled Long to get rid of his bothersome lieutenant governor but also allowed him to take his Senate seat early. Instead of waiting for his lawsuit against Long to take its course, Cyr acted hastily. On October 13, he went to the Caddo Parish clerk of court and had the man administer him the gubernatorial oath. That proved a blunder and gave Long an opening for retaliation. Long announced that since Cyr considered himself governor, the lieutenant governor's office was vacant. Long summoned the senate president pro tempore, Alvin O. King—next in the line of succession—to Baton Rouge to be sworn in as lieutenant governor.

A state court would rule in December that only the legislature could remove the governor. In January, the state supreme court, by a vote of four to three, dismissed Cyr's suit. He was out of a job. And Long boarded a night train for Washington in late January 1932 to take his oath of office. Upon Long's swearing in, King became governor, an office he held until May, when O. K. Allen began his term.[20]

Some may have assumed Long's new office and his apparent shift toward national affairs meant he would devote less attention to directing Louisiana government and daily business at LSU. The following February, after less than a month in the Senate, he told a reporter he had moved to Washington to "rest" from Louisiana politics. Anyone who believed that did not know Long well—and he would soon prove them wrong.[21]

14

SELL THEM PLUGS

In December 1931, President James Monroe Smith summoned the LSU cadet commandant, Major Troy Middleton, to discuss the school's football program now that Russ Cohen was out. Besides wanting a solid play caller, Smith and others believed the team needed a disciplinarian. Smith listed some potential replacements, including Tennessee's enormously successful coach, Robert Neyland. Middleton said Neyland—whose Volunteers had lost only two games under his leadership since 1926—was not interested. But he mentioned someone who might be: former Army head coach Lawrence "Biff" Jones.

The staid, earnest Jones was respected as a defensive specialist and student of the game. "We doubt if any instructor has a better knowledge of football strategy than this mild-mannered army chieftain," a national sports columnist wrote about Jones in 1928. "Every one at the famous army school has full faith in the leadership of their coach." During his West Point coaching tenure, from 1926 to 1929, Jones compiled an impressive 30–8–2 record. Over his first two seasons, the team lost only two games. Army regulations, however, prevented an officer from remaining at the academy more than four consecutive years. At the end of the 1929 season, the Army shipped Jones, an artillery captain, to Fort Sill, Oklahoma. After his brief sojourn there, officials planned to make him West Point's athletic director. But Middleton thought he and Smith could persuade Jones to consider LSU instead.[1]

With Smith's permission, Middleton called the thirty-six-year-old coach to discuss the coaching position. Jones promptly demurred, protesting "there would be too much politics in the job." Long's meddling with LSU football was no secret, especially in college football circles, but Middleton said he was confident Long would not be a problem. He stretched the truth when he told Jones the newspapers had exaggerated the Kingfish's role with the team and that, in fact, the governor was more interested in the band. That seemed to weaken Jones's resolve, and he yielded to Middleton's insistence that he visit New Orleans to talk with Smith, Middleton, and dean of administration James Broussard, who chaired LSU's Athletic Council. Jones met the group at the Roosevelt Hotel, Long's New Orleans headquarters. Toward the end of the meeting, Long burst into the room. "Well, Coach," Long asked, "have you got everything you want?" Jones told Long his every request, except a public relations man for the Athletic Department, had been approved. Jones argued that a good publicity agent could help LSU with the New York and national press. "Don't worry," Long replied, "I'll get you all the publicity you need." Jones may not have found that reassuring.

Next, Jones went to Baton Rouge to continue talks with Middleton and to explore the town and the LSU campus, but he was still unsure about the job as he left Louisiana. On his return to West Point, he stopped in Nashville to see Russ Cohen, who had written to Jones and urged him to take the position. "[Cohen] said I shouldn't have the problems he had because Huey would be in Washington so much," Jones recalled. "He said to keep Huey at arm's length, yet close enough to give us the help we needed." Cohen also told Jones that Long "was always in his hair—on the bench, at squad meetings." And he added, "Huey's idea of a coach was somebody who coached the team in the week and turned it over to him on Saturday." Wary of Long's heavy hand, Jones declined LSU's offer. Smith, however, was unwilling to accept that answer. He implored Jones to meet him in St. Louis for one more discussion. Jones agreed, but in this meeting, he presented a set of preconditions. These included that LSU make him an instructor of military science, so he would have a job at LSU if the school fired him as head coach. Jones assumed LSU would reject this and his other demands. To his surprise, Smith accepted them all. Assured that he could coach the LSU team with no interference from Long, Jones took the job.[2]

As a commissioned officer, however, Jones could not leave West Point without the Army's permission. But Smith and Broussard hoped they could persuade Army leaders to let them have Jones. In early January 1932, the men traveled to Washington to meet with the Army chief of staff, Major General Douglas MacArthur. Jones and MacArthur were friends, but the general was skeptical about sending him to LSU. As Smith and Broussard explained the arrangement they wanted for Jones, MacArthur puffed on a cigarette as he stared out his office window. Finally, he broke his silence. "I like Biff Jones," MacArthur said. "How much does this job pay?" Seventy-five hundred dollars, Broussard replied. "If a poor Army captain can make that much in addition to his [Army] salary," MacArthur said, "I'll let you have him. But don't you ever come back to this office and ask for a single thing."[3]

At six feet, three inches, the clean-cut Jones was a square-jawed, imposing man of military bearing, comfortable on the football field, on the battlefield, and in social settings. "Prepossessing was the best way to describe him," said one person who knew Jones. A *Times-Picayune* reporter who observed the coach for the first time wrote, "One look at him is enough to convince any observer that he is a man who won't stand any foolishness." Jones was the taskmaster and disciplinarian that Long and Smith wanted. And he applied his discipline to Long. In his first meeting with the LSU Athletic Council, Jones insisted he did not want Long stalking the sidelines during games. Jones, who believed rousing speeches by coaches "only incite players to do unsportsmanlike things," asked Long to back off. "You've cried to them, coaxed them, and cursed them," the new coach told the senator. "Now, let's try it my way. We'll teach them how to play football, get them in good physical and mental condition, and then let them play it. It's their game and not a case of life and death."[4]

Long put a positive spin on his diminished role. "I've been the advertising agent for LSU in the past," he told attendees at an LSU athletic banquet in mid-February 1932. "It is up to the coach now. Rome wasn't built in a day, and I stood by Russ Cohen until such a time that he had a chance to make good. We are all good advisers. I expect to do some advising myself, but the sooner the coach tells me that he is running that job, the more I'll like him."[5]

Long did not allow his new US Senate responsibilities to distract him from running Louisiana government or LSU. Over the next three years, his grip on the state became tighter and more extensive, as almost no aspect of local or state politics escaped his attention. Critics in and beyond Louisiana called him a dictator. "I'm a small fish here in Washington," he told the reporters in January as he welcomed them to his suite at the Mayflower Hotel, his DC headquarters. "But I'm the Kingfish to the folks down in Louisiana."[6]

Long made it clear he would scrutinize events in Baton Rouge, especially at his beloved university. Asked in January when he would move to Washington, he had joked, "I don't know. I've got a lot of things to do first, and one of them is to go back and teach that band some new tunes." And when he occupied his Senate office in Washington, the *Reveille* treated it like the death of a benefactor, perhaps believing Long would no longer issue orders to Smith, the LSU Board, or Band Director Wickboldt. "Living in the midst of the changes which have taken place in the school," the student paper said in a February 19 editorial about Long's accomplishments, "students are less likely to take cognisance [*sic*] of their blessings than reporters in Washington who take the whole list at a glance." The paper argued that "no student can be ignorant of the material advancements which have taken place at the university since it came to be 'the pet of the state.'"[7]

Despite having moved to the US Senate, Long was still comfortable in his command of Louisiana because he had a reliable and pliable successor in the Governor's Mansion. A close associate from Winnfield, O. K. Allen, took office in May 1932. A sycophant, the forty-nine-year-old Allen knew well that Long still commanded the loyalty of lawmakers and the support of the public. Long did not want a partner, but an underling. He knew Allen was agreeable to anything he wanted.

Long's abuse of Allen was legendary. When Long spoke to Allen, it was as a domineering boss to a wayward employee. "Huey used to cuss him unmercifully," Allen's top assistant recalled. "Huey felt that was necessary to keep Oscar in line." One day, during the summer 1932 legislative session, Long arrived in Baton Rouge from New Orleans and went to Allen's office, where he planted himself in the governor's chair and began issuing orders. "Oscar," he directed, "go get me those goddam bills we was talking about." Embarrassed by Long's dismissive tone, Allen pretended not to hear the instruction. "Goddam you, Oscar," Long shouted, "don't you stall around with me! I can break you as easy as I made you! Get those goddam bills and get 'em on the jump." Allen hurried from the office to fetch the documents.[8]

The following year, Long's younger brother, Earl, from whom he was then estranged, testified before a US Senate committee investigating charges of corruption in Louisiana. Speaking to Huey, the younger Long described Allen's subservience: "I don't think Allen went to the picture show, talked to his wife, or let his children change their clothes until you told him all about it. I think you took charge of the mansion and everything about it, and they were

When Long went to the US Senate in 1932, he remained in control of Louisiana government through his puppet governor, Oscar K. Allen (*left*), a longtime friend and ally from Winnfield. (Huey P. Long Photograph Album, LSU Special Collections)

bowing and scraping to you as if you were the governor." That description of Allen's deference was exaggerated, but only slightly. The fact was Huey Long was away from Baton Rouge for much of the year, and he could not issue daily orders to Allen or make the less-important decisions that required the governor's attention. But that did not mean he was not still in charge of Allen and interested in his underling's every move. For that reason, Long had installed Richard Leche, a New Orleans lawyer he trusted, to serve as Allen's top aide and to report on his activities.[9]

Among Long's and Allen's immediate concerns was the influence of the worsening Great Depression and its impact on state revenues. By spring 1932, a university once awash in revenue for its ambitious building program was experiencing what the LSU Board called "financial stringency." In February, the board allowed Smith to borrow up to $200,000 to keep the university afloat. Then, in March, board members authorized up to $1 million in warrants, a financial instrument similar to a US Treasury bill. They could be used for payment to contractors who were finishing the Medical School building, the women's dormitory, the Music and Dramatic Arts Building, the Field House and Recreation Center, and the Home Economics Practice House. Paying 5 percent interest, the warrants would finance furnishings for the new buildings.[10]

It was not long before the new governor pledged to come to LSU's rescue. At the university's spring graduation in May, Allen promised he and the legislature would ensure that LSU was well funded. "This is not my year," the governor said, perhaps referring to the current state budget proposed by Long. "Next year is my year. You can depend on O. K. Allen. We want to help you." Speaking to ROTC graduates at LSU a few days later, the new governor pledged to help make the university "greater, bigger, and better."

That summer, still needing construction money, the LSU Board authorized Smith to apply for a loan of $1.2 million from the federal Reconstruction Finance Corporation. The repayment would be derived from Athletic Department proceeds and dormitory and dining hall fees.[11]

Despite the leaner times, the university was nearing completion of its second wave of new buildings. In May, Long and other officials—joined by the LSU Regimental Band—dedicated the Medical School building in New Orleans, at ceremonies held to coincide with the national convention of the American Medical Association. By July, the rest of the buildings on the Baton Rouge campus were completed and furnished. The total expenditure for five structures was $2.9 million.[12]

Despite LSU's temporary cash shortfall, the school also announced plans in July to enlarge Tiger Stadium. When Skipper Heard, the graduate student who managed the Athletic Department's business affairs for Coach Russ Cohen, learned that Smith planned to spend $250,000 to build new dormitories, he approached him with an idea that university officials had first considered in 1925: Why not put some of those dorm rooms into Tiger Stadium and give the stadium a simultaneous expansion? Heard proposed raising the stands on the east and west sides of the stadium. The plan involved adding 10,000 seats to the stadium—giving it a seated capacity of 23,000—and putting housing for 480 undergraduates under the new bleachers.

"What it meant was," Heard later said, "for $250,000, the president got his dormitories, and we increased the seating capacity." Long approved the plan, including building a second floor in the University Dining Hall (soon to become Murphy J. Foster Hall) to accommodate more students. "These

Tiger Stadium in the late 1920s.
(LSU Photograph Collection, LSU Special Collections)

improvements and additions," Smith said, "will enable the university to offer to a number of students room and board at a price ranging from twenty to
twenty-four dollars." Smith explained that the expansion work would open
LSU to "a large number" of men and women. Asked where he would find
the $250,000 for the projects, he acknowledged the school did not have the
funds. The expected enrollment increase, he said, would generate additional
fee revenue to finance the projects.[13]

Long's and LSU's enthusiasm for a bigger and bolder Tiger Stadium reflected a growing attitude in college towns throughout the South beginning
in the 1920s, as football grew in popularity and assumed greater cultural significance. "Southerners of the 1920s saw college football as a public relations
vehicle that could present an image of progress and respectability to the rest
of the nation," historian Andrew Doyle observed, adding that the condition
of many southern college stadiums were far below the standards of playing
fields in other parts of the country. "After World War I, civic leaders across
the South led campaigns to finance the construction of modern concrete
and steel stadiums that local boosters invariably proclaimed to be southern versions of the Yale Bowl." For a political leader like Long, who believed

The Great Depression made it difficult for students to afford fees and living expenses at LSU. In 1932, the school began accepting cotton, produce, and cattle in lieu of fees. In September 1932, Elena Carter Percy, a seventeen-year-old student from West Feliciana Parish, drove nine head of cattle onto campus and turned them over to President James Monroe Smith. (LSU Photograph Collection, LSU Special Collections)

that his growing national profile and reputation were tied to the success of the LSU football team and the magnificence of its facilities, pouring money into Tiger Stadium was irresistible. There was another factor that facilitated building and expanding such stadiums around the country: As automobiles and modern highways became more prevalent in the 1920s and early 1930s—including the roads Long built—football fans found it easier to make a day trip to watch their favorite college team.[14]

Long and Smith were making a safe bet on LSU's growth and the increased revenue it would provide for the stadium expansion. When Smith became president in 1930, enrollment at LSU was about 2,300. By the 1932–33 school year, it was more than 3,500. Hundreds of new students flocked to campus, lured by the free tuition, low fees, and the ease of paying for their expenses with cotton, produce, or cattle. In September, for example, Elena Carter Percy, a seventeen-year-old student from West Feliciana Parish—just north of Baton Rouge—rode onto the campus on horseback driving nine cows and turned them over to Smith in lieu of her fees.[15]

Long's pride was the Field House, which still bears his name.
(LSU Photograph Collection, LSU Special Collections)

The swimming pool of the Huey P. Long Field House.
(LSU Photograph Collection, LSU Special Collections)

As the lawsuit over his funding scheme for financing LSU's building program dragged on (a state court dismissed the legal challenge in November 1932), Long took pride in the grand features of the buildings he helped fund and build. These included the large, elaborate Huey P. Long Field House, in which he invested special interest. Down the street, the new Music and Dramatic Arts Building had a large theater that would seat 750, along with dressing rooms and a workshop theater. Another section offered dozens of individual studios and practice, sewing, and costume rooms. For other students, the building contained a hundred pianos and several pipe organs. "Had it not been for the interest Senator Long manifested in the university while he was governor," the *Reveille* said in an editorial, "possibly none of these achievements would have been possible."[16]

Long also continued directing affairs at the Medical School. In summer 1932, worried that the school might not be accredited by the Council on Medical Education, Long engaged in a messy, sometimes-public spat with the school's chair of surgery, Emmett Irwin. Long wanted to oust Irwin to make room for Urban Maes, a respected New Orleans physician. He offered Irwin a patronage position: head surgeon for the New Orleans Dock Board. "To hell with it. I quit," Irwin said, refusing the deal. Two faculty members left with Irwin, but Long got what he wanted. With Maes in place, the school earned accreditation in 1933.[17]

Maes was not the only big name Long lured to his new Medical School that year. In January, the school announced it had hired a respected physician from London, Aldo Castellani, as dean of the School of Tropical Medicine. In announcing the appointment of Castellani, who once chaired the Tropical Medicine Department at Tulane, LSU officials noted the doctor was "one of the only two men in the world, not British subjects, knighted by King George for service to humanity." The other was Nobel laureate Guglielmo Marconi, the Italian inventor of the radio.[18]

D espite Long's new duties in Washington, President Smith soon learned that the former governor still knew about almost everything happening on his campus. Long had relationships with football players, band members, and student leaders, particularly those in the secretive Theta Nu Epsilon Society. Long's network informed him that Smith's wife, Thelma, had a grandiose view of her role at the school. A former cafeteria manager, Thelma moved up in the world and considered herself "LSU's First Lady." She threw herself into hosting extravagant parties at the president's home. For these elegant affairs, Thelma supervised the construction of an extensive, formal garden behind the president's house and transformed a terrace into a stage for dances and musical performances by university students and professors. In her garden, she installed "a movable moon," which she could set into motion with the press of a button. The gossip about the moon found its way to Long's ears. He called President Smith. "Get rid of that godammed moon," he ordered. It disappeared. In any era, news of such expenditures might have turned heads. During the Great Depression, it was a potential scandal, as were reports that Thelma also was the social sponsor of an elite, new horse-riding club. For a fee, LSU students could learn about horsemanship from a retired cavalry officer. When Long learned about the riding school, he fired off a terse telegram to President Smith: "SELL THEM PLUGS." Confused, Smith showed the message to his friend and LSU Board member George Everett. "Why show it to me"? Everett replied. "I don't know whether I'm on the board or off. He fires me every other day." But, Everett added, "I know what you're going to do: Sell them plugs."[19]

Another source of information about James and Thelma Smith and LSU may have been Long's thirteen-year-old elder son, Russell, called Bucky by family and friends. When Long vacated the Governor's Mansion in early 1932 to take his US Senate seat, Rose made plans to take her children to New Orleans, where Long owned a large home on Audubon Boulevard, near the Tulane University campus. Then an eighth grader at LSU's University High School, Russell did not want to move to New Orleans in the middle of the school year. So Long and Rose allowed him to finish the term in Baton Rouge. The young man lived for a few weeks in Long's suite at the Heidelberg Hotel in downtown Baton Rouge. Long assigned two Louisiana state troopers to protect and accompany Russell wherever he went. "I was living the life of Riley," he later recalled. But Smith frowned on this arrangement and persuaded the Longs to let their son live with his family in the president's home until summer. The friendship between Russell and Smith's son, Jimmie, had not prevented the two boys from some friendly competition. Already a poised, budding politician, Russell defeated Jimmie for freshman class president the previous fall.[20]

Long with his elder son, Russell, who attended LSU after his father's death.
(Photo by Leon Trice, Louisiana State Archives)

15

WHO IS THAT AWFUL MAN?

Troy Middleton and others had assured Biff Jones that Long, ensconced in the US Senate, would not have time to meddle with his football team. Although Long abided by their arrangement—he could sit on the sidelines, but no play calling, pep talks, or theatrics—it did not mean he would be absent from Baton Rouge during football season. In the 1930s, Congress recessed for the year in summer. For example, in 1932, Senate and House members went home in mid-July, not to reconvene in Washington before December 2. Long was free to return to Louisiana, where he could issue orders to Governor Allen in person, roam the LSU campus, and attend every game he wished.

Long pledged to let Jones coach without interference, but he never promised to stay away from team practices. True to form, on the Tuesday afternoon before the September 24 LSU–Texas Christian University (TCU) game, Long—accompanied by Allen—appeared at the team's practice. Asked by reporters if he would attend Saturday's contest, Long said, "You know I wouldn't miss it—where is this fellow Biff?" At that, Long wandered toward the players, but stood at a respectful distance as the new coach put the squad through drills. Deciding not to pester Jones, Long walked over to speak with assistant coaches Bernie Moore and Harry Rabenhorst and grilled them about the team's progress. After about thirty minutes, he was off to tour the expanded stadium. Then, he went to the band hall where, baton in hand, he led students in "Shine On, Harvest Moon," a tune the band learned for him the previous year.[1]

Jones's first game as LSU coach, attended by about ten thousand fans in Tiger Stadium, ended in a 3–3 tie against a strong TCU team. During the game, Long avoided the players. "Senator Long, Governor Allen and other officials," the *Times-Picayune* reported, "were on the sidelines, but none of them interfered with Jones' boys." The experience was unpleasant for Long. Afterward, his close friend (and the university physician) Dr. Clarence Lorio, pulled Jones aside to say that Long's friends had teased him about being "kicked off the bench." Serving as Long's emissary, Lorio promised that, if Long were allowed back in the team's orbit, he would not move beyond the thirty-five-yard lines. Jones approved the proposal. "He observed this for three years," Jones later said. "Never came in the dressing room or squad meetings."[2]

The following week, Long led the team, the band, and two trainloads of LSU fans to Houston for the Tigers' game against Rice University. "We're coming to lick you," Long told Rice fans in a newspaper interview that week. "We'll arrive Saturday noon and we'll stage a parade that will give Houston its biggest thrill since Sam Houston whipped Santa Anna." Long arrived, as advertised, on the self-styled "Kingfish Special." As he stepped from the train, dressed in a cream-colored suit and hat and white shoes, he swung his walking stick as thousands of curious onlookers crowded around him. A reporter overheard a young boy ask as he looked up at Long, "Mama, I see the Kingfish, but where's Amos?"

Long was eager to start his parade. "Let me get back to the band!" he barked, pushing his way through the throng. He found them and, marching alongside drum major Lew Williams, he led the 140-piece unit through downtown to the Rice Hotel, as members played a variety of "Southern songs." At the stadium, before the game, Long conducted the band in "Shine On, Harvest Moon," flapping his arms to the music's beat. Despite a large, loud contingent of LSU fans in attendance, the Tigers lost to the Owls, 10–8. Afterward, Long returned to the hotel with the band and handed each member a dollar bill, telling them he wanted, in return, more music. "Boys," he said, "I just gave you a dollar each, but that ought to last you a long, long time in Louisiana." He then led them in a medley of tunes.[3]

Long skipped several LSU games that October. As much as he loved LSU football, he seized the opportunity to insert himself into national politics and claim some credit for electing the 1932 Democratic presidential nominee, New York governor Franklin D. Roosevelt. That June, Long attended the Democratic National Convention in Chicago and, as an enthusiastic FDR supporter, helped put Roosevelt over the top by intervening to stop a dam-

Long led the LSU Regimental Band through the streets of Houston
before the 1932 LSU–Rice University game.
(LSU *Gumbo* yearbook, 1933)

aging fracture in the Mississippi delegation. New Deal historian William E. Leuchtenburg believed "it is even arguable that without [Long] Roosevelt would not have been nominated." Despite this crucial help, Roosevelt was wary of the tempestuous Louisiana political boss. He later told an aide that Long was one of the two most dangerous men in America. (The other, FDR said, was Major General Douglas MacArthur.)[4]

Ready to throw himself into the fall presidential campaign, Long went to New York that summer to meet with FDR's top political adviser and the Democratic National Committee chair, James Farley, who later wrote that Long "was itching to perform a stellar role; he wanted to steal the national spotlight; and there is no doubt on earth that, in the back of his mind, he was already looking forward to the day when he himself would be a candidate for the Presidency." Long lobbied Farley on a plan to give him a special train he would use to campaign for Roosevelt. Farley thought the proposal was too expensive and might allow Long to overshadow Roosevelt. The campaign offered to send the Louisiana senator, Farley recalled, "into states believed already lost or so firmly committed to Roosevelt that he couldn't possibly do any harm." If Long was aware of this, he revealed no irritation to Farley.[5]

In the meantime, Long went to Hyde Park, New York, for his first meeting with the nominee. He appeared at FDR's home wearing a brightly colored suit, an orchid shirt, and a pink necktie. T. Harry Williams speculated that Long, who tended toward flamboyant clothing, chose this outfit "deliberately to insult" Roosevelt and his aristocratic relatives and "to let them know that Huey Long would not conform to their standards." During lunch, Long overheard Roosevelt's mother ask, "Who is that *awful* man sitting on my son's right?" When he returned to Louisiana after the visit, Long told a friend about FDR, "I like him. He's not a strong man, but he means well. But, by God, I feel sorry for him. He's got even more sonsofbitches in his family than I got in mine."[6]

In mid-October, on Roosevelt's behalf, Long stormed through North and South Dakota, Nebraska, and Kansas with sound trucks, all financed by his Louisiana organization. The Democratic National Committee gave him no financial support. In each of twenty-six cities and towns where he spoke over nine days, Long drew large, enthusiastic crowds. Afterward, a group of state Democratic Party chairs wired Farley, "If you have any doubtful state, send Huey Long to it." Farley later acknowledged that he underestimated Long and said he believed the Louisiana senator could have helped FDR carry Pennsylvania. "We never again underrated him."[7]

Back in New Orleans on Saturday, October 29, Long confessed to exhaustion. "I came home today so I could go to Baton Rouge tonight to see LSU play Sewanee, but I don't think I'm going," he told reporters who greeted him at the railroad station. "What I want most of all is rest." Long then went straight to his home on Audubon Avenue. He skipped one of LSU's best performances of the season. The Tigers beat Sewanee, 38–0.[8]

Because he was away campaigning for much of the time—and so well behaved when he attended—the 1932 LSU football season was a mostly Kingfish-less affair. The newspapers always mentioned Long's presence at games, but, unlike previous seasons, there were no stories about his sideline antics. Although he roared from the stands and the sidelines as LSU fell 6–0 to Centenary College in Shreveport on November 12, his only impact on the game was his loud cheering. He did not, however, miss a chance to play drum major. After arriving in Shreveport, he led the LSU band in a parade from the train station to the Caddo Parish Courthouse.[9]

Long's only contribution to the annual grudge match between LSU and Tulane that year was to mock the rival team when Tulane officials asked LSU to reschedule the November 26 game because two-thirds of the school's forty-one players had influenza. LSU declined to set another date for the game, asserting that hundreds of fans from around the country made plans to attend. Long ribbed the Green Wave for "alibi-ing." He declared that "we have a board of health at LSU that is willing to certify that 95 percent of our [LSU] men are sick with the influenza, two are down with cholera, and one is despondent because his girlfriend jilted him last week." Long was joking, but made it clear he did not believe the Tulane players were ill. "Tulane may beat us playing football," he added, "but they don't need to try to beat us alibi-ing. We've had very good experience cooking up alibis for the past five years [meaning LSU had not beaten Tulane since 1926] and we're all prepared to put out another one if things went the wrong way." With the apparent help of a flu-reduced Green Wave squad, LSU beat Tulane, 14–0. Long, Allen, and other dignitaries watched without incident from the stands.[10]

In December, Long was back in Washington for the second session of the Seventy-Second Congress. The day before, as the Tigers played their last game of the season against the visiting University of Oregon, the new senator was on the Senate floor threatening to filibuster a bill to place conditions on independence for the Philippines. In Baton Rouge, meanwhile, a few hundred miserable, shivering LSU fans watched in twenty-four-degree weather as Oregon's "Mighty" Mike Mikulak rushed for two touchdowns, handing Biff Jones and his team a 12–0 loss.[11]

That disappointing defeat aside, LSU's 6–3–1 season was a triumph. On the cusp of joining the new Southeastern Conference, the Tigers could boast about winning each of their four Southern Conference games. None of their conference opponents—Mississippi State, Sewanee, South Carolina, or Tulane—scored a point against LSU. In fact, over the season's ten games, the Tigers allowed only 31 points. "Tiger adherents now unqualifiedly admit the football season has been a success," an Associated Press writer observed after LSU beat Tulane. Although Tennessee played seven conference games and won six of them, while also winning its two nonconference games, Long insisted LSU deserved the Southern Conference title because it was the only team undefeated or tied in conference play. "I feel that LSU is clearly entitled to the championship," he told the sports editor of the *Atlanta Constitution*. "The school has had a difficult year. The new building plan has handicapped the students. We have gone forward with a lot of spirit in LSU. It's a great student body." Long was also delighted with Jones's first year as coach. "I am proud of the team. I think Captain Jones has done a great job."[12]

Despite the distractions of his first year in the US Senate and the presidential campaign, Long had not forgotten about his beloved university. Although he spent much of the next two-and-a-half years away in Washington, Louisiana state government and LSU were never far from his mind.

16

TELL THEM THEY CAN GO TO HELL

In Washington, as in Louisiana, Long made a fashion statement most days with his colorful attire. He wore a somber suit sometimes, but more days found him strolling into the Capitol in something louder, perhaps a white linen suit with a bright tie. He entered the Senate chamber one morning in late January 1933 wearing a purple wool sweater with a large "L" emblazoned across the front, identical to that worn by LSU football players and one he often sported while leading the school's band or at campus pep rallies.[1]

LSU might have been on Long's mind, but the demands of national and Louisiana politics consumed him for the first half of the year. For much of January, he filibustered a banking bill supported by leaders of both parties that its author, Senator Carter Glass of Virginia, argued would rescue the Depression-plagued banking industry. Long and a few allies claimed the legislation favored the powerful eastern banks and that it would do nothing to achieve what he and President-elect Franklin Roosevelt wanted most—the decentralization of wealth. Long prevented a vote on the bill for a week and forced senators to accept an amendment to prohibit national banks from establishing new branches, except in the nine states that already permitted them. He hoped to kill the bill, but the best he could say was that he had wounded it. "We have dressed it up and crippled it up. We have taken off the right leg of the corpse and its right arm and chiseled into its lungs." The "carcass," he said, should be removed and buried. Although the bill cleared the Senate, the House rejected it after Roosevelt sent word he also opposed it.[2]

Confident, as always, in his powers of persuasion, Long believed he could work with Roosevelt. At least, he thought so after FDR's election and before his March 1933 inauguration. Long traveled to the president-elect's winter retreat in Warm Springs, Georgia, in December 1932, hopeful Roosevelt would accept his advice on programs to address the deepening national depression. But Long left disappointed in Roosevelt's evasiveness. "When I talk to him, he says, 'Fine! Fine! Fine!' But Joe Robinson [a Long nemesis and the Senate's Democratic leader] goes to see him the next day and again he says, 'Fine! Fine! Fine!' Maybe he says, 'Fine!' to everybody."[3]

Roosevelt moved to Washington before his inauguration and set up temporary quarters in the Mayflower Hotel, where Long also lived. He and FDR met on January 19 for the third time. "He's the same old Frank," Long told reporters after their meeting. "He's just like he was before the election. He's all wool and a yard wide." Asked if Roosevelt would "crack down" on him, Long bellowed, "Crack down on me?! He don't want to crack down on me. I came out of his room happy and satisfied. He told me, 'Huey, you're going to do just as I tell you,' and that's just what I'm going to do. He's a great president."[4]

Long had his own ideas about addressing the Depression, and he was unafraid to oppose many of Roosevelt's policies in the early months of the administration. But he devoted much of his time in 1933 to promoting his own audacious economic program. It was his trademark policy proposal until his death from an assassin's bullet two-and-a-half years later. In mid-March, about two weeks after Roosevelt took office, Long introduced three tax bills. As he described them in a national radio broadcast, they "allow[ed] no one man to own more than $100 million; allow[ed] no one man to have an earned net income in excess of $1 million per year; and allow[ed] no one child to inherit more than $5 million from the estate of a father or mother." Long acknowledged that Roosevelt had not endorsed his proposals. "He has a hard task ahead. We must be patient and not expect too much too quickly."[5]

Long disguised only thinly his national ambitions from the early days of his Senate service. And while he and Roosevelt made a show of cooperating at the beginning of their tenuous relationship, both men knew they would eventually part ways. Long wanted the office that Roosevelt would soon occupy, so their parting was quick. A few weeks after his January meeting with FDR, Long mounted a public effort to dissuade the president from appointing Senator Carter Glass as Treasury secretary. In a provocative move, he went public with his views and urged supporters to write the president-elect and urge him to select a Democratic congressman from Alabama, Henry Steagall, who chaired the House Banking Committee.

Within days of the inauguration, Long also pushed Roosevelt to act more decisively to address the national economic crisis. He opposed the president's bank holiday (aimed at stopping bank failures), urging him to subsidize the banks, instead. Then, he fought Roosevelt's Government Economy Act, legislation to cut $500 million from the federal budget on the backs of veterans and government employees. The bill passed, but Long was one of thirteen senators to vote against it. Long supported Roosevelt's National Industrial Recovery Act in principle, but he assailed the bill's wage-and-price provisions, which he believed large businesses would use to drive smaller competitors out of business. He also attacked several FDR appointees, including Treasury secretary William Woodin, who he ridiculed as being "mired with the mud of Wall Street and the House of Morgan." He called Mordecai Ezekiel, the assistant Agriculture secretary, an "enemy" of farmers. And he said Hugh Johnson, Roosevelt's director of the National Recovery Administration, was engaged in a "corrupt alliance" with the major banks.

Although Long voted for much of Roosevelt's agenda, he often did so after giving the legislation a backhanded compliment. By the end of the session, in June 1933, Long told the Senate he would not celebrate the administration's perceived successes. "I do not care for my share in a victory that means that the poor and the downtrodden, the blind, the helpless, the orphaned, the bleeding, the wounded, the hungry, and the distressed, will be the victims."[6]

Despite his growing dispute with Roosevelt, Long was careful not to attack him. "The trouble is," he said in August, "Roosevelt hasn't taken all of my ideas; just part of them. I'm about one hundred years ahead of him. We're on the same road, but I'm here and he's there." But their disagreements over policy were not the only problems brewing between the two leaders. For months, Long had pushed James Farley, Roosevelt's top political adviser and now his postmaster general, to persuade the president to appoint his allies to federal positions in Louisiana. These included jobs like US attorney and federal marshal. Farley, however, claimed that he and Roosevelt were alarmed by "hundreds of pleas and petitions [that] were pouring in from citizens in Louisiana who said their rights were being invaded by the policies written into law by the Long regime." It did not help Long that some of those complaining were his prominent, well-connected critics, including former governor John Parker (friends with Harold Ickes, a top New Deal official), former governor Jared "J. Y." Sanders (friendly with two of Roosevelt's cabinet members), and former US senator Edwin Broussard (recently defeated for reelection by a Long ally, John H. Overton). New Orleans mayor T. Semmes Walmsley, head of the Old Regulars machine, also made it clear to his friends in Washington that Long was to be denied patronage.[7]

Roosevelt and Farley summoned Long to the White House in June for a showdown. Long arrived in a light summer suit and a sailor straw hat with a bright-colored band. "Huey had come in with a chip on his shoulder," Farley concluded, "and although his words were courteous enough it was obvious from his attitude that he was there for the purpose of testing the mettle of the President of the United States." Most appalling to Farley—but not to the apparently unabashed FDR—was that Long refused to remove his hat during the conversation. "At first," he wrote, "I thought it was an oversight, but soon realized it was deliberate." When Long doffed the hat, it was to tap the president on the knee or elbow. He laid it on his lap only when he noticed that Roosevelt's aides were incensed by his disrespect for their boss. Farley and Roosevelt made it clear as the meeting ended that Long would have no input into federal patronage in Louisiana. "There was nothing said that could give offense to Senator Long," Farley claimed, "and, at the same time, there was nothing said that could be construed as a promise even to consult him on patronage matters." It was the last time Long and Roosevelt met.[8]

Long said he was unconcerned about the results of the White House meeting. "The president and I are never going to fall out," he said in August. "I'll be satisfied whichever way matters go." But relations between the two men grew more contentious. In October, Interior secretary Ickes, who also ran the federal Public Works Administration, announced that Louisiana had spent only half of its $5.8 million appropriation for highway construction that year. Long likely prevented the state from accepting all the money because he knew the projects would be administered by his political enemies. Publicly, he offered a different excuse: FDR's appointees might steal it. "Under the set of conditions that have been imposed and the character of the men that the national administration has put in charge of affairs in Louisiana," he said, "it is almost impossible to get the federal funds without some of it being stolen like they used to steal state funds." Long urged Roosevelt "to fire the whole gang he has put in charge down here and give us fifty cents where he has allowed the other gang a dollar [and] we will do more in one week than that gang would in five years." Long's parting shot at the White House, via the reporters taking down his words, were, "And while you are at it, pay them my further respects up there in Washington. Tell them they can go to hell."[9]

In Baton Rouge, meanwhile, LSU's campus kept growing as Long, Smith, and other officials worked to keep up with a student body that had increased 72 percent since 1931. "We can only marvel at the expansion of the University in the space of one year," the editors of the LSU yearbook, the *Gumbo*, wrote in their 1933 edition. While praising the opulence and modernity of the women's dormitory (Smith Hall), the Huey P. Long Field House, and the Music and Dramatic Arts Building, the editors observed, "there is still a need for additional buildings and plans for the construction of such are now in process. This insatiable need for more equipment is more easily understood in the face of the tremendous increase in enrollment." To meet the increasing demand, the university built a new men's dormitory in fall 1933. Dubbed the "F building," it was a green-painted wooden structure that housed forty students and offered few of the amenities found in other dormitories. For example, it had no hot running water. "The boys living in the building do not seem to mind the lack of comforts," the *Reveille* reported, "treating the whole matter as a joke. Roughing it is just another means of getting an education to them." And it was not only undergraduates who were flocking to LSU. In 1929, the university's graduate school had only ninety-five students. By the 1933–34 school year, there were 365.[10]

The new campus three miles south of the new Capitol was also becoming better connected to the city. In February 1933, 150 previously unemployed men began building a new paved road (now Nicholson Drive) to connect St. Louis Street in downtown Baton Rouge with the campus.[11]

"The thing that caused our rapid growth in the early thirties was the depression and the student aid," Fred Frey, then dean of the College of Arts and Sciences, recalled. "It was cheaper for a student to come down here than to stay at home. The university was helping, and then the federal government [through the Federal Emergency Relief Act] was helping them." (By 1934, the Federal Emergency Relief Administration employed 458 LSU students.) President Smith reported LSU's enrollment increase to the LSU Board of Supervisors in early 1933. He could not promise it would grow unabated, but he said, "It is my belief that as the University gains in prestige and improves its facilities, it will continue to make an appeal to the young people of

Smith Hall (now Ruffin G. Pleasant Hall) in 1934, the first
undergraduate women's dormitory built on the new LSU campus.
(LSU Photograph Collection, LSU Special Collections)

the state and to their parents as being the logical place for securing a higher education." Noting that 10,000 Louisiana high school students graduated recently, he added, "I think it safe to say that at least 10 to 15 per cent of these young people will seek the facilities of the University." It went without saying in 1933, of course, that none of the new students would be Black, and neither Long, nor any other prominent Louisiana politician favored doing anything to open the doors of LSU or any other all-white institution to Black students. The first Black undergraduate student at LSU, A. P. Tureaud Jr., would not attend there—and then only for fifty-five days—until 1953.[12]

University officials hoped to fund the next round of construction—including an east-wing expansion of the women's dormitory, a new Arts and Sciences building, and a campus waterworks system—with a $1.7 million loan from the federal Reconstruction Finance Corporation. Officials in Washington approved a loan for LSU in July 1933 but cut the amount to $508,000, explaining the university did not have the legislative approval necessary to service the larger figure. State lawmakers gave LSU permission to borrow the full amount in June 1934.[13]

From Washington, Long bragged about the success and growth of his pet institution. In a Senate speech in February 1933, defending his organization against charges of fraud in the election of his ally John Overton to the other Louisiana US Senate seat, he veered into a discussion about LSU. Long declared he had transformed the university—once "a third-rate college"—into "an A-number-one university of the United States, as good as Harvard, Yale, Johns Hopkins, or any other university." LSU was making great strides, but no objective observer would have placed it on par with Harvard or Yale. Long also boasted about the LSU Medical School. "That medical college only a few days ago was given the highest rating that can be given by the American Medical Association to a medical college." The assertion was accurate but did not tell the full story. The AMA recognized LSU as having an "acceptable medical school," which was its top rating. Prospective physicians were eager to gain admission, as Long expected. Smith reported that fall the school had one hundred applicants for that year's eighty slots.[14]

Not everyone approved of the attention that Long, Governor Allen, and other officials in the Long regime showered upon LSU. For much of 1933, daily newspapers in New Orleans, Shreveport, and Monroe—each owned by anti-Long publisher John Ewing—carried front-page "investigative" pieces attacking what they claimed were the Long organization's abuses and excesses, some of them at LSU. A few of the stories were long on innuendo and short on specific proof. In June, the *New Orleans States*, the *Shreveport Times*, the *Monroe Morning World*, and the *Monroe News-Star* accused Long and his lieutenants of awarding LSU money and attention at the expense of other schools. "Money is being poured into the coffers of the state university, and it is evidently not enough," the report asserted. "The public schools must get along with half rations and, because of this, teachers in every part of the state go unpaid." The papers claimed, "ornate buildings are constantly being added" at LSU while the university struggled to pay its bills. "The most difficult thing in Baton Rouge is to get a line on the expenditures of the state university." In particular, the papers alleged, "fifty thousand dollars worth of pianos [purchased for the Music and Dramatic Arts Building] staggered the good citizens of Baton Rouge." There is no evidence, however, that Baton Rouge citizens were outraged by LSU's piano budget.[15]

Later that month, the papers addressed the state's bonded indebtedness, which increased dramatically under Long. It had swelled to $140 million for construction of new highways and bridges, a new Capitol, and for improvements at LSU. (Since 1931, LSU had accumulated $1 million in bond debt, less than 1 percent of the state's total.) "With the advent of Mr. Long came the new bond order," the papers complained. "Bonds were issued thenceforth with an abandon and recklessness that soon deprived them of their original character."[16]

The most biting of the stories came in August, under the headline, "Canker Worm of Politics Bites Deep and Expensively at L.S.U." The unbylined story claimed, "The general charge is made that while the university has expanded in student strength and equipment, it has fallen in public confidence and gone back in successful business management." The papers accused Long's organization of politicizing LSU while bloating its budget. They argued that Smith's $12,000 annual salary was exorbitant and that he drove a luxurious automobile "at a time when university professors were not drawing their pay." The story also contained suggestions that Smith had hired relatives to work at the school, which "have led certain students to facetiously refer to it as the 'Smithsonian Institute.'" The charge was true. Smith appointed one of his wife's nephews, J. Emory Adams, as manager of the university bookstore and other concessions at the Huey P. Long Field House. The cost of the new LSU Medical Center, the papers claimed, was also excessive. An article in August explained how LSU officials undervalued the worth of the university's buildings to save on fire insurance.[17]

Another story in August attacked Long for the inflated cost of operating Charity Hospital in New Orleans and for politicizing the facility. In this article, the newspapers revealed their blindness to the role that politics had played in the facility's operation. "This is something altogether new in the conduct of the hospital," the writer asserted. "The word politics was never dreamed of in connection with the Charity Hospital until Huey Long became governor." The story also attacked Long's organization for its "overweening predilection for [employing] men and women of the creole race [at the hospital]."[18]

Among the other charges against Long in the Ewing papers' series was that he meddled in the hiring and firing of faculty and staff members at LSU. The evidence for this charge included Long's role in the Kemble K. Kennedy/ *Whangdoodle* case, his alleged influence in the 1931 dismissal of English professor John Earle Uhler, and his attempts to force Law School dean Robert Tullis into retirement. One story in early August mentioned the name of another LSU employee Long had allegedly targeted: Murphy J. Sylvest, a former member of the state house of representatives from Washington Parish who voted for then-governor Long's impeachment in 1929. Once a high school teacher and principal in Franklinton, Sylvest was an LSU graduate with a law degree from New York's Hamilton College. LSU hired him as an instructor in the school's Department of Government in 1931. When Long learned of the appointment, he reportedly demanded that Smith fire him. Whoever was behind his exit from campus, Sylvest did not last long on the LSU faculty after the school announced his hiring.[19]

A friend of Long's also appeared on the school's payroll in 1933. In 1931, Long had hired away LSU's frugal business manager, Robert L. "Tighty" Himes, naming him as general manager of the state penitentiary at Angola. His permanent replacement at LSU, Edgar N. Jackson, was a native of Long's hometown of Winnfield. From 1914 to 1933, he was a partner in a grocery store in the small town. A former member of the Winn Parish School Board, Jackson had studied business at Louisiana Polytechnic Institute for three years, but never graduated. He had no experience managing the finances of any large enterprise, much less a state university. His presence on the LSU campus attracted little or no public attention until March 1934, when the *Monroe News-Star* mentioned him in a story about politics at LSU and identify him as a Long "protégé."[20]

Long's occasional meddling in LSU's hiring practices was not in dispute in 1933. So far, however, he had not ordered Smith to do much that attracted unfavorable press attention. That would change when Long forced LSU to award Kemble K. Kennedy his long-desired law degree.

17

A LAUGHINGSTOCK

After his expulsion from LSU in summer 1930, Kemble K. Kennedy took a job with the Louisiana Tax Commission, no doubt a result of Long's patronage. But he was still not a lawyer, something he hoped Long would change. In November 1932, the state Board of Pardons and Governor Allen erased his 1930 criminal libel conviction. It was his first step in returning to LSU's good graces.

The next step came in June 1933, when the LSU Board ordered his reinstatement as a student. If Kennedy could pass three examinations, President Smith told a reporter, LSU would give him his law degree. But this offended Dean Robert Tullis, who informed Smith and the board he would not sign any diploma the school awarded to the disgraced student. To end the impasse, board members forced the aging Tullis into retirement and appointed Professor Ira S. Flory as acting dean. In fall 1933, Kennedy received what the university called a "special diploma." Signed in secret—not by Tullis or Flory, but by Smith and Allen—Kennedy's unique diploma would not become public knowledge until the following summer. Although Long could force LSU to award a law degree to his young friend, the Louisiana State Bar Association was not so pliable. Long's determination to help Kennedy would embarrass the university and trigger national sanctions for LSU's Law School when the unusual arrangement became news in 1934.[1]

With Tullis gone, Long hoped to replace him with someone he believed could confer greater respectability on the university's law program. Unfortunately for LSU, Long's reputation for meddling in the school's affairs was well known in academic circles, which made it difficult to find an esteemed scholar. Long eventually consulted one of Roosevelt's top advisers and part-time speechwriters, Raymond Moley, then a prominent law professor at Columbia University on leave to serve as an assistant secretary of state. One day in August 1933, Long appeared in Moley's State Department office. "If I could suggest a man [to replace Tullis]," Moley recalled, "he [said he] would not inquire into his politics, he would pay him a good salary, higher if necessary than that of the dean of the Harvard Law School, and he would give him money enough to build a law school on a par with the Louisiana State University Medical School." Moley believed Long, but he observed that "his utter contempt for the ordinary process of making such appointments was obvious."

Moley was initially unsure if he should help the Louisiana senator. "In the university, as in politics, he was a dictator." But he offered his advice. Among those who came to mind was Wayne Morse, a former student of his at Columbia and who was now the dean of the University of Oregon Law School. In 1929, at thirty-one, Morse became the nation's youngest dean of an accredited law school. As Long waited in his office, Moley phoned Morse. "I've got a new deanship for you at Louisiana State University," Moley told him. Morse asked Moley why he should consider LSU. "Here's a man who can tell you all about that," Moley said, before handing the phone to Long, who began firing questions at Morse, including, "How much are you getting now? I'll double that." Morse insisted he would not tolerate political interference. "That's what we want to get you down here to do: Run the school and build it up." Morse promised to consider the offer but sent Moley a telegram that night asking why the university president had not offered him the job. "That's the way they do things," Moley replied, assuring him if Long made the offer, "it was his for the taking." Morse later said Long phoned him "in the middle of the night" to discuss the job further, an occurrence that helped the young dean decide. "If he could call me in the middle of the night to hire me, he could call me, also, in the middle of the night to fire me," he said years later. Morse—who would be elected to the US Senate in 1944 and serve in that body for twenty years with Long's elder son, Russell—declined the job. LSU would not choose a permanent dean until 1935, when the school hired thirty-one-year-old Frederick K. Beutel, a law professor from Tulane University.[2]

L ong kept his finger on LSU's pulse, but national and state politics and the fallout from his reckless personal behavior made 1933 one of the more trying periods of his career. For the early part of the year, a US Senate Special Committee on Campaign Expenditures held hearings into the questionable election of Senator John Overton, the Long-backed candidate who defeated Edwin Broussard in 1932. After Overton's Senate election, the committee investigated alleged corruption by Long and others that Broussard said had undermined his candidacy. The committee conducted hearings in Washington in October but went silent until early 1933, when it announced members would hold a public inquiry in New Orleans in February. Those sessions—and another round the following November—produced smoke, but no fire. Witnesses presented little hard evidence that committee members could use to prove Overton's victory resulted from corruption. When the investigation was over, the committee's exasperated chairman, Senator Thomas Connally of Texas, commented, "I advise anyone who thinks he knows something about politics to go down to Louisiana and take a postgraduate course."[3]

Long had other woes in 1933. In August, he went with a friend to a banquet at the Sands Point Bath and Country Club on Long Island, New York. The evening ended in disaster when someone assaulted Long in the club's men's room. It is not clear what occurred, but an inebriated Long may have said or done something to a patron, who hit him. Bleeding from a cut above one of his eyes, Long fled with his host. When the New York newspapers learned of the incident, they made it a national sensation, and Long a laughingstock. Long suggested a political enemy mugged him. "A member of the house of [banker J. P.] Morgan slipped up behind and hit me with a blackjack," he told a reporter. To another, he said, "I realize that I have powerful enemies." The only positive outcomes from the episode were that Long quit drinking, adopted a healthier diet, and started an exercise regimen. He shed twenty-five pounds.[4]

Back home, Long had other troubles. The November 1932 statewide elections to approve a series of constitutional amendments were mired in charges of political corruption. After voters approved all the amendments, Long's opponents noticed irregularities in New Orleans, where each passed with massive majorities. In sixteen precincts, not one person voted against any of the amendments. In twenty-eight other precincts, the votes for and against each amendment were identical. Later that year, juries convicted three local officials for election fraud and, in 1933, Governor Allen pardoned them all.[5]

Long's political fortunes suffered further in 1933 after he endorsed the state Tax Reform Commission's proposal to impose seven new state taxes to fund his education and roads programs. The commission proposed offsetting the levies on personal income with new taxes on crude oil produced in Louisiana, natural gas, tobacco, lubricating oil, liquor, and public utilities. To compensate for the increased sales taxes on poor and middle-income residents, Long supported a $2,000 homestead property tax exemption. On a statewide speaking tour in October to sell the plan, voters greeted Long with indifference and, sometimes, hostility. Some hecklers mocked him about the Sands Point affair. The Senate investigation into charges of corruption in his organization was not only harming Long's psyche but also his standing with the public. Long began responding to hecklers with threats of violence by the time his caravan arrived in northern Louisiana. At the courthouse square in Minden, he confronted a crowd of armed opponents, even though the head of the State Police begged him to cancel the appearance. To Long's relief, the speech ended without incident. During his tour's last event, in Alexandria, hecklers hurled raw eggs at him. None reached Long, but they struck several people on the stage.[6]

L ong took refuge in aspects of his job that did not involve partisan politics or investigations into allegations of political corruption. In fall 1933, at least, that meant LSU football and the team's second season under Coach Biff Jones. With its 7–0–3 record, it would be the Tigers' best season since 1921, when Coach Branch Bocock led them to a 6–1–1 record. The best record any LSU football team had posted over the previous ten years was the 6–2–1 season of Russ Cohen's 1928 squad, the first year of Long's term as governor. Long attended many of the games in 1933—all but three of the season's ten contests were played in Tiger Stadium—but selling his tax program often kept him away from Baton Rouge. But even when at the games, he remained in the stands or sat on the players' bench, well out of Jones's way. For the second year in a row, there were no newspaper stories about his sideline antics, pregame pep talks, or halftime speeches. True to his word—and perhaps because his popularity seemed at a low ebb—he did not make a spectacle of himself at football games.

In fact, the most outrageous story about Long's behavior in 1933 was mythical. The tale about Long and LSU's 1933 game against Rice University has persisted for decades. Long was said to have noticed a poster advertising the Ringling Brothers, Barnum & Bailey Circus in Baton Rouge on the same day as the September 30 LSU-Rice game. The circus, the story went, had scheduled an afternoon parade and performance. Concerned that the circus events might reduce attendance for the Tigers' season opener, Long supposedly phoned a circus executive to demand he move the performance to another day. As journalist Harnett T. Kane wrote in his 1941 book, *Louisiana Hayride,* Long said, "I don't think you're a-gonna like Baton Rouge, anyway." The executive reportedly asked why. "Did you ever try to dip a tiger?" Long replied. "You got vats big enough for your elephants?" Long elaborated, "Brother, we got health laws in Louisiana. The way I interpret 'em, every one of your animals will have to get dipped in sheep dip before they cross the [state] line. We can't take no chances." To that, Kane observed, "There was no dipping. There was no circus show before night." Other journalists, biographers, and historians have repeated various versions of the story. (The tale seems to have appeared in Louisiana for the first time in an October 1938 sports column in the *Times-Picayune.*) Others claimed Long made the phone call before a game in Tiger Stadium against Southern Methodist University (SMU), which would have placed the incident in 1934.[7]

Judging by the Ringling Brothers' schedules in 1933 and 1934, it is difficult, if not impossible, for the story to be true. The circus did not book appearances in Baton Rouge on the same day as an LSU football game. A news story in the *Baton Rouge State-Times* on September 15, two weeks before the game, announced the circus would arrive for afternoon and evening performances on Friday, September 29, the day before the LSU-Rice contest. And the circus scheduled performances in New Orleans on Saturday, September 30—the day of the Rice game—and October 1. The schedule for the Louisiana performances of the circus the following year also makes it difficult to support the story about Long's threatening phone call. Ringling Brothers' shows were set for October 6 and 7 in New Orleans, and for October 8 in Baton Rouge, two days after the LSU-SMU game in Tiger Stadium. The story is delightful—and credible because it fit Long's personality and style—but it is only an entertaining fable.[8]

The rest of the 1933 football season was no more remarkable than Long's illusory call to the circus executive. Subdued by scandal and sinking popularity and distracted by his need to sell an unpopular tax plan, he was more than a little preoccupied as the Tigers embarked on their banner season.

Now living in New Orleans, Long sometimes made the drive to Baton Rouge on Saturdays to attend LSU games. He remained in the stands for the Tigers' 13–0 win over Rice on September 30. Although he skipped the next week's home game with Millsaps (LSU won 40–0), he was in Tiger Stadium on October 14 for LSU's annual match against Centenary. He sat in the governor's box with Allen and Lieutenant Governor John B. Fournet as Centenary battled LSU to a 0–0 tie.[9]

Long mixed business with pleasure the following week. He took a special train with the band to Shreveport to campaign for his tax plan before attending the annual State Fair game against Arkansas. Upon arrival, he left for a ceremony dedicating a new $750,000 bridge spanning the Red River between Shreveport to Bossier City. He joined Allen on a flatbed truck for the ceremonies (only one city official showed up for the dedication) but passed on the opportunity to discuss the bridge and, instead, pitched his taxes. "Long's reception was the least impressive of any accorded him here," the anti-Long *Shreveport Times* reported the next morning. "Only occasional laughter greeted his attempts at humor, and only scattered applause was won by his political promises." As a cutting aside, the *Times* observed, "There were many negroes in the audience." Long, the paper reported, "plunged heatedly into a tirade against his Shreveport opposition and the promulgation of the proposed seven-point state taxing program." After Long's and Allen's wives cut the ribbon to open the span, the two men climbed into a car for the ride across the river. Long then left to play a more enjoyable role—leading the LSU band through downtown. In unusually hot weather that night, Long watched LSU defeat Arkansas, 20–0.[10]

Long was present in Tiger Stadium the next week when LSU hosted Vanderbilt for the Tigers' homecoming game. It was the first time former LSU coach Russ Cohen—now an assistant coach at Vanderbilt—returned to Tiger Stadium. Although Long joined Allen and President Smith at an elaborate banquet that day in honor of players from LSU's remarkable 10–0–0 season in 1908, he declined an invitation to address the group. He was also well-behaved during the game, watching from the stands as the game ended in a 7–7 tie. Long was less subdued during the next week's 30–7 win against South Carolina in Tiger Stadium. The *New Orleans Item* reported that he "rode the bench with the Tiger squad throughout the game, and during one time out led the Tiger cheering section as it sang 'Shine On, Harvest Moon.'"[11]

Preoccupied with the special Senate investigation into his organization

Long, *second from right,* sits on the sideline at an LSU-Tulane game, probably the 1934 game that LSU lost, 13–12. (Photo by Leon Trice, Louisiana State Archives)

and the 1932 US Senate election, Long did not attend another LSU football game until December 2, when the Tigers went to New Orleans for their annual game against Tulane. Long led the LSU band through the city's business district before the contest. And he sat on the LSU bench for much of the game. Unlike previous years when he made a spectacle of himself, Long controlled any urge to inject himself into events that day. One observer thought he looked "dejected" as the team failed to score for most of the first half. He drew attention only briefly, at the end of the second quarter. Tulane's student section showered Long with loud boos as he walked off the field with the squad, likely a response to his well-known affinity for LSU football. The game's only drama occurred near the end, when LSU's Pete Burge completed a spectacular catch in the Tulane end zone, hauling in a pass from halfback Abe Mickal. "When that happened," the *New Orleans Item* reporter wrote, "Senator Long, probe or no probe [meaning the US Senate investigation] . . . joined everyone else in the stadium in a brief but heartfelt trip to dementia." After Mickal kicked the extra point for a tie, neither team scored again. The game ended in a 7–7 draw.[12]

Long ended the Tigers' phenomenal season riding the bench one last time for the December 9, 7–0 win against Tennessee. Writing in the *New Orleans Item,* sportswriter Fred Digby praised Biff Jones's coaching and, in an unspoken rebuke to Long's past antics, suggested the team's success that year was because Jones abstained from theatrics. "This theory is that results can be obtained in football without 'firing up' or arousing the boys to a high mental pitch through pep talks, crying to or cussing 'em." Digby congratulated Jones for resisting advice to deliver fiery pregame speeches. "I don't think that's ever been done by an LSU coach in the 40-odd years of battle with Tulane," he wrote. Digby also batted down reports in an Associated Press story that Long delivered a "fight talk" to players at halftime. "No one 'talked' to the Tigers," he insisted.[13]

Long may not have received credit for the Tigers' remarkable football season, but his relentless boosting of the team and his sideline conduct in years past—not to mention his unrelenting support of the band—meant the university and its team were now a part of his national identity. "LSU has every reason to look toward the football future with high hopes," sports columnist Bob Murphy wrote in the *Knoxville Journal* on December 12. "They have a wonderful coaching staff. They have a first-class grid plant [stadium]. They have the football players, and, above all, they have the backers headed by the imitable one—Huey Long."[14]

As he thought about Long's behavior at football games the past two seasons, Biff Jones may have assumed Long would continue to honor his promise not to interfere with his team. Jones might have reflected on the assurances Troy Middleton and Russ Cohen gave him about the unlikelihood of Long's continued meddling in the football program and decided they had been right. Maybe he even thought he would coach his squad through another banner season without the interference of Louisiana's senior US senator. To his dismay, however, Jones soon discovered he and others had badly misjudged Long's willingness to remain calmly on the sidelines.

18

IT WAS HUEY LONG'S UNIVERSITY

Long now faced an array of challenges to his leadership, beyond the US Senate investigation into the 1932 election of his ally Senator John Overton. Those included his organization's heavy-handed efforts to elect Lallie Kemp, the widow of the late US representative Bolivar Kemp, to replace her husband in an early December congressional election. Long's and Allen's conduct during the campaign prompted charges of foul play.

For months, Allen had resisted calls to schedule the election. A former LSU Board member and sometimes–Long supporter from Amite who represented Louisiana's Sixth Congressional District (in and around Baton Rouge), Kemp had died in June. State law required a quick election to fill his seat, but Long feared that a political enemy—state senator Jared Y. Sanders Jr., son of former governor Jared Y. Sanders Sr.—would prevail in the state's least pro-Long congressional district. Allen followed Long's orders and delayed setting an election date. That angered Sanders's supporters, who called a mass meeting in Baton Rouge in late November to conduct a rump "citizens election." The vote would not be binding, but it was a challenge to Long's leadership. In response, the day before the meeting, Allen convened the Sixth District Democratic Committee to make Lallie Kemp "the unopposed Democratic nominee because there will not be time to hold a primary." Allen then set a general election for eight days later.

The result was growing anger in southeastern Louisiana against Long and an electoral mess that attracted unwelcome national attention. The two elections in December only sowed more confusion. In the official balloting, Kemp led by 4,801 votes, but only after anti-Long mobs in St. Francisville and Clinton seized the ballots and burned them. Long's opponents in Hammond hung him in effigy. In the rump "citizen's election" a few weeks later, however, Sanders—the only candidate on the ballot—received 15,000 votes. Both candidates claimed victory. In January 1934, the US House declared neither election valid. In yet another special election in April, voters elected Sanders over the new Long organization candidate, state agriculture commissioner Harry D. Wilson.[1]

The election debacle was not Long's only problem in early 1934. Worried about the growing danger of what he regarded as Long's potential to become a fascist dictator in Louisiana and beyond, President Franklin Roosevelt continued to deny the Long organization federal patronage in Louisiana. And, in 1934, the Roosevelt administration cracked down on Louisiana's refusal to match federal grants with state funds. By January of that year, the Federal Emergency Relief Act (FERA) supported almost 400,000 needy Louisianans with no accompanying appropriations from the state. FERA administrator Harry Hopkins warned Allen in May 1934 that federal relief support for Louisiana would cease unless Louisiana established and funded a Department of Public Welfare and other relief offices. Allen waited until the last day of the 1934 legislative session to propose the appropriations for that, only to have Long allies kill it in committee. Hopkins kept his promise in August. He halted all FERA funds to the state, forcing a special session that month to generate modest state matching dollars for FERA spending in Louisiana. A subsequent session in November provided additional unemployment funds for parish governments.[2]

Concerned about Long as a threat to his 1936 reelection, Roosevelt approved the renewal of a moribund federal investigation into the Kingfish's taxes which the US Treasury Department began in 1932 under the administration of President Herbert Hoover. "Get all your agents back on the Louisiana job," acting treasury secretary Henry Morgenthau Jr. told Elmer Irey, director of the department's Intelligence Division, in late 1933. "Start the investigation of Huey Long and proceed as though you were investigating John Doe. Let the chips fall where they may." Irey, who had led the inquiry that put mobster Al Capone in prison for tax evasion in 1931, was delighted to reopen the case. He sent about fifty investigators to Louisiana to search for evidence that Long associates had demanded kickbacks from contractors and other business working for LSU. Louisiana newspapers eventually reported the probe.[3]

In response, some observers began preparing Long's political obituary. "One of the most encouraging symptoms of political renaissance comes from Louisiana where Huey Long lies weltering in the chaos of his own political doings," the *Bee* of Danville, Virginia, editorialized in December 1933. "When the constituency begins to burn you in effigy on election eve, it is a fairly strong indication that you have run your vicarious political course and that political security is at an end." The paper predicted Long was all but finished. "Huey Long has been going downhill rapidly for some time. The debacle now is all but complete."[4]

Faced with adversity, Long followed his instincts, which always tended toward the audacious. In February 1934, he proved that Roosevelt's worries about him as a potential national rival were well founded. During a national radio address, Long unveiled his Share Our Wealth Society, a proposed network of local clubs around the country that supported his wealth-distribution program. Long promoted his new organization in other radio speeches throughout 1934 and 1935. As he preached his message of taxing the rich to provide for the poor, clubs sprung up in cities and towns all over the United States. By early 1935, he boasted of 3.6 million members. *New York Times* columnist Arthur Krock observed in January 1935, "It is more and more evident in Washington that many Democrats feel [Long] is getting ready to pounce upon their party and absorb all or a large part of it in 1936."[5]

L ong waged a multi-front war with the Roosevelt administration, but he also sought every available federal dollar to continue expanding LSU's campus. Smith announced in March 1934 that because of rapid enrollment growth—the Baton Rouge student body for the coming 1934–35 school year would be 4,348, including Long's daughter, Rose—LSU would seek $2 million in financing to embark on another building program. That included more living space for men and women students, the Arts and Sciences Building (now O. K. Allen Hall), a "French House" to serve as home for the school's romance language programs, and a meat-curing and refrigeration plant. "Housing facilities for the co-eds at present are very inadequate," Smith told the Baton Rouge Lions Club, explaining that many women made living arrangements in town. He said the school needed rooms to accommodate an additional 500 coeds.[6]

LSU also constructed buildings that year under a new protocol inspired by Long, who believed the contractors' bids on the Arts and Sciences Building were exorbitant. Present when university officials examined the documents, Long erupted when the lowest bid was for $600,000. "You buzzards are conniving," he scolded the contractors in attendance. "You know you can build that building cheaper than that. I'm not going to give it to any one of you. We'll build it ourselves." The university hired George Caldwell, a contractor and an executive with his family's firm, Caldwell Brothers, to supervise all new construction on the campus. As the superintendent of construction of LSU, Caldwell presided over work on nine new buildings during the next five years.[7]

Because of steady, upward enrollment over recent years, LSU officials also asked the legislature in 1934 for an increased appropriation to cover the university's mounting expenses. Lawmakers granted the request for an extra $200,000 to support LSU's operations for the coming school year. Lawmakers also approved legislation in June that allowed LSU to borrow up to $1.7 million from the federal Reconstruction Finance Corporation (RFC) to pay off existing loans on previous construction and to fund some or all of the planned new construction. LSU's explosive growth, however, rankled lawmakers from other parts of Louisiana. Although Smith assured them the loans would be serviced from student fees, and not with state revenues, some were skeptical. "The schools are closing over the state," one house member complained, "and we are getting ready to give LSU the right to borrow $1.7 million." In New Orleans, the anti-Long *New Orleans States* attacked the proposed borrowing. "Apparently, under its present control, Louisiana State University is never to be operated under a pay-as-you-go policy," the paper declared, adding, "Is it any wonder that there is a growing protest of the people against the exploitation of higher education at the expense of the community institutions, the kindergarten, primary, grammar and high schools, which have been so sorely neglected by an administration that pretends to be the friend of the masses?"[8]

Even though the university had permission to borrow the money, the RFC would not approve a $1.77 million loan for LSU until July 1935. In the meantime, Long and Allen persuaded the state's Board of Liquidation in late December 1934 to borrow $1.16 million to start the building program. It expanded to include seven new buildings: the Arts and Sciences Building, five new residence units for students (including Highland Hall for women and more dorm rooms in Tiger Stadium), and the French House. Long appeared before the board to request the loan, telling members that some students were sleeping under paper sheds in the school's overcrowded dormitories. The school, he said, needed room for an additional 1,000 students. Long also announced he would use part of the loan to establish dental and pharmacy schools at the university's Medical Center in New Orleans.[9]

Other work continued apace on campus while Long and Smith worked to secure funding for the new buildings. In January 1934, workers employed by the federal Civil Works Administration (CWA) began dismantling Alumni Hall on the south end of the old LSU campus. Using the materials from the original building, workers reassembled the structure on the bluff next to the Gym Armory, near Tiger Stadium. Now the Journalism Building, Alumni Hall would house the offices of several university officials, including the Alumni Federation, bursar, auditor, dean of student affairs, the news and military departments, and the school's athletic offices. The $204,000 Alumni Hall project was one of eight buildings funded by the CWA at LSU in 1934, employing local workers, including almost 400 LSU students who earned $15 a month. CWA workers completed a new campus-wide sewerage disposal system by March and were nearing completion of the school's botanical gardens, the beautification of an area behind the Greek Theatre, the installation of wooden seats in Tiger Stadium, and the construction of sidewalks and parking lots around the stadium.[10]

Long was proud of the buildings he helped fund, particularly the Music and Dramatic Arts Building, one of several he considered his own and which he visited often in the days after its dedication. Composer and bandleader Gene Quaw—who later wrote the words to a popular LSU football fight song, "Hey, Fighting Tigers"—was a frequent visitor to the school in the mid-1930s. He recalled observing Long's arrival at the building one day in 1934 or 1935. Director Henry Stopher rushed out to greet Long. "Good day, Senator, how are you?" Stopher said. "Let me show you around this beautiful building." Long scoffed. "Show me around? Hell, I built it. Run around and look at it yourself if you want to."[11]

With Long's support, the university continued to expand beyond the borders of its Baton Rouge campus. In June, the state legislature approved a bill by a Long ally—senate president pro tempore James A. Noe—that made Ouachita Parish Junior College in Monroe part of the LSU system. Located three miles east of downtown Monroe, the thirty-eight-acre campus would be known as the Northeast Center of LSU (now the University of Louisiana at Monroe). The school's courses corresponded with the first two years of study in Baton Rouge and served as a feeder for the larger school. The bill to subsume the college passed over protests of some northern Louisiana senators and public neutrality by Long. "If you are going to let LSU go out and take over the schools in our parishes, you might just as well abolish the state Department of Education," state senator E. B. Robinson of Lincoln Parish (home of Ruston's Louisiana Polytechnic Institute) said. State senator Waldo Dugas of Lafayette (home of Southwest Louisiana Institute) agreed, as did the president of the Board of Education, H. H. White of Alexandria, who called the plan "unwise."[12]

Most distraught was the daily paper in Ruston. "Charges of L.S.U. Is 'Octopus' of the State," the *Ruston Daily Leader* screamed in a front-page banner headline on September 1. "This is the most far reaching and insidious proposition ever offered the educational interests of the state," writer E. H. Fisher asserted. "It means that sooner or later, if this proposition is allowed to go over, the virtual elimination of the other state schools of Louisiana." Fisher added, "If this plan goes through, the State University would dominate the social thought and life of the state; the economic thought and the political life of this state would be in the hands and power of this octopus."

Tech supporters in Ruston were not the only ones worried about what they considered Long's lopsided support of LSU. In Hammond, for example, patrons of Southeastern Louisiana College had suspected for years that Long supported LSU at their school's expense. Among his first vetoes as governor in 1928 was rejection of legislation providing an annual $75,000 appropriation for the fledgling college. Long had offered no explanation for killing the funding.[13]

Long seemed unfazed by the scattered criticism. To a visiting reporter, William Dean of the *Greenville News* in South Carolina, he bragged about supporting his beloved university. "Louisiana State University is among the greatest schools in the country," Long boasted. "And the school of music over there is second to none. The Boston and Cincinnati conservatories are the only ones that can even compare with it." A university that was once "a Class-C outfit before I came along," he said, was now "Class A, even in athletics." Long also crowed about how he made the school accessible to a wider swath of Louisiana's young people. "A student can go through LSU for $20 a month and pay for everything. We've fixed it up so a fellow can go to the medical school without paying tuition charges of any kind." Asked to describe his aspirations for LSU and the state, Long replied: "My program is very simple. It is to relieve the poor of all taxes, to give everyone free schools and free textbooks through the secondary schools and a fighting chance to get through college, and to cover the state with good roads. We've about done them last two. God willing, I'm gonna get the first one done in this present session."[14]

Long's devotion to LSU did not mean he ignored events at other college campuses. In January 1934, he demanded the resignation of his third cousin, W. W. Tison, as president of the Louisiana State Normal College in Natchitoches. Long had engineered Tison's hiring in 1929 after he ordered then-president Victor Roy's dismissal. But Long's relationship with his cousin deteriorated. He was angry that Tison refused his entreaty in 1932 to reinstate a student and political supporter, William Dodd, whom Tison had expelled. Dodd, who became Louisiana's lieutenant governor in 1948, tangled with Tison over students' demands for an extended Easter break in 1932. When Long phoned his cousin to urge him to drop the charges against Dodd, Tison balked. He told Long the young man was a troublemaker and added, "Huey, the State Board of Education is my boss," to which Long replied, "Who the hell do you think is the boss of the State Board of Education?" Dodd won reinstatement to the college and, in 1934, Long urged the board to force out Tison. The embattled president resisted but bowed to reality and stepped down in July.[15]

For most of his time running Louisiana state government—as governor and now as a US senator—Long focused on expanding the LSU campus, supporting the football team (including hiring its coaches), and building a bigger, better Regimental Band. To be sure, he had blocked Campbell Hodges from becoming president in 1928; he hired President James Monroe Smith and a new band director in 1930; he approved firing Professor John Earle Uhler for writing his "scandalous" 1931 novel, *Cane Juice;* he pushed Law School dean Robert Tullis into retirement and tried to hire Wayne Morse of Oregon to replace him; and he schemed to help his protégé Kemble K. Kennedy earn a law degree. Still, LSU leaders did not regard Long's involvement in LSU's affairs as excessive and improper. Because the governor was entitled to sit on the LSU Board as ex officio chair, his attendance at board meetings was not considered unusual or inappropriate. When Governor Allen appointed Long—then a US senator—to the LSU Board in November 1934, it turned a few heads, but it created no scandal.[16]

"He had nothing to do with the academic program that I know about," Troy Middleton, the cadet commandant and, later, dean of men in the 1930s, recalled in 1961. "He did not interfere or put people in jobs, except maybe a few in the business staff. He never asked me for anything, jobs, etcetera. He loved the band, and he loved the cadets and built them up. In doing so, he helped LSU." Another dean of men in the early 1930s, Fred Frey, shared Middleton's forgiving recollection of Long's role in the university's academic and business affairs. Except for his initial involvement in choosing Smith as president, Frey insisted, "as far as I know, he never did come back after that time [to meddle in the university's daily business]." Frey, who worked at LSU into the early 1960s and would serve as acting LSU president in 1947, maintained, "We had less political interference during Huey's time than we ever did." He later elaborated: "In all of the appointments I was making at the time, I had not one single suggestion from the governor . . . as to whom I should appoint. I certainly cannot say this about some of our other governors who have indeed tried to engineer appointments."[17]

One academic department on campus that Long meddled with was the School of Music. When a faculty member Long had known since childhood, A. M. Culpepper, approached him in summer 1934 about creating a "brass choir," Long was supportive. Long may have been unaware that Smith had already rejected the idea. Smith told the school's dean that LSU did not have funds for the instruments needed to fill out the unit. Without consulting Smith, Long approved the purchase of $6,000 worth of new horns from the Werlein's Music Store in New Orleans. When Smith learned of Culpepper's insubordination, he instructed the music school to cancel the order. That news reached Long, who summoned Smith to his suite in the Heidelberg Hotel in Baton Rouge and berated him for canceling the purchase. One observer said Long told Smith "never again to interfere with the delivery of anything sent to any department of the university upon his order."[18]

Because Long was so involved in the finer points of the band, the football team, and the construction of buildings—and because he was on campus so much—it was not unreasonable for a casual observer to conclude that he was acting as the school's de facto president. Long also bragged often to reporters about the outsized role he played in the university's operation. But there were only scattered stories before 1934 about Long's meddling in LSU's academic affairs. "He did not concern himself with what was taught in the classroom," biographer T. Harry Williams concluded. "This was not because he understood the concept of academic freedom and respected it, but because he did not think that the exercise of academic freedom could possibly affect him." Although he did not cite his confidential source for this finding, Williams maintained that university professors worked under only one major restriction by Long: "They could not publicly criticize Huey Long. Academic freedom did not include the privilege of denouncing the man responsible for the splendor that was LSU."

Williams was correct, although the prohibition against public criticism of Long would have been implicit. That no university employee criticized Long during these years may have been because he earned the respect and affection of many faculty members and staff for his generous support of LSU. But it was more complicated than that. No political leader, much less someone as controversial and divisive as Long, could have commanded universal admiration among a university's faculty. Because Long rewarded his allies and punished his opponents, the risks involved in disparaging him was well understood by every state employee, including LSU professors.[19]

Long was not oblivious to the fact that the LSU faculty had among its ranks some who were not his political supporters. To the University Graduate Club on campus in October 1934, he joked he had made LSU "perfect, except for one thing—the faculty, which still has some anti-Long teachers on it." Long explained that he allowed these faculty members to remain employed to create "diversity of opinion on the faculty."[20]

As LSU's campus and its enrollment grew, so did its need for new (white) faculty members. One faculty member, English professor John Palmer, later reflected on the influx of new professors from around the country and described Baton Rouge of the 1930s as "one of the most socially congenial places that has ever been on this earth." Palmer recalled that by the mid-1930s "there were at least 35 or 40 young family people on the campus whose talk I still remember as the most stimulating I have ever heard." Cleanth Brooks, an assistant professor of English who arrived in Baton Rouge in 1932, remembered a campus that "threw its net wide, and it swept in all sorts of people: those who could only be regarded as so-so; those who were undistinguished but solid and useful . . . and those—they were in considerable number—who were intelligent, imaginative, and intelligently vigorous."[21]

Edwin P. Embree—head of Chicago's respected Rosenwald Fund that supported Black education in Louisiana—visited Baton Rouge in March 1934 and left with a favorable opinion of LSU. "I have been impressed with the amazing growth of LSU," he wrote afterward. "From an unknown place twelve years ago, it has risen to be included in the nationally known universities. If the state will stand by, LSU has every right to come to be included in the first 12 or 15 universities in the United States, which means inclusion in the first 20 universities in the world." When Smith and Long quoted him later that year to imply that LSU was already among the top twelve universities in the country—he only suggested the university had the *potential* to reach such heights—Embree clarified his statement. He insisted that no southern university was among the nation's top twelve. LSU, he said, "is not even among the best Southern institutions."[22]

Whatever Embree meant, few could deny that LSU's reputation had grown. Charles Pipkin, dean of the Graduate School, worked hard to attract better professors and instructors. Among the first of Smith's promotions in 1931 as he set about to renovate the school's faculty, Pipkin proved one of the new president's best decisions. A thirty-two-year-old Arkansas native and Rhodes Scholar, Pipkin arrived at LSU in 1925 from the University of Illinois, where he was a respected professor of government and authority on international law. As one observer at the time wrote of Pipkin, he "blew like a bracing current of arctic air into a campus which for decades had gone its languid way amid the faint smell of magnolia blossoms." Pipkin was a force of nature who, one colleague recalled, "deferred to no one, acknowledged no sacred cows, and spoke his mind with a startling lack of regard for what was considered discreet academic policy." Buoyed by Long's promises to continue increasing funding for the school, Smith pressed Pipkin to recruit top scholars for all the university's departments, an assignment the dean took to heart.[23]

Among those who arrived in 1934 to teach that fall was a respected young scholar, Robert Penn "Red" Warren, a wiry, red-headed Kentuckian lured from Vanderbilt University to take a position as an assistant professor of English. "It was 'Huey Long's university,'" Warren later wrote, "and definitely on the make—with a sensational football team and with money to spend even for assistant professors at a time when assistant professors were being fired, not hired—as I knew all too well." In the 1940s, Warren wrote one of the great American novels of the twentieth century, *All the King's Men*—a book inspired by Long. Warren came to Baton Rouge, assured by Pipkin that the senator "would never mess with my classroom." And Warren insisted Long never did. "He was far too adept in the arts of power to care what an assistant professor might have to say."

Like many of his enlightened peers, Warren was no fan of Long's methods, but he acknowledged Long had helped make LSU available to thousands of young people who would never have dreamed of entering a classroom there. Among Warren's new colleagues on the LSU English faculty was Cleanth Brooks, his former associate from Vanderbilt. A bespectacled Kentucky native who earned a master's degree at Tulane before winning a Rhodes Scholarship at Oxford University, Brooks was one of Pipkin's first recruits. Along with Warren, Brooks—who became a renowned literary critic—came to symbolize the academic and literary renaissance at LSU in the 1930s. By March 1935, Warren, Brooks, and Pipkin had a $10,000 grant which they used to launch a literary journal, the *Southern Review*, that Smith conceived and which the LSU Board of Supervisors approved in August 1934. It would be among the most respected English-language literary journals in the world, further burnishing LSU's academic reputation. In 1934, LSU also gave birth to the Southern Historical Association and began making plans to publish its *Journal of Southern History*, which debuted in summer 1935. Also in September 1935, less than a week after Long's death, the university announced the creation of what would become another venerable literary institution, the LSU Press.[24]

LSU was growing in stature and reputation. "It was a university on the make," Brooks later observed. And much of that growing reputation rested on a foundation that Long began laying in 1930 and upon which he built in the years since. The story of LSU until 1934 was the phenomenal growth and success of a once-small university in a provincial southern capital which, a few years earlier, had only a football team to earn it any notice beyond the state's borders. People were taking note. Emerging scholars were willing to move to Baton Rouge and give the university a chance. Maybe, university leaders thought, they were on the cusp of the greatness that Edwin Embree predicted. By the end of 1934, however, Huey Long jeopardized many of those dreams.[25]

19

I. O. HUEY

SU and Huey Long had become synonymous in the minds of many Americans by 1934. During the 1933 football season, sportswriters around the country had referred increasingly to the university and its football team as "Huey Long's LSU," "Huey Long's LSU Tigers," "Huey Long's LSU Eleven," or "Huey Long's boys." His goal to merge his national profile with LSU's was almost complete. "Folks over the land read about Huey and his football Hueys," a columnist for the *Raleigh (NC) News and Observer* wrote in late October. "Saturday night arrives, phones ring in newspaper offices, and subscribers ask: 'How did Huey Long's team come out today?'" New Orleans journalist Harnett T. Kane observed: "Huey's football shows could not be kept out of the newspapers, no matter how much the papers hated Huey. They were spectacles in the Billy Rose–Roxy tradition: 2000 cadets, 200 musicians, 50 'purple jackets'—coeds in white pleats, blazers, and 50 smiles—octettes of dancing boy and girl cheer-leaders, and 50 sponsors in a row. And the star of the troupe, Huey swinging, roaring, high-tailing it at the head of the march. He led his boys and girls down the main streets of the invaded towns, razzle-dazzled over the field between halves and remained, as usual, perilously close to the players during the game."[1]

Long did not travel with "his" team for the 1934 season opener on September 29 against Rice in Houston, where the Tigers wrestled the Owls to a 9–9 tie. Nor did he appear in Tiger Stadium on October 6 for the team's first home game of the season, against Southern Methodist University (the game ended in another tie, this one, 14–14). Instead, he was on the hustings in early October, campaigning for a close ally, Lieutenant Governor John B. Fournet, running for the state supreme court. Long rode with Governor Allen from New Orleans to Baton Rouge on October 13 to watch with twelve thousand other fans as LSU defeated Auburn, 20–6. As usual, the Kingfish cheered from the sidelines. The *Morning Advocate* reported no senatorial antics, only Long's presence on the Tigers' bench.[2]

Long made his customary trip to Shreveport the following week for the annual State Fair game against Arkansas. When the teams trotted toward their locker rooms at the half, deadlocked 0–0, Long followed the Tigers inside for a pep talk. It may have been the first flagrant violation of his promise to Biff Jones that he would refrain from meddling with the team. "Huey wasn't satisfied with the first half and went into the dressing room during the intermission and gave the boys a talking to," *Times-Picayune* sportswriter Pete Baird reported the next morning. Whether or not Long's encouragement had any effect on the Tigers, LSU left town with a satisfying 16–0 victory.[3]

Long had worked hard to increase the renown of LSU football during the previous seasons. But for all he did to associate himself with the team, nothing approached the national spectacle that he and LSU staged for the season's next game, at Vanderbilt.

F or weeks, Long had planned a massive decampment of LSU students and supporters to Nashville for the October 27 game. It would be only the fourth time the two teams had played each other. In its three previous matchups against Vanderbilt—in 1902, 1910, and 1933—LSU had never beaten its occasional Southeastern Conference rival. The Tigers' best showing was in 1933, when they fought the Commodores to a 7–7 tie.

In early October, Long summoned Major Troy Middleton to his suite at the Heidelberg Hotel in Baton Rouge to inquire about taking the entire LSU Cadet Corps to Tennessee for the game. Middleton said the cost was prohibitive. "You worry too much about expenses," Long told him. "I'll take care of that." Long was more concerned about keeping everyone safe, asking, "Can you take 'em without killing 'em?" Middleton thought he could, "if I was properly supported and if the right restrictions were observed. Notably, no civilians in trains with cadets." Long asked how many trains would be needed to transport the 1,500 cadets and the 120-piece band to Nashville. "I said at least four," Middleton recalled telling Long, adding, "That shocked him."[4]

When Long phoned the Illinois Central Railroad to inquire about the cost per cadet, a representative offered a nineteen-dollar round-trip fare.

"That's too much," Long snapped. "I'll give you six dollars per person." The railroad agreed only after Long hinted he might persuade the state Tax Commission to reassess the value of bridges the company owned in Louisiana. The next day, Long had his six-dollar fare. On Monday, October 15, he went to LSU's Greek Theatre to tell cadets the good news. Attending the game would not cost them "a thin dime," he said, explaining that the school would pay for the Cadet Corps and band to travel to Nashville.

Long stood in the hot, midday sun for forty-five minutes, describing the journey to students. He said the trip would cost the school about $18,000. "It's going to be tough to raise that much money, but we have raised more than that down here," he assured them, adding that the excursion would be a "splendid advertisement" for LSU. Long soon revealed that he had already found the funds. He told reporters LSU had planned to spend $17,000 on a double-page advertisement in the *Saturday Evening Post,* money that would now be devoted to travel for the cadets and the band. "There are going to be quite a few people there," Long said. "Some will come to see you, some to see the football game, and I'll draw a few myself, and I want you to give the university a good name." That meant, he said, they must promise not to consume "a drop of liquor from the time they left until they got back."[5]

Vanderbilt officials reported a rush on tickets for the contest within days of the announcement. "Many of those who purchased tickets," a *Times-Picayune* sportswriter, William McG. Keefe, wrote on October 19, "did so with the understanding 'Huey Long would be there.'" Keefe added that Long "is in such demand that Alabama University is seriously considering switching its [schedule] of 1935 to get a game with L.S.U. if Senator Long keeps his promise to come here for a game." Keefe noted that Long's trip to Vanderbilt "is the first time in the history of football that athletic departments of universities have been able to commercialize the drawing power of anyone outside of a football team or its coaching staff." Long's "box office appeal," Keefe concluded, would help pay off "many a stadium bond."[6]

A week before the game, LSU announced arrangements for up to six trains (only five were needed), each with fourteen cars, to carry cadets, the band, students, university and state officials, and other fans to Nashville. Those preferring a first-class Pullman berth paid $26.85 for the round trip. Besides the thousands who departed for the game from Baton Rouge, special trains would also leave from New Orleans and Shreveport to bring even more fans to the Tennessee capital.[7]

By October 23, the Tuesday before the Saturday game, Long learned that hundreds of non-cadet students were eager to make the trip but could not afford the fare to Nashville. Late that morning, he summoned those students to the Greek Theatre to say he would lend them six dollars each for the train and one dollar for meals. Students needing such loans, he said, could speak to him in private. "The gold rush started," the *Morning Advocate* reported the next morning. "The students didn't wait to see him privately. They advanced upon him as he left the speaking rostrum in a phalanx formation and, in football terms, he was 'stopped by the mass.' Very quickly 'I. O. Huey' became a general campus phrase."

In the rush, Long asked students to sign their names on whatever slips of paper they had so their loans could be recorded. After he ran out of money—he had only about $200—Long turned to President Smith. "Jim, let me have some money." Long plucked fifty dollars from Smith's wallet. When that was gone, he barked to an aide, "Get me two or three hundred more." When that cash was disbursed, Long announced that needy students should come to his hotel room.

Word of the gold rush spread throughout campus. Hundreds of people poured into the Heidelberg Hotel that evening, lining up along the hallway as Long stood at his door and dispensed cash as students and others filed by. "What's your name?" he asked as he handed out laundry slips. "Write it down." Long soon realized that not all his transactions were with students. "Salesgirls, office boys and townspeople were joining in," the *Morning Advocate* reported. "Too many persons claimed to be 'one of the Jones boys.'" Later that night, as he thumbed through his stack of slips, Long grumbled, "I never saw so many Joneses and Smiths in my life. There aren't but five thousand students in the university and ten thousand must have been here already." Long and LSU tightened up the lending program by the next day, requiring students to show identification and sign a proper form with the correct name. The university also arranged its own loan process for students unable to visit Long's hotel, while also threatening disciplinary action against any student who signed an I.O.U. with a false name. When it was over, Long had lent 500 students $3,500 in $7 increments.[8]

That night, after he made his last loan, Long returned to campus to see the Regimental Band. He took the baton from Director A. W. Wickboldt as members rehearsed for the concert they planned to give upon arrival in Nashville on Saturday morning. "Let those horns go to hell! Drown out them saxophones!" Long shouted. Later, he surrendered the baton to Wickboldt and sauntered around the room as the band played. When he disliked a note, he rushed back to the director's stand to correct the offending player. "Wring his neck!" he yelled at one student who blew a discordant note. Long "made innumerable changes in the vocal arrangement of several feature numbers," a *Morning Advocate* reporter wrote. After leading the students in his beloved "Shine On, Harvest Moon," Long pronounced, "They sound pretty good to me," and sent the band home.[9]

The next day, Thursday, the football team left for Nashville by train from Hammond. In Nashville, meanwhile, enthusiasm grew for the LSU visit, not just because Long and thousands of students and fans would soon arrive, but because of a rumor spreading through the city. On Friday, October 26, as Long and his traveling party prepared to board their train for Nashville, the city's evening paper, the *Nashville Banner*, announced, "LONG IS EX-PECTED TO ANNOUNCE FOR PRESIDENT IN NASHVILLE." The story

LSU Band members and other students gather in the Greek Theatre in November 1934, awaiting Long's announcement about the LSU-Vanderbilt game. (Photo by David R. McGuire Jr., David R. McGuire Jr. Memorial Collection, Tulane Library)

Long speaks to LSU students from the Greek Theatre stage. He says that cadets and the band would accompany the football team to Nashville for the LSU-Vanderbilt game. President James Monroe Smith stands in the background. (Photo by David R. McGuire Jr., David R. McGuire Jr. Memorial Collection, Tulane Library)

After he learned that many students could not afford the Vanderbilt trip, Long returned to the Greek Theatre to announce he would lend needy students seven dollars each. Students swarmed him as he began handing out cash. (Photo by David R. McGuire Jr., David R. McGuire Jr. Memorial Collection, Tulane Library)

Before Long and the LSU Regimental Band left for the game in Nashville, Long appeared at the band hall to help lead the musicians in a final rehearsal. Bandmaster A. W. Wickboldt is to Long's right. (Photo by David R. McGuire Jr., David R. McGuire Jr. Memorial Collection, Tulane Library)

Long and LSU cadets in Baton Rouge on October 26, 1934, before their departure for the game with Vanderbilt. (LSU Special Collections)

In Nashville for the 1934 Vanderbilt game, Long leads the LSU band and Cadet Corps as they march from the train station to the Tennessee War Memorial. Major Troy Middleton, commandant of cadets, is to Long's right. (Photo by David R. McGuire Jr., David R. McGuire Jr. Memorial Collection, Tulane Library)

At the Mississippi Capitol in Jackson, Long directs the LSU band in a concert before the 1934 LSU-Ole Miss game. (Photo by Leon Trice, Louisiana State Archives)

reported that Long "scoffed at the rumor and subtly replied that he was really going to announce for the 'presidency of Mexico.'" Whatever Long planned, he was doing little to tamp down expectations. He dispatched a fleet of campaign sound trucks ahead of his arrival and said he would deliver a pregame speech at the stadium. Asked by a reporter what he would say, Long responded, "I'm not even thinking about it because I am afraid the devil will read my mind and prepare the people against me."[10]

On Friday afternoon at five o'clock, the first of five trains carrying about 3,200 passengers left Baton Rouge. An official with the Illinois Central System later called the caravan "the largest movement of football players and their friends that has ever been seen in the South." The *Nashville Banner* compared the scene to "a gigantic minstrel show" and a "Roman holiday." Wearing a light tan suit and sporting a purple-and-gold boutonniere with long streamers, Long joined his party (including his wife, Rose, and fifteen-year-old son, Russell) in a car on the second train to leave town. As his train pulled out, Long waved his hat to the crowd that gathered to see the cadets off. An enormous banner across the side the last car in each train announced, "Ole War Skule." Hung on the back of the same cars were huge, illuminated likenesses of a tiger's head. As passengers settled into their seats, they read a flier handed to them as they boarded:

> These trains are under the direction of Louisiana State University and the authorities of the state of Louisiana acting for the Old War Skule. We are going to Tennessee to help our state and our school and not one thing is going to be allowed to mar that good work. Not one drink of liquor and not one bottle of liquor will be allowed on this train or by anyone who rides this train. If one violation of this order is found, the guilty party will be put off at once. Do not try to avoid this rule. It will not work. You can now give your ticket back and get your money if you do not want to observe these rules, but if you go on this train, it is with the above as your rule and law.

Not long into the journey, around six o'clock, Long summoned a group of seven band members he had selected to serve as his personal orchestra. After they played for a few minutes, he sent word forward for Wickboldt to find him a piccolo and two clarinet players. "We need more wood," he ordered. "There is too much brass. The notes are too deep. What we really need is a banjo." At that, Long beckoned the trainmaster and asked him to radio ahead to Vicksburg and instruct his longtime friend Charlie Scott to locate a banjo. Then he began his search for a banjo player. Three young men volunteered. About two hours out of Baton Rouge, Long's train stopped at Harriston, Mississippi, where several hundred locals gathered to watch his train pass. Long stood on the bottom step of the car and chatted with the crowd as an attendant aimed a flashlight at his face. Then, he called his orchestra and directed them to play "Shine On, Harvest Moon." Further north, around Port Gibson, Mississippi, Long decided the ensemble had too many trombones. "One of you will have to quit," he commanded, inviting two young men to demonstrate their trombone playing before deciding which one would remain in his unit. When the train pulled into Vicksburg around nine o'clock to pick up about 200 more passengers, Long left his car to speak with the locals who assembled to view the spectacle. Then, out of the darkness, Charlie Scott appeared with a banjo. Back onboard, Long's mood turned sour as two strings on the instrument snapped when the player strummed the first notes.[11]

Passengers settled in for the long night's ride. Some played cards, others gathered in one of the two dining cars attached to each train, and many slept. Long was not among the sleeping. "I feel like a fighting cock," he said as the train plowed through the darkness. "I don't need but a couple of nods." Long padded through the cars all night, chatting with the cadets and band members. Whenever the train chugged through a small town or settlement, small groups of people were there, hoping for a glimpse of the Kingfish. "Hi, Huey!" or "Hello, Kingfish!" they shouted to the passing train.[12]

Long's train rolled into Nashville's Union Station the next morning around nine. Wearing a cream-colored flannel suit and a tan hat, Long stood on the platform of his car as it stopped. Waiting in the large crowd were twenty Tennessee highway patrolmen sent for Long's protection. Long's aides asked state officials in Nashville to allow Louisiana state troopers and the senator's personal bodyguards to enter the state with their firearms, a request the state initially refused. The two sides worked out a compromise: Members of Long's security detail were considered "game wardens," deputized to guard "whatever wild life you may see fit to import into our State." When Long stepped from the car, the state's top game warden, Damon Headden, was ready to commission him and his entourage. Long soon wore a large purple ribbon emblazoned with "Deputy Game Warden" in gold letters, accompanied by the image of a fish. On the ribbon's upper corner was a Tennessee game warden's badge. On his lapel, Long sported a purple-and-gold rosette with streamers. Among those greeting Long was Mayor Hilary Howse, who exclaimed, "The city is yours, Senator." Long replied, "I hope we leave you some of it."[13]

Long assembled his band and the cadets and led them on a two-mile parade from the train station to the Tennessee War Memorial. On his left, at the head of the parade, were Long's bodyguard, Joe Messina, and Howse. On his right was his friend Dan McGugin, the longtime, legendary Vanderbilt football coach. The crowds along the route were massive, most there to glimpse the Kingfish. Howse later told reporters that Long and LSU attracted the largest turnout of citizens since the return of Tennessee soldiers at the end of the World War. As Long led the band and cadets through the streets, he told a reporter, "I've got to tell 'em [the LSU team] what to do." He gave McGugin a jovial punch. "The only difference between me and Dan is that he tells them what to do before the game and I tell them what to do while the game is going on."

When the parade reached the memorial, Long scurried around, arranging his band as members prepared to perform in concert. After he announced the program, he threw himself into duty, serving as water boy for the group and passing out drinks to the musicians. Cadets performed a variety of tunes: "Meet the Band," "Hold Me," "Road Is Open Again," "River Stay 'Way from My Door," "Yea, Team," "Blue of the Night," "Tiger Rose," "Mah Lindy Lou," and "Shine On, Harvest Moon." Long snatched the baton from Wickboldt several times to lead the band, including when it played its last tune, "Vanderbilt Forever." He had not planned to make an address at the concert but relented after the crowd kept demanding remarks from him. His "speech" was brief—no more than three sentences—and without substance.[14]

Long arrived at the football field early that afternoon, now wearing a dark blue business suit. Standing on a speaker's box on the five-yard line, McGugin introduced Long to the crowd of twenty thousand as "the all-American football rooter of all time." The two sound trucks Long brought to Nashville, parked in the nearby end zone, amplified his voice. When he stepped to the microphone, he did not mention politics, and he had no plans to announce his candidacy for president. Instead, his remarks were brief and light. He pointed to the eastside stands, filled with about seven thousand LSU fans, who he said traveled to Nashville to see an exciting football game. "We even set up all night in chair cars to get here," he said. "We came seven thousand strong because we felt that we owed Tennessee more than we can ever repay, because it was the companies of mountaineers from Tennessee that followed Andrew Jackson to Louisiana and gave us our territorial possessions by beating the same army that had beaten Napoleon at Waterloo. If by any accident, Vanderbilt should beat LSU, and we may have scowls on our faces, let me assure you that they would not come from our hearts. I hope we have a good game and a good time." Then, Long marched toward the cadets, as his aides removed the speaker's stand.

Long remained on the bench throughout the game, which LSU won, 29–0, on the strength of halfback Abe Mickal's passing, punting, and kicking. Long had already drawn attention to himself with his pregame speech and by posing with the LSU and Vanderbilt cheerleaders. But he did not interfere with Biff Jones's coaching. His only role in the game was to lead the LSU side in cheers whenever the fans' enthusiasm waned. Perhaps Long behaved so well because the game went so well. Whatever the case, he could not have judged the trip to Nashville, and his leading part in it, as anything but a brilliant success.[15]

The happy-but-weary LSU contingent left Nashville on Saturday evening for a restless night of travel back to Baton Rouge. When Long's train pulled into Vicksburg Sunday morning to allow several hundred fans to disembark, he led the band into the streets for a brief parade through the city—up the hill toward the business district. The sight and sound of the musicians startled two white mules hitched to an ice wagon. When they bolted, a ten-pound block of ice fell off, slid down the street, and went between Long's legs. According to the Associated Press reporter on the scene, "[Long] grabbed it up and, much like a half-back going around end, outran the runaway mules and pitched the ice back into the wagon as the crowd howled in glee." Soon, everyone was back on the train and bound for Louisiana. The last group of exhausted travelers from Nashville arrived in Baton Rouge after three o'clock that afternoon.[16]

The Vanderbilt trip was a national sensation. Papers across the country, including the *New York Times,* covered the spectacle for days. One *Morning Advocate* reporter described it as "the greatest peace time long-distance railroad excursion in the history of America." In Raleigh, North Carolina, *News and Observer* columnist Anthony J. McKevlin noted, "It wasn't just another football game. It had much advance notice—not only on the sports pages, but on the front pages—in newspapers throughout the land. Huey Long put the game on the front pages." An Associated Press story about Long and the game ran in dozens of newspapers around the country in the days after LSU's invasion of Nashville. "Huey Long's Circus Thrills Nashville," the headline in the *Palm Beach (FL) Post* declared. The headline over the same story in the *Jacksonville (IL) Daily Journal* announced, "Huey Long's Boys Beat Vanderbilt." In the *Fort Worth Star-Telegram,* the headline was, "Huey Long Steals Show as L.S.U. Meets Vanderbilt."[17]

In his college football roundup the next week, syndicated sports columnist H. I. Phillips assessed the game thus: "Among the interesting football scores was: Huey Long, 29; Vanderbilt, 0." But the press coverage was not all glowing. An Associated Press sportswriter, Kenneth Gregory, worked Long's authoritarian rule of Louisiana into his lead: "'Kingfish' Huey Long and his colorful entourage celebrated joyously tonight the success of a gala gridiron party. Louisiana State, pride and joy of the political dictator of 'the Creole state,' unloosed a crush offensive that swept Vanderbilt aside."[18]

A few weeks after returning from Nashville, Long revealed plans for another LSU traveling circus, this time to Knoxville for the December 8 game against the University of Tennessee. He told reporters that, while he would pass up the Tigers' November 17 Ole Miss game in Jackson, he guaranteed the railroad company that twelve hundred passengers would make the trip to Knoxville. And he announced he had negotiated a seven-dollar round-trip rate. Long cautioned that this trip would not be "quite as good" as the Nashville excursion because he would not bring the Cadet Corps.[19]

As Long reveled in the glow of his Vanderbilt triumph, *Morning Advocate* sportswriter W. I. Spencer noted the senator's increasing use of LSU football to burnish his national image. "Taking advantage of football as an entrée into the pages of national importance for publicity, Senator Long has temporarily abandoned his other means of getting before the eyes of the public, one of which was the celebrated Sands Point affair. The question then arises: Can this football team that Captain Biff Jones has put together and polished into Swiss-watch perfection hold up under Senator Long's ambition for it and himself?" The answer to that question, as Long and the rest of the nation soon discovered, was a resounding "no."[20]

20

SENATOR ABE MICKAL

Long planned to attend LSU's next football game, against Mississippi State in Tiger Stadium, the Saturday after the Vanderbilt excursion. But first, he attended to some Louisiana politics. He went to Shreveport on Friday, November 2, to defend the fourteen constitutional amendments his organization placed on the statewide ballot for the following Tuesday. Explaining amendment one—to abolish the state's one-dollar annual poll tax—Long insisted removing the tax would not enfranchise Black citizens. "The [repeal of the] poll tax don't help the negro to vote. In fact, if they have property, we make 'em pay the tax. What keeps them from voting is the Democratic Party and the control of the registration rolls." In a sometimes-belligerent presentation to a large crowd at the city's Municipal Auditorium, Long said he would soon call a special legislative session to apply the "iron clasp."[1]

The "clasp" to which Long referred was an expansion of his power over state government and a deepening conflict with leaders in the recalcitrant city of New Orleans, over whom he sought to extend his authority. During the regular legislative session in May, Long and his allies rammed through a series of bills aimed at giving his organization even more power and diminishing New Orleans and its mayor, T. Semmes Walmsley, a former ally from whom he split in 1933. Long maintained that New Orleans was rife with corruption and illegal gambling, but his real problem was that the city's leadership rejected his dominance. With Long away in Washington, however, much of his and Governor Allen's program failed or was dropped in the face of determined anti-Long opposition. Long returned to Baton Rouge by June to take charge. He muscled through most of the program, including legislation giving him control of the New Orleans Police Department. Walmsley, meanwhile, spurned Long's growing authority.

Long escalated his conflict with New Orleans, worried that the mayor's organization might rig a special election for Public Service Commission and defeat his chosen candidate. At Long's direction, Allen sent the state's National Guard into New Orleans on July 30 to occupy the parish's Registrar of Voters office. Allen also declared limited martial law in the city, precipitating an armed standoff with its police force. T. Harry Williams doubted that Long and Allen invaded New Orleans because they were afraid of losing an election. After all, the state controlled the parish's voting rolls. "There is only one possible explanation of Huey's action: he thought that by a crude display of power he could awe his opposition in New Orleans, probably in the coming election and perhaps permanently," Williams wrote. "Awing his enemies had become a preoccupation with him."

Again, through Allen, Long called a four-day special session for August. With stunning speed, his legislative leaders railroaded to passage a series of bills that astounded some allies for their audacity. The consolidation of power into the governor's office was breathtaking, making Allen—and, by extension, Long—the de facto dictator of Louisiana. Not finished acquiring power, Long ordered Allen to call another special session for November 12. The forty-four bills rushed through over five days gave Long, through his puppet, even more authority over local governments. One bill allowed the governor to fill any vacancy in state and local offices until the next scheduled election. Long also created the new State Bar of Louisiana in retribution for the Louisiana State Bar Association's expulsion of an ally, Attorney General Gaston Porterie. Opponents had accused the attorney general of undermining the 1933 investigation into alleged voter fraud in Orleans Parish. Creating a new bar association allowed Porterie to continue practicing law, as the bill made him the association's president. The legislation also opened another path for Long protégé Kemble K. Kennedy to enter the legal profession.

Long also took over the city of Alexandria, passing a bill declaring vacant the offices of mayor, commissioner of streets and parks, and commissioner of finance and utilities. The legislation authorized the governor to appoint their replacements, new officials who would serve until the 1936 election. Most dramatically, he sneaked through legislation raising taxes on a nemesis, the Standard Oil Corporation. "This is the time to pay [back] the Standard Oil for the impeachment," he told allies. He passed the measure using a dummy bill his leaders amended at the last minute to include the tax increase. The company's lobbyists did not discover the gambit until it was too late to object.[2]

Long's absolute control of the state—combined with his resentment over the Roosevelt administration's attacks on his political organization, including a federal tax evasion investigation—led him to visions of grandeur and overstatement. In a telephone interview with a New Orleans reporter in early November, he declared that Louisiana should leave the Union. "The only way for us to get out of this here depression is to secede from the United States—sever all connections and make a clean start." Long ventured that secession might be accomplished through "a friendly agreement" with the federal government, allowing Louisiana to become a sovereign nation "or join us with Mexico or something." It might take up to six years, he added, "but we'll set up a real Utopia in this state. But we've got to get out of the United States. We've got to run our own business and not have any of those damn folderols that's goin' on up there."

He also boasted about LSU's football prowess. Wading into the debate over whether the universities of Minnesota or Alabama had the year's best football team, Long bellowed, "Louisiana State University!" adding, "I'll tell you what we'll do. We'll play both teams at any place they pick in the same week. We'll play 'em both the same day." In fact, Long added, "We'll play 'em both at the same time—and if they're still afraid, we'll let 'em pick any eleven men they want out of our squad and we'll beat 'em with what's left, just provided they'll leave us four backs."[3]

Long's audacious, fanciful pronouncements were often treated as just that. In preparing for the November special session of the legislature, however, his penchant for dramatic moves got the best of him. Long plunged his beloved LSU into a series of damaging disputes that caused weeks of embarrassing controversy and recrimination. It began with Long's desire to have a little fun with a vacancy in the state senate.

No LSU player had created more enthusiasm for the Tigers in 1934 than halfback Ibrahim Khalil "Abe" Mickal, a modest, twenty-one-year-old premedical junior from McComb, Mississippi. An immigrant from Talia, Lebanon, Mickal had arrived in the US with his family at age seven. His parents had once disapproved of his love of football and hoped he would stay in McComb and help manage the family's general store. But Mickal, a high school gridiron star, eventually won them over. He had been the Tigers' most celebrated player over the past two seasons with his thrilling passes, punts, and laser-perfect field goals and extra-point kicks. Some fans called him "Miracle Mickal."

With Long watching from the bench, Mickal suffered a minor injury to his left knee in the second quarter of LSU's November 3 home game against Mississippi State. The Tigers won, 25–3, but Mickal's availability for the team's next big, showcase game—in Washington, DC, against George Washington University (GWU)—was uncertain. Long and the university physician, Clarence A. Lorio, downplayed the star player's injury after he did not return to the field during the second half of the Mississippi State game. "Well, he's all right," Long told reporters afterward, speaking as if he were a coach, "we just wanted to give him a rest."[4]

Mickal was not all right. Although he traveled with the team, he did not play against GWU. Long missed that game, too, unable to leave Baton Rouge, as his special session was set to begin the following Monday. On the Friday before the game, Long sent a telegram to Washington, where Biff Jones and his team were preparing for the next day's contest. He released the text to the press: "Please tell any of your boys who make a touchdown or otherwise distinguish themselves in Saturday's game that Governor O. K. Allen has authorized me to say they will be made a colonel, a rank much higher than that of Kentucky under present circumstances." Long also promised that "special equipment will be provided on the top floor of the state Capitol for the luxury and ease of all stars on their return. Nothing is too good for the Tigers." But when the Tigers beat GWU 6–0, Long was displeased, and declared it was the team's "low point, our worst day" of the season. "We played strictly a defensive game with Mickal, [center Lloyd] Stovall and me out," he told reporters. That Long linked his absence from the sidelines as a reason for the team's disappointing offensive performance should have been a warning to Jones that the senator's hands-off relationship to his football team would soon end.[5]

Long had shown his hand before the game. Making colonels was not the only honor he hoped to bestow on a player. On November 7, he had joked to reporters about appointing Mickal lieutenant governor if he played well in LSU's upcoming game against Tulane. When a reporter reminded Long that Mickal was a Mississippi resident, Long shot back, "Well, didn't Napoleon live in Corsica?! Hell, it don't matter where Mickal lives. Mississippi is just a province of Louisiana, anyhow." What started out as a joke quickly spun out of control while the Tigers were in Washington. On Saturday, November 10, the day of the game, Long revealed that he planned to appoint Mickal to the Louisiana senate.[6]

That morning, the *Reveille* editor, Jesse Cutrer of Kentwood, received a phone call from Helen Gilkison, a twenty-five-year-old former *Reveille* and *Gumbo* editor and 1930 LSU journalism graduate who covered Capitol news for the *New Orleans Item*. Gilkison told Cutrer that Long wanted to ask a favor: Would he sign a proclamation calling a mass meeting of LSU students to "elect" Mickal to the state senate? She added Long hoped Cutrer would chair the convocation. Gilkison said Long would summon students to the Greek Theatre. There, he would stage a burlesque version of the "mass meeting" that anti-Long forces held in December 1933 to nominate an archrival, state senator Jared Y. Sanders Jr., for the Sixth District congressional seat, left vacant when US representative Bolivar Kemp died. After Governor Allen refused to schedule an election to replace Kemp, Long opponents had convened a rump meeting of local voters to perform the work they claimed the governor would not do. After a long, bitter fight, Sanders won the congressional seat the previous April, which left his state senate seat vacant. As Allen had yet to schedule an election to choose Sanders's replacement, Long sought to have some fun at his opponents' expense. He would mock their "mass meeting" by "electing" Mickal as a state senator.

Cutrer hesitated when Gilkison asked him to meet Long at the Capitol but agreed to see the senator. It was not clear why a journalist was making the request on Long's behalf, except that Gilkison had been friends with Long since her days as an LSU student, when she and two other journalism coeds had knocked on the door of the new Governor's Mansion and persuaded Long to give them a personal tour.

When Cutrer arrived, Long handed him the proclamation and urged him to sign it. "After reading it," Cutrer later wrote in an affidavit about the episode, "I told the senator that it was not my place to sign it and asked that he get the president of the student body to sign the proclamation." When Long told him the student body president, William Lobdell, was out of town, Cutrer asked why he did not ask the vice president to sign the document.

"What's the matter with you?" Long asked. "Are you scared?" Cutrer said he told Long, "I did not consider that it was my duty or position to sign

LSU star halfback Abe Mickal.
(LSU Photograph Collection, LSU Special Collections)

the proclamation." At an impasse with Long, Cutrer left without signing the proclamation.[7]

That afternoon in the Greek Theatre, Long's burly, omnipresent body-guard, Joe Messina, opened the meeting as temporary chair before turning the proceedings over to a student, Ed Khoury. To the six hundred students in attendance, Khoury read a proclamation declaring the right of "a citizens' committee" to gather to "name, nominate and elect a state senator for the twentieth senatorial district for the parish of East Baton Rouge to serve out the unexpired term now vacant in the Louisiana state senate."

With that, Khoury announced, "Nominations are in order!" Someone called out the name of football player Jesse Fatherree. Next, prodded by Long, drum major Burns Bennett rose to nominate Mickal.

"I second it!" Long, seated amid a group of coeds, shouted.

"All in favor, say aye," Khoury said. "All opposed, keep quiet!"

"Meeting adjourned!" Long commanded, as the amused students demanded that he deliver a speech.

At the rostrum, Long explained his reason for the burlesque. "Governor Allen's been a friend of mine, but he's been too high-handed about not setting an election for the senate from East Baton Rouge [Parish]," Long said, leaving unspoken that Allen did whatever Long ordered. "We just had to fill it. If I have anything to do with it, Abe will be seated at this extra session."

As Long prepared to leave campus, a reporter asked him if Mickal could serve, given that he was a Mississippi resident and not a US citizen by birth. "Oh, that doesn't make any difference," Long said, admitting he did not know whether Mickal was eligible. As one historian of the period observed, "It was the Roman emperor touch, the next thing to Caligula's appointing his horse a consul."[8]

Mickal and Coach Jones were both surprised when news of the mass meeting reached them. Arriving by train in Baton Rouge on the afternoon of Monday, November 12, Mickal ducked into the team bus to avoid the crush of students and townspeople who gathered at the train station to greet the returning team. When a reporter followed him onto the bus and asked for his reaction to the "election," a red-faced Mickal responded, "I—I don't know. I better not say anything." When the reporter asked if he would appear at the legislature that evening to take his seat, Mickal said, "Well, yes, if you see me."

It was an open question at LSU and the Capitol if the whole thing was a joke. The *State-Times* noted, "Nobody took Mickal's 'election' seriously, because the planned 'induction in office' before the legislature meets will not be in accordance with the Senate rules." The same story, however, suggested that Long regarded Mickal's election as legitimate. That night, when lawmakers convened, several hundred LSU students and others crammed the senate gallery to await the star halfback's swearing in. Legislative staffers prepared a desk with his name on it, and the chamber's electronic voting board listed him among the senate's members. Long announced that Mickal would receive the legal ten-dollar-a-day stipend to which each lawmaker was entitled during a legislative session.[9]

Soon, however, an agitated Biff Jones appeared and asked to see Long. "These are all fine boys, giving their all to the university, making sacrifices every day to prove their loyalty," Jones told Long. "And I won't have them made fun of." Jones also reminded Long that Southeastern Conference rules prohibited professionalism and that if Mickal were seated in the senate, he might lose his amateur status. When their meeting ended, *Times Picayune* reporter Frank Allen observed, "Senator Long stalked off, displeased." Leaving the Capitol, Jones told reporters, "You know, [Mickal's] been on football trips and has been missing some class attendance." In response to Jones's protest and Mickal's failure to appear at the Capitol, senators granted their new member a five-day leave of absence (the session lasted only five days). "His time is going to be consumed with work at the school and preparation for the next football game," Senator Harvey Peltier of Lafourche Parish, also an LSU Board member, said. Asked by reporters about Mickal's absence, Long explained, "Well, he had to study in his dormitory tonight." Mickal never took his appointment seriously, regarding it as a gag by Long that took on a life of its own. Whatever the case, if the incident ended only with Mickal's "leave of absence," the damage to LSU's reputation would have been minimal. What happened next ensured that it was anything but.[10]

21

THE *REVEILLE* SEVEN

everal days after the Mickal episode, Duyane R. Norman, a sophomore commerce major from Bienville Parish, submitted a letter to
the *Reveille,* defending the star halfback's conduct after Long tried
to appoint him to the Louisiana senate. Editor Jesse Cutrer approved it for
publication. It was typeset and placed on page four of the Friday, November 16, edition. Norman wrote:

Is there one serious minded student in the university that is in sympathy
with the proposed attempt to seat a popular member of the L.S.U. football
squad in the Louisiana Senate? What a mockery of constitutional government and democracy to elect by mass meeting a member of Louisiana's governing body.

Yet that is all right. It was only a burlesque. What kept this action from
moving out of the category of a burlesque into a serious mockery of our legislative body? The answer to this question lies in the intelligence of the so-
called "Senator-Elect" and in the foresight of the athletic director of L.S.U.

The student body as a whole should thank these parties for preventing
the use of L.S.U. students as a mockery to our government. Those who know
Abe Mickal realize that he is not only a football player but also a competent
student of the university.[1]

On Thursday night, *Reveille* reporter Frank Cayce went to the paper's
printer, the J. E. Ortlieb Printing Company on Florida Street, to oversee
production of the next day's edition. As Cayce left the printer for his ten-
minute walk to the Capitol to check on events there, he grabbed the first part

of the paper's eight-page edition. When he arrived at the press table in the senate chamber, Cayce handed the section to a former *Reveille* reporter and editor, David McGuire. A senior journalism student, McGuire worked for Helen Gilkison, the *Item* reporter who had phoned Cutrer days earlier about Long's mass meeting at LSU. McGuire scanned the paper and shared it with Gilkison.

A few minutes later, Long wandered by. "Watchya reading, Helen?" he asked. Gilkison handed him the *Reveille* section. According to about twenty witnesses, when Long saw Norman's letter, he exploded with a torrent of curses. "This is my university!" he thundered. "No one down there dares say a word against Huey Long. I will fire a thousand of them if they say a word against Huey Long. Get me Jim Smith. I'll get a new editor for that paper by morning." Long reserved his worst profanity for Cutrer, the editor who had rebuffed Long's request to sign the proclamation for the mass meeting of LSU students the previous week. "This Cutrer's a rotten little son of a bitch, just like that rotten uncle of his," he said, reminding those around him that an uncle of the student editor, former state representative William Cutrer of Tangipahoa Parish, voted for Long's impeachment in 1929. "All them Cutrers are rotten," he said, "and I told President Smith not to make that boy editor of that paper." Then, Long added, "That letter's not going to be in that paper tomorrow. I'll make 'em tear it out and run the damn paper over."

Smith and LSU's business manager, Edgar Jackson, scurried to the Capitol to see Long. Hoping to calm him, Smith agreed to order the *Reveille* to reprint the section without Norman's letter. He phoned Ortlieb Press and spoke to Grace Williamson, a journalism student from New Orleans who was the Friday-issue editor. Norman's letter must not appear, he said, and instructed her to destroy the forty-two hundred copies of the section already printed. Meanwhile, Cutrer, who rushed back to the press to deal with the matter, learned about Smith's phone call when he arrived. He and Williamson removed Norman's letter and began reprinting that section of the paper. Jackson showed up a few minutes later to retrieve a copy of the reprinted paper for Long. "[Jackson] told me that I should go to Senator Long and apologize," Cutrer later said, "adding that if I ever said he told me to do so, he would say that I was lying."

Cutrer did as he was told. He made the one-block walk to the Heidelberg Hotel, Long's headquarters in Baton Rouge, where he found Smith and Jackson waiting for him in the lobby. The men accompanied Cutrer to his meeting with Long. Cutrer recalled that they "coached me all the way up in the elevator not to resent it if Senator Long got mad and cussed me." When the trio arrived at Long's suite, the editor explained he did not write the letter; it was a student's opinion. By then, Long was calmer. He asked only if the press had destroyed the papers. Cutrer assured him they had.[2]

Because Long erupted in front of several reporters and dozens of legislators, it was no surprise that Friday's newspapers contained stories about his censorship of the *Reveille*. An Associated Press story in several major Louisiana daily newspapers reported, "A sophomore's criticism of the antics of United States Senator Huey P. Long in dubbing Abe Mickal, star football player, a 'state senator' was eliminated from today's issue of the 'Reveille' ... as it was about to roll from the press last night." Contacted by the reporter, Cutrer engaged in some diplomatic dissembling. He said neither LSU nor Long censored the letter. "It wasn't suppressed. We just decided not to run it."[3]

Cutrer and Williamson went to Smith's office the next morning for a meeting that included James Broussard, the dean of administration, and several journalism faculty members. All the participants hoped to quell the previous night's tumult. Cutrer recalled that Smith told them, "These are abnormal times," and added that Long was "virtually a dictator of the university" and that for "the good of the university" he would never defy him.

At this meeting, Smith presented his plan for settling the matter. He informed Cutrer and Williamson that he would appoint Helen Gilkison as a journalism faculty member charged with overseeing the *Reveille*'s production. Cutrer and Williamson, who likely knew about Gilkison's friendship with Long, were wary of the unorthodox arrangement. "I specifically asked [Smith] if she was to act as a censor, to which he definitely stated that she was not," Cutrer recalled. With that assurance, the two students agreed to collaborate on the production of future editions, so long as Gilkison acted only in an "advisory capacity."[4]

The arrangement fell apart the following Monday night, November 19, when Gilkison arrived at the Ortlieb Press and demanded to see the proofs for the Tuesday paper. Angry at this apparent violation of their agreement with Smith, the *Reveille* editors prepared a front-page box for the next edition, which read: "This issue of the Reveille has been censored by Miss Helen Gilkison, who was authorized by Dean Broussard to examine the pages before the edition went to press." That forced Gilkison to back down. She offered not to censor the paper if the students deleted the box. Both sides relented, and the next day's *Reveille* appeared absent the box and without Gilkison's editing. Alarmed at the idea of someone censoring their publication, Cutrer and two other student reporters went to Broussard's home that night. The dean of administration told them that, as the supervisor of all student publications, he wanted Gilkison as the *Reveille*'s censor.[5]

It was not the first time Broussard, a *Reveille* reporter during his undergraduate days at LSU, had interfered with the student paper. In February, he wrote to an associate professor of journalism, Marcus Wilkerson, to complain about a column on a Southeastern Conference meeting at LSU in which reporter David McGuire referred to visiting delegates as "lads," "boys," and "partners in crime." In his indignant letter, Broussard suggested canceling McGuire's column "unless his articles show first, that he is informed on what he writes about and second, that he refrain from a certain humor that is neither interesting nor dignified." Broussard also summoned McGuire to his office for a reprimand.[6]

With Smith away for the week, the paper's editors met with Broussard again the next day. This time, they told him they would stop writing for the *Reveille* if the university continued censoring their work. It was not the first time they had asserted their free speech rights. In May, editors had boasted, "In some universities suppression of the student press is exercised by the administration. At L.S.U. there is no official censorship." In their meeting that morning, they reminded Broussard of the language of the Constitution's First Amendment, to which Broussard replied, "What has that to do with Louisiana State University?" He urged them to accept Gilkison's role until Smith returned to campus. They refused. Faced with this defiance, Broussard may have worried that in Smith's absence he was taking too much responsibility for a system of censorship that Long and Smith had devised. Whatever the case, later that day, he backed down and allowed the students to publish what they pleased.[7]

An Associated Press story the next morning about the controversy appeared in newspapers around the state, informing readers of the episode and adding that Broussard had countermanded Long's censorship of the *Reveille*. That arrangement lasted only until Smith returned to Baton Rouge. Smith convened a meeting on Monday, November 26, with the *Reveille* staff and top LSU administrators. He urged the students to agree to Gilkison's review of their work. Cutrer asked if Gilkison would allow any criticism of Long in the paper. "The president stated that 'no criticism of Long or any other university officials would be permitted,'" Cutrer told reporters that evening.

Rather than bow to Smith's demands, Cutrer and five staff members resigned from the paper. Later that day, students hung a sign on the door to the *Reveille*'s office in the basement of Allen Hall: "Killed by Suppression." Explaining himself to the press the same day, Smith said, "The question is whether I, as president of the university, or a student editor, shall have the last say. I have held that I will have it." Smith denied that Long's anger over the letter to the editor had anything to do with his decisions. "Whether Senator Long is here or isn't here makes no difference."[8]

The paper's editors were not the only students dismayed by Long's and Smith's assault on their freedom of speech. A group of about forty journalism students convened on Tuesday, November 27, to discuss their response. "Huey Long has gone too far to back up," journalism student Wes Gallagher, who became president of the Associated Press in 1962, told the group. Another student, Sam Montague, insisted "if something was not done" by students "we will be branded as cowards who are told what to do and a degree from the School of Journalism will not be worth the paper it is written on." The students called themselves the "Students of the School of Journalism," and issued a petition, which twenty-six of them signed. It stated:

> To President James Monroe Smith and the faculty committee on student publications:
>
> We, the undersigned members of the school of journalism, do hereby respectfully request the reinstatement of the *Reveille* staff with the full rights of student self-expression. If such is not forthcoming, we, as a body united, refuse to contribute one word to any student news organ.
>
> This is not a protest against reasonable faculty supervision, but a protest against the suppression of student opinion and freedom of speech of a student news organ.

Twenty-six journalism students distributed a handbill around campus in the afternoon that complained, "This university has seen fit to suppress [the *Reveille*] through censorship." The students declared, "The university is virtually without a newspaper," and requested the student body's support for the publication. "This is a call to battle by students for the return

The staff of the LSU student paper, the *Reveille*.
(LSU *Gumbo* yearbook, 1934)

of rights to L.S.U. which are enjoyed by students on every other American college campus." Outraged that the students had not presented the petition to him first, Smith suspended the group of twenty-six for "gross disrespect" in sharing the document with the press. And Broussard backed him. "I am opposed to objectionable censorship in the sense of rewriting everything that goes into student publications," the dean said. "On the other hand, if the kind of noncensorship that students demand means that they must be given free rein to attack and criticize state officials, university officials and members of the faculty, then I am for censorship in the strictest sense of the word." Meanwhile, two new signs appeared on the *Reveille*'s door. One declared: "Defunctus—By Order of Huey, The State, The God." Another said: "For Sale, One Key to Reveille Office."[9]

As Louisiana and some national newspapers—including the *New York Times*—began noticing the story, Long backtracked and blamed everything on Smith. "I didn't know what was going on," he told a reporter on November 28. "I was out of touch with the whole thing." Long speculated that, "Maybe Dr. Smith got impatient. You know, this [student suspensions] is one way to solve the problem of [campus] overcrowding." Long insisted he "never interfered with university officials." To another reporter, he suggested that he had lost control of the university. "Maybe he's [Smith] sore at me because I haven't raised the money and is taking things into his own hands. Maybe he's going to expel enough students to relieve the overcrowded conditions."

To both reporters, Long mentioned his inability to help Kemble K. Kennedy in 1930 after LSU expelled him. "That boy was wearing a suit of my clothes, with my name inside it," he said. "I appealed to the president to reinstate him, but he refused, and I never could get that boy back. There ain't nothing I can do in this case." That explanation strained credulity. Anyone with even passing knowledge of Louisiana politics understood that LSU officials had censored the *Reveille* and punished the students to please Long.[10]

Smith remained immovable as journalism students boycotted their classes to protest their classmates' suspensions. "If the Board of Supervisors does not see fit to back me up, they can get a new president. I'm going to stick with it, and I don't give a hang what any board member thinks." Smith said students who "make the proper representation" could be reinstated.[11]

Meanwhile, the students' travails drew national attention. The president of the American Association of University Professors (AAUP) speculated that the situation might be an infringement on academic freedom and said his organization could drop LSU from its list of accredited schools. About the same time, the Western Conference College Editors, during its convention in Chicago, adopted a resolution condemning Long for "unwarranted censorship of The Reveille." Long responded in a telegram, insisting, "I have never censored nor undertaken to censor anything published at L.S.U." A few days later, the Big Ten Editorial Association chimed in, charging that Long was politicizing LSU and "meddling in purely educational affairs." In another telegram, Long bragged about his role in elevating the university. "Before the days of Huey Long, the Louisiana State University would never have been heard of, much less to excite such notice by such high and worthy surveillance as you give it." Long scolded the association: "I believe every one of you would be ashamed of your action in lending your arm to such an effort if you understood the truth."[12]

Long feuded and defended while Smith expelled. To the twenty-six students who signed the petition, Smith said he would reinstate them only if they signed a statement retracting their criticism of him. Twenty-two did so on Tuesday, December 5. The following day, Smith ordered Troy Middleton, dean of men and commandant of cadets, to expel Jesse Cutrer ("for uttering as true . . . that which is false") and David McGuire (for "attempting to incite insubordination of students, reporting to the Press the proceedings of a closed meeting, and for making himself a general nuisance"). Smith and Middleton "suspended indefinitely" five other journalism students: Cal

Abraham of Baton Rouge; Carl Corbin of Houma; Sam Montague of New Orleans, L. Rea Godbold of Brookhaven, Mississippi; and Stanley Shlosman of Marshalltown, Iowa. LSU said their offenses included "issuing statements derogatory" about LSU and "subjecting it to unjust and unwarranted criticism," "giving out statements to the Press which were misleading and likely to be damaging to the good name of the University," and "forcing freshmen to distribute circulars."[13]

The *Reveille* reappeared on Tuesday of that week with a new editor, Grace Williamson, who, after her scuffle with Gilkison and Smith, had made peace with them. The paper's masthead, which once named most members of the paper's staff, now listed only one person by name: "Grace Williamson . . . Editor. Assisted by a Volunteer Staff."

Williamson's portrayal of the dispute over Gilkison's censorship role was nothing like the story Cutrer and McGuire shared with reporters. In a signed editorial, "To the Students," the new editor wrote, "It has been said that the editors resigned in an effort to combat censorship. This statement is incorrect." Williamson claimed the students quit because they refused to accept "faculty supervision." She added, "The question at issue has not been so much one of press freedom as of responsibility that accompanies such a privilege." Williamson asserted the dubious proposition that LSU could control what the *Reveille* published because "the public, by and large, accepts what appears in The Reveille as reflecting University opinion."

Montague was unsparing in his criticism of what he and the other expelled and suspended students regarded as Williamson's betrayal. "I think the name of the university publication should be changed from *Reveille* to *The Retreat*," he told the *Times-Picayune*. "Miss Williamson is trying to absolve herself by maintaining that if it had not been for her, the School of Journalism would be lost." Montague also called out the journalism faculty for failing to stand up for the rights of the expelled students. "It is apparent that all the things which they have taught us have not meant a thing to them."[14]

If Long and Smith thought that suspending and expelling the students would end their woes over control of the student newspaper, they were mistaken. The Southern Association of Colleges and Secondary Schools (SACS), LSU's main accrediting body, announced on December 4 that it would investigate allegations that Long "is running Louisiana State University." The students released sworn affidavits the same day, which attested to the perception of LSU administrators that Long controlled LSU. Cutrer swore that Smith informed him Long "would fire me, my staff, destroy the School of Journalism, and fire 4,000 students before he would offend the senator." He said in his affidavit that Broussard said, "When you get to be my age, you'll learn that principles don't mean much." Abraham also said LSU business manager Edgar Jackson (the former grocery store owner from Long's native Winnfield) told him, "You know we can't do anything that would offend the senator."

Meanwhile, student newspapers at other universities around the country editorialized against LSU's punishment of the student journalists. The *Hustler* of Vanderbilt called their expulsion a "mean and tyrannical attitude" and blamed Long for the scandal. The University of Tennessee's *Orange and White* declared that "this reactionary action at L.S.U. represents a potential threat to college journalism throughout the country," and condemned Long's "blighting touch." Members of the Theta Nu journalism fraternity at Tulane declared themselves "fully in sympathy with the courageous stand of the *Reveille* staff and the journalism students who support it," and denounced the school's "unduly severe treatment of the *Reveille* staff."[15]

In Shreveport, the editors of the *Conglomerate,* the student paper of Centenary College, bragged that their administration did not interfere with its publication. "The fact that there is no censorship is especially appreciated since the disturbance over the Louisiana State University publication has shown what chaos and worry can be caused by censorship, which in most cases is entirely unnecessary." The Kentucky Intercollegiate Press Association sent a telegram to Cutrer, expressing approval of "your commendable action and objecting to the censorship." Other student papers that condemned Long and LSU included the *Daily Iowan* at the University of Iowa, and the *Daily Maroon* at the University of Chicago, which wrote in an editorial, "Huey claims to have done more for Louisiana than anyone else. Why then, if this superman is so mighty, that at the first hint of criticism, must he reach out and squelch the offenders?" The Louisiana Press Association also denounced LSU.[16]

In Washington, President Franklin Roosevelt even entered the fray with an indirect swipe at Long. In late December, the president hosted thirty-seven editors of college newspapers at the White House. Before the students departed, Roosevelt inquired if any student from Louisiana was present. Introduced to Roosevelt as the editor of the *Reveille,* Cutrer—now the former editor—chatted with the president and later with White House reporters covering the meeting.[17]

Besides the national and regional criticism, Smith worried about potential student unrest at LSU. On December 5, he averted an outright revolt when the Student Council issued a statement of support, declaring, "President Smith and his faculty advisors are right in the stand he and they have taken in reference to faculty supervision of the Reveille." Between 200 to 300 students converged on the Gym Armory two days later for a rump mass meeting after student body president William Lobdell, who also worked for LSU as a coach of the freshman football team, refused to call a convocation. After student body vice-president James Arceneaux called the meeting, students descended on the building, only to be told that Smith forbade their gathering.[18]

The LSU campus awoke to a disturbing scene on Saturday, December 8. A student corporal patrolling the campus around 6:45 discovered Smith had been hanged in effigy the night before. His likeness dangled about twelve feet high on a flagpole greased with lard near the center of campus. A placard attached to the effigy's chest read: "James Monroe Smith, 'Jimmy the Stooge,' hanged in effigy December 7, 1934." Middleton ordered a detail of cadets to remove the likeness before students and others on campus saw it. Asked later that day about the effigy, Smith said, "I didn't know there was one." For the rest of the day, a Louisiana state trooper stood watch near the flagpole.[19]

A *New Orleans Item* reporter who visited LSU found the campus less than distraught about the controversy. Most students, busy with their studies and work, were not absorbed with the political intrigue unfolding on their campus. "The student at large who discusses the matter at all treats it rather impersonally, as a farce by now a bit tiresome, being enacted before him," reporter Edmond LeBreton wrote in the paper's December 9 edition. As one premedical student told LeBreton, "Most [students] don't care, but some who pose as being indifferent and others who just say, 'It's a hell of a situation,' would talk more if they weren't scared." The student refused to share his feelings with the reporter. "I'm not talking," he said. "I want to get through here and go down to the medical center." At least two students told LeBreton that Long was in the right. "After all," one said, "Long did build this place up. He's got a right to some gratitude, hasn't he?" Another student said, "Sure, we know Huey's running the university. What of it? If it wasn't Huey, it would be somebody else. He's made it a good place to go."[20]

In a column carried in the *New Orleans Item* and picked up by the North American Newspaper Alliance syndicate, Sam Montague, one of the seven expelled students, explored the question of "why our student body has not made their voice heard in this controversy." Montague's reasonable conclusion was that "the students, in the majority, are afraid. They are afraid for themselves, or for their friends and relations." Montague listed student constituencies whose scholarships or postgraduation livelihoods depended on not offending the Long organization. "The Law school students cannot voice themselves because they have to pass the bar examination in Louisiana, and they are afraid that if they incur the disfavor of the present administration, they will be failed." Engineering students, he wrote, were hoping to work for the state Highway Commission. Future teachers wanted jobs with the state. "Students in general are afraid to say anything because their scholarships, or their university jobs might be taken away from them. Most of the scholarships in the university have come from a political source, and they are given away quite freely. And the sad part about it is, that the students really need them to go to school." Montague and others might also have noted that another reason students were not passionate about the *Reveille*'s treatment was that the paper did not cover the story. Although interested students could have learned about the dispute from the Baton Rouge and New Orleans papers, the news source most available to them—and free—ignored the unfolding scandal.[21]

Meanwhile, Long stoked the controversy, delivering a speech on WDSU radio in New Orleans in which he alleged, without evidence, that "New Orleans newspapers" paid the LSU students to generate the dispute. Long was no doubt stung by the extensive coverage of the episode in the city's papers, particularly the *Times-Picayune*. But most other daily papers in the state also covered the story with gusto. "The newspapers can't get grown people to believe their lies anymore, so they are starting on boys too young to know better," Long charged.[22]

The expelled students, who came to be known as the "Reveille Seven," found the greatest support from the School of Journalism at the University of Missouri. Officials there offered to admit the students so they could complete their studies. "Without freedom of the press," the school's associate dean, Frank Martin, said in a statement, "the sovereign people cannot retain or exercise sovereignty." Others offered help, too. An anonymous individual in New Orleans (some suspected a former *Reveille* editor) established an account from which the seven could borrow, interest-free, the funds to finish their educations elsewhere. And the journalism school at the University of

Virginia invited the students to enroll there, too. The seven opted for Missouri, where each earned a bachelor's degree in journalism. (The LSU Board of Supervisors apologized to the former students and cleared their records of all disciplinary charges in 1941.)[23]

Long had overreacted and overreached in response to a benign letter to the *Reveille* that never mentioned him by name. "That was bungled," Troy Middleton acknowledged years later, adding that he asked Smith and Broussard "to turn it over to me, but they wouldn't. I would have gone to Huey and laid it on the line, which is what Smith should have done. Huey would have seen it. He was smart." Joe Cawthon, a student close to Long who distrusted editor Jesse Cutrer's motives, admitted, "The *Reveille* incident was an error on [Long's] part." David McGuire later said Long "managed it horribly for a smart man. He got himself into a situation that he need not have done." McGuire did not regard Long's attack on the *Reveille* as a matter of press freedom. "He viewed it solely as a personal attack upon him and he was outraged in his feeling that he had done a great deal to help the university, and in a physical way, he did."[24]

One Long biographer, however, argued that Long forced Smith to censor the *Reveille* because he had "no respect for the principle of academic freedom." T. Harry Williams wrote that Long "viewed LSU as a personal or political possession and interfered with it whenever he saw fit." It was not, Williams believed, that Long was hostile to academic freedom, per se. "He knew little about the principle and cared less." Long was usually tolerant or disinterested in what happened in the university's classrooms. His only standard was that *his* university could not be used as a vehicle to attack or criticize him (which was a standard hostile to faculty and student free speech).

That Long controlled LSU was not in dispute in 1934. But some Long critics also charged that he co-opted the university to such a degree that only his political supporters could get, or keep, their jobs at the university and that its employees were coerced into making political contributions to his organization. The belief that Long had transformed LSU into a political organization—a charge that the *Reveille* episode did nothing to dispel—was so prevalent that a committee of LSU faculty members in late 1934 or early 1935 sent a confidential survey to 174 of their colleagues to inquire about the extent of the Long organization's political influence at LSU. Whether truthful—they were promised anonymity, but respondents may not have trusted the committee to guard their identity—the 173 faculty members who responded reported no political pressure or coercion from LSU to support Long's political organization. "The evidence presented . . . needs no explanation," the nine-member committee wrote in a pamphlet it published to share the results of the survey. "It is sufficient to convince impartial persons that the charges and insinuations referred to are unfounded and untrue."[25]

The following year, Long revealed more about his attitude toward higher education and LSU. In a brief interview with a Socialist Party of America–affiliated student magazine, *Student Outlook,* he answered a question about the growing practice in other states of requiring college students to swear loyalty oaths. "Well," he replied, "there hasn't been any of that in Louisiana, and there won't be. All the radicals and reds in the colleges won't do any harm. It's a mighty good thing that they are beginning to do a little thinking. I wish there were a few million radicals."[26]

Whatever Long's attitude about free speech and academic freedom at LSU, his clash with the *Reveille* was not without cost to him or to the university. Newspapers across the country covered the students' plight in stories that were sympathetic to the seven young men and disdainful of Long's imperious actions. Amplified by news reports of the so-called "dictatorship laws" that Long imposed on the state during several legislative sessions in 1934, the growing, unflattering image of Louisiana's political boss was that of a dictator.

"The Louisiana dictatorship of Huey Long stands as a monument to disorganized opposition in the path of his march to power," Associated Press writer Ralph Wheatley, of the news service's New Orleans bureau, wrote in early December. Wheatley's story—headlined "Dictator-American Style"—ran in dozens of newspapers around the country and described Long's ruthless rise to absolute power in Louisiana. Another AP story focused on Long's iron-fisted control of LSU. A sub-headline of the story declared, "Huey Long Dictator." The anonymous writer noted Long was "enthroned with dictatorial authority in political Louisiana." A year-end roundup by the Newspaper Enterprise Association syndicate listed "Huey Dictates" as 1934's ninth biggest story: "For the first time in many years a single man arose to be uncontested master of a great American state. He was Huey Long, 'Dictator of the Delta.'" Editorials in newspapers across the country often described him as the "dictator of Louisiana." For example, an editorial in the *News-Herald* of Franklin, Pennsylvania, on December 27, began: "While one may wax warm about the ruthlessness of the dictatorship in Germany under the regime of

Adolf Hitler, or criticize severely the bloodthirsty policy of Soviet Russia . . .
he only has to look at Louisiana and view a spectacle of personal control
gone mad."[27]

Midway through December, Long and LSU administrators might have
hoped they could put the unpleasantness of the *Reveille* scandal behind them
and end 1934 on a more positive note. That, however, would have required
Long to remain on the sidelines at LSU's remaining football games. And this
was something the Kingfish refused to do.

22

THAT BUNCH OF
BUZZARDS AND VARMINTS

P ublic interest was high in Louisiana and Mississippi for LSU's November 17 game in Jackson against Ole Miss, and not only because the teams were rivals from bordering states. LSU's 1934 squad featured six players from Mississippi, including Abe Mickal, Jesse Fatherree, and Walter Sullivan. Long planned to travel with the team and the band but changed his mind the week before the game. "I'm too tired. I've been hitting it hard," he told reporters. He knew his presence in Jackson would raise the game's national and regional profiles, especially considering the number of Mississippi natives on the squad. "Huey P. Long's gridiron argosy to Nashville last week has brought him into demand as a football crowdgetter," the Associated Press reported in early November. The AP quoted a source at the University of Georgia who said the school hoped to schedule a game with LSU for the 1935 season. If Long attended, the Georgia official said, the university might agree to a match between the two SEC powerhouses.[1]

On Friday, November 16—the day before the Ole Miss game—Mississippi governor Martin S. "Mike" Conner issued a lighthearted public appeal for the Louisiana senator's attendance. In a telegram to Long he released to the press, Conner wrote: "Province of Mississippi is entitled to a visit from Kingfish and if you don't come with LSU team Saturday we are going to rebel and keep those Mississippians here. Thousands are anxious to see and welcome you and Governor Allen but prefer for Senator Mikal [sic] to be left in charge of Louisiana province."

With that, Long changed his mind. The next morning at 6:30, he joined the 36-man squad, the 112-member Regimental Band, and hundreds of fans and students on a special Illinois Central train as it departed Baton Rouge's Yazoo and Mississippi Valley Company depot. Around 8:30, the train chugged into McComb, Mississippi, Mickal's hometown. Long and the band poured off for a thirty-minute parade up the town's Main Street. Mickal's mother and father—waiting at the station when the train arrived—marched with Long, one parent on each arm, as the band made its way to the couple's general store for a brief concert. "That day," Mickal said years later, "he could have been elected to any office in Pike County."[2]

When Long's train reached Jackson late that morning, eight Louisiana State Police troopers on motorcycles wheeled out of a baggage car and led Long and the band up Capitol Street from the station to the Capitol. The *Jackson Clarion-Ledger* reported, "Huey and his band completely paralyzed lower Capitol Street activity." Over 10,000 onlookers lined the route. As the parade passed the Governor's Mansion, Long stopped the band to serenade the governor. He sent two aides to knock on the front door. "Go in there and arrest Mike," Long told them. Conner "surrendered" and joined the procession. Flanked by the drum majors, Long and Conner led band members to the steps of the Mississippi Capitol. Upon arrival, Long busied himself with distributing cold water to parched band members. And then, with Long conducting from a dry-goods box placed on the Capitol steps, the band opened with his favorite song, "Shine On, Harvest Moon." Long next directed the band in another of his beloved tunes, "Mah Lindy Lou," as many in the crowd sang along. As the band played, Long also chatted with Conner, engaging in a bit of pregame bravado for the press. When Conner joked, "We like your band better than your darn football team," Long replied, laughing, "I bet you do." Then, tugging at Conner's lapel, he pointed to the band. "Now, just listen to this. That's a symphony orchestra there, and this afternoon you'll hear a real football band." After the concert, Long escorted the musicians to the Edwards Hotel for a luncheon, paid cash for the meal, and then gave each member a dollar in spending money. "He took the town by storm and left it with the citizenship from Jackson and all parts of Mississippi wondering what manner of man this 'Kingfish' really is," the *Clarion-Ledger* observed.[3]

To Biff Jones's certain consternation, Long was no less demonstrative during the game, which LSU won while an injured Mickal sat on the bench. Long marched into the stadium at the head of the band but peeled off to greet friends in the stands. "I didn't come up here to politic," he protested when some fans begged for a speech. "I came up here to see a football game." He

Long led the LSU team and band to Jackson, Mississippi, in November 1934 for the LSU–Ole Miss game. After arriving by train, Long led a parade to the Governor's Mansion, where he invited Mississippi governor Sennet "Mike" Conner, *second from left,* to join the procession. (Photo by Leon Trice, Louisiana State Archives)

also came to stick his nose back into Jones's business. With LSU leading 14–0 at the half, Long approached Jones to suggest sending in substitutes. "How about putting in the wrecking crew?" Long whispered to Jones, who responded that the LSU lead was not yet big enough. In the second half, Jones was startled to observe Long on the Ole Miss sideline, speaking to Coach Ed Walker. After the game, Jones asked Walker what Long told him. Walker reported that Long said, "I've just spoken to Biff. We're not going to beat the hell out of you if you don't try to pull anything." LSU left town the winner, 14–0.[4]

Going into its December 1 contest with Tulane, the Tigers had not lost a game since December 17, 1932, when they fell to Oregon, 12–0. Over the next eighteen contests, LSU won thirteen and tied five. Tulane's record was also impressive, coming into Tiger Stadium for this showdown boasting a season record of eight wins and one loss. "Interest in the game seethes," *Morning*

Advocate sportswriter W. I. Spencer wrote. "It is the renewal of the rivalry between two of the oldest football enemies of Dixie. . . . Prospects for one of the greatest games ever to be played between the two crack football teams . . . loom stronger than ever." Seven trains brought 8,000 Tulane fans to Baton Rouge on a cool, clear December afternoon.[5]

The LSU-Tulane game was always a personal affair for Long. And Tulane supporters were aware of his affinity for their Baton Rouge rival. A few years earlier, Long had tried to remain neutral at this annual contest. By 1934, he was impartial no more, and the Tulane crowd did not let him forget it. Some students applauded as Long entered the stadium wearing a navy-blue double-breasted suit and a dark felt hat. Others jeered. Fans from the Tulane section booed him. One cheer took aim at Long's censorship of the student newspaper, a scandal still unfolding in early December: "Rah, rah, rah. Rah, rah, rah. Reveille! Reveille! Reveille!"

Long behaved for much of the game between the evenly matched teams. "He jumped up and raced to a position of vantage whenever Louisiana [State] worked the ball within scoring distance," the *Morning Advocate* reported, adding, "He was happy." Another reporter noted: "He was a reserved, dignified rooter. He committed no antics, he stayed away from [Jones] and rarely rose from his sideline seat." A group of students presented Long with a gold watch at halftime. A student committee—chaired by Long loyalist Joe Cawthon, and which had included then–*Reveille* editor Jesse Cutrer—raised money for the fifty-dollar timepiece in appreciation for Long's role in organizing the celebrated Nashville excursion in October. But he made no speech, and many fans did not notice the brief ceremony.[6]

Long was dejected by game's end. Mickal, who had not played since November 3, did not enter the game until the second quarter. The star halfback performed well—he threw a dramatic touchdown pass in the third quarter—but also missed two extra-point kicks that cost the Tigers the win. Even worse, Mickal went down on a defensive play later in the quarter and left the field on a stretcher. With LSU leading 12–7 near the game's end, Tulane scored on a spectacular run by halfback Monk Simons. In the excitement, Simons's mother fainted, and a forty-eight-year-old LSU supporter, Ben E. Day, died of a heart attack. LSU lost, 13–12. Stunned, tearful Tigers fans departed the stadium in silence. A few weeks earlier, Long had crowed about the likelihood LSU—like Tulane, Alabama, and Georgia—might finally win a bid to the prestigious Rose Bowl. "We're the greatest in the world at this

Long was close to LSU Law School student Joe Cawthon of Logansport. Cawthon delivered Long a copy of the 1935 *Gumbo* yearbook, an edition dedicated to Long. (LSU *Gumbo* yearbook, 1934)

time," he bragged after LSU beat Vanderbilt. Now, however, such an invitation was unimaginable.[7]

The loss crushed Long. "Well, they just beat us," he said through a forced grin as he left the stadium. One jubilant Tulane fan taunted him, "Well, Huey, we beat you, didn't we?" Long muttered, "Yeah." Long was stoic but confessed to friends he was losing confidence in Jones. "Biff Jones may not be the worst coach around, but he sure ain't the best."[8]

In the game's immediate aftermath, Long was most concerned about Mickal's well-being. As the halfback lay recuperating in the campus infirmary the next morning, the Kingfish dropped by for a visit and lingered for forty-five minutes. Mickal, who became a respected obstetrician and served on the faculty of LSU's Medical School, recalled that Long encouraged him to continue pursuing a medical education. In 1936, the Detroit Lions chose Mickal in the sixth round of the National Football League draft, making him the first LSU player ever drafted by an NFL team. He declined the Lions' offer and entered medical school. In 1967, Mickal was inducted into the College Football Hall of Fame.[9]

The Tigers' next game was in Knoxville, against the University of Tennessee. Even in his absence, the attention-hungry senator dominated the headlines about the coming contest. Long once planned to lead another large contingent of LSU fans to the game but called it off in a pique in mid-

Long with LSU head football coach Lawrence "Biff" Jones.
(Photo by Leon Trice, Louisiana State Archives)

November when the *Knoxville News-Sentinel* printed syndicated columnist Westbrook Pegler's criticism of the Kingfish's autocratic rule of LSU. "Senator Long has assumed control of the football team of Louisiana State University as an instrument of political ballyhoo," the New York–based columnist asserted. "He recruits and hires players in pursuit of a determination, arrived at several years ago, to win a national football championship for Louisiana State, no matter how." Pegler wrote that, under Long, football games were political rallies and that he appropriated the band, the student body, and "the university itself." Pegler alleged Long had recruited football players to LSU by promising them jobs at the Louisiana Highway Department. "Huey is the first statesman with the gall or originality to take over a state university, complete with football team, band, cheer-leaders, traditions and all as a political circus."[10]

Pegler's column was tough, but fair, and not unlike the criticism of Long that appeared in some Louisiana newspapers. And it was not the first time the columnist had attacked Long. In August, Pegler had enraged Long with a series of articles critical of his authoritarian tactics. One on the front page of the *New Orleans Item* on August 18 was headlined, "It's Heil Huey in Louisiana! Just Putsch-Over for Der-Kingfish."[11]

Pegler's new attack on Long was not a product of the Knoxville paper. It ran in dozens of other newspapers around the country. But Long reacted with irrational anger to the columnist's words, just as he did when the *Reveille* published the LSU student's letter that same month. The day after the column's appearance in Knoxville, Long called off his excursion, telling the Tennessee athletic director he would not lead his contingent of fans and the band unless the school corrected the record. "If that bunch of buzzards and varmints wants to say things like that, we're not going to Knoxville," he said. It was not clear why Long believed the university should accept responsibility for a syndicated column in a local newspaper. Asked what Tennessee officials could do, Long replied, "They can correct the impression circulated."[12]

Pegler's column was not the only criticism of Long's sideline conduct in the national press. The week after the column appeared, the board of the Touchdown Club of New York—an organization of former college football stars—adopted a resolution condemning Long's politicization of college football "to further his own ambitions and self-aggrandizement." The club said it "resent[ed] the poor sportsmanship as exemplified by Sen. Huey Long in ballyhooing for his own selfish political ends the fine team representing Louisiana State University."[13]

Hoping Long would change his mind about attending the December 8 game, the Knoxville Chamber of Commerce tried to quell the dispute. "By unanimous vote of our board today you are hereby requested to disregard Pegler's article and to come on up here," the organization said in a telegram to Long in mid-November. The editors of the *News-Sentinel's* rival paper, the *Knoxville Journal*, made their bid, too. City editor Harry Clark sent Long several telegrams in which he offered him space in the paper to rebut Pegler's charges. "The *Journal* thinks the comment [was] patently unfair, and wants a statement from Senator Long denouncing it," Clark wrote on November 11. The paper's sports editor, Marvin Thompson, agreed. "Naturally, you can't blame Huey for feeling a grave injustice has been done him," Thompson wrote in a column a few days after Pegler's piece. "He has meant more to L.S.U. football than any other one person with the possible exception of Capt. Biff Jones."[14]

Long wavered but decided against the trip. "Pegler is an infamous liar," he told a reporter, "and he is seeking publicity for himself." After the Knoxville papers "played up" Pegler's "scurrilous" article, Long said, "I couldn't go to Tennessee now." As an afterthought, Long added, without apparent irony, "I didn't want no publicity." Long's decision was just as well. LSU lost to Tennessee, 19–13. In the aftermath, Long was not only disappointed in LSU's second successive loss but also that Jones had played Mickal, despite the senator having ordered the coach to keep his injured player on the bench. Wearing a brace, a wounded Mickal limped off the field late in the game after he booted a punt.[15]

In New Orleans, where Long was unpopular for his animosity toward city leaders (not to mention his cheerleading for LSU over Tulane), there was jubilation over LSU's loss. "The feeling of satisfaction felt by many Orleanians—some Tulanians—over the defeat of Louisiana State University by Tennessee perhaps was a bit unusual, but it can be attributed almost entirely to a desire to see Senator Long suffer," *Times-Picayune* sports columnist William McG. Keefe wrote. "I have no doubt that 99 per cent of those Louisianians who were glad to see the Tigers lose will, in their broader-minded moments, feel proud of the desperately game battle the Tigers waged." Looking forward to the next week's season finale against Oregon in Tiger Stadium, Keefe observed, "If it would be possible for those who pulled against L.S.U. to get Senator Long out of their minds for a while, I'm sure L.S.U. would have almost 100 per cent moral support next Saturday."[16]

For most of the past two football seasons, Long had kept his nonintervention promise to Biff Jones. He seldom strayed from the bench during games and rarely suggested plays to Jones. His role before, during, and after games was that of head cheerleader and band director. That began to end when Long embarrassed Jones and his team by appointing Mickal to the state senate. And it terminated in spectacular fashion during the Tigers' 1934 season finale.

23

HOLLYWOOD'S IDEA OF A UNIVERSITY

On the afternoon of Saturday, December 15, with the Tigers trailing Oregon by two touchdowns in Tiger Stadium as halftime approached, a frustrated Long finally broke the nonintervention pledge he made to Jones three years earlier. Before the game, Jones got an inkling of what was coming. He was surprised to find Long sitting in the coach's spot on the bench. By the second quarter, Long was out of his seat and exhorting the players. When a group of players left the field after Jones sent in substitutes, an agitated Long goaded them as he denigrated Jones's coaching. Seated nearby, Jones could not help but hear and see Long's antics. Whatever forbearance he had about the Kingfish's presence on the sideline evaporated. The normally calm coach rose, flung his hat to the ground and, shaking his finger in Long's face, ordered him to stop his meddling.

A few minutes later, with LSU behind 13–7 at halftime, Long and Baton Rouge federal bankruptcy judge Edmond Talbot marched into the locker room as Jones diagrammed a defensive play on a blackboard.

"Can I talk to the team?" Long asked Jones.

Jones's reply was curt. "No."

"Who's going to stop me?"

"Well, you're not going to talk."

A stunned Long spat back, "You'd better win this game."

"Well, if I don't, I guess I'm through."

"Yes."

With that, Jones snapped. "Well, get this! Win, lose, or draw, I'm through!"

"Okay!" Long growled as he stormed off.

Asked years later why he prevented Long from speaking to the players, Jones said, "If Huey had talked two minutes and we'd won, he would have thought he was responsible and he would have been in my hair like he was in [Russ] Cohen's." As Jones returned to his team, Long encountered a bevy of fans gathered around the dressing room entrance. He implored them to understand that he only wanted to help. "Ain't I part of the organization?" he sputtered. "Why can't I talk to the boys? Why do we have to spot the other team two touchdowns?" One bold fan, a Jones supporter, told the senator, "Why don't you run the band and lay off the football team?" A surly Long did not return to the field until midway through the third quarter and, even then, sat sullen on the bench for most of the second half.[1]

Meanwhile, in the dressing room, an angry Jones abandoned diagramming defensive plays and addressed his players. Abe Mickal said he never saw his coach so disturbed. His voice quivering, Jones delivered an uncharacteristically emotional speech. "I've never asked a personal favor of you, but I am now. I want to win this game more than anything else in the world."[2]

After Jones's passionate halftime oration, the Tigers' defense held the line, but LSU remained down by six points as the fourth quarter began. Shortly thereafter, Tiger Stadium erupted when halfback Jesse Fatherree sprinted thirty-eight yards for a touchdown. The extra-point kick put LSU ahead by one point, sending a jubilant Long into what a *Morning Advocate* writer called "an Indian dance." LSU kept the lead for a 14–13 win.

The next day, Long pretended not to understand the fuss over his halftime spat with Jones. "The first I knew of it was when I read it in the papers this morning," he told reporters. "Jones is a fair coach. Some are better and some are worse." Asked about the incident, Jones had no comment, except to offer, "I am planning to go fishing."[3]

Long had pushed Jones to the limits of his endurance. He had few options, as he knew Long would not stop meddling with a team that he considered his personal possession. "There are only two paths open to Biff," W. I. Spencer wrote in the *Morning Advocate* the Monday after the Oregon game. "He has to have full control with absolutely no interference such as the ballyhoo and injurious publicity with which Senator Long helped break down the morale of the squad in the closing weeks of the past season. Or else he has to quit." Spencer noted that Long also had a decision to make. "Senator Long can laugh it off and use better judgment in his dealings with the football team in the future on and off the field. Or he can go ahead and try to run the squad—very much to his eventual sorrow."[4]

Jones and Long both thought better of their quarrel in the game's immediate aftermath, but when news of their confrontation hit the local newspapers, neither man backed down. Smith and others tried to persuade them to bury their differences, fearing that the fallout from Long firing the football coach—on the heels of the *Reveille* episode—would inflict irreparable harm on LSU's reputation. "Biff does not want to hurt the university for which he has already done much good," *New Orleans Item* sports editor Fred Digby wrote the day after the Oregon game. "Everyone closely in touch with the athletic situation at L.S.U. knows that Jones has been responsible for the enviable reputation the Tigers have gained for the last three years for sportsmanship on the field and gentlemanly conduct off it."[5]

By Monday afternoon, however, the break was complete. Jones asked President Smith to relieve him of coaching duties, leaving him employed at LSU, at least temporarily, as an assistant professor of military science and tactics. He soon departed to coach at the University of Oklahoma. In 1954, having finished his 87–33–15 coaching career at the University of Nebraska, Jones was inducted into the College Football Hall of Fame.[6]

Before he left town, Jones went to see Long. "They had a friendly chat," LSU athletic director Skipper Heard recalled. "The last thing Huey said was, 'Biff, if I can ever do a favor for you, please let me know.' They shook hands and parted friends." Asked by a reporter why he resigned, Jones said that Long "simply couldn't understand that a coach doesn't like to be interfered with." The *State-Times* reported that "congratulatory telegrams from all parts of the country poured into Captain Jones' office. All of them commended his stand against the kingfish's dictatorship and many offered him coaching jobs."[7]

As Jones departed, he left behind not only a stellar record (20–5–6, during three seasons at LSU); he also stood out as the only prominent LSU official willing to rebuke Long. It may have cost him his job, but Jones arrived in Oklahoma with his dignity intact. "The faculty of Louisiana State," columnist George Currie wrote in the *Brooklyn Daily Eagle*, "dedicated to seek truth where it may be found to the confusion of ignorance has steadfastly said neither yes nor no to Huey's brainstorms. It remained for a football coach to have the gumption to stand up to the brass band Senator and in effect tell him to go jump into the lake."[8]

L ong's feud with Jones and his role in pushing the coach out of his job angered football players and others around LSU's football program. "A campus uprising was averted only by Captain Jones' refusal to make any statement on the 'break' with Long or to discuss the situation with the players," Fred Digby wrote in the *New Orleans Item* on December 21. Digby quoted one source at LSU who said faculty and athletic leaders had counseled players, "Forget Long and Jones and their quarrel and think of the university. The Senator and the Captain will be gone and forgotten eventually but the university is here to stay." That message assuaged a few players, but Digby reported that most of the team, "loyal to Jones and sick and tired of having Long dinned into their ears, are ready to kick over the traces." It was not just those around LSU who were appalled by Long's recent behavior. Early in 1935, Hal Reynolds, chairman of the Rose Bowl, told the sports editor of the *Atlanta Constitution,* "as long as Huey Long is at LSU, LSU will never play in the Rose Bowl, no matter what its record is."

Long and Smith averted the potential player uprising by quickly announcing that LSU would hire a "nationally known" coach to replace Jones. Long floated the names of prominent coaches like the University of Chicago's Clark Shaughnessy (a successful former coach at Tulane and Loyola), Alabama's Frank Thomas, and Manhattan College's Chick Meehan. But Smith and Heard knew that the unfavorable national headlines that Long created made it impossible to hire such a coach. Even after the embarrassment of Jones's resignation, Long insisted he would continue supervising the football team. "I have fired the Third Street coaches [downtown Baton Rouge naysayers] and transferred the coaching to the state Capitol," Long announced the Thursday after the Oregon game. He complained about outside advice he received from LSU supporters. "There was a bunch of 'em in here a little while ago trying to tell me about a new coach," he said. "I wouldn't let 'em tell me." Long was serious. He offered the job to Thomas and Shaughnessy, among others. Shaughnessy and Vanderbilt coach Dan McGugin told Long that the best candidate for the position was LSU assistant coach Bernie Moore.[9]

Long and LSU bowed to reality by Christmas. Smith announced the school had hired Moore, the popular yeoman who was Cohen's chief scout and coached the freshman football squad. Moore had also been LSU's successful head track-and-field coach since 1930. His team won the 1933 national track championship, and he was the assistant coach of the 1932 US Olympic track team. Long supported Moore's hiring, while pretending he

Biff Jones's replacement as head football coach was Bernie Moore (*left*), who was tolerant of Long's interference with his team. (Photo by Leon Trice, Louisiana State Archives)

had not participated in the selection. He claimed Moore "was the choice of university officials and the football team, so he's okay with me."[10]

Moore may have won the job partly because he was so agreeable to interference from Long. He told a reporter after his appointment that Long was always welcome to speak to his team. "It's his team, isn't it?" he said. Asked to elaborate, Moore explained, "Why, don't you know that a great many very fine boys are now getting the best possible education at LSU? They talk about our football team being recruited, but don't you believe it. They're not at school to play football. They're on the campus to study. Their marks prove that." Moore pointed to Abe Mickal, who majored in premedical education. "Mr. Long made these things possible for us," Moore said. "So, if he wants to give pep talks, why shouldn't he? He can give a better pep talk than I can, anyhow." Moore was a brilliant choice and one of the most successful football coaches in LSU's history, even though Long would not live to see it. In Moore's first three seasons, LSU lost only one SEC game and amassed an overall 27–5–1 record. Moore remained LSU's coach through the 1947 season. His record at LSU—83–39–6—earned him membership in the College Football Hall of Fame in 1952. From 1948 to 1966, he served as commissioner of the Southeastern Conference.[11]

L ong may have pretended that he had nothing to do with Moore's employment, but he entertained no such pretense about hiring a new director for LSU's Regimental Band. For several years, Long had known the leader of the house orchestra at the Roosevelt Hotel in New Orleans. José Castro-Carazo was a thirty-nine-year-old native of Costa Rica. A musical prodigy and a child of privilege—his father had been chief justice of Costa Rica's Supreme Court—Carazo studied music at his country's National Conservatory (now the University of Costa Rica's School of Music), graduating at thirteen. By his eighteenth birthday, Carazo had earned an advanced degree in composition and orchestration from Spain's respected Royal Conservatory of Music. He was an accomplished violinist, conductor, and arranger. Before arriving in New Orleans in 1922, he had toured the United States with several orchestras and bands. In New Orleans, he adopted the stage name "Castro Carazo" and was music director for the Saenger Amusement Company's Grand Orchestra, working first at the company's Strand Theater, then at its newer Saenger Theater. In the early 1930s, Carazo went back to Costa Rica, where he served as general director of military bands. He soon returned to New Orleans and, in 1933, became orchestra conductor for the Roosevelt Hotel's new Fountain Room. The venue was popular for elegant dining and dancing, and WWL radio, with its new studios in the hotel, often broadcast his orchestra's performances.[12]

Among Carazo's new patrons was then-governor and, later, senator Huey Long. "Although I had known Governor Long for quite a while," Carazo recalled, "it was more or less in a 'passing acquaintance' manner. Occasionally, we would meet downtown, or at social gatherings and notwithstanding the fact that he always was nice and kind to me, yet it was a polite, distant attention." One afternoon in August 1933, during rehearsal with his eighteen-member dance orchestra, Carazo noticed Long slip into the dining room and take a seat at a table. After listening for a while, Long asked if Carazo had the sheet music for "Smoke Gets in Your Eyes," a song from a Broadway show, *Roberta,* that he had attended in New York. When Carazo could not find the

In late 1934, Long hired Castro Carazo, conductor of the Roosevelt Hotel's Fountain Room orchestra, to direct LSU's Regimental Band.
(LSU *Gumbo* yearbook, 1936)

music, Long suggested they search for it in Carazo's eleventh-floor room. Long sat on the floor as the two men combed through piles of music until they found the song. When they returned to the ballroom, Carazo led the band in playing the tune. And then he turned to Long and asked, "Would you like to conduct the orchestra, Senator?"

"Do you think I could?" Long said as the bandleader placed the baton into his hands.

An amused Carazo watched as a delighted Long, often with eyes half-closed, "directed" the musicians in the song. "He was in seventh heaven."[13]

Thus began a warmer friendship between the two men. When Carazo and his orchestra performed in Baton Rouge, Long occasionally summoned the bandleader to his suite at the Heidelberg Hotel to play the piano for him. "He liked to sit on the bench beside me while I played," Carazo recalled. Long invited Carazo to accompany him to an LSU football game in late 1934, probably the December 1 game with Tulane. "He said there was something wrong with the LSU band," Carazo said. "He wanted me to listen with him, tell him what was wrong." Carazo's diagnosis was simple. "I told him it was too small, didn't put on as much of a show. It should be big, colorful, should advertise LSU." Long, always receptive to audacious displays, told Carazo, "I'd like to get the best director in the world. Where can I find him?" Carazo joked in response, "You're talking to him now."

On a Saturday, about two weeks later, Carazo encountered Long in the lobby of the Roosevelt Hotel. "Where are you going?" Long asked.

"To the Fountain Room."

"You can't. You're fired. Didn't you know [general manager] Seymour [Weiss] fired you? You're the new LSU band director."

The next day, in Governor O. K. Allen's office, Long summoned President Smith and Major Troy Middleton for a meeting. (This may have been the morning after Long's dramatic showdown with Biff Jones during the LSU-Oregon game.) There, he introduced Carazo to them as the university's new band director. "You got three bosses," Long told Carazo. "Dr. Smith, Major Middleton, and me. Don't listen to anybody else. I want you to build and buy the best band in the country."[14]

LSU announced Carazo's appointment—and A. W. Wickboldt's sudden resignation because of ill health—several days later. With Long's enthusiastic support, Carazo set about reorganizing the Regimental Band. To increase the size of the 112-person unit to Long's goal of 250—making it the largest university band in the country—LSU began offering scholarships to prospective members. "The ability to play an instrument well was not always a firm prerequisite" to band membership, Tom Continé and Faye Phillips observed in their history of LSU's band. The unit grew to 150 by fall 1935. By the end of 1936, it boasted 200 students.[15]

"I want to create a band that can play any type of music and make it an asset to LSU," Carazo told the *Reveille* after his appointment. Besides forming a concert band and a symphonic dance orchestra, Carazo said he hoped to "go on concert tours through Louisiana." And he made the band more accessible to the student body. In early April, he published in the *Reveille* the score for a melody he composed—"a dreamy fox trot"—and invited LSU students and alumni to enter a contest for the best lyrics. He promised to share the copyright with the winner, as well as half the profits from any sales of the sheet music. Within a few months, a writer for the *Reveille* noted a difference in the band after hearing the unit's performance in the Greek Theatre on April 5. "The change in the character of the playing is evident," the anonymous reviewer observed. "There is more precision, more musical rhythmic feeling. The German characteristic, of mere definite beats, has been discarded. The band is becoming more and more of a symphonic band."[16]

Carazo's presence at LSU energized Long and heightened his already intense interest in the band and the School of Music. Students and faculty members did not find it unusual to encounter Long in their building. One day, composer Gene Quaw entered the building and followed the sounds of swing music emanating from a studio. When he turned the corner, he found Long standing by a grand piano with "a girl cheerleader on each arm." Carazo was playing the piano. Long, leading the band, was also singing "in rich, low baritone," the song "Hello, Tennessee." As the band played, Long exhorted, "Get hot! We got to beat Tennessee. Everybody swing it. Dammit, I said swing it!" A Montana native who became LSU's director of social recreation, Quaw was enchanted. "I had never seen such a place," he said later. "It was like Hollywood's idea of a university."[17]

LSU *was* like a movie. In fact, a few years later, 20th Century Fox produced a musical satire on college football, based loosely on Long and LSU. The 1938 film "Hold That Co-ed" starred legendary actor John Barrymore, playing a Long-like governor, Gabby Harrigan, who exploits the football team for a local school, "State College," to generate favorable publicity for his US Senate campaign. Among other things, the governor rushes the field to offer advice to the coach (played by song-and-dance man and future California US senator George Murphy), orders the coach to put a woman place kicker on the squad, and persuades the legislature to fund a new 100,000-seat stadium. State's first game after Harrigan adopts the team is against LSU, a contest that ends in a tie. The film concludes with a game-winning touchdown by the woman placekicker against State's rival, Clayton, a cross-town, Tulane-like private university.[18]

For the eight months that they worked together, Long and Carazo enjoyed a remarkable and productive partnership. In early 1935, the two men began composing marches and other songs for LSU. Their work that year included "Darling of LSU" and "Touchdown for LSU," written two months before Long's September 1935 death, and a tune still played at LSU football games. After the 1934 LSU-Vanderbilt game, Long also composed the words to a song that he and Carazo called "Miss Vandy," and which Long dedicated to the coeds of Vanderbilt. The photograph of the Vanderbilt coed Long selected to grace the cover of the sheet music, published in summer 1935, was Lucy Ann McGugin, daughter of one of Long's friends, Vanderbilt football coach Dan McGugin.

According to Carazo, Long wrote the words to songs, to which the composer supplied the music. "He had no technical knowledge of music," Carazo maintained. "He couldn't tell one note from another. But he had an inherent love for music." As for his voice? "He had no voice for singing," Carazo recalled. As another bandleader friendly with Long remembered it, "It was a lawyer's voice." Carazo saw in Long a man with simple tastes in music, but who found it relaxing and a diversion from his stressful political life. "It was the soft, tender part of him," the bandleader believed. "He liked music that was soft, not boisterous. He didn't particularly like marches." One of Long's sisters, recalling his lifelong love of music, quoted her brother once saying, "The best way to relax is to lie down, turn on a music player, let your mind go blank and follow the music."[19]

Amid all their frenetic, intense work in 1935, Carazo said, Long never discussed politics or LSU business. Sometimes, however, Long told him, "Castro, when I'm elected president, I'm going to make you director of the Marine Band." Long enlisted Carazo in only one political chore. "He thought he needed a national number [song] to identify his [Share Our Wealth] program." In January 1935, as Long plotted his 1936 presidential run, he gave Carazo the lyrics he had written for a campaign song, "Every Man a King." Carazo provided the music overnight. The LSU band played the song, and led students in singing the words, at assemblies in the Greek Theatre in March and April. And the two men arranged for singer Ina Ray Hutton and her all-women band, the Melodears, to record it for play on a national newsreel service. Later that year, Long invited a singer to perform the song as a musical interlude during one of his national radio speeches.[20]

Despite its historical and cultural significance (singer/composer Randy Newman revived the song in his well-received 1974 album, *Good Old Boys*), "Every Man a King" was not popular during Long's lifetime. "Although the air was pleasing," biographer T. Harry Williams observed, "it lacked 'punch,' and the lines were pretentiously political and awkward to sing." Eight months later, however, Carazo would arrange the song into a minor-key dirge for Long's funeral. Carazo remained at LSU until 1941. In his post-LSU years, he gave piano lessons in his Baton Rouge home. Two of his students in the 1950s were Long's granddaughters Katherine and Pamela Long.[21]

L ong's rule over the football team and his censorship of the *Reveille* were not the only headaches the state's senior US senator caused for LSU in late 1934. His years-long insistence on rescuing Kemble K. Kennedy and ensuring that the young man enter the legal profession caught up with LSU's Law School. Long and Smith had short-circuited the Law School's degree process in June 1933. Over the objection of the school's dean and its faculty, they had persuaded the Board of Supervisors to approve a "special diploma" for Kennedy, signed not by the Law School dean, but by Smith and Governor Allen. Kennedy received his diploma in fall 1933. These machinations, however, did not become known to the public until Kennedy appeared before the Louisiana Supreme Court's bar examining committee in early 1934. Kennedy only gained bar admission because Long forced the legislature that year to create the new State Bar of Louisiana, whose board of governors were loyal to him. Kennedy passed his bar exam on the second try in summer 1934.[22]

Kennedy may have deserved a second chance for his *Whangdoodle* misconduct and, considering that his coeditors were never penalized, his punishment was harsh by almost any standard. Long and Smith, however, did not rescue Kennedy by making an argument on the merits. Instead, they settled their scores against Dean Robert Tullis—forced by Long to retire in 1933—and then awarded Kennedy his degree by employing raw political power. By December 1934, Long's rough treatment of the Law School attracted the attention of accrediting organizations. When the Southern Association of Colleges and Secondary Schools (SACS) began investigating Long's influence over LSU—mostly because of his censorship of the *Reveille*—the Law School case also played a role. By spring 1935, the American Bar Association also took an interest in Kennedy's case.[23]

L SU was not Long's only problem in late 1934 and early 1935. The noose of federal agents who were investigating Long and his associates tightened in December 1934. Federal prosecutors in New Orleans charged eight of Long's confidants for income tax evasion, including his political treasurer and close adviser, Seymour Weiss. Prosecutors also indicted other Long intimates: Abe Shushan, president of the Orleans Levee Board, and state senator Jules Fisher and his nephew, state representative Joe Fisher, both Long legislative leaders from Jefferson Parish. (Joe Fisher, tried in April 1935, was the only Long associate convicted before the Kingfish died.)[24]

Busy planning to run for president in 1936, Long pretended not to worry about the investigations, because, as biographer William Ivy Hair noted, "Huey knew how to sidestep paper trails. He scrupulously paid taxes on all income that came to him by checks (about $25,000 in 1934)." As one of the federal prosecutors later admitted, "We have no income tax case against Huey Long. We've traced the money coming in, but it all stops at one of his lieutenants."

Despite the efforts of the US Treasury Department's chief investigator, Elmer Irey, to indict Long for tax evasion, the federal prosecutor that Roosevelt cajoled to take the case, former Texas governor Dan Moody, refused to bring charges. "We are not going to convict Huey Long before a Louisiana jury by proving he cheated on his taxes," Moody told Irey. "We may not be able to convict him if we can prove he murdered his mother, but we'll never do it on an income-tax charge." Moody added, "We might embarrass him, but he embarrasses hard, and anyhow we aren't trying to do that. We want a conviction." Irey continued pushing Moody to prosecute Long. In his memoir, he claimed that in summer 1935 he collected enough evidence to charge Long and his association over their creation of the Win or Lose Oil Corporation, which had acquired state oil leases, and that Moody promised to seek an indictment. Long died before Moody could present the evidence he had to a federal grand jury. Whatever the facts about Long's finances, it was also evident that the case against him was shot through with politics. And, as Moody had noted, it is difficult to imagine a Louisiana jury convicting Long of a crime, no matter what evidence prosecutors might have presented.[25]

Far from assuming a defensive posture, Long fought back against what he perceived as partisan attacks on him and his organization by Roosevelt's prosecutors. He helped defeat Roosevelt's proposal for US membership in the World Court and led the Senate fight to amend the president's work relief bill to require the federal government to pay a "prevailing" wage. Then, he turned his sights on Roosevelt's postmaster general, James Farley. Long baited the administration and its Senate allies into a bitter, protracted argument over what he alleged was Farley's corruption. He also challenged the Roosevelt administration's attempts to withhold federal funds for public works projects in Louisiana. "No public works money is going to build up any share-the-wealth machine," Interior secretary Harold Ickes vowed in April 1935. Long responded that Ickes could go "slam bang to hell." Regarding Farley, Long said that if he "must kneel to such crooks as may be employed by men like Jim Farley, God send me to hell before I bring myself to go through that kind of thing to get patronage."[26]

24

MAKE THEM STEAL FOR
THE SCHOOLS

Long was rarely so distracted by national and state politics that he neglected LSU. In early January 1935, for example, he made two remarkable announcements, reported in newspapers across the state: "Sen. Huey Long said tonight that Louisiana State University doctors had discovered a cure for cancer and that [LSU] had bought radio station WDSU New Orleans for $100,000 to broadcast the cure to the world." Asked to explain, Long boasted that researchers had "developed a cancer treatment with marvelous results and we expect to get hold of people in time to treat them." Later, Long elaborated, "They speak of doctors searching for a cancer cure all the time, but everyone is going to know that Dr. LSU has found that cancer cure." As for the radio station purchase, authorized by the legislature in December, Long said, "I believe everything is settled." What would the university broadcast on its new station? "Everything," Long replied, adding, "Right now, a good bit of attention will be directed to medical treatment developed" at LSU.[1]

Long misunderstood or misspoke. Although willing to talk with LSU about a deal, WDSU's owners had no desire to sell. And LSU had no cancer cure. "We have a cancer clinic which is constantly being improved to keep abreast of developments in the treatment of the disease," Arthur Vidrine, dean of the Medical School, explained when asked about Long's announcement, "and we use the approved modern methods and equipment, but we have not ourselves worked out a specific cure."[2]

Long was on firmer ground in February, when he bragged about board approval for new LSU schools of dentistry and pharmacy within the larger entity now called the LSU Medical Center. In December, the state's Board of Liquidation authorized Governor Allen and the LSU Board to borrow $1.1 million to construct a building for the two new schools, as well as to build more undergraduate dormitories on the Baton Rouge campus. Long said that revenue generated from increasing the state's corporation franchise tax, which he pushed through in a special session in late 1934, would service the loan. President Smith announced in January that LSU would not only create new dental and pharmacy schools but also a graduate School of Medicine and a School of Nursing.[3]

By 1935, Long could be satisfied with what he and Smith had accomplished at LSU since early 1931. He was pleased with the new buildings and programs, new and more prestigious faculty, and increased enrollment (for the LSU system, it grew to 6,065 for the 1935–36 school year).[4]

When LSU hosted a three-day convention of the National Association of Deans and Advisers of Men in February, the four-hundred-member group invited Long to address a banquet on the gathering's first day. Long told the deans he envisioned a time when education—from grammar school through college or vocational—was free to every young person. He said he hoped to translate his success at LSU into a national education program. Such a plan, he said, would be financed by taxing "from the top" and, if implemented, could end poverty in the United States. "Go back home and get hold of your politicians," he exhorted. "If they are thieves, make them steal for your college."[5]

In March 1935, during a radio address over the National Broadcasting Company's network, Long sold his Share Our Wealth plan, pitched his national Share Our Wealth Society, and portrayed his education accomplishments in Louisiana as his aspiration for the rest of the country.

How happy the youth of this land would be tomorrow morning if they knew instantly their right to a home and the comforts of a home and to complete college and professional training and education were assured! I know how happy they would be because I know how I would have felt had such a message been delivered to my door.

I cannot deliver that promise to the youth of this land tonight, but I am doing my part. I am standing the blows; I am hearing the charges hurled at me from the four quarters of the country. It is the same fight which was made against me in Louisiana when I was undertaking to provide the free schoolbooks, free buses, university facilities, and things of that kind to educate the youth of that state as best I could. It is the same blare which I heard when I was undertaking to provide for the sick and the afflicted.

When the youth of this land realizes what is meant and what is contemplated, the billingsgate and the profanity of all the [James] Farleys and [Hugh S.] Johnsons in America can't prevent the light of truth from hurling itself in understandable letters against the dark canopy of the sky.[6]

The following month, at ceremonies on campus to celebrate LSU's seventy-fifth anniversary, Long reviewed what he considered his accomplishments at the university. Educational leaders from around the country and other dignitaries (including the French ambassador) had come to Baton Rouge for several days of events marking the school's milestone. When Long addressed an anniversary luncheon on April 12 at Foster Hall, he was in no mood to pretend his role at LSU had been ceremonial. He began by dismissing the notion, propounded by Smith in his introduction, that Long had not meddled with LSU. "It seems many have asked when I have interfered in the operation of the university and Dr. Smith has said that I haven't," Long said. "I am slandered by the president when he says I did not interfere." Long then launched into a lengthy and passionate defense of involvement with LSU since 1930:

I want to assert that as a matter of fact that I have interfered. I interfered when they were reducing salaries of teachers all over the United States, and I stepped in and prevented the reductions at LSU. Following that time, we found we had several lawsuits [challenging funding for the university]. It is imperative to an institution that it must have a scapegoat. Whoever builds has to get licked, so we formed a little entente down here to make Dr. Smith as white as perfection and, provided that if anybody had to be blackened up, it would be me. . . . I interfered and gave them some more money. I'm going to quit this interference at the first opportunity and give the job to Dr. Smith and let him and the others stay up nights with legislators getting the additional votes necessary to put the legislation over. . . .

You will find out that you cannot do without politicians. They are a necessary evil in this day and time. You may not like getting money from one source and spending it for another. But the thing for the school people to do is that if the politicians are going to steal, make them steal for the schools.[7]

Not at this or other anniversary events was a representative of Pennsylvania's Washington and Jefferson College. The college's president declined Smith's invitation in a letter, explaining that he believed "the high purposes of the university seem, at a distance, to have been subordinated to the political objectives of Mr. Huey Long." One university president who attended the ceremonies, Glenn Frank of the University of Wisconsin, offered implicit criticism of Long during his visit to Baton Rouge: "A too politically intimate domination of our state universities will, in time, produce 'a reptile university' to serve current political ends as [late German Chancellor Otto von] Bismarck's 'reptile press' served the political ends of the German government." Long made no public comment about the reproach.[8]

Near the end of the 1934–35 school year, law student and Long ally Joe Cawthon and the yearbook manager, Al Brumfield, called on Long at his suite in the downtown Heidelberg Hotel. They were there to deliver a copy of the 1935 yearbook, the *Gumbo,* and ensure that Long saw the effusive praise the student editors wrote in their "Tribute to Senator Huey P. Long." The *Gumbo* listed Long's accomplishments at LSU, which included "five major buildings recently erected," "securing means for the erection of others," and a two-fold increase in enrollment. "His efforts for its welfare have been unceasing. His zeal, untiring. While possessing a genuine appreciation for the past traditions and brilliant record of Louisiana State throughout the long years of its existence, this steadfast patron of the capstone of the state's educational system is eager for the realization of the greater university of tomorrow." Cawthon and Brumfield found Long barefoot and in pajamas as he welcomed them. They handed him the yearbook. "He sat on the side of his bed and when he saw the dedication," Cawthon recalled, "he cried like a baby."[9]

There was little question about Long's impact on the university over the previous four years. Even harsh critics like journalist Raymond Gram Swing, who regarded Long as "a plain dictator," acknowledged his achievements. "Taken all in all," Swing wrote in the *Nation* in January 1935, "I do not know any man who has accomplished so much that I approve of in one state in four years, at the same time that he has done so much that I dislike. It is a thoroughly perplexing, paradoxical record." Swing described LSU as "a flourishing, wealthy institution, with a first-rate faculty, doing work which marks it

Grade A among the universities of the country. It has 4,000 students [actually about 6,000, including graduate students], as against 1,500 when Huey became Governor. Its equipment is superb, and it is taking a leading place in education in the South." A March 1935 editorial in the monthly university publication, the *Louisiana Leader,* was not exaggerating with this claim: "The greatest progress in the history of Louisiana State University has been made during the greatest financial upheaval in the history of the world. . . . While the development of many state institutions throughout the country has been retarded because of the lack of funds, Louisiana State University has grown and expanded as never before."[10]

The results about which Swing and others wrote were impressive, and they continued into 1935 and beyond. The university's English Department—which attracted bright lights like Robert Penn Warren, Cleanth Brooks, and Robert B. Heilman—was growing in size and stature. Other departments and colleges that expanded with the addition of distinguished faculty in the mid-to-late 1930s included the Department of Government (now Political Science), which appointed noted scholars Alex B. Daspit in 1934 and Charles S. Hyneman in 1937. By the late 1930s, the department lured gifted students from across the country, including future US senator and vice president Hubert H. Humphrey, who arrived in Baton Rouge from Minnesota in 1939 to earn a master's degree and serve on the school's debate team with Long's elder son, Russell. (Less than ten years later, the two LSU graduates would take their US Senate seats within four days of each other.)

Also flourishing was the Law School, which hired Thomas A. Cowan, a prominent administrative law specialist from Catholic University, as well as Harvard University Law School graduates Gordon Ireland, Jerome Hall, and Leavenworth Colby, the school's first law librarian; the College of Commerce, which appointed former Penn College president Harlan L. McCracken to teach economics; the Department of Fine Arts, which named as chair a well-known artist, John Sites Ankeney; the Department of History, which hired Harvard graduate John D. Barnhart; the Department of German, which appointed noted scholar Karl J. R. Arndt; and the School of Music, which added to its faculty several respected artists, including Stefan Sopkin, a renowned concert violinist from the Cincinnati Conservatory of Music; Louis Hasselmans, a prominent cellist and conductor from the Metropolitan Opera; and a world-famous opera baritone, Pasquale Amato. By 1939, LSU's faculty ranks grew to almost six hundred (all white).[11]

And the campus continued growing. LSU had sixty-two new buildings by the end of 1935, well beyond the halfway mark of the ninety-six structures the university hoped to construct when officials approved plans for the new campus in the early 1920s. From 1934 through 1935, the school opened or expanded ten buildings. Those included the Arts and Sciences Building (now Oscar K. Allen Hall); the French House; an enlarged west side of Tiger Stadium to include dormitory rooms for an additional 295 men; reconstruction of the old Alumni Hall (now the Journalism Building); and five other dormitory units, including the Graduate Women's Dormitory (since demolished, but which sat near the current Law Center building). In May, the university borrowed $526,000 for another stadium expansion, as well as to remodel and enlarge the cafeteria building, Foster Hall.[12]

Meanwhile, 110 men, employed by the Louisiana offices of the Civil Works Administration and the Emergency Relief Administration, cleared a swampy area east of the campus (now the University Lakes). Workers cut cypress trees from the swamp and sawed them into lumber, which they used in construction projects at LSU (including the rebuilt Alumni Hall) and around town. Next, they dug a canal to drain the water, removed tree stumps, and converted the former swamp into a series of shallow lakes. On another part of campus, behind the Greek Theatre, workers supervised by dean of administration James Broussard and local landscape architect Steele Burden were excavating the area to build a sunken azalea garden. The university expanded by an additional 665 acres in August, when LSU bought a tract of alluvial land three miles south of the new campus (part of the former Hope Estate Plantation) for use as a "student farm."[13]

As good as this news was for Long, there was still the matter of the national condemnation of his appalling behavior in late 1934, particularly his censoring the *Reveille*. There were also the various investigations by accrediting bodies into whether the university was governed, not by its Board of Supervisors, but by the state's senior US senator. In March, a committee of the Southern Association of Colleges and Secondary Schools (SACS) arrived in Baton Rouge as its investigation into Long's dominance of LSU intensified. That month, the Association of American Law Schools also sent a representative to the campus (the second visit since fall 1934) to inquire about Long's control of the Law School and his role in awarding Kemble K. Kennedy his diploma. Instead of pretending he had little or no say in the school's administration (he was now serving on the LSU Board), Long seemed to double down on the notion that he oversaw the school. "I am the head of Louisiana State University," he said in late March when he visited the University of South Carolina.[14]

The American Bar Association made its move in May, placing LSU's Law School on probation and questioning the process by which Kennedy received his diploma. Long responded with venom, labeling the group "a bunch of corporate lawyers." He claimed the organization had no legitimate jurisdiction in the matter. "The American Bar Association has no more legal status to control schools and colleges than I have in the government of China. Louisiana will tell them to go slap dab to hell. They haven't got a damn thing to do with Louisiana."[15]

The scandal resulting from LSU's expulsion of the "Reveille Seven" continued to attract unwelcome attention from national organizations. In April, representatives from about seventy-five southern universities—the Allied Associations of Southern Student Leaders and Editors—met in New Orleans and issued a statement condemning LSU's "subserviency" to Long. They also praised "the courage and fearlessness" of former *Reveille* editor Jesse Cutrer.[16]

Long's dominance at LSU even found its way into a speech by Rhode Island governor Theodore Francis Green when he accepted an honorary law degree from Rhode Island State College in June. "We have seen within the past year the evils of demagoguery pounding upon a state college," Green told graduates on June 10, declining to refer to Long by name. "When the day comes that a political boss of the most flagrant sort can dictate to the administration, the faculty, and even the opinions of a student publication then, indeed, we have come about as far from democracy as we can without entirely submerging ourselves in the tyranny of fascism." Green, who later served in the US Senate with Long's son Russell, vowed, "We are not going to allow that sort of thing to happen here in Rhode Island."[17]

Among those on the LSU campus worried about the way Long was tarnishing the university's reputation were the editors of the school's new literary journal, the *Southern Review:* Graduate School dean Charles Pipkin, and English faculty members Cleanth Brooks and Robert Penn Warren. Soon after the journal's debut in July 1935, the three men realized that some critics associated their publication with Long. "Generally," wrote one historian of the journal, "there was surprise that anything coming from LSU, the 'darling' of the senator, could be so markedly 'liberal.'" Brooks and Warren later acknowledged they fretted about the possibility Long might interfere with their work, which never happened. Brooks believed Long "had bigger fish to fry."

The exiled former editors of the *Reveille,* now finishing their studies at the University of Missouri, may have disputed Warren's and Brooks's view of Long's inattention to what LSU published. In summer 1935, however, Pipkin and his colleagues could not be so sure Long would leave them alone, or that critics would believe it when they asserted that he exercised no control over their work. In particular, they worried Long might notice the *Southern Review.* If he did, how would he react? With indifference, incomprehension, or retribution? To assert their editorial independence, Pipkin suggested the journal publish an article in which the editors declared, obliquely, their opposition to Long's policies. For that article, they recruited one of Long's fierce critics, Norman Thomas, the Socialist Party of America's presidential candidate in 1928 and 1932. Thomas, who had lectured on "Aims of Socialism" at LSU in February 1934, was invited to review a new book, *The Need for Constitutional Reform,* by historian (and Franklin Roosevelt advisor) William Yandell Elliott. The editors encouraged Thomas to discuss Long's rule of Louisiana and his Share Our Wealth proposal. Thomas agreed to draft the essay, which would run in the journal's December 1935 issue. The editors knew that, with even the mildest criticism of Long in a university-subsidized publication, they could seal their fate and that of their new journal. Long, however, would not live to see the publication's second issue.[18]

Investigations and public condemnation by political leaders, like Rhode Island's governor, were not the only problems Long was causing LSU. The Roosevelt administration continued withholding funding for public works projects in Louisiana. FDR's aides argued that, because Long's organization controlled Louisiana government, the federal government lacked assurance that federal dollars would be spent properly. In 1934, the Public Works Administration (PWA) rejected LSU's application for a $1.5 million construction grant. University officials were now back with another funding request, hoping the PWA would approve a million-dollar grant to finance a building for LSU's planned schools of pharmacy and dentistry. PWA administrator Harold Ickes, who engaged in a public feud with Long for months, refused to consider the LSU application.[19]

A delegation of Louisiana officials, including President Smith, went to Washington on July 16, hoping to persuade Ickes that the funds would not be misspent. "They assured me that there would be no interference by any state board with these two projects," Ickes wrote in his diary about the meeting. Ickes told the group such assurances were meaningless until Long relinquished control over federal projects in Louisiana. "I explained that we would not allow ourselves to be put in the position of being permitted to go ahead with a project in Louisiana merely by grace of one of Huey Long's boards." Ickes noted that Long argued Louisiana was well off "and didn't need any help from the Federal Government." When Smith asked why Ickes's agency had not yet ruled on grant applications from LSU, Ickes said, "I told him that some people believed that this wasn't so much an educational institution as it was a political institution." Ickes recalled that Smith "took great exception to that statement." As the group prepared to leave, Ickes reminded them he imposed the same rule on Louisiana that he applied to other states: "I said so long as this was Federal money, we would exercise the right to allot and supervise its expenditures without any interference from any outside authority."[20]

A mid his battles with Roosevelt and with other political adversaries in the Senate (not to mention his constant attention to political events in Louisiana), Long still found time to nurture his beloved football team. He instructed LSU's Athletic Department in early 1935 to hire *Washington Times* sportswriter Harry Costello to generate national publicity for the school's sports programs, particularly its football team. A beefy former Georgetown University quarterback—he played from 1910 to 1913—Costello later coached at the University of South Carolina and the University of Detroit before enlisting in the Army at the beginning of the First World War. After the conflict, he went into sports journalism, writing for the *New York World* before moving to Washington, where Long noticed him. "He's a man of strong feelings," a *New Orleans Item* columnist wrote about Costello. "Has boundless enthusiasm. Is entranced with his new job. Thinks L.S.U. is a grand institution. And his purpose is to acquaint the world with that fact." Long no doubt hired Costello because he thought the journalist-cum-pitchman would also better acquaint the world with Huey Long. Given that Long often declared his oneness with the football team, that obvious point went unwritten in most columns about the reporter's job at LSU. Assistant Coach Harry Rabenhorst understood the move: "Costello built up LSU in his stories—and Huey."[21]

Now that he had a coach in Bernie Moore who was tolerant of his meddling, Long began appearing at team practices again. He arrived at a spring practice in early March in a cloud of dust, just as the offensive and defensive squads were lining up. Moore did not seem to mind as Long leaped from his car, sprinted onto the field, and crouched near the offensive line. "I always like to stand behind the attacking team," Long told reporters after the practice, "and these LSU boys [offensive linemen] are always better than they are on defense." Long also boasted about his hopes for the team's upcoming season. "They'll whip any team in the country this season." Long raised expectations later that month for another train trip like the caravan he led to Nashville the previous October—this time to New York City for the October 12 game against Manhattan University. "I'm trying to get a twenty-dollar round-trip rate for you students," he said on March 19, after he summoned the student body to the Greek Theatre. So keen was Long to win that year's game with Tulane—a team LSU had not defeated since 1932—that he promised Moore a $5,000 bonus if his squad could beat the Green Wave on November 30. Just as Long hoped, LSU would defeat Tulane, 41–0, to cap off its best regular season since 1908. But there would be no bonus for Moore from Long. In fact, the Kingfish would not live to see the Tigers' first football game of the 1935 season.[22]

25

BLOOD ON THE POLISHED MARBLE

L ong surely knew what his authoritarian control of Louisiana government might cost LSU. His dictatorial rule of the legislature, every state board, and cities like New Orleans and Alexandria had made it impossible for university leaders to persuade federal officials that they were running an institution free of his authority. It did not help that Long often bragged about his domination of the university. "He's going to ruin our college," one Baton Rouge woman, a leader of the anti-Long Square Deal Association's women's auxiliary, told the group in mid-January 1935. "Would you want your children to go to a school where they couldn't express their opinion?" Through tears, the woman concluded, "I believe all this will end in bloodshed, and in someone being hurt."[1]

During the legislature's regular session in April, Long reached for even more power, proposing legislation to allow the state—and, therefore, the governor—to select local election commissioners and poll watchers. Long's organization now counted the votes in all Democratic Party primary elections. The stunning move prompted state representative Mason Spencer of Morehouse Parish to tell Long: "I am not gifted with second sight, nor did I see a spot of blood on the moon last night, but I can see blood on the polished marble of this Capitol, for if you ride this thing through, you will travel with the white horse of death." House members approved the bill, 61–27.[2]

Long called a new session for July 4. "Huey Long's Louisiana 'dictatorship' celebrated Independence Day by preparing for another special session of the legislature tonight in military guarded Baton Rouge," an Associated Press reporter wrote. The story described the state of quasi–martial law that existed in the capital for much of 1935 after Long summoned the Louisiana National Guard to deter an armed citizens' insurrection aimed at toppling his authoritarian rule. In five days, he muscled through twenty-five bills with little or no debate. "This special session," the Associated Press reported on July 13, "gave Senator Long virtually every power imaginable in the Democratic state of Louisiana." Among the powers of Long's puppet governor was authority to hire and fire all public school teachers and parish and municipal employees. Opposition legislators, especially in New Orleans, were so demoralized that many did not bother to vote. Other anti-Long lawmakers surrendered to Long, understanding that the only way to persuade the state to spend money in their districts was to support him. "The last extra session of the Senator-Dictator Long's legislature has driven the final rivet in the shackles of Louisiana's white Democracy," the anti-Long district attorney of Orleans Parish, Eugene Stanley, declared, "and the Dictator-Senator Long has driven the final nail in the coffin of the political, financial, economic, and moral life of Louisiana's people."[3]

New Orleans suffered most. For years, Long had tried to bring the city's ruling machine, the Old Regulars, to heel. Now he had the power to do so, and after securing the loyalty of many former opponents in New Orleans, his new allies stripped Mayor Semmes Walmsley of his powers. When Long and the state legislature were done with the city, journalist Thomas O. Harris wrote, "the New Orleans city administration did not have enough patronage or revenue left to support the government of an incorporated village." As T. Harry Williams observed, "Huey had brought a great city almost to ruin so that he could force his will on its government. After the surrender of the Old Regulars, Huey was almost absolute in Louisiana. He wielded power such as no other American boss or leader had ever had."[4]

At Long's behest, Governor Allen called another special session in early September to further consolidate power. Long did not plan to attend the entire session, but when one of his legislative leaders summoned him on September 8, the Sunday morning after the session began, he left New Orleans for Baton Rouge. When he arrived at the Capitol, Long went to his apartment on the building's twenty-fourth floor. Instead of diving into legislative business, Long invited Castro Carazo, the LSU band director, to join him. For several hours, the two men worked on a new song that they called "Under the Louisiana Moon."[5]

Late that afternoon, Fred Frey, the dean of LSU's College of Arts and Sciences, left Our Lady of the Lake Sanatorium, where his wife was recovering from surgery. On his way home, he stopped by the Capitol's ground-floor restaurant for an early dinner. As he sat at the counter and ate his soup, Frey watched as Long, an aide, and eight to ten bodyguards swept into the room and sat near him. If Long recognized Frey as the LSU official he had accosted in November 1930 when arriving at the campus to see then-president Thomas Atkinson, he showed no sign of it. "I could hear them talking, but I could not hear what they were saying." The anxious looks of the menacing men who surrounded Long unnerved Frey. "I got so nervous I couldn't eat," he said, adding that he soon got up to leave. As he went to pay, Frey recalled, "I was afraid to reach for my [coin] purse." Frey went home, where his wife's brother told him of rumors floating around town that Long might be shot. Meanwhile, at about 5:30 p.m., an exhausted Carazo left the Capitol for his home.[6]

A few hours later, Frey returned to the hospital to see his wife. Then, after eight o'clock, he headed home. As he passed the Capitol, however, Frey stopped his car. "I thought I would go in and see how things were going," he said, adding, "And I said to myself, 'I don't have any business in the legislative hall. I better go home and see about those kids.'" He drove away into the night.[7]

Inside the building, observing the legislative action from the house of representatives' visitors' gallery, was Robert Heilman, a recent PhD graduate of Harvard University and now on the English faculty at LSU. With him was his wife, Ruth. The Heilmans had moved to Baton Rouge over Labor Day and rented a home two blocks from the Capitol. From their perch above the house floor, the couple watched in wonder as Long strode around the room, issued orders, and seemed to run the entire show. Around 9:15, as representatives prepared to adjourn for the evening, the Heilmans saw Long leave the chamber.

Long was heading for the governor's office with a group of lawmakers and bodyguards in tow. After entering Allen's outer office, the Kingfish returned to the hallway. On the opposite side of the corridor stood a young man waiting for his chance to confront the senator. Carl Austin Weiss was a twenty-nine-year-old respected ear, nose, and throat doctor who had attended LSU during his freshman and sophomore years (1921–23) before leaving for medical school at Tulane. He and Long had never met, although Long appeared at his Baton Rouge office in November 1932, demanding treatment for an irritated eye. Weiss's father, also a physician, tended to the senator, and recalled being offended by Long's persistent cursing.[8]

The younger Weiss was married to a daughter of state judge Benjamin Pavy of St. Landry Parish, about sixty miles west of Baton Rouge. The former Yvonne Pavy met Weiss—then practicing medicine at the American Hospital in Paris—in summer 1931 when she had attended the International Colonial Exposition. Yvonne and Carl married in 1933 and, in June 1935, the couple's only child, Carl Austin Weiss Jr., was born.

Weiss was at the Capitol on this night, some believed, because of a bill Long planned to push through the legislature, aimed at his enemies in St. Landry Parish. To an ally in the parish, Long once complained, "I can run hell, but I can't run St. Landry." When a group of Pavy's opponents had suggested removing St. Landry Parish from the anti-Long judge's district, Long agreed. The legislation would make it almost impossible for Pavy to be re-elected. It was a move so bold and scandalous that one of Long's aides urged him to drop the idea. "I live and die for my people," Long replied. But there was another reason Weiss may have come to the Capitol that night. One intimate believed that Long had sent word to Judge Pavy "to lay off him [or] he would say the Pavys have 'coffee blood.'" As Long understood, in 1935, the suggestion that a white man's child might be part Black was an ugly slur to most Louisiana whites.[9]

Around 9:20 p.m., Weiss pushed through the crowd huddled around Long in the hallway. According to witnesses, the physician pulled a .32 caliber pistol, aimed it at his target, and fired. Hit in the abdomen, Long staggered away and stumbled alone down a nearby stairwell. From their seats in the house gallery, Robert and Ruth Heilman heard the gunshots. "There was a strange outburst of sounds in a rapid but irregular sequence." At first, they thought it was firecrackers. "Then men came running back into the chamber below us and ducking behind desks. It had to be gunfire, though to a new young Ph.D., fresh out of Harvard, this was unbelievable." Later, Heilman learned, "We were hearing the shots that killed Dr. Carl Weiss and [Weiss's shot that] fatally wounded Senator Long."[10]

Indeed, the Heilmans heard Long's furious bodyguards empty their guns into Weiss's body. The young doctor died instantly. Meanwhile, a friend who encountered Long as he emerged from the stairwell flagged down a car and rushed him to the nearby Our Lady of the Lake Sanatorium, where Fred Frey's wife lay recovering from her surgery. At the Capitol, the State Police and other officials cordoned off the building and guarded Weiss's lifeless body until the East Baton Rouge Parish coroner, Dr. Thomas Bird, could arrive. When he appeared, Bird deputized *New Orleans Item* correspondent Helen Gilkison—Long's friend and the former *Reveille* editor and, later, censor—to help him identify the gunman. "Why, that's Dr. Weiss," Gilkison said, leaning over the body, before helping Bird search his pockets for identification.[11]

At the hospital, meanwhile, Long was still conscious as a group of worried physicians hovered over him. Among them was Charity Hospital administrator Arthur Vidrine, in Baton Rouge for legislative business. Joining Vidrine was LSU's doctor, Clarence A. Lorio, and his brother, Dr. Cecil Lorio. Long had requested that two respected surgeons from LSU Medical Center in New Orleans operate on him. But when the men failed to show—their car ran off the road en route—Vidrine commenced surgery, concerned that his patient might bleed to death without immediate intervention. "If I was going to be operated on," Dr. Isidore Cohn, then at Tulane Medical School, later said, "I would not have picked Vidrine."[12]

The Lorio brothers and another local doctor assisted Vidrine. "It was surely one of the most public operations in medical history," T. Harry Williams observed. One person present marveled, "I thought then and have since, 'What a scene.' Here was a man maybe dying, and the room was full of politicians." Clarence Lorio later said the operation "was a vaudeville show." Long's hour-long surgery at first appeared to have been successful, but it was botched. Vidrine failed to probe for damage to one of Long's kidneys. He was bleeding to death, and Vidrine may have missed a torn renal duct. By the time doctors realized their mistake, it was too late. They could have operated again but believed Long would not survive a second surgery. Instead, they made him comfortable and hoped for the best.[13]

The next day at St. Joseph's Cathedral, just two blocks from where Carl Weiss had died in a Capitol hallway the previous night, family members and hundreds of mourners gathered for the physician's funeral. Presiding over the mass was Monsignor F. Leon Gassler, the Baton Rouge priest who had been so scandalized by Professor John Earle Uhler's 1931 novel about LSU, *Cane Juice.* And seated in the pews of the packed church to pay their respects were former governor John Parker, US representative Jared Y. Sanders Jr., East Baton Rouge Parish district attorney John Fred Odom, and Robert Tullis, the former LSU Law School dean Long had deposed several years earlier. Among the dozens of floral arrangements honoring Weiss was one from Parker. To one reporter present, it appeared that every physician in the city was in attendance. It was undoubtedly the best-attended funeral of an alleged political assassin in American history.[14]

The same day, Dan McGugin, the former Vanderbilt football coach and now the school's athletic director, arrived at the nearby hospital. He had rushed to Baton Rouge from Nashville and offered his blood for a transfusion. Five students and several football players from LSU did the same. In all, Long received five transfusions, including one from state senator James A. Noe of Monroe, given before surgery. It was all for naught. A few minutes after four o'clock on the morning of Tuesday, September 10—about thirty-one hours after the shooting—Long died. He was forty-two.[15]

Speaking to reporters at the hospital, moments after Long's death, Governor Allen said, "His last idea in public affairs concerned the poor boys attending the state university. When he was being brought to the hospital after he was shot down Sunday night, he said, 'What will those boys do without me?'" Other Long associates echoed that theme. The same day, one of his closest associates, Seymour Weiss, told the *New Orleans States* what he claimed were Long's last words. "The last thing he said when he was still conscious was, 'I wonder what will happen to my poor university boys.'" The next day, E. L. Sanderson, a physician who treated Long, wrote an account for the Associated Press of his final hours. The superintendent of Shreveport's Charity Hospital, Sanderson described Long's "heroic" fight for life and what he said were his last words. "One [remark] referred to the Louisiana State University when he said: 'What will the boys and girls do if I should die?'" Sanderson also recalled that when Long's wife, Rose, entered the room a few hours before his death, he said, "Oh, Lord, don't let me die, for I have a few more things to accomplish." Sanderson, however, concluded, "I really believe his last words were those pertaining to the LSU school."[16]

In the weeks after his death, letters to Long's Senate office were answered by his secretary, Earle Christenberry, with a message that emphasized the late senator's devotion to LSU. "During his only conscious moments, his comments concerned his family and the poor boys he was educating through Louisiana State University." When he announced his candidacy for governor later that year to replace O. K. Allen, New Orleans appeals court judge Richard Leche also described Long's passing. The Long intimate who once served as Allen's top aide, Leche was among those in Long's hospital room before he died. "The school children of Louisiana and the advancement of the Louisiana State University were almost the last thoughts in the mind of Senator Long," Leche reported in December 1935."[17]

But reality differed greatly from the myth of a dying Long who cried out about his beloved university and its students. As Leche admitted in a 1960 interview, "Huey was in a coma, apparently. I never heard him utter a sound." James O'Connor—a member of the state's Public Service Commission, one of Long's closest allies, and the person who drove him to the hospital in the minutes after the shooting—did not recall any profound last words. "I don't think he said a word," O'Connor said. "Remember, he was in awful shape." Theoda Carriere, a nurse assigned to Long's hospital throughout his ordeal, had a similar recollection. "About the only thing he wanted was to get up and go to the bathroom." This does not mean that it was implausible that LSU would have been on Long's mind had he been conscious in his last hours. The university was never far from his thoughts. Only days before, on September 4, he had visited the LSU football team for the last time, dropping in to watch the squad's practice. And, among Long's personal effects when he arrived at the hospital after the shooting was the gold watch LSU students presented him at halftime during the LSU-Tulane game the previous December.[18]

O n the LSU campus—largely empty because most students were away on summer break—faculty members, staff, and a few students mourned their school's most prominent patron. A grieving Castro Carazo started work on the music for Long's funeral, to be held at the Capitol, where he would direct the state's National Guard Band. (Most LSU Regimental Band members were not attending summer school.) Taking the campaign song that he and Long created earlier that year, "Every Man a King," Carazo rearranged the piece into a minor key dirge for two measures. Next, he transitioned into a tune reminiscent of the hymn, "Nearer My God to Thee," then to the "Star-Spangled Banner," before returning to end with the minor-key version of the campaign tune.[19]

Elsewhere on campus, football star Abe Mickal, now also the LSU student body president, delegated the duty of arranging the students' expression of sympathy to one of Long's favorites, senior law student Joe Cawthon. Cawthon and two other students, Dave Herman and Harry Kron of New

Orleans, ordered a large wreath of purple and gold flowers to be placed on Long's casket. And they arranged for a unit of twelve LSU band members to serve as a guard of honor around Long's bronze casket in the Capitol's Memorial Hall while he laid in state. Band members also sent a floral replica of a harp made of purple asters and marigolds.[20]

On the afternoon of Thursday, September 12, LSU football coach Bernie Moore canceled practice to allow players to attend Long's funeral. "The L.S.U. football squad will attend the senator's funeral in a body," Mickal said on behalf of the team. "His death is a personal loss to all of us. I'm only sorry that the whole university is not here so that it could demonstrate its esteem and respect."[21]

All activity halted in Long's honor across the campus that afternoon. In New Orleans, even the rival Tulane football team stopped its practice at four, the hour Long's funeral was to begin. In Baton Rouge, as pallbearers carried Long's enormous casket down the Capitol steps toward his grave in the nearby sunken gardens on the building's grounds, the state's National Guard Band played the dirge Carazo had arranged.[22]

A few days after the funeral, LSU announced plans for its own memorial service for Long after the fall semester began. And the faculty, in a statement, mourned him as a "benefactor and friend . . . who cannot be replaced." Noting the many physical reminders of Long on the campus and conveying its sympathy to his family, the faculty statement concluded, "it is seldom that there has been a leader in government who had taken such a personal interest in the welfare and development of the university." Long's sudden death left some wondering what his disappearance from Louisiana politics would mean for the university. "The pomp and ceremony of Huey Long's pet project—Louisiana State University—has lost its master's touch," a United Press reporter observed. "Whether the school will continue as he outlined, to become one of the outstanding academic centers in the country, was a matter Long himself couldn't foresee."[23]

The day before Long's funeral, LSU released figures on enrollment for the fall semester, set to begin on September 22. A record 6,065 students, the largest number so far in LSU history, were expected on the school's campuses (Baton Rouge, the Medical School in New Orleans, and the junior college in Monroe). On the Baton Rouge campus, 5,500 students would attend, joined by seventeen new faculty members. The numbers made LSU the tenth largest public university in the country.[24]

If anyone worried that Long's influence and legacy might disappear from LSU now that he was dead, they were wrong. A tangible reminder of the late senator was on his way to campus. Long's sixteen-year-old son, Russell—still in mourning—was beginning his first year at LSU, after his father had forbidden him from enrolling at Princeton University. "My God," Huey had complained when Russell told him he did not wish to attend LSU, "here I have worked and strived and risked impeachment to build a university here that a state can be proud of, that people can send their sons and daughters to, and it's not good enough for my own son." That semester, Russell was elected freshman class president.[25]

26

THE SECOND LOUISIANA PURCHASE

Not much changed at LSU in the weeks after Long's death. The fall semester began on schedule. The football team practiced for its September 29 season opener in Tiger Stadium against Rice University. And the Southern Association of Colleges and Secondary Schools (SACS) and the Association of American Law Schools (AALS) pressed their cases against LSU's administration for having submitted to Long's iron will. A SACS committee visited Baton Rouge in mid-October to collect evidence, which encompassed more than Long's domination of LSU. SACS also wanted to know more about Long's influence over hiring and firing teachers in Louisiana's public elementary and secondary schools.[1]

Hoping to end the SACS probation, the LSU Board of Supervisors voted on November 30 to affirm the university's autonomy and vowed that it would "continue to resist all types of outside interference with curricula or extracurricular activities." The board authorized President Smith "to protect in every legal way at his command the University from such interference." Now that Long was gone, and the LSU Board declared its independence, the impetus for the SACS inquiry dissipated. In early December, the organization dropped its investigation of LSU.[2]

LSU's Law School was not so fortunate. Meeting in New Orleans for its annual convention in late December, the AALS censured the school. Over the university's fierce protests, the association released an extensive, scathing indictment of the university. It said, in part:

> The executive committee is thoroughly convinced that the late Huey P. Long, while governor and senator of Louisiana, exerted undesirable and far-

reaching political influence over the educational institutions of the state, giving rise to problems by no means confined to the college of law. This pernicious influence permeated the whole educational structure. The [state's] budget law empowered the administration to control the selection of teachers in the parish schools and this power was exercised for political ends. Moving upward from the base of the educational pyramid of the State University, the executive committee finds there is political interference with academic freedom and proper administration.

The committee criticized LSU for Long's role in the "Reveille Seven" episode; the involuntary retirement of Law School dean Robert Tullis; offering the Law School dean position to the University of Oregon's Wayne Morse "by long distance telephone"; the forced resignation of Coach Biff Jones; and awarding Kemble K. Kennedy a law diploma without the dean's approval. Smith also admitted to investigators that the university physician, Clarence A. Lorio, "was a political appointee" that Long had forced him to hire. "In the opinion of the executive committee," the AALS wrote, "these instances indicate impingement of political pressure upon the affairs of the university in general and at the college of law in particular, contrary to the ideals, standards and traditions for which this association stands." The organization's report concluded:

> It is true that death has removed the personal influence of Huey P. Long. It is also true that, in certain matters not directly responsive to the criticism above stated, gratifying improvements have occurred in the college of law. Since the incidents above summarized, salaries have been raised, the faculty enlarged, library expenditures increased, library administration improved, office accommodations and secretarial service provided, but these are material things and not things of the spirit. . . .
>
> Whatever confidence [this] committee has as to the future of the College of Law of Louisiana State University rests principally on the fact that Senator Long is dead. But the committee is by no means sure that a successor to his ambitions and influence may not arrive, and nothing in President Smith's past record has appeared which indicates that he would make a courageous fight for independence. We think an attitude of anxious solicitude for the college of law should be maintained and recommend that this association instruct the incoming executive committee accordingly.[3]

LSU Law School dean Frederick Beutel rejected the association's conclusions, declaring "there is no political influence" at LSU. He insisted that the university was in "perfect shape" and that he welcomed weekly investigations by the association. Smith's response to the report, which singled him out for special scorn, was more cutting and suggested that he was not worried about losing the support of Long's political organization. "The university is but little concerned with the findings of the committee, as it is evident that the report was drawn up and presented by the inspectors after hobnobbing with certain politicians, and that does not represent an impartial investigation of the law school or affairs of the university." Kemble K. Kennedy echoed Smith, telling a reporter the AALS statement "was hatched in the brains of Yankee law professors . . . after consultation and collaboration by the alleged investigators with rabid anti-Long and disgruntled politicians." The leader of the investigation, the dean of Ohio State University's Law School, called Smith's criticism "absurd," adding, "Most of the facts found were deduced from statements of, or admissions by, President Smith himself to various investigators." Another AALS official added, "This institution is getting off extremely light and should consider itself lucky."[4]

L ong's death was a tragedy for his family and friends but a boon for LSU, despite the troublesome, lingering investigations. In Long's absence, less-divisive leaders emerged to guide his organization and repair relations with President Roosevelt. In January 1936, Richard Leche, the New Orleans appeals court judge who had been Governor Allen's top assistant, won the Democratic Party primary for governor. A tall, pudgy, gregarious thirty-eight-year-old politician, Leche had attended Tulane University before he volunteered for the US Army during the First World War. After the war, he spent a few years in the Midwest selling cars before returning to New Orleans and entering Loyola Law School. After practicing law for several years, he lost a state senate election in 1928. Leche entered Long's orbit shortly thereafter and helped manage the Kingfish's 1930 US Senate race.[5]

Leche's true role in Allen's office had been to help Long monitor the figurehead governor. In the weeks after Long's death, the leaders of his organization had feuded over who would take the political reins. Self-described as "252 pounds of Huey Long candidate," Leche claimed Long had anointed him successor. Several others asserted their claim to Long's blessing. But,

Governor Richard Leche in front of the LSU Law School building, which the school named after him. (Richard Leche Papers, LSU Special Collections)

with the support of his former boss—a term-limited Governor Allen—Leche won the grudging loyalty of most in Long's organization. He ran for governor, and Long's younger brother, Earl, for lieutenant governor. Both won. Allen, however, did not live to see Leche take office. He died of a brain hemorrhage on January 28, 1936, just three months before his term ended. (Because the lieutenant governor, John B. Fournet, had resigned to take a seat on the state supreme court, the senate's president pro tempore, James A. Noe of

Monroe, became governor and served out the remaining fifteen weeks of Allen's term.)[6]

Although Leche was head of Long's political organization, his election signaled the end of Washington's punishment of Louisiana and LSU over Long's autocratic control of the state. Leche hurried to repair relations with President Franklin Roosevelt. He went to Washington in April, before his May inauguration, to meet with the president and interior secretary Harold Ickes. "While I am not taking home any federal money in my grip," Leche said after his White House meeting, "I am convinced that in the future Louisiana will get from the federal government everything the state reasonably may expect."[7]

Once in office, Leche persuaded legislators to repeal many of the oppressive so-called "dictator" laws that troubled Roosevelt and Ickes and which had stopped federal Public Works Administration and Works Progress Administration money from flowing to Louisiana. In June, Leche, Lieutenant Governor Long, and US senator-elect Allen Ellender led the legislature to Dallas, where Roosevelt attended the Texas Centennial Exposition. Convening in an unprecedented special session at the Cotton Bowl, Louisiana lawmakers adopted a resolution endorsing Roosevelt's reelection. In a flash of showmanship reminiscent of Huey Long, Leche brought along the LSU Band, whose members serenaded Roosevelt as he departed the exposition. Leche went to Washington the following month to continue courting Ickes. He told reporters as he left that "the atmosphere had completely changed."[8]

In November 1936, Leche invited Harry Hopkins, one of Roosevelt's closest aides, also the administrator of the Works Progress Administration, to Baton Rouge for the annual LSU-Tulane game. The WPA financed the latest stadium expansion, a $700,000 project that completed the horseshoe shape of the stadium, added new dormitory rooms for 1,000 more students, and installed 4,000 additional stadium seats. (By 1938, the stadium housed 1,754 students.) Leche and LSU feted Hopkins, gave him an honorary degree, and invited him to speak during the stadium's dedication ceremonies, carried across the country by radio on the National Broadcasting Company. To signal the university's affinity with Roosevelt's WPA, the LSU Band marched onto the field and formed the letters "WPA" while playing the "Star Spangled Banner." A promising day was complete when LSU beat Tulane, 33–0.[9]

In March 1937, university officials hosted First Lady Eleanor Roosevelt, who delivered a lecture, "A Typical Day at the White House," to students in

At the 1938 LSU-Tulane game in Tiger Stadium, university officials feted Harry Hopkins, one of President Franklin Roosevelt's top aides. To recognize the role that Roosevelt's Works Progress Administration had played in the recent stadium expansion, the LSU Band formed the letters "WPA" on the field while playing "The Star-Spangled Banner." (Richard Leche Papers, LSU Special Collections)

the Gym Armory. Leche showed up to welcome President Roosevelt the following month when he and Eleanor visited New Orleans to dedicate a WPA project at City Park. In late May, LSU hosted another former Long nemesis, Postmaster General James Farley. The Roosevelt administration official who Long once attacked as corrupt now praised Long and his university. "[LSU] is, in truth, an institution which embodies the democratic principle of opportunity for all, rich and poor, young and old, men and women," Farley said in his commencement address at the Greek Theatre. "It is fitting, therefore, that adequate recognition be given by the state and by the nation to the part played by one of your outstanding leaders in the development of this institution. Some of his accomplishments may grow dim with the passing of time, but this university will remain for centuries as a monument to the unselfish zeal in the cause of education of your late distinguished United States senator Huey P. Long."[10]

Farley's effusive praise for Long was the result of the relentless self-effacement of Leche, Smith, and other state officials who labored to ingratiate themselves with Roosevelt and his aides. "Louisiana State University was lucky in that it got the advantages of dictatorship without getting all the disadvantages," journalist Don Wharton wrote in *Scribner's* in September 1937. "It was saved from having to pay in full for Huey's services rendered. One doesn't like to say so, but it can't be avoided: Huey's death was a boon to the University. Had Weiss missed ... L.S.U. would hardly be worth examining today—save as a curiosity. Huey Long was building its physical plant, but he was undermining everything else."[11]

The result of the rapprochement between Roosevelt and the Leche-run Long organization was a flood of federal money into Louisiana, particularly at LSU. Some called it "the second Louisiana purchase." Now, there was money to complete the LSU Medical Center complex in New Orleans. The federal WPA-funded construction of the Physics and Math Building (now Nicholson Hall), an expanded agricultural complex (now Dodson and Audubon halls), expansion of the Sugar Plant to include a new chemical engineering laboratory, the Panhellenic Building, the Infirmary, the baseball stadium (named in 1943 for an LSU graduate and World War II hero, Alex Box), and the Coliseum (later named for Governor John M. Parker). Other federal money went to building more sidewalks, paving streets, and for drainage projects. PWA grants paid for the Commerce Building (now Himes Hall), the Faculty Club, three new dormitories in the so-called "Evangeline group," and the Law School building (briefly named Leche Hall and modeled after the US Supreme Court building). By the end of 1938, the campus had seven dormitories for over 1,200 women students to accommodate the rapid growth of coeducation on the campus. More than half of the 2,700 male students on campus in 1938 lived in four-person rooms in Tiger Stadium. Enrollment at all the LSU campuses—in Baton Rouge, New Orleans, and Monroe—continued to grow, from about 7,000 in the fall of 1936 to over 7,600 the next school year.[12]

With Long out of the picture, LSU's future appeared bright, and uncomplicated by the undue influence of a powerful politician. Despite what seemed like a new era of progress for the state's leading university, however, scandal lay just around the corner.

27

THE LOUISIANA SCANDALS

Huey Long once told a colleague, "You know, my friends are the ones who get me in trouble. I can take care of my enemies." To another associate, he remarked, "If those fellows ever try to use the power I've given them without me to hold them down, they'll all land in the penitentiary." Long told journalist Forrest Davis in 1935, "I ain't the dictator of Louisiana. I have my ideas, my program, and my organization down there. I mess around with what goes on a good bit. Things get out of hand when I don't." Most pointedly, speaking about his associates, he once warned a lawyer for the Louisiana Highway Commission, "If I lay down and die tomorrow, half these bastards will be in the penitentiary before day after tomorrow." As journalist Alva Johnston wrote in the *Saturday Evening Post* in 1940: "Huey was a mixture of genius and larceny; his successors had no genius." Long dynasty biographer Stan Opotowsky put it best: "Whereas Huey had the touch, all these men had was the grab."[1]

Among those without touch or genius was James Monroe Smith. Without Long as a check on his worst instincts, Smith and his wife, Thelma, graduated to a glamorous life. They hosted lavish parties at the president's well-appointed campus home. Those around him noticed he handed out handsome tips, more than might be expected from a university leader of relatively modest means. Smith's ostentatious ways may have been the reason some LSU students and others in Baton Rouge referred to him as "Jingle Money Smith."[2]

Smith had outsized aspirations for the wealth and prestige that the mere presidency of LSU would never bring him. He also had outsized confidence that he could obtain such wealth and prestige by clever investing. Smith traded stocks and made other investments during his time in Lafayette, when he was a dean at Southwestern Louisiana Institute. He began with small real estate purchases and later borrowed $300 to purchase Morrison's Cafeteria stock. After Long's death, however, his appetite for magnificent wealth would be his undoing.

In December 1936, he used an agent to approach the New Orleans representatives of a national brokerage firm, Fenner & Beane, with a creative investment proposal. The agent informed the firm that Smith represented "a group of individual investors, who were people of means" who wished to invest in wheat futures, believing that when the looming war in Europe broke out, the commodity's price would skyrocket. "Their names were not disclosed to us," Fenner & Beane said later in a statement, "but the fact was impressed upon us that the trading would be on a large scale and that funds or collateral would be available at all times to meet our requirements." Smith's agent stipulated that all transactions with the firm should be recorded under the pseudonym "J. Monroe." The firm's director said Smith's plan "filled me with joy." He explained Smith "belonged to the political crowd. They had all the wherewithal in Louisiana. The old people, our former customers, were out. I felt that we were going to see the color of real money at last."

Among Smith's early misdeeds was using LSU bonds as collateral for investing $500,000 in wheat futures. He expected that the imminent outbreak of war and a spike in wheat prices would make him a wealthy man, but the conflict did not unfold as Smith expected. The Munich Agreement in September 1938 averted the higher wheat prices that Smith expected. The brokers demanded more collateral, which a desperate Smith supplied in counterfeit bonds. When the brokers insisted on proof of the bonds' legality, Smith submitted doctored LSU Board of Supervisors minutes to secure $500,000 in loans from three banks and used the money as collateral. It was not the first time Smith acted improperly. In 1937, he also used $50,000 in New Orleans Levee Board bonds, acquired from a friend on the board, to purchase a thousand barrels of Kentucky whiskey, expecting a large profit after three years.

By early 1938, warning signs abounded that all was not well in Louisiana government and at LSU. That spring, Rufus W. Fontenot, an LSU graduate who was Louisiana's federal revenue collector, picked up rumors about Smith's whiskey investments. Such speculation was not inherently illegal, but Fontenot thought, if true, it was strange behavior for a university president. He would monitor Smith. In December, Fontenot learned of Smith's activities in the wheat market. Now his antennae were up. He wanted to know where Smith acquired the money for these purchases. In January 1939, Treasury Department officials gave Fontenot permission to launch a formal investigation.[3]

Meanwhile, a disgruntled former pro-Long lawmaker, state senator James A. Noe of Monroe, was conducting his own investigation, targeting Governor Leche and other Long organization members he suspected of criminality. Long had been a close friend and business partner of Noe, who served briefly as governor after O. K. Allen's death in early 1936. In 1934, Long, Noe, Allen, and others had formed an enterprise that would make most of them and their heirs wealthy—the Win or Lose Oil Company. To Noe's lasting disappointment, however, the Long organization made Leche its leader and gubernatorial candidate in 1935. And a bitter Noe became estranged from his former political allies. In 1938, now back in the state senate, the former governor introduced eighteen measures to reign in the excesses of the Long era. His bills included civil service reforms and requiring voting machines to eliminate election fraud. Lawmakers rejected them all. "Noe methodically set about to break up the Long people," Noe's friend F. Edward Hébert, then city editor of the *New Orleans States,* recalled. "He meant to get them, and he was willing to spend God knows how much money to do it." Believing Leche's ruin was his ticket to the governor's mansion in the 1940 election, Noe resolved to destroy his erstwhile ally. Leche was an enticing target. Almost since his first days as governor, he made no secret of his desire to profit from the office, even bragging to friends, "When I took the oath as governor, I didn't take any vow of poverty." Among Leche's money-making schemes, he had paid $38,000 for Long's newspaper, the *American Progress,* and used the publication to milk businesses and local governments for advertisements and subscriptions. After inflating its value by urging Louisiana politicians to buy stock in the newspaper, he sold it to Earl Long for $200,000, realizing a handsome profit.[4]

Noe probed the Leche administration for a year and a half, amassing almost one thousand affidavits that alleged myriad crimes by officials at LSU and throughout state government. This included the organization's shake-downs of state employees—5 to 10 percent deducts from the salaries of workers in the months before statewide elections—to finance its political operations. "LSU was being mined," New Orleans journalist Harnett T. Kane wrote later. "It was a gold-rush center, with pay dirt on all sides, there for the scraping up by the favored ones. For the lesser aides, the flakes were available." Noe had urged the US Justice Department for months to turn its attention to Smith and Leche. James H. Morrison, an anti-Long congressional candidate from Hammond, also waged a public war against Leche. He questioned how the governor—a "relatively poor man"—could afford a luxurious new home in St. Tammany Parish, north of New Orleans. The *New Orleans States,* its sister paper, the *Times-Picayune,* and the *Morning Advocate* also raised questions about the Long organization under Leche.[5]

Noe also tried for months to persuade other Louisiana newspapers to investigate the Leche administration's alleged crimes, based on the sensational details of avarice and larceny in his mountain of affidavits. He had photographs of stolen hogs, grain, and gravel. But nothing he had seen was stamped "L.S.U." The photographs could not prove an association with the university or the state. But Noe was sure he had uncovered crimes and that he would find the conclusive proof. In summer 1939, he got a tip that such evidence would soon be available. An employee at LSU's Building Department informed Noe about a large quantity of university materials—including concrete, gravel, and lumber from university WPA projects—that were being diverted for the personal use of university employees, including Smith, and friends of Leche. The employee told Noe that a truckload of window frames, milled in an LSU shop, would be delivered to the Metairie home of a Leche friend, James McLachlan, on June 7. Noe tipped off his editor friend, F. Edward Hébert, at the *New Orleans States.* Lying in wait in nearby bushes as the LSU employees unloaded the frames from a university truck was a photographer for the newspaper who took dozens of photographs.

The *States* published an explosive front-page story on June 9, 1939, replete with damning pictures. Syndicated investigative journalist Drew Pearson revealed days later that the US Justice Department was investigating possible corruption in the handling of WPA funds in Louisiana. Pearson quoted from an affidavit (acquired from Noe) by a WPA assistant foreman in Louisiana who disclosed another aspect to the growing story of corruption at LSU: He said the university's construction superintendent, George Caldwell, ordered him and his crew to build a barn and a log house for Leche on property the governor owned in Covington, about sixty miles east of Baton Rouge. Another foreman said that WPA workers had fabricated sections of two small buildings at LSU and erected them on Leche's property. Pearson reported that Caldwell also presided over LSU crews that performed substantial improvements to the home and property of LSU's business manager, Edgar N. Jackson.[6]

At first, Leche and Smith dismissed the story. Leche said the newspapers "will stop at nothing calculated to injure me or my friends." Smith said the delivery to McLachlan was appropriate. "I'm sure proper compensation was made," he said. "I will look into the matter." On July 11, the *Times-Picayune* added one more confusing wrinkle. It reported on a "$464,000 mystery Geology Hall" being built on the LSU campus (the west and middle sections of what is now the Howe-Russell-Kniffen Geoscience Complex). The paper could find no one who claimed to know the source of the building's funding.[7]

Within days, everything came crashing down around the two men and others at LSU. On June 26, Smith told Leche about the illicit loans in hopes the governor would persuade the LSU Board to give him retroactive approval. Leche did not at first understand that Smith had borrowed the money for his personal investment schemes. He ordered Smith to "go on home and rest up while we look into the matter." After a quick investigation, Leche comprehended the extent of Smith's misconduct. When Smith returned later that day, he acknowledged that, besides the unauthorized loans on LSU accounts, he had "opened up a little trading account" on behalf of the university. "Well, Doc," Leche told Smith, "do you want to do it the hard way or the easy way?" Smith resigned. Several hours after Smith left, Leche ordered the State Police to arrest the former president. But the delay offered Smith and his wife time to flee before troopers could apprehend them. As a nationwide manhunt for the wayward president mounted, Leche knew his alleged crimes would soon be revealed. Citing poor health, he resigned the following day. Earl Long became governor, announcing that he supported investigating Smith and LSU "in full force," adding, "Let the chips fall where they may."[8]

For days, the Smiths' disappearance was national news. On July 1, the couple surrendered to authorities in Brockville, Ontario, on the Vermont-Canada border about one hundred miles southwest of Montreal. After waving extradition, they were soon back in Louisiana, landing in New Orleans on a commercial flight accompanied by the assistant State Police superintendent, Murphy Roden, one of Huey Long's former bodyguards. Present to cover their return were two former journalism students that Smith expelled from LSU in 1934: David McGuire (with the *New Orleans States*) and Carl Corbin (with the *Times-Picayune*). McGuire had the first question.

"Will you name your associates in your grain speculations?" he asked, as Smith and his wife waded through the throng. Smith ignored him. Then Corbin peppered Smith with more questions. "What have you got to say about the criticism of the university this case has brought about?"

"I'll answer those questions later."

Corbin persisted. "Do you think there will be another investigation of the university by the Southern Association of Colleges and Secondary Schools?"

"If there is, we will win like we did before," Smith replied, adding with rising irritation, "I don't know who you are, but you are very impertinent."

"Oh, I thought you would remember me. You kicked me out of school four years ago."

The next morning, in his story, McGuire wrote, "Five years ago when the resigned president expelled seven journalism students at the order of Senator Long, one of the reasons he gave was 'subjecting the university to unjust and unwarranted criticism and acting against the best interests of L.S.U.' He was asked by [Corbin] if his recent actions had been for the best interests of the university. He remained silent."[9]

Waiting in Baton Rouge as deputies booked Smith into the parish prison was the LSU professor Smith had fired in 1931, after his novel *Cane Juice* offended a local Catholic priest. John Earle Uhler, still a member of the English faculty, joined ten other locals, including seven LSU faculty and staff members, in signing Thelma Smith's $7,500 bail bond. "I can't help but remember that, 'There, but for the grace of God, go I,'" Uhler told a reporter when asked why he helped Thelma. Meanwhile, the former LSU president spent the night behind bars.[10]

It soon became public knowledge that, besides altering LSU Board minutes to get $500,000 in bank loans, Smith also forged Governor O. K. Allen's signature to a $1,000 LSU bond. And Smith changed board minutes to give himself and the university business manager, Edgar N. Jackson, pay raises and to award LSU's construction superintendent, George Caldwell, a 2 percent kickback on all building construction on the campus. "In addition to Smith's operations, there was a private building boom at Baton Rouge," a *Saturday Evening Post* reporter wrote. "Trainloads of material arrived for university construction projects; fleets of trucks carried it off in all directions for private use by politicians of the Long machine." By one estimate, as much as 60 percent of the concrete LSU purchased for construction after Huey Long's death went to help build nonuniversity structures.[11]

By mid-July, a state grand jury indicted Smith, Caldwell, and Jackson for diverting state-owned building materials for personal use. Also indicted in the scheme was Long's close friend and the LSU physician—now a state senator—Clarence Lorio. Smith's wife, Thelma, was indicted for "harboring, concealing and assisting" her husband's flight from Louisiana. State officials also charged several WPA foremen at LSU for stealing building materials.[12]

Investigators caught Smith and other LSU and Leche administration officials in another illegal scheme: the sale of the Bienville Hotel in New Orleans to LSU. The university bought the rundown hotel for $575,000, ostensibly to provide housing for students at LSU Medical Center. Included in the price was the hotel's $75,000 in furnishings. Smith, Seymour Weiss, and several New Orleans associates devised a scheme for making money off the deal by selling the building's furnishings to the university twice.[13]

Some corrupt officials, like Smith, went to trial in state courts. But the real action in 1940 occurred in federal court after assistant US attorney general John Rogge, a tall, idealistic, thirty-six-year-old Harvard graduate, charged many of the men with federal crimes. At first, Rogge expected to indict the officials for income tax evasion, but he and his assistants—the Justice Department assigned seventeen agents to the investigation—were stunned to find that most of the major players had paid taxes on their ill-gotten gains. Perhaps the US government's creative and successful 1931 tax evasion prosecution of Mafia boss Al Capone informed their behavior, or they were naive enough to believe they would never be caught. Whatever the case, they also broke a host of state laws, including those against kickbacks and bribes. Some of Leche's associates violated federal "hot oil" statutes (overproduction of crude oil in violation of federal quotas), but the federal crimes that Leche and others committed were not obvious.

The depth and breadth of the corruption within Louisiana government and at LSU offended Rogge's sensibilities. He worried that state officials might decline to prosecute Leche, Smith, and their coconspirators. To put these individuals in federal prison required creativity. Undeterred by the lack of evidence for tax evasion, Rogge relied on a novel legal approach that survived appeal: He charged most of the officials with mail fraud. Even though many of them had not used the mails to further their schemes, in most cases at least one person engaged in their conspiracy had. That was enough for Rogge and the courts to try them. To those who protested that he was trying to send people to prison for minor transgressions, Rogge retorted, "Major criminals should not commit minor crimes."[14]

A federal jury convicted Leche of various offenses, including mail fraud in a kickback scheme involving the purchase of trucks for the state. Among others convicted in federal court of using LSU building materials for personal use were George Caldwell; LSU's assistant construction manager, Eugene Barksdale; and Edgar Jackson, the university business manager. Senator Clarence Lorio, the LSU physician, was convicted of mail fraud connected to kickbacks on electrical contracts at LSU. Smith, Seymour Weiss, and several others were found guilty for their roles in the Bienville Hotel scheme. Juries also convicted Smith, Weiss, and Caldwell for tax evasion. Rogge and his assistants charged 149 people associated with the Long organization and LSU. Julia Welles Hawkins, a 1938 LSU graduate in teaching, recalled more than eighty years later, "Everyone who signed my diploma went to prison."[15]

A federal judge sentenced Leche to ten years for his crimes. In 1945, the former governor won his parole, and President Harry Truman pardoned him in January 1953. Smith, also sentenced to eight to twenty-four years on state charges of misusing LSU funds, attempted suicide in November 1939 on the night before his transfer from the East Baton Rouge Parish Prison to the Louisiana State Penitentiary at Angola. Smith was not the only person implicated in the "Louisiana scandals" to despair to the point of suicide. Four others took their lives before trial or before they could begin their prison sentences. Smith spent almost six years in state prison and another ten months in a federal penitentiary in Georgia. After his release in 1946, he served as the principal of an all-boys' preparatory school in Tennessee. At the time of his death in 1949, he was director of vocational rehabilitation at the Louisiana State Penitentiary.[16]

Although Governor Earl Long was part of the Leche-Long organization, he skirted the scandal. The public believed Long's story that the two estranged brothers had reconciled in the months before Huey's death. As lieutenant governor, Long had not been a central figure in the administration. And investigators could find no evidence to link him to Leche's and Smith's schemes. Long, Noe, and the others in Long's organization who were not charged with crimes maintained the scandal was a shocking betrayal of everything their martyred leader represented. They argued Leche was not the logical conclusion of Long's alleged corruption and avarice, but a subversion of his lofty principles. Earl Long also declared his independence from

Leche and his conspirators, signaling that his administration was dedicated to honest governance and accountability. He pledged to continue governing "like Huey P. Long, Oscar Allen, Jesus Christ, and God Almighty would have me do." Long and his political associates claimed Leche's criminality was an aberration. "Smith is only one man," the new governor insisted. "Don't blame everybody. Look at Jesus Christ. He picked twelve. And one of 'em was a sonofagun!" Louisiana historian Allan P. Sindler, however, observed that "the Scandals were, in reality, not a betrayal of Huey but a natural and logical fulfillment of the mass acceptance of amoral politics induced by the kingdom of the Kingfish."[17]

At LSU, the scandal was barely two months old before the university began scrubbing Smith's and Leche's monikers from its buildings. Leche's name was on plaques attached to thirty-three buildings, including the $1 million Law School building named after him and dedicated in 1938. Workers erased the former governor from the edifice by pulling out several large stone blocks onto which his last name was chiseled. They reversed the blocks and pushed them back into place. The school also removed a large bronze medallion featuring Leche's profile, installed above the building's main entrance. Bronze plaques with Leche's name also adorned almost every pillar in Tiger Stadium and the baseball stadium, as well as most buildings on campus that were built during his term. The university removed them all. Smith's name came off the women's dormitory, Smith Hall (now Ruffin G. Pleasant Hall). In the wake of the two men's indictments, the LSU Board voted to stop naming buildings after living individuals.[18]

I n the days after Smith's resignation in July 1939, Governor Long and the LSU Board appointed E. S. Richardson, president of Ruston's Louisiana Polytechnic Institute, as LSU's acting president. Richardson accepted the position but changed his mind almost immediately. The board then gave the unenviable job of righting the university to quiet, boyish thirty-one-year-old Paul Hebert, dean of the LSU Law School. A Baton Rouge native, Hebert was a 1929 law graduate of LSU who earned a doctorate in law from Harvard and joined the Loyola Law School faculty in 1930. After a year on the LSU law faculty, he returned to Loyola in 1932 as dean. He was all of twenty-four. LSU hired Hebert again in 1936, this time as the dean of administration, and he became the university's Law School dean the following year.[19]

Helping Hebert to rehabilitate the damaged university was Colonel Troy Middleton, the former cadet commandant and now the dean of administration, who took over as comptroller and acting vice president. Hebert and Middleton stabilized the university's finances. "It was pure chaos at first," Middleton, who became LSU's president in 1951, recalled. "The university had been operating on a cash basis. We didn't know whom we owed, if we owed anyone. As I recall, we ran an advertisement in Louisiana newspapers saying, in essence, 'If the university owes you, come talk to us.'"[20]

One of the first problems Middleton discovered was that many revenue-producing units on campus—including the Athletic Department, bookstore, cafeteria, campus creamery, and the meat production facilities—generated more than a million dollars a year for LSU but had never been put under the supervision of LSU accountants. "The only real evidence that the receipts turned in by the various departments were correct," the state's supervisor of public funds had written to Leche in 1938, "is the word of the person in charge of the collections." An audit of LSU's practices by a New York public accounting firm concluded, "Practically no methods of internal check were provided" before 1940. Other problems, the firm found, included "flagrant dishonesty on the part of [LSU] officials and employees, loose methods of operation, a failure to obtain bids for large purchases, a lavish and extravagant manner of conducting operations, extreme carelessness and laxity in accounting, and an intentional or unintentional burying of items in 'dumping-ground' accounts existed to an almost unbelievable extent." With a deficit of $586,000 in June 1939, LSU was functionally bankrupt. In late summer 1939, Governor Long and Hebert won approval from the legislature for a $550,000 bank loan to keep the university solvent.[21]

Hebert declared in early August at the summer commencement that the new LSU would be a "better, but not necessarily a bigger institution," and he vowed to eradicate "partisan political influences" in LSU's affairs. "Our recent troubles should serve as a powerful stimulant to greater effectiveness. The sound foundations of a strong educational institution are now here, and the university will continue to gain respect and recognition."[22]

Meanwhile, a group of nineteen faculty members recommended a seven-point program to rescue LSU. Among their suggestions were a university free of political influence and ending censorship of the *Reveille*. They also demanded the resignation of the LSU Board. The chair of LSU's alumni organization agreed, noting there were at least five board members "who hold political jobs and thus should not be in the position of handling the affairs of LSU." At issue was the degree to which board members supervised the university's affairs. "It has been alleged that tampering with the minutes of the board made it possible for some of the major irregularities to occur," the *Times-Picayune* observed in an editorial. "It has not been made clear whether the board ever exercised its right to hear the minutes read back—a boring procedure sometimes dispensed with." One board member, Theo S. Landry, general manager of the Louisiana State Penitentiary, confessed to devoting "entirely too little time" to LSU business. "We, as members of the board, failed by having placed too much confidence in one man. We should have been more careful and more watchful." Landry resigned from the board. By October, nine of the fifteen LSU Board members quit.[23]

Among Hebert's first policy changes was to end "long jaunts" by the Cadet Corps and students to football games. Students had hoped for a reprise of the 1934 trip to Nashville for the 1939 Vanderbilt game. That would not happen, Hebert announced in October. "We do not have the money that would be required," he said, adding that the school spent as much as $25,000 on out-of-town trips. "Such an expenditure at this time, if we had the money, would be ridiculous." Hebert eliminated another practice from the Long years: lending money to students. Middleton added to Hebert's reforms by announcing the construction program at the university would conclude as soon as the last new building was finished. And, he said, any student who held a campus job was be expected to work for his or her pay. Dead-head jobs would end, he said, explaining LSU would no longer tolerate "any monkey business like that." The university would have no "extensive student aid program unless the federal government gives the university the money."[24]

The LSU that Hebert and Middleton salvaged in 1939 and 1940 was a university in crisis, but also transformed. In the nine years prior, Louisiana and the federal government spent $13.5 million on expanding LSU (about $275 million in 2022 dollars), turning a once-modest university with meager ambitions into a large, growing institution with a favorable national reputation. Despite its dreadful press coverage in summer 1939—some took to calling LSU a "school for crime"—the university recorded an enrollment that fall of 7,796, including 6,580 on the Baton Rouge campus, down only 251 from the previous year.[25]

Even after Hebert's and Middleton's efforts to purge the excesses of the Long-Smith era from the LSU system, Long's legacy was never far from the minds of anyone who walked the campus in 1939. The names of Leche and Smith were erased from the buildings, but the Huey P. Long Field House remained. Oscar K. Allen Hall survived, as well. Over eighty years later, the buildings still carried the men's names. Everywhere students walked on the lush, growing campus, they encountered evidence of Long's influence at LSU. Despite the damage his meddling had inflicted on the school's reputation in 1934–35, the modern LSU was his dream and among his most important accomplishments. And it was not only Long's spirit that pervaded the Field House, the Quadrangle, the Greek Theatre, and Tiger Stadium. Many of his children, grandchildren, and great-grandchildren would attend and graduate from LSU. In the short term, the most significant evidence of Long's legacy at LSU was his older children—daughter, Rose, and elder son, Russell. In spring of 1937, the campus coeds elected Rose as president of the Association of Women Students. The following year, Huey's twenty-year-old son was elected as LSU's student body president.[26]

CONCLUSION

NEITHER SAINT NOR DEVIL

Huey Long's influence on Louisiana higher education, particularly at LSU, was considerable and long-lasting. By one accounting, Long, Allen, and Leche (the Long organization's leaders) spent more than $62.5 million (about $1.2 billion in 2022 dollars) on the state's seven institutions of higher education from 1930 to 1940, the darkest years of the Great Depression. This included $18.8 million in new buildings—$5.6 million of them at LSU. Not all the spending on Louisiana's colleges and universities came from state appropriations. The federal government supplied $7.3 million. Still, Louisiana's commitment to providing a college education for its youth was impressive. It also produced results, especially at LSU. Louisiana put a college degree within the reach of tens of thousands of young people who might never have imagined such an opportunity. In the decade of the 1930s, the enrollment at universities nationwide grew an average of 28 percent. LSU's systemwide enrollment in the same period swelled by 333 percent.

LSU's exploding growth compared to other schools in Louisiana and around the country was no mystery. Long and his successors showered the school with revenue and attention. For ten years, few of LSU's needs went unmet. LSU's total revenue from 1930 through 1939 was $43.7 million, compared to the combined $18.7 million Louisiana spent on the other six state institutions during the same period. LSU was, by far, the largest public university in the state and Long's personal project.[1]

Long's tenure—and those of his immediate successors—produced results and reforms, but maybe not the results that many hoped for and not the reforms that those committed to democratic government could have sup-

263

ported. "In reality," the *New York Times* wrote in an editorial the day after his death, "Senator Long set up a Fascist government in Louisiana. It was disguised but only thinly." This characterization was too strong. Long's ideology might have sounded fascistic to some, but, as historian Alan Brinkley observed, he was not a fascist "in any meaningful sense of the term." Peter H. Amann, a prominent social historian of modern France who studied fascist ideologies, viewed Long as an authoritarian, but not a fascist. "If Long had an undoubted authoritarian streak, this reflected his vanity, impatience, ambition, and reaction to the equally unscrupulous methods of his opposition in Louisiana, but not a considered ideological stance as was the case of European Fascists," Amann wrote. "His nationalism at most mirrored the prejudices of his southern constituents and was limited to helping defeat the proposal for America's entry into the World Court."[2]

The fact of Long's authoritarianism, however, was not widely disputed. "Long achieved much—certainly more than the oligarchy ever had," historian Arthur M. Schlesinger Jr. wrote. "But his achievement should not be overestimated. Like an agent emperor or modern dictator, he specialized in monuments. He sprinkled the state with roads and buildings. But he did little or nothing to raise wages for the workers, to stop child labor, to reduce the work day, to support trade unions, to provide pensions for the aged, to furnish relief to the unemployed, even to increase teachers' salaries. He left behind no record of social or labor legislation." As biographer T. Harry Williams wrote, "In striving to do good he was led on to grasp for more and more power, until finally he could not always distinguish between the method and the goal, the power and the good."[3]

Some criticisms of Long's larger record are valid, as are common critiques of his involvement with LSU: He cared more about the football team and the band than academics and showed less interest in improving Louisiana higher education, writ large; he used LSU to generate positive, nonpolitical coverage for himself, in Louisiana and nationally; and, his constant meddling in LSU's affairs almost cost the university its accreditation. As journalist Carleton Beals wrote the year of Long's death: "On the basis of an illiterate state, a poverty-stricken teaching force, a politically vitiated school-system of shameful meagerness, Huey erected the showy edifice of his great university with an extravagant budget. The millions spent on L.S.U., much of the money in an improper form, and in a manner far worse than that for which Long earlier attacked former governor Parker, were for the purpose of show, political power, and to provide a basis for a nationwide conquest of student and professorial support. With this false glitter he was laying plans to seduce higher education everywhere."[4]

There was some truth in Beals's critique, but while using LSU as a vehicle for his political aggrandizement, Long knew he had to produce tangible results for the institution. For example, he could have co-opted the football team and the band and ignored the rest of campus. Instead, he saw LSU's larger success—educating thousands more Louisiana youth, and expanding its scope, including training physicians—as a crucial part of his ability to boast that the university was on par with the best state schools in the South and beyond. He could not have made that claim with only a renewed band and a winning football team as his evidence. He needed more and, so, he demanded and produced it. Long and President James Monroe Smith achieved lasting accomplishments at LSU, including increased enrollment, expansion of the campus, more and better faculty, and new academic departments. "No matter how adept Long was in the arts of power, he could never have sustained himself or his organization merely by manipulation," as T. Harry Williams wrote in 1961. "He had a program. He promised something, and he delivered it."[5]

As his harsh critic Thomas O. Harris observed in 1968, "In sum, Huey Long provided great utilities for public use, but he insisted on employing them for his own political benefit." Harris, who considered Long a "dictator," also agreed that his rule was not without positive results for Louisiana. "Neither saint nor devil, he was a complex and heterogeneous mixture of good and bad, genius and craft, hypocrisy and candor, buffoonery and seriousness." The renowned scholar of southern politics V. O. Key understood Long's contribution to Louisiana best. "The choice of the Louisiana electorate is not in reality one between black and white, between a do-nothing government and a venal administration with a program, as some observers would have us believe," Key wrote in 1949. "Long left a lasting imprint on the conservative element in the state by showing the people that government could act." Although Key did not single out LSU in this critique of Long, one could add to the observation that Long also showed Louisiana that the state could provide a sound college education for its young people.[6]

During his years ruling Louisiana, Long enacted programs that helped Louisianans of all races (for example, all citizens benefited from the roads and bridges he built), but his emphasis was always on helping white voters. Long abolished the poll tax in 1934, but that reform did not result in greater numbers of Black voters because of the refusal of parish registrars and other local officials to allow them to vote. And Long did not force them to do so. In fact, he signaled that he accepted the status quo on Black disenfranchisement. He attacked the Ku Klux Klan, but did so only after the organization's influence in Louisiana had waned. And when he arrived in the US Senate, he opposed legislation to outlaw lynching, as did other southern senators. "You can quote me as saying I'll vote 100 percent against" the bill, Long said. "We just lynch an occasional nigger. No federal anti-lynching law would help that."

Long's attention and funding helped transform LSU from an insignificant state school into a university with a respected faculty and a growing national reputation. The only group in Louisiana who benefited from Long's devotion to LSU, however, were white students. For its first ninety years, the school was a whites-only institution. This was not Long's doing, of course. Segregation was the law decades before he became governor. And desegregation of schools at all levels, in Louisiana and elsewhere, was still decades away. Long may not have been a race-baiter, but he was like many other politicians throughout the country who did not challenge the status quo on race.[7]

And LSU in the 1930s was very much part of that status quo. A review of the university's yearbook, the *Gumbo,* from its inception in 1910 through the 1960s, is a bracing and disheartening experience—a sea of white faces. The first Black undergraduate to attend classes at LSU, A. P. Tureaud Jr., withdrew before the end of his first and only miserable semester at the school in 1953. LSU did not enroll another Black undergraduate until 1964.[8]

In almost every way during its first 90 years, LSU was an integral part of Louisiana's white supremacist economy and culture. Only whites could benefit from an education at LSU's law school, medical school, dental school, and other colleges and departments. The university also barred Blacks from serving on the faculty. LSU's only Black employees for its first 110 years were staff members, custodial and cafeteria workers, and other personnel working menial jobs. LSU did not hire its first Black professor—Julian T. White in the Department of Architecture—until 1971.[9]

Long's social and educational programs helped many Black Louisianans, but his priority was winning white votes. The sad fact was that Louisiana during the Long years did little to prepare Black students for high school, much less college. When Long became governor in 1928, Louisiana had only three state-approved, four-year high schools for Blacks and 353 for whites. In the 1928–29 school year, only 434 Black students graduated from public high schools in Louisiana, compared to 6,548 whites (although over 35 percent of the state's population was Black.) Ten years later, conditions had improved, but Black students still lagged far behind those attending white schools. At the end of the 1938–39 school year, Louisiana funded 378 state-approved four-year high schools for whites, and 39 for Blacks. But the disparity between whites and Blacks graduating from high school in 1938–39 was a stark reminder of racism's rule over Louisiana education: 74,416 whites and only 1,128 Blacks.[10]

Even if Long, Allen, and Leche had supported admitting Blacks to LSU or the state's other higher education institutions, there were precious few Black high school graduates to apply. Those with a high school diploma (or who could pass an entrance exam) and the desire and means to attend college either enrolled at one of the two public, four-year universities for Blacks: Southern University in Baton Rouge or, beginning in 1936, Louisiana Negro Normal (now Grambling State and not a four-year school in the early thirties). Others attended one of the four private Black colleges—New Orleans University (now Dillard University), Xavier College, Straight College (subsumed by Dillard in 1934), or Coleman College (in Gibsland and, later, Shreveport). But Louisiana's Black public colleges had low enrollment. For the 1929–30 school year, for example, Southern University reported 299 students. That grew to 876 for the 1938–39 school year, a 192 percent increase. LSU's enrollment from 1930 to 1940, meanwhile, increased by more than 300 percent. At decade's end, only 7 percent of all students attending four-year public universities in Louisiana were Black, compared to 5 percent ten years earlier.

Those who beat the odds and made it to Southern University or Louisiana Negro Normal encountered underfunded campuses. The two public Black universities suffered by comparison to LSU in other measures, too. Southern's expenditures for 1929–30 were $95,685, compared to LSU's $940,669. By the end of the decade, LSU's annual budget swelled to $2.6 million (a 178 percent increase), compared to Southern's $138,871 (a modest 45 percent increase). The record is clear: Whatever Long accomplished for

Louisiana higher education accrued primarily to the benefit of LSU and almost always to white students. And, over the succeeding years, that changed only slightly. Even through the first two decades of the twenty-first century, total Black enrollment at LSU never surpassed 15 percent.

But it was not only Black universities that suffered from the state's emphasis on LSU. The rest of Louisiana higher education was funded more modestly during the 1930s. For example, during the decade, the budgets of Louisiana State Normal College (now Northwestern State) grew by 104 percent and Louisiana Polytechnic Institute's by 68.5 percent while LSU's almost tripled. LSU's enrollment grew by more than four times during the 1930s, but the State Normal College's student body expanded 30 percent and Louisiana Polytechnic's 126 percent.[11]

A mong Long's fiercest critics in academia was historian Glen Jeansonne, who argued Long "was both insincere and ineffective." Jeansonne scoffed at notions that Long built anything great and valuable at LSU. "Long constructed only three buildings at LSU: a women's dormitory, a student union, and a music building; his predecessors built far more." Jeansonne's math was off. His criticism ignored Long's vital role in creating LSU's medical and dental schools, and he discounted Long's dominance over his puppet, O. K. Allen, and the progress made at LSU under Allen's administration. If one condemns Long as a dictator or authoritarian, then Long deserves some blame and credit for the actions of his underlings. Jeansonne also denigrated Long's contribution to increasing LSU's national profile with the spectacle of an enlarged Regimental Band and his relentless promotion of the football team. Historian Allan Sindler also downplayed Long's role at LSU, arguing that "credit for arousing public interest in an expanded state university must be assigned" to Long's predecessors, particularly Governor John Parker. Other critics noted that longtime state education superintendent Thomas H. Harris deserved recognition for helping Long make the case for expanding institutions of higher education.[12]

Long left much unfinished or untried upon his death in 1935. He did not accomplish as much as his supporters claimed, nor was his rule as benevolent as friendly biographers and historians maintained. Even at LSU, he undermined academic freedom and emphasized nonacademic pursuits to a sometimes-damaging degree. Had he lived longer, LSU might have been sanctioned by an accrediting body or, worse, lost its accreditation. That said, it is also indisputable that LSU's rapid growth and transformation in the 1930s were primarily results of Long's efforts. Others deserve credit for their contributions to LSU during this period, but many of those contributions happened because Long made the school his priority. Like Governor John Parker before him, Long laid a foundation upon which others built.

I n September 1934, after LSU offered him a position on its English faculty, Robert Penn Warren and his wife, Emma Brescia, left Nashville for Baton Rouge. They drove south in a beat-up green 1931 Studebaker that Warren called "Original Sin." As the former Vanderbilt professor reached the Louisiana side of the Mississippi River in northeastern Louisiana, he pulled over to pick up a hitchhiker who clutched a parcel wrapped in old newspaper held together with twine. The man was, Warren remembered, "a country man, the kind you call a red-neck or a wool-hat, aging, aimless, nondescript, beat up by life and hard times and bad luck."

As they drove, the old man told the couple about Huey Long. "The roads, he said, were shore better now. A man could git to market, he said. A man could jist git up and git, if'n a notion come on him." The man prattled on about "Huey," recounting mythical tales of the leader's political prowess, fearlessness, wisdom, and his love for the downtrodden. "There were a thousand tales, over the years, and some of them were, no doubt, literally and factually true," Warren later wrote. "But they were all true in the world of 'Huey'—that world of myth, folklore, poetry, deprivation, rancor, and dimly envisaged hopes." But, Warren observed, "there was another world—this a factual world—made possible by the factual Long, though not inhabited by him. It was a world that I, as an assistant professor, was to catch fleeting glimpses of, and ponder." Warren meant that "provincial" Baton Rouge and LSU in the mid-to-late 1930s existed in "a world of a sick yearning for elegance" and "pretentiousness, of bloodcurdling struggles for academic preferment, of drool-jawed grab and arrogant criminality."

At LSU, Warren discovered a diverse faculty, "some as torpid as a gorged alligator in the cold mud of January and some avid to lick the spit of an indifferent or corrupt administration, but many able and gifted and fired by a will to create, out of the seething stew and heaving magma, a distinguished university." The students, too, were varied. Many of them poor, awkward country boys with "burning ambition," and "a thirst for learning." And the college education of those poor young people, "you reminded yourself, with whatever complication of irony seemed necessary at the moment, was due to Huey, and to Huey alone." Warren believed that "the 'better element' had done next to nothing in fifty years to get that boy out of the grim despair of his ignorance." The "good families" of Baton Rouge, Warren learned, hated Long, "sometimes for good reasons and sometimes for bad and sometimes for no reason at all, as a mere revulsion of taste."

But those families, Warren realized, "never seemed to reflect on what I took to be the obvious fact that if the government of the state had not previously been marked by various combinations of sloth, complacency, incompetence, corruption, and a profound lack of political imagination, there would never have been a Senator Huey P. Long, and my old hitchhiker by the roadside would, in September 1934, have had no tale to tell me."[13]

NOTES

ABBREVIATIONS

HPL   Huey P. Long
LLMVC   Louisiana and Lower Mississippi Valley Collections, LSU Libraries
LRC   Louisiana Research Collection, Tulane University Special Collections
LSUA   Louisiana State University Archives
THWP   T. Harry Williams Papers, Louisiana and Lower Mississippi Valley
         Collections, LSU Libraries

PREFACE

1. "At LSU, Football and Politics Converge in a Way That's Uniquely Louisiana," *Sports Illustrated,* October 15, 2019.

2. "Louisiana Gov. Bobby Jindal Tweets His Support for Les Miles," *USA Today,* November 28, 2015; "LSU Coach Les Miles in Crowd at Bobby Jindal Event That Raises Half a Million Dollars," *Advocate,* December 3, 2015.

3. "Times Do Change," *Monroe News-Star,* October 20, 1977; "LSU Rejects Edwards' $1 million," *Times-Picayune,* November 22, 1983; "Edwards Enters Unknown Area," *Town Talk,* November 23, 1983; "Remembering a Louisiana Original: John McKeithen," *Tiger Rag,* May 2, 2016.

4. John McKeithen interview, T. Harry Williams Center for Oral History, LSU Libraries; "A Big Night in a Li'l Ol' Town," *Sports Illustrated,* September 30, 1968; "Times Do Change," *Monroe News-Star,* October 20, 1977; "Remembering a Louisiana Original: John McKeithen," *Tiger Rag,* May 2, 2016; "Huge Crowd Witnesses Earl Long Inauguration," *Richland Beacon-News,* May 15, 1948.

5. "The Big Issue at LSU," *Shreveport Times,* February 25, 1953; "Board Has Resignation from Stoke," *State-Times,* December 28, 1950; "LSU Board Members Comment on Change," *Times-Picayune,* December 30, 1950.

6. Stanley R. Tiner, "Louisiana Governors and LSU Football," *Shreveport Journal,* December 9, 1983.

7. I encourage readers who want more information about Long's assassination to start

here: Lamar White Jr., "The Final Days of the Indefatigable Huey P. Long Jr.," *Bayou Brief,* August 25, 2021, www.bayoubrief.com/2021/08/25/the-final-days-of-the-indefatigable-huey -p-long-jr/2/.

1. I WANT A BAND

1. *University Bulletin,* Baton Rouge: Louisiana State University, May 1931, 239; "President Atkinson of L.S.U. Ill, Has Influenza," *Town Talk,* November 6, 1930; Frey interview, T. Harry Williams Center for Oral History, LSU Libraries; Frey interview, THWP; "Four New Members Selected By Blazers," *Bunkie Record,* May 17, 1929; *Gumbo* yearbook, class of 1930, Louisiana State University, digitalcommons.lsu.edu/gumbo/39; Long's walking stick described, "How Gov. Long Inspired L.S.U. Team to Fight," *New Orleans States,* November 28, 1930; "Reminiscences of Fred C. Frey," Fred C. Frey Papers, Box 1, LLMVC; Continé and Phillips, *The Golden Band from Tigerland,* 9–10; *University Bulletin,* May 1929, 20.

2. Morgan, *Redneck Liberal,* 44–45; "Ole Miss Dropped by Universities Group from Accepted List," *Clarion-Ledger,* October 31, 1930; "Ole Miss Students Burn Governor Bilbo in Effigy," *Clarion-Ledger,* December 7, 1930.

3. Frey interview, THWP; Williams, *Huey Long,* 286; *University Bulletin,* April 1930, 365; "Gov. H. P. Long Plays Host in New Mansion," *Ruston Leader,* June 4, 1930; Continé and Phillips, *The Golden Band from Tigerland,* 12; "Tiger Team of 26 Players Leaves to Battle Arkansas in Shreveport Sat.," *State-Times,* November 2, 1928.

4. Middleton said Long appeared in his office one afternoon in September 1930. During their conversation, Middleton said, Long asked, "Can I do anything for you?" Middleton said he replied, "Yes, how about giving me a band?" (Price, *Troy H. Middleton,* 105).

5. Frey interview, THWP; "Reminiscences of Fred C. Frey," Fred C. Frey Papers, box 1, LLMVC; "Major Middleton Assumes Duties as Commandant," *Reveille,* July 11, 1930; "Maj. Middleton Comes to L.S.U. as Commandant," *Morning Advocate,* February 28, 1930.

6. Middleton interview, THWP.

7. Fred Frey interview, THWP; "Reminiscences of Fred C. Frey," Fred C. Frey Papers, box 1, LLMVC; Continé and Phillips, *The Golden Band from Tigerland,* 18.

2. I AM ON MY WAY

1. Long, *Every Man a King,* 6–7; Hair, *The Kingfish and His Realm,* 37; "The High School Rally," *St. Tammany Farmer,* March 5, 1910; Holeman, *Winn Parish,* 9–20, 43–49.

2. "The High School Rally," *St. Tammany Farmer,* March 5, 1910; *University Bulletin,* June 1910, 55–56; "Rally Events Were Spirited," *State-Times,* May 1, 1909; "High School Rally," *University Bulletin,* February 1910, 4–8.

3. Harley B. Bozeman, "Winn Parish as I Have Known It," *Winn Parish Enterprise,* April 25, 1957; Williams, *Huey Long,* 38; "High School Rally Events," *Daily State,* April 25, 1910; "High School Rally," *University Bulletin,* February 1910, 5; Long, *Every Man a King,* 8; "The High School Rally," *St. Tammany Farmer,* March 5, 1910; "High School Rally," *University Bulletin,* February 1910, 7–8; Bozeman, "Winn Parish as I Have Known It," April 25, 1957; Bozeman, "Winn Parish as I Have Known It," May 2, 1957; "Crowley High School Team Wins First Place

in State Field Meet," *Crowley Signal,* May 7, 1910; Long, *Every Man a King,* 7; Harris, *The Memoirs of T. H. Harris,* 125.

4. Williams, *Huey Long,* 39; Long, *Every Man a King,* 8; "Requirements for Admission," *University Bulletin,* February 1910, 33–36; Lucille Long Hunt interview, THWP; Bozeman, "Winn Parish as I Have Known It," July 11, 1957.

5. Bozeman, "Winn Parish as I Have Known It," April 11, 1957.

6. Williams, *Huey Long,* 39–40; "Winnfield High School Opening," *Comrade,* September 9, 1910; Hunt and Davis interviews, THWP; Bozeman, "Winn Parish as I Have Known It," April 11 and May 2, 1957; "Huey Pierce Long," biographical essay by Long organization, Jack B. McGuire Collection of Huey P. Long Papers, box 1, LRC.

7. *University Bulletin,* June 1910, 267–79.

8. Williams, *Huey Long,* 43; Schlesinger, *The Politics of Upheaval,* 68.

9. "Who's Huey Now?" *Time,* October 26, 1931; Martin, *Dynasty,* 26.

10. "Huey Comes Home," *Comrade,* November 11, 1910; Wall et al., *Louisiana: A History,* 282; Dunbar interview, THWP; White, *Kingfish,* 11–12.

11. Bozeman, "Winn Parish as I Have Known It," November 7, 1957; Williams, *Huey Long,* 87.

12. Hair, *The Kingfish and His Realm,* 86–87.

13. Williams, *Huey Long,* 121–25; Talbot interview, THWP; "Editorial Rambles," *Telegraph-Bulletin,* June 4, 1884.

14. "The Boyhood Chum of Huey Long," *Shreveport Times,* May 17, 1959.

15. Long, *Every Man a King,* 41–43.

16. "Hot Well Crowds Receive Attacks on City Silently," *New Orleans States,* July 5, 1919.

3. THE FATHER OF LSU

1. Wilkerson, *Thomas Duckett Boyd,* 310–11; Hoffman, *Louisiana State University and Agricultural and Mechanical College,* 328; "State Federation of Agricultural Interests Formed," *Times-Picayune,* March 5, 1918; Schott, "John M. Parker of Louisiana," 322–24.

2. Williams, *Huey Long,* 132; Wiegand interview, THWP; Schott, "John M. Parker of Louisiana," 3, 93–94; "The Real Teddy Bear Story," Theodore Roosevelt Association, www.theodoreroosevelt.org/content.aspx?page_id=22&club_id=991271&module_id=333084; "The true, tangled tale of the teddy bear, Theodore Roosevelt and the resurgence of a threatened species," *Washington Post,* March 11, 2016; Brinkley, *The Wilderness Warrior,* 439.

3. Wilkerson, *Thomas Duckett Boyd,* 310–11; *University Bulletin,* May 1920, 33–36, 67–232.

4. Wilkerson, *Thomas Duckett Boyd,* 310–11; Hoffman, *Louisiana State University and Agriculture and Mechanical College,* 282–83, 328–30.

5. Schott, "John M. Parker of Louisiana," 17–19.

6. Schott, "John M. Parker of Louisiana," 350; "State Federation of Agricultural Interests Formed," *Times-Picayune,* March 5, 1918; "14 Laws to Aid State Farmers Will Be Asked," *New Orleans Item,* March 5, 1918.

7. Wilkerson, *Thomas Duckett Boyd,* 309–14; Hoffman, *Louisiana State University and Agriculture and Mechanical College,* 299, 329, 333–34; Ruffin, *Under Stately Oaks,* 47–48; "River News," *Daily Advocate,* May 4, 1883; "New Cotton," *Daily Advocate,* August 8, 1897; "Injunction Suit Filed against LeBlanc in District Court," *Daily State,* June 1, 1908; "North Part of Cam-

pus Once Southern Plantation Site," *Reveille,* March 26, 1958; "First Day Enrollment at L.S.U. Near 900 Mark," *Times-Picayune,* September 26, 1921; Hoffman, *Louisiana State University and Agricultural and Mechanical College,* 327–34; "LSU Bought a Farm, Got a Beautiful Campus," *Shreveport Times,* March 27, 1960; "Act No. 6," *State-Times,* June 6, 1918.

8. Schott, "John M. Parker of Louisiana," 253, 350; Wall et al., *Louisiana: A History,* 277; Hair, *The Kingfish and His Realm,* 12–13.

9. Williams, *Huey Long,* 132; Sindler, *Huey Long's Louisiana,* 40; Long, *Every Man a King,* 47–48; "Long Announces Support of Parker," *Times-Picayune,* October 26, 1919.

10. Schott, "John M. Parker of Louisiana," 363–65; Herman B. Deutsch, "New Orleans Politics—The Greatest Free Show on Earth," in Carter, *The Past as Prelude,* 318.

11. Schott, "John M. Parker of Louisiana," 367–68.

12. Williams, *Huey Long,* 137–45; Matthew J. Schott, "Huey Long: Progressive Backlash?" *Louisiana History,* Spring 1986, 142.

13. "Huey Long Target of Legislator for Issuing Circular," *Shreveport Journal,* September 29, 1921; "The Kingdom of the Kingfish," *New Orleans Item,* July 25, 1939.

14. "Long's 'Empire Invisible' Fight Carried to N.O.," *New Orleans Item,* September 29, 1921; "The Kingdom of the Kingfish," *New Orleans Item,* July 30, 1939.

15. "Gel 'All Het Up' When They Romp Pleasant and Long," *Clarion-Progress,* October 1, 1921; "Lawmakers Bitterly Condemn Authors of 'Oil Tax' Circulars," *Shreveport Journal,* September 29, 1921; Williams, *Huey Long,* 146–47.

16. "Sheriff Seeks Huey Long for Alleged Libel as to Parker," *Monroe News-Star,* October 3, 1921.

17. "Long Here Tuesday A.M.," *State-Times,* October 3, 1921; "Bond of $5,000 Made By Long in Criminal Libel," *State-Times,* November 4, 1921.

18. Williams, *Huey Long,* 149.

19. Williams, *Huey Long,* 150.

20. "Long Guilty of Criminal Libel Brunot Decides," *State-Times,* November 8, 1921; "Fight in State Just Beginning Says Huey Long," *State-Times,* November 10, 1921.

21. "Long Case Develops Candidate in Palmer," *New Orleans States,* November 13, 1921.

22. Schott, "John M. Parker of Louisiana," 376–77.

23. Ruffin, *Under Stately Oaks,* 49.

24. "Parker Plan to Finance Big College Is Opposed," *New Orleans States,* April 6, 1921; "Parker Fights Hard for His College Plan," *New Orleans States,* April 7, 1921.

25. "Convention's Work May Not Be Ended on Scheduled Time," *Shreveport Journal,* May 9, 1921; "Convention Is Getting into a Real Stride," *State-Times,* May 14, 1921; Ruffin, *Under Stately Oaks,* 49–50; "Funds Available at Present for New Univ. Small," *Reveille,* July 18, 1924; "University Loses $300,000 through Court's Decision," *Reveille,* January 9, 1925; Schott, "John M. Parker of Louisiana," 372; "Greater A&M Plan Adopted," *Shreveport Times,* April 14, 1921; "3 Per Cent Rate on Oil Approved," *Times-Picayune,* May 25, 1922.

26. Schott, "John M. Parker of Louisiana," 372; "S.L.I. Industrial Building to Be Parker Hall," *Daily Advertiser,* May 11, 1940; Williams, *Huey Long,* 137; Schott, "John M. Parker of Louisiana," 373.

27. Schott, "Huey Long: Progressive Backlash?" 143.

28. "Reminiscences of Fred C. Frey," Fred C. Frey Papers, box 1, LLMVC; Williams, *Huey Long,* 137; "The Kingdom of the Kingfish," *New Orleans Item,* July 31, 1939.

29. Dalrymple, *A Brief Sketch—Illustrated of the Louisiana State University and Agriculture and Mechanical School,* 29.

30. *University Bulletin,* May 1924, 7–15, 314–47; "Biennial Report of the President of Louisiana State University to the Governor and Members of the Legislature for 1932–34," *University Bulletin,* May 1934, 18; "Engineering Is Popular Course with L.S.U. Men," *State-Times,* October 29, 1923; Cutrer, *Parnassus on the Mississippi,* 4. Enrollment figures reported by LSU and in the local news media often differ, probably because the newspapers reported preliminary figures or enrollment totals for only one semester. Sometimes the numbers reported included the Medical School and summer-school enrollment, with no total reported for just the Baton Rouge campus. When possible, I use the official enrollment numbers for the Baton Rouge campus as reported by LSU in its *University Bulletin* or the president's report to the governor and the legislature.

4. THIS TEMPLE OF VANITY

1. "Sentiment for Greater College Grows Swiftly," *Times-Picayune,* May 3, 1921; "Governor Backed on Agricultural College Support," *Times-Picayune,* May 31, 1922; "Governor Scores Critics in Speech at LaPlace Rally," *State-Times,* August 27, 1923; "Schwing Scores Governor on Agricultural College Support," *New Orleans States,* November 18, 1923.

2. "Huey Long Picks Taxes, State Boards and Oil as Targets in Campaign Opener," *New Orleans States,* September 2, 1923.

3. "Mr. Long Explains," *Times-Picayune,* September 21, 1923.

4. "Which?" *Times-Picayune,* September 21, 1923.

5. *University Bulletin,* May 1904, 4; "Board of Supervisors," *University Bulletin,* May 1905, 8; "Board of Supervisors," *University Bulletin,* April 1909, 8; "Fuqua Defends His Penitentiary Record," *New Orleans States,* September 30, 1923.

6. Davis, *Huey Long,* 85; "Lake Charles Hears Long," *Shreveport Times,* November 20, 1923.

7. "Louisiana Departs for Arkansas Fray at Shreveport Fair," *Times-Picayune,* October 31, 1924; "Old Rivals to Meet on Field of New Stadium at State Fair," *Shreveport Times,* November 1, 1924; "Many Followers Coming with Tiger and Razorback Teams," *Times-Picayune,* October 31, 1924.

8. "Old Rivals to Meet on Field of New Stadium at State Fair," *Shreveport Times,* November 1, 1924; "Record Made by Crowd in Seeing Shows," *Shreveport Times,* November 2, 1924.

9. Carriere interviews, THWP.

10. Lawliss, *The Master List of Design Projects of the Olmsted Firm, 1857–1979,* 46, 117–31.

11. "Plans for New State College," *Weekly Town Talk,* December 24, 1921.

12. After Link died in November 1923, the Baton Rouge–New Orleans firm of Toledano, Wogan & Bernard took over architectural work for the campus; Desmond, *The Architecture of LSU,* 43; "Link Resigns to End the Fight over Architect in Charge at University," *Daily Advertiser,* August 9, 1924; Ruffin, *Under Stately Oaks,* 55; "Plans Complete for Moving New Site in September," *Reveille,* April 17, 1925; "Parker Tells of Dreamers' Aim Realized," *Morning Advocate,* May 1, 1926.

13. "Call for Higher Standards in Universities Sounded as Great Plant Is Dedicated," *Morning Advocate,* May 1, 1926; Bledsoe and Richard, eds., *Louisiana State University,* 46–54; Ruffin, *Under Stately Oaks,* 51–53; "Last Of Work On New L.S.U. Being Started," *State-Times,* Janu-

ary 5, 1924; "New University, One of Finest in the Land, Built with Little Cost to Taxpayers of the State," *State-Times,* April 30, 1926; "Greek Theatre on New Campus Being Used for the First Times of Rally, Dedication Visitors," *State-Times,* April 30, 1926; Desmond, *The Architecture of LSU,* 86.

14. Chad Seifried, "The Development of 'Death Valley' in Louisiana: Modernization and Tiger Stadium, 1924–2013," *Louisiana History* 57, no. 2 (Spring 2016): 189; Schmidt, *Shaping College Football,* 40.

15. "L.S.U. Contracts for Buildings Let," *New Orleans States,* January 6, 1924; Seifried, "The Development of 'Death Valley' in Louisiana," 189–91; "Tigers Tackle Auburn Today in Birmingham," *State-Times,* October 25, 1924.

16. "Greenies Score on Touchdown in Second Period of the Game," *State-Times,* November 27, 1924; "Record Crowd Here for Game Well Handled," *State-Times,* November 28, 1924.

17. "Glorious in Victory Sublime in Defeat," *New Orleans States,* November 28, 1924; "Record Crowd Here for Game Well Handled," *State-Times,* November 28, 1924.

18. "Three New Sections Planned for L.S.U. Concrete Stadium," *New Orleans States,* December 25, 1924.

19. "Inspect New L.S.U. Grounds and Buildings," *Town Talk,* May 1, 1926.

20. "Long Brings Campaign to Baton Rouge," *State-Times,* September 24, 1927; "2500 Hear Long at Baton Rouge," *New Orleans States,* September 24, 1927.

21. Harris, *The Kingfish,* 38.

5. WE MUST GET A PRESIDENT

1. Williams, *Huey Long,* 493; Cutrer (in *Parnassus on the Mississippi,* 7) claimed "Governor Long did not so much as set foot on LSU's campus until 1930." Fred Frey (in "Reminiscences of Fred C. Frey," Fred C. Frey Papers, box 1, LLMVC) had a similar recollection: "From 1928 to 1930 the university had not seen or heard much from Huey." In a 1973 journal article about Long and the *Southern Review,* Albert J. Montesti wrote, "For the first two years after his election, Long paid little if any attention to LSU" ("Huey Long and 'The Southern Review,'" *Journal of Modern Literature,* February 1973, 65).

2. "Gov. Long Addresses L.S.U. Cadet Regiment," *Weekly Town Talk,* May 26, 1928; "Long to Address Cadets Today at the Final Parade," *Morning Advocate,* May 25, 1928.

3. "Segregation of Boys, Girls for L.S.U. Advanced," *Morning Advocate,* June 12, 1928; "Steps Taken for Bettering of University," *State-Times,* June 11, 1928; "Seniors Bid L.S.U. Adieu on Day Ends," *Morning Advocate,* June 10, 1928.

4. White, *Kingfish,* 61–64.

5. Hair, *The Kingfish and His Realm,* 173–86; White, *Kingfish,* 66.

6. Schlesinger, *The Politics of Upheaval,* 47–48.

7. "Reminiscences of Fred C. Frey," Fred C. Frey Papers, box 1, LLMVC; Mitchell, "Growth of State Control of Public Education in Louisiana," 417–18; "Mrs. Cooper Appears in Role of Dominant Figure in Rift at Louisiana Normal School," *Shreveport Journal,* March 16, 1929; "Students Say Long's Sister Assailed Act," *Shreveport Times,* March 16, 1929; "President Tison of Normal Is a Third Cousin of Gov. Long," *Shreveport Journal,* March 16, 1929; Dodd, *Peapatch Politics,* 15; "Roy Cheered by Students," *Weekly Town Talk,* March 9, 1929.

8. "Hodges Moves Selection of Congressman," *Shreveport Times,* July 9, 1927; "Bossier Par-

ish Unit of League to Save State Formed," *Shreveport Journal,* June 29, 1929; "Long Tries to Put Harris at Head of L.S.U.," *Shreveport Times,* March 24, 1929; J. Y. Sanders Jr. interview, T. Harry Williams Collection, LLMVC.

9. "Louisiana Man Slated to Be Commandant of U.S. Military Academy," *Shreveport Times,* March 11, 1926; "Col. Hodges of West Point New L.S.U. President," *Crowley Daily Signal,* November 18, 1926; "C. B. Hodges Is Named Boyd's Successor," *LSU Alumni News,* December 1926; "Choice of Hodges as President Appears Wise One," *Reveille,* December 4, 1926; "Ruling on Hodges Is Reversed," *Daily Advertiser,* March 4, 1927; "The Commandants," *LSU Alumni News,* October 1944; *Gumbo* yearbook, class of 1913, digitalcommons.lsu.edu/gumbo/17; "War Department Will Determine Hodges' Course," *Shreveport Times,* November 20, 1926; "Leave of Absence for Major Hodges to Accept L.S.U. Presidency Refused," *Weekly Town Talk,* January 24, 1927; "Justice Department Rules Hodges Cannot Be Granted Leave," *Weekly Town Talk,* April 2, 1927.

10. "State University Alumni Honor Col. Hodges at Banquet," *Shreveport Journal,* December 29, 1926.

11. "Long Tries to Out Harris at Head of L.S.U.," *Shreveport Times,* March 24, 1929.

12. Harris, *The Memoirs of T. H. Harris,* 168.

13. "Hodges, L.S.U. President Designate, Hoover's Aide," *Morning Advocate,* March 23, 1929; "Board Elects Atkinson as Head of L.S.U.," *Weekly Town Talk,* June 15, 1929.

14. "Fail to Oust E. L. Stephens," *Shreveport Times,* June 15, 1929; "Issue over Dr. Stephens as S.L.I. Head Up at Meet of Board," *Daily Advertiser,* May 21, 1929; "The Stephens Case," *Shreveport Times,* June 17, 1929.

15. "Centenary Grid Team May Lose Almokary," *Shreveport Times,* March 29, 1929; Gottlieb interview, THWP.

16. "Long Said to Have Tried to Sway Almokary to Enter LSU," *Shreveport Journal,* March 28, 1929; "Almokary Says No Job Offered Him at L.S.U.," *Shreveport Journal,* March 30, 1929; "Oil City News," *Shreveport Journal,* June 12, 1929; Otis Harris, "As We Were Saying," *Shreveport Journal,* March 29, 1929; "Tiger Gridders Loyal to Jones; Threaten to Quit," *New Orleans Item,* December 21, 1934.

17. "Head Coach Cohen Arrives Thursday to Assume Duties," *Reveille,* January 6, 1928; "Rabenhorst, Enis Will Assist with Coaching Duties," *Reveille,* January 13, 1928; Finney, *The Fighting Tigers,* 88–89; "Fluke Touchdown Fails to Win for Wake Forest Boys," *Wilmington Morning Star,* November 28, 1919; "State College Beats Wake Forest 21 to 7," *Greensboro Daily News,* November 28, 1919; MacCambridge, *ESPN College Football Encyclopedia,* 976.

18. "Local Enthusiast Knew 'Pooley' Would Get Mad after While and Win for Bama," *State-Times,* January 1, 1926; "Go to It Boys Gov. Fuqua Tells Alabama Heroes," *Morning Advocate,* January 2, 1926; "Alabama's Crimson Tide Sweeps over Champions of West Coast, 20–19," *Times-Picayune,* January 2, 1926; Bowling, *Wallace Wade,* 67–108.

19. Andrew Doyle, "Turning the Tide: College Football and Southern Progressivism," *Southern Cultures,* Fall 1997, 28–51; Doyle, "Causes Won, Not Lost," 196; Walsh, *Where Football Is King,* 135; Bailey, "Games That Will Pay," 166–72; "Georgians Turn Back Yale Attacks and Win, 14 to 10," *Nashville Banner,* October 9, 1927.

20. Watterson, *College Football,* 183–85.

21. Gottlieb, Bowman, and Rabenhorst interviews, THWP.

22. Rabenhorst interview, THWP; "L.S.U. Humbled by Razorbacks at State Fair," *Shreve-*

port Times, October 30, 1927; Finney, *The Fighting Tigers,* 89; McManus, "Sharing the Hate," 49–50.

6. I DON'T FOOL AROUND WITH LOSERS

1. "Governor Sanders Shakes the Louisiana Plum Tree," *Times-Picayune,* May 22, 1908; "'Marse Henry' was Sportsman as Well as Statesman, Loving Call of Great Out-of-Doors," *Morning Advocate,* October 12, 1926.

2. "Governor Was Loyal Alumnus to End," *LSU Alumni News,* October 1926; "Tigers Lose Ardent Friend in Passing of Henry Fuqua," *Reveille,* October 16, 1926.

3. "Tiger Team of 26 Players Leaves to Battle Arkansas in Shreveport Sat.," *State-Times,* November 2, 1928; Bowman interview, THWP.

4. Rabenhorst interview, THWP; Silverman, *New York Sings,* 90; Harrell, "The Ku Klux Klan in Louisiana," 398–400.

5. Rabenhorst interview, THWP.

6. Bowman interview, THWP.

7. "Sidelights," *Shreveport Times,* November 4, 1928; Sidney Bowman interview, T. Harry Williams Collection, LLMVC; "Fifty-Five-Yard Run from Intercepted Pass in Third Period Wins for Arkansas," *Shreveport Times,* November 4, 1928.

8. "Eighty-First Annual Report for the Session 1929–30," State Department of Education of Louisiana, *Bulletin* no. 186 (October 1930): 28–29, 151.

9. "Baton Rougeans Report a Fine Trip to New Orleans with Weather Ideal and No Accidents," *State-Times,* November 30, 1928; "On The Sidelines at Grid Classic," *Times-Picayune,* November 30, 1928.

10. "Tulane Signs with Vandy for Games in 1931 and 1932," *New Orleans States,* January 8, 1930.

11. "Long Denounces Parker, Ballard in Hot Address," *Times-Picayune,* October 21, 1929; Hair, *The Kingfish and His Realm,* 190.

12. Carriere interview, THWP.

13. Williams, *Huey Long,* 37; Gottlieb interview, THWP; Davis, *Huey Long,* 21–22.

14. Rabenhorst interview, THWP.

15. "Don Zimmerman, Track, Grid Star to Enter Tulane," *Times-Picayune,* June 18, 1929; Carriere interview, THWP.

16. Rabenhorst interview, THWP; "Bedlam Reigns in Baton Rouge as Tulane Wins," *Times-Picayune,* November 29, 1929.

17. Hargrave, *LSU Law,* 20–21; "Tullis' Eyesight Vastly Improved after Operation," *Shreveport Journal,* December 12, 1929.

18. "Pity Huey over Protégé's Plight," *New Orleans States,* June 4, 1930; "Kennedy Made President of Student Body," *Reveille,* May 18, 1928; "Council Posts Given to Cole and Kennedy," *Reveille,* November 22, 1929; "K. K. Kennedy Made President of New Law Club," *Reveille,* October 18, 1929; Williams, *Huey Long,* 496.

19. "K. K. Kennedy Made President of New Law Club," *Reveille,* October 18, 1929.

20. "Student Row at L.S.U. Settled," *Shreveport Journal,* November 23, 1929; Kennedy to Long, November 1, 1929, Kemble Kennedy Scrapbook, Kemble Kennedy Papers, LLMVC.

21. "Long to Call L.S.U. Board to Retire Tullis," *State-Times,* December 10, 1929; "Long Discusses State Project with Visitors," *Crowley Daily Signal,* December 10, 1929.

22. "Law Students Express Faith in Dean Tullis," *State-Times*, December 11, 1929; "Law Students Attack Letter of K. Kennedy," undated, unidentified newspaper clipping, Kemble Kennedy Scrapbook, Kemble Kennedy Papers, LLMVC; "Students' Opinion on Dean Tullis Removal Divided," *Weekly Town Talk*, December 11, 1929; Williams, *Huey Long*, 496; "Ask Retention Of R. L. Tullis," *Shreveport Times*, December 21, 1929.

23. "Long Proposes to Make Tullis Dean Emeritus," *Times-Picayune*, December 22, 1929; "Law Students Send Letter to President," *Reveille*, December 13, 1929; "'Nothing I Can Do,' Declares Huey Long," *Times-Picayune*, November 29, 1934.

24. "Rating of Law School and L.S.U. Threatened by Long's Dickerings," *Morning Advocate*, January 2, 1930.

25. "Letters from the People," Kemble K. Kennedy letter to the editor, *State-Times*, December 19, 1929.

7. THE *WHANGDOODLE*

1. *Whangdoodle* 1, no. 2, LLMVC.

2. *Whangdoodle* 1, no. 1, LLMVC; "'The Whangdoodle' Editors Sought by L.S.U. Authorities," *Weekly Town Talk*, April 8, 1925; "Libel Is Charged to L.S.U. Student," *Times-Picayune*, April 9, 1925; "Indicated T.N.E. Group Exists on L.S.U. Campus," *Reveille*, March 6, 1925; "Concerning Theta Nu Epsilon," *State-Times*, March 11, 1925; "Two Suspects In 'Pink Sheet' Case Accused of Libel," *Reveille*, April 17, 1925; "Theta Nu Epsilon Disowns Chapter at University," *Times-Picayune*, April 22, 1925; "Stir at State University Created by Reports Organization Secret Outlaw Fraternity Here," *State-Times*, March 7, 1925; "Third Man Held in 'Whangdoodle' Libel Sensation," *Times-Picayune*, April 21, 1925; "'Whangdoodle' Shocks Baton Rouge," *Rayne Tribune*, April 25, 1925; "A Disgrace," *State-Times*, April 7, 1925; "Jury Fails to Make Report on Whangdoodle," *Weekly Town Talk*, May 30, 1925.

3. "'Tattler' Appears Inauguration Day, Passes Unnoticed," *Reveille*, May 26, 1928; *Whangdoodle* 1, no. 2, LLMVC.

4. *Whangdoodle* 1, no. 3, LLMVC; "Scandal Sheet Issued at L.S.U.," *Crowley Daily Signal*, April 24, 1930; "Kennedy Found Guilty of Libel for Each Count," undated, unidentified newspaper clipping, Kemble K. Kennedy Scrapbook, LLMVC.

5. "The Whangdoodle," *Reveille*, May 2, 1930; "L.S.U. Cadets Seek Scandal Sheet Probe," *Daily Advertiser*, May 1, 1930; "Students Voice Regrets for Pink Sheet Appearance," *Morning Advocate*, May 8, 1930; Thomas W. Atkinson to Kemble K. Kennedy and Paul G. Borron, May 5, 1930, Kennedy Scrapbook.

6. "'Whangdoodle' Inquiry Under Way at L.S.U.," *Shreveport Times*, May 6, 1930; "Students Ask Whangdoodle Investigation," *Reveille*, May 2, 1930; "Student Indicted in 'Whangdoodle' Quiz at Capitol," *Times-Picayune*, June 3, 1930; Atkinson to Kennedy, May 5, 1930, Kennedy Scrapbook.

7. "Pledge of Secrecy Relative to Publishing and Distributing the 'Whangdoodle' and Other Business of T.N.E. Fraternity," Kennedy Scrapbook; *Whangdoodle* 1, no. 3, LLMVC.

8. "Student Indicted in 'Whangdoodle' Quiz at Capitol," *Times-Picayune*, June 3, 1930; "Kennedy Is Indicted on Libel Count," *Morning Advocate*, June 3, 1930; Executive Order by Walter Prichard, LSU Dean of Men, June 3, 1930, Kennedy Scrapbook; "Long Denies Any Threats to L.S.U., Atkinson," *New Orleans States*, June 5, 1930.

9. "Assert Long after Scalp of Atkinson," *Shreveport Times,* June 6, 1930; "'Hot Time' Threats by Long Failed to Impress Atkinson," *Shreveport Journal,* June 6, 1930; "Long Denies Any Threats to L.S.U., Atkinson," *New Orleans States,* June 5, 1930; "Suspension of Kennedy Is Endorsed," *New Orleans States,* June 9, 1930.

10. "Kennedy Found Guilty of Libel for Each Count," undated, unidentified newspaper clipping, Kennedy Scrapbook; "Kennedy Gets Year for Criminal Libel," *Weekly Town Talk,* November 15, 1930.

11. Kennedy to LSU Board on May 11, 1931, in Proceedings, LSU Board of Supervisors, June 8, 1931, Board of Supervisors Records, box 2, LSUA.

12. "Long Petitioned by Hundreds to Reprieve Kennedy," *Shreveport Journal,* November 15, 1930.

13. Cawthon, Corbin, and McGuire interviews, THWP; Beals, *The Story of Huey P. Long,* 386.

14. "Long Weighs Many Petitions to Free Kemble K. Kennedy," *Shreveport Journal,* November 18, 1930; "Reprieve Frees Kemble Kennedy for 12 Months," *Clarion-News,* November 27, 1930

15. "Long Denies Any Threats to L.S.U., Atkinson," *New Orleans States,* June 5, 1930; "New Board for L.S.U. Confirmed," *Morning Advocate,* July 11, 1930; "George Everett Named to L.S.U. Board Vacancy," *Morning Advocate,* August 2, 1930.

16. "Before Governor's Denial," *New Orleans States,* June 5, 1930.

17. Doles interview, THWP; "Long Denounces Ransdell's Work in U.S. Senate," *Times-Picayune,* August 25, 1930; Vincent J. Marsala, "U.S. Senator Joseph E. Ransdell, Catholic Statesman: A Reappraisal," *Louisiana History,* Winter 1994, 41–42; *Beaumont Journal,* August 4, 1930; Sindler, *Huey Long's Louisiana,* 69–71; White, *Kingfish,* 102–4; "The Kingdom of the Kingfish," *New Orleans Item,* August 24, 1939; "Senate Approves New LSU Board," *Daily World,* July 11, 1940.

18. Sindler, *Huey Long's Louisiana,* 75.

8. I DID MY DAMNDEST

1. "More Than 6,000 See L.S.U. Cross Goal Dozen Times," *Morning Advocate,* September 21, 1930.

2. "More Than 6,000 See L.S.U. Cross Goal Dozen Times"; "Team from North Louisiana Unable to Check Heaving Foe in Baton Rouge Game," *Shreveport Times,* September 28, 1930; "Louisiana State Tigers Romp over Southwestern," *Shreveport Times,* October 5, 1930; Finney, *The Fighting Tigers,* 472.

3. "Looking 'Em Over with Fred Digby," *New Orleans Item,* October 6, 1930; "Tigers Coach Is Confident Team Will Put Up Fight," New Orleans *States,* October 9, 1930; "Spoutings In Sportdom," *New Orleans States,* October 9, 1930.

4. "Cohen Sees Tiger-Carolina Game Saturday as 'toss up,'" *New Orleans Item,* October 10, 1930; "Kicked Gives South Carolina Edge," *New Orleans Item,* October 12, 1930; "Looking Forward," *State-Times,* October 13, 1930.

5. Finney, *The Fighting Tigers,* 95.

6. "Foot Ball . . . Rules. . . ." *Northwest Oklahoman,* September 21, 1934; "Side-Line Coaching Heavily Criticized," *Whittier News,* November 27, 1926; "Football Coaches Would Stand Pat on Present Rules," *Wilkes-Barre Times Leader,* December 29, 1925; Lambert, *Football Officiating and Interpretations of the Rules,* 219; Oriard, *King Football,* 131.

7. Finney, *The Fighting Tigers*, 95–96; Finney wrote that Long persuaded Cohen to call the 1099 play late in the game and that it resulted in a score. This could not be the case, however, as both of LSU's touchdowns came in the first half; "L.S.U. Defeats Sewanee 12 to 0 in Stiff Battle," *Morning Advocate*, October 26, 1930; "L.S.U. Defeats Sewanee 12 to 0 in Stiff Battle," *New Orleans Item*, October 31, 1930.

8. "Mixing with Mickey," *State-Times*, October 31, 1930; "L.S.U. Tigers Leave for Arkansas Game," *New Orleans Item*, October 31, 1930.

9. Finney, *The Fighting Tigers*, 96; Bowman interview, THWP; "The Game Play-by-Play," *Morning Advocate*, November 2, 1930.

10. "Post Mortems in Sports," *Morning Advocate*, November 2, 1930.

11. Finney, *The Fighting Tigers*, 96–97.

12. "Atkinson Resigns L.S.U. Presidency," *Weekly Town Talk*, November 17, 1930; "Dr. J. M. Smith Named New Head for University," *Morning Advocate*, November 18, 1930; Williams, *Huey Long*, 501–2; James Monroe Smith Diary, 29–30, James Monroe Smith Papers, LLMVC; Everett interview, THWP.

13. Bozeman, "Winn Parish as I Have Known It," February 4, 1960; James Monroe Smith Diary, James Monroe Smith Papers, 29–32, LLMVC.

14. "Dr. J. M. Smith Named New Head for University," *Morning Advocate*, November 18, 1930.

15. "Smith Assumes L.S.U. Presidency as Atkinson Quits," *Times-Picayune*, November 18, 1930.

16. "Dr. J. M. Smith Named New Head for University," *Morning Advocate*, November 18, 1930.

17. "Dr. James Monroe Smith Named President of L.S.U.," *Reveille*, November 21, 1930.

18. "Dr. J. M. Smith Named New Head for University," *Morning Advocate*, November 18, 1930; "New State Capitol on Long's Program," *Weekly News*, October 11, 1930.

19. "Looking 'Em Over," *New Orleans Item*, November 18, 1930.

20. "Many Complexities of Status of Two Schools and the Dope Making More Annual Interest Than Usual," *Morning Advocate*, November 25, 1930; "Tiger Mentor Turns toward Game with Tulane Thanksgiving," *Morning Advocate*, November 18, 1930.

21. Finney, *The Fighting Tigers*, 97–98; Butler interview, THWP; "How Gov. Long Inspired L.S.U. Team to Fight," *New Orleans States*, November 28, 1930.

22. Zimmerman was the star Tulane halfback from Lake Charles that Long had suggested poaching in 1929. In Tulane's November 16, 1930, game against Georgia, the sophomore halfback made a thrilling fifteen-yard run for a touchdown at the end of the first half. Tulane beat Georgia, 25–0; "Tulane Routs Georgia Eleven in Bid for Second Title," *Morning Advocate*, November 16, 1930; "How Gov. Long Inspired L.S.U. Team to Fight," *New Orleans States*, November 28, 1930.

23. "How Gov. Long Inspired L.S.U. Team to Fight," *New Orleans States*, November 28, 1930.

24. Digby interview, THWP; Williams, *Huey Long*, 507; "Long Says Cohen Will Stay but Russ Is Silent," *New Orleans Item*, November 28, 1930; "Governor and New Head of University Well Pleased," *New Orleans States*, November 28, 1930.

25. "Hey, Rockne!" *Daily Chronicle*, December 11, 1930; Butler interview, THWP; "Tigers Elated over Showing with Greenies," *Morning Advocate*, November 28, 1930.

26. "How Gov. Long Inspired L.S.U. Team to Fight," *New Orleans States*, November 28, 1930; "Tigers Elated over Showing with Greenies," *Morning Advocate*, November 28, 1930; Butler interview, THWP; Finney, *The Fighting Tigers*, 98; "Hey, Rockne!" *Daily Chronicle*, December 11, 1930; Williams, *Huey Long*, 507.

27. "Cohen Made L.S.U. Head Coach," *Morning Advocate,* December 2, 1930; "Coach Cohen Signs Three Year Contract," *Reveille,* December 5, 1930.

28. "Signed Statement Expressing Team Confidence in Coach Was to Appear before Monday Night's Conference," *Morning Advocate,* December 3, 1930; "Congratulations, Cohen," *Reveille,* December 5, 1930.

29. "J. P. Luker Is Chosen Most Valuable Player on 1930 Eleven at Business Men's Banquet Held Monday Night," *State-Times,* December 9, 1930; Williams, *Huey Long,* 508; "For He's a Jolly Good Fellow," *Reveille,* December 5, 1930.

30. "Hey, Rockne!" *Daily Chronicle,* December 11, 1930.

9. A COW COLLEGE

1. Long claimed in his autobiography, "In November 1928, [LSU] was given 'A' rating by the Association of American Universities which established it on a parity with the best in the country" (*Every Man a King,* 246); Don Wharton, "Louisiana State University," *Scribner's,* September 1937, 34; Carriere interview, THWP; Jerry P. Sanson, "'What He Did and What He Promised to Do . . .': Huey Long and the Horizons of Louisiana Politics," *Louisiana History* 47, no. 3 (Summer 2006): 268.

2. Some Louisiana historians, including Matthew J. Schott, have argued that Louisiana's educational system was not markedly worse than other southern states. "Louisiana's high rate of illiteracy must partly have reflected the problem of the Cajuns with their unwritten language," he observed. "And the marked increase in literacy in later years must have reflected this group's Anglo-American acculturation." ("Huey Long: Progressive Backlash?" 137); William A. Link, "Making the Inarticulate Speak: A Reassessment of Public Education in the Rural South, 1870–1920," *Journal of Thought,* Fall 1983, 69; Joan Malczewski, "Weak State, Stronger Schools: Northern Philanthropy and Organizational Change in the Jim Crow South," *Journal of Southern History,* November 2009, 976–78; "Eighty-First Annual Report for the Session 1929–30," State Department of Education of Louisiana, *Bulletin* no. 186 (October 1930): 28–29; Williams, *Huey Long,* 493; V. O. Key Jr., "Louisiana: The Seamy Side of Democracy," in Dethloff, ed., *Huey P. Long,* 57; Wall et al., *Louisiana: A History,* 304.

3. "Biennial Report of the President of Louisiana State University to the Governor and Members of the Legislature for 1932–34," *University Bulletin,* May 1934, 18; "L.S.U. Has Near 2000 in Classes as Work Starts," *Clarion-News,* September 25, 1930; "L.S.U. to Begin 1930–31 Session September 15," *West Carroll Gazette,* September 12, 1930; "Over 1900 Enrolled in University," *Reveille,* October 19, 1928; "New L.S.U. Enrollment Record Seen," *Morning Advocate,* September 16, 1930; *University Bulletin,* May 1931, 285; The school set a record for incoming freshmen in the fall of 1930, enrolling 777 first-year students; "L.S.U. to Get $250,000 from Severance Tax," *Reveille,* July 7, 1926.

4. "Reminiscences of Fred C. Frey," Fred C. Frey Papers, box 1, LLMVC

5. "Student Expenses," *University Bulletin,* May 1931, 48–51; "Police Jury to Finance 3 Boys' Tuitions L.S.U.," *Daily Advertiser,* August 8, 1930; Davis, *Huey Long,* 39–40; "Proceedings of LSU Board," June 8, 1931, Board of Supervisors Records, box 2, LSUA; Watterson, *College Football,* 183–85; "Out-of-State Old Students Pay No Tuition," *Morning Advocate,* August 16, 1931; "L.S.U. to Give Scholarships outside State," *State-Times,* August 18, 1931; "L.S.U. Students

May Use Cotton to Pay Fees," *Times-Picayune*, September 17, 1931; "Thirty Percent of Student Body Is Employed in Wage-earning," *Reveille*, April 26, 1929; Cawthon interview, THWP.

6. Harris, *The Kingfish*, 38; "Steps Taken for Bettering of University," *State-Times*, June 11, 1928.

7. Williams, *Huey Long*, 512; Bowman interview, THWP.

8. White, *Kingfish*, 21–22; Watterson, *College Football*, 143.

9. Georgacopoulos, "How 'Lyingnewspapers' Made Huey Long the Ruler of His State: A Model of Press-Populist Dynamics"; "'Hey, Rockne'—Watch Your Step! Huey Long Is on Your Trail," *Bay City Times*, December 14, 1930.

10. "Louisiana Governor Apologizes for His Pajamas and German Cruiser Booms 17-Gun Salute," *St. Louis Post-Dispatch*, March 4, 1930; Davis, *Huey Long*, 122–23.

11. Leuchtenburg, *Franklin D. Roosevelt and the New Deal*, 97; Schlesinger, *The Politics of Upheaval*, 50; Gamble interview, THWP.

12. "Huey Long Promises Pot-Likker Lessons on Reaching Senate," *Selma Times-Journal*, August 3, 1930; "Potlikker and Cornpone May Split Solid South if Huey Long Wins Out," *Atlanta Constitution*, February 17, 1931; "Cornpone and Potlikker Involve Dixie Governors in Hot Dispute," *Orlando Evening Star*, February 16, 1931; "Roosevelt Is a Crumbler," *Huntsville Times*, February 23, 1931; "Amos 'n' Andy Divided for First Time in Dixie's Cornpone-Potlikker Etiquette," *Atlanta Constitution*, February 21, 1931; Huey Long to Robert E. Scott, April. 12, 1932, Jack B. McGuire Collection of Huey P. Long Papers, LRC; William F. Mugleston, "Cornpone and Potlikker: A Moment of Relief in the Great Depression," *Louisiana History*, Summer 1975, 279–86.

13. McLeod, *The Original Amos 'n' Andy*, 72.

14. Butler interview, THWP; Williams, *Huey Long*, 512; Beals, *The Story of Huey P. Long*, 395.

15. Kane, *Louisiana Hayride*, 216–17.

16. "Governor Plans State Medical School at L.S.U.," *Times-Picayune*, December 23, 1930.

17. Cawthon interview, THWP; Salvaggio, *New Orleans Charity Hospital*, 109–11; Klein and Harkin, *A History of LSU School of Medicine New Orleans*, 3; "The Huey P. Long Years and Louisiana Politics," *Tulane University School of Medicine and Charity Hospital*, Tulane University Health Sciences Center Rudolph Matas Library, History and Archives, www.tulane.edu/~matas/historical/charity/charity6.htm.

18. "Arthur Vidrine Slated for Charity Hospital Superintendent at N.O.," *Opelousas News*, August 2, 1928; Salvaggio, *New Orleans Charity Hospital*, 109–11; Klein and Harkin, *A History of LSU School of Medicine New Orleans*, 3–4.

19. Salvaggio, *New Orleans Charity Hospital*, 110.

20. "Governor Plans State Medical School at L.S.U.," *Times-Picayune*, December 23, 1930; "Medical School Promised L.S.U. within the Year," *Morning Advocate*, December 23, 1930.

21. "Tulane Denies Turning Away Medical Pupils," *Times-Picayune*, December 24, 1930; "Phelps Refuses Reply to Remark from Governor," *Times-Picayune*, December 25, 1930; "Long Hints at Tulane Funds Investigation," *Shreveport Times*, December 28, 1930.

22. Cohn interview, THWP.

23. "Dr. Vidrine Is Named Head of Medical School," *New Orleans States*, January 4, 1931; Klein and Harkin, *A History of LSU School of Medicine New Orleans*, 2.

10. YOU HAVE TO DARE A BIT

1. James Monroe Smith Diary, 49–50, James Monroe Smith Papers, LLMVC.

2. Long, *Every Man a King,* 247; James Monroe Smith Diary, 39–43, James Monroe Smith Papers, LLMVC.

3. "Capitol Building Contracts Reach Nearly $3,000,000," *Times-Picayune,* December 11, 1930.

4. "New School to Be Discussed," *Crowley Daily Signal,* January 3, 1931; "Dr. Vidrine Is Named Head of Medical School," *New Orleans States,* January 4, 1931; "Make Plans for Buildings for Medical School," *State-Times,* January 5, 1931.

5. "Million Dollar Building Plans Held at L.S.U.," *Morning Advocate,* January 24, 1931.

6. James Monroe Smith Diary, James Monroe Smith Papers, LLMVC.

7. Nugent interview, THWP.

8. "Contracts Let for New L.S.U. Medical School," *Times-Picayune,* March 31, 1931; "Contract for L.S.U. Medical Building Let," *Rayne Tribune,* April 10, 1931.

9. "L.S.U. Receives $2,150,000 for Sale of Lands," *State-Times,* April 21, 1931; "L.S.U. Sells 22 Acres of Land for $1,800,000," *Times-Picayune,* April 22, 1931; "Old Campus Land May Be Given State," *State-Times,* May 24, 1950; "Complete Finance Plans for L.S.U. Building Program," *Morning Advocate,* April 21, 1931; "Alumni Aid L.S.U. Land Sale Plans," *Morning Advocate,* June 9, 1931.

10. "Suit Filed to Set Aside Sale of L.S.U. Lands," *State-Times,* June 5, 1931; "Sale of 22 Acres to Highway Body Attacked in Suit," *Times-Picayune,* June 6, 1931; *United States Naval Institute Proceedings,* July 1926, vol. 52, no. 281, 2507.

11. "Alumni Aid L.S.U. Land Sale Plans," *Morning Advocate,* June 9, 1931.

12. "Caldwell Firm Gets Contracts for University," *Morning Advocate,* August 1, 1931; "Contracts for Two University Buildings Given," *Morning Advocate,* August 8, 1931; "Dormitory Ready Next Month for Co-Ed Group," *Morning Advocate,* November 3, 1931; "New Dormitory Begins Its Part in Campus Life December 5," *LSU Alumni News,* January 1932; Middleton interview, THWP; "New Swimming Pool Will Be Largest in U.S.," *Reveille,* October 16, 1931; James Monroe Smith Diary, James Monroe Smith Papers, 65, LLMVC.

13. "Governor Claims Road Body–L.S.U. Deal Was Proper," *Times-Picayune,* November 28, 1931.

14. Cutrer, *Parnassus on the Mississippi,* 11; Middleton interview, THWP; "Two Selected on Faculty of Newly Formed Medic School," *Reveille,* February 6, 1931; "3 Departments Are Elevated to Schools," *Reveille,* February 20, 1931; Williams, *Huey Long,* 514; "Alumni Aid L.S.U. Land Sale Plans," *Morning Advocate,* June 9, 1931.

15. McGuire interview, THWP.

16. Huey Long speech excerpt (Con. Rec. 73, 2nd, vol. 78, pt. 6, 6190), found in T. Harry Williams Papers, Research Material, Box 17, LLMVC.

17. James Monroe Smith Diary, 62, 70–72, James Monroe Smith Papers, LLMVC.

18. James Monroe Smith Diary, 30–38; Frey interview, THWP.

19. Williams, *Huey Long,* 503.

20. Don Wharton, "Louisiana State University," *Scribner's,* September 1937, 37; James Monroe Smith Diary, 29–51, James Monroe Smith Papers, LLMVC.

21. James Monroe Smith Diary, 39–43; Williams, *Huey Long,* 502; Butler interview, THWP.

22. According to Leche, in telling this story Long had used, repeatedly, the word "nigger," not "man" (Leche interview, THWP).

23. "Reminiscences of Fred C. Frey," Fred C. Frey Papers, box 1, LLMVC; "Dean Hebert Begins Duties," *Reveille*, September 18, 1936; Ruffin, *Stately Oaks*, 69.

24. Hébert, *Last of the Titans*, 125; "Dignified Pomp Marks Ceremony of Inauguration," *Morning Advocate*, November 13, 1931; "Smith Installed with Ceremonies as L.S.U. Leader," *Times-Picayune*, November 13, 1931; "Long Speaks to Teachers," *Weekly Town Talk*, November 12, 1931.

25. "L.S.U. to Begin New Session on September 21," *Morning Advocate*, September 1, 1931; "Sidewalks to Be Laid on Campus," *Reveille*, October 30, 1931; "Library School Is Accredited," *Reveille*, April 6, 1934.

26. "Tigers Will Practice Twice a Day with Night Work Planned Later," *Times-Picayune*, August 30, 1931; Seifried, "The Development of 'Death Valley' in Louisiana," 195–98.

27. *Gumbo* yearbook, class of 1931, digitalcommons.lsu.edu/gumbo/38.

11. *CANE JUICE*

1. "Eight Educators Added to Faculty for Next Session," *Reveille*, March 23, 1928; "Dr. Uhler to Leave Hopkins Faculty," *Baltimore Sun*, March 19, 1928; Cutrer, *Parnassus on the Mississippi*, 17; "Hell in Scene for New Play by Dr. Uhler," *Reveille*, March 1, 1929; "Uhler Now Has Proofs of His Book on Drama," *Reveille*, April 5, 1929; "Row, Peterson Co. Publishes Play by Dr. J. E. Uhler," *Reveille*, April 19, 1929; "Dr. J. E. Uhler's Book on Drama Is Published," *Reveille*, November 1, 1929; "'Louisiana's Own' Songs Are Written," *Reveille*, November 8, 1929; "Dr. Uhler's Play Just off Press," *Reveille*, December 6, 1929; "Play by Uhler Presented by Guild Members," *Reveille*, February 21, 1930; Winchell, *Cleanth Brooks and the Rise of Modern Criticism*, 82–83.

2. Uhler to Hewitt Howland, May 30, 1931; Howland to Uhler, June 15, 1931; Howland to Uhler, July 20, 1931, John Uhler Papers, Correspondence, 1921–60, box 1, LLMVC.

3. Watterson, *College Football*, 158; Hewitt Howland to Uhler, March 10, 1931, John Uhler Papers, Correspondence, 1921–60, box 1, LLMVC; "Cane Juice," *Time*, October 26, 1931.

4. "Some Pertinent Remarks on CANE JUICE," Father F. L. Gassler, October 3, 1931, John Uhler Papers, Correspondence, 1921–60, box 1, LLMVC; "Father Gassler's Attack on Novel 'Cane Juice' Answered by Dr. Uhler," *Morning Advocate*, October 5, 1931.

5. "Professor Uhler Pens Sharp Reply to Moral Attack," *Morning Advocate*, October 6, 1931.

6. "Uhler Dismissed by L.S.U. Board Because of Novel," *Morning Advocate*, October 11, 1931; "Long, Smith Comment on Uhler Tangle," *Morning Advocate*, October 10, 1931.

7. "Long, Smith Comment on Uhler Tangle," *Morning Advocate*, October 10, 1931.

8. Forrest Bailey to "Our Friends in Louisiana," October 9, 1931, and Roger Baldwin to "interested friends," October 10, 1931; telegram to Uhler, October 12, 1931; Henry R. Linville to Smith, October 13, 1931, John Uhler Papers, Correspondence, 1921–60, box 1, LLMVC.

9. "Uhler Plans to Sue Priest for Damages," *Monroe News-Star*, October 12, 1931.

10. "University Pays $4000 to Uhler," *Reveille*, November 20, 1931.

11. Llewellyn Jones, "Academic Freedom in Old Louisiana," *Chicago Evening Post*, January 8, 1932; "John Uhler, 'Cane Juice' Author, Busy at Work on Political Novel," *Shreveport Times*, February 28, 1932.

12. James Monroe Smith to Uhler, April 5, 1932, John Uhler Papers, Correspondence, 1921–

60, box 1, LLMVC; "Dr. Uhler Is Re-instated in Former Position on Faculty as English Professor Next Year," *Reveille*, April 15, 1932; "Uhler Re-instated," *Reveille*, April 15, 1932.

12. WHAT DOES THE BAND THINK?

1. Betty M. Field, "Louisiana and the Great Depression," in Conrad and Baker, eds., *Louisiana Gothic: Recollections of the 1930s*, 18–25; Glen Jeansonne, "Challenge to the New Deal: Huey P. Long and the Redistribution of National Wealth," *Louisiana History*, Autumn 1980, 337; Glen Jeansonne, "Huey Long and Racism," *Louisiana History*, Summer 1922, 273; Williams, *Huey Long*, 307–10; Hair, *The Kingfish and His Realm*, 191–92, 227, 231; John W. Scott, "Highway Building in Louisiana before Huey Long: An Overdue Re-Appraisal," *Louisiana History*, Winter 2003, 5–38; "Biennial Report of the President of Louisiana State University to the Governor and Members of the Legislature for 1932–34," *University Bulletin*, May 1934, 6.

2. Continé and Phillips, *The Golden Band from Tigerland*, 11–12; *University Bulletin*, April 1930, 365.

3. Hood interview, THWP.

4. "New Uniforms Will Be Given Band at L.S.U.," *Morning Advocate*, January 28, 1931.

5. "L.S.U. Team Will Have New Uniforms," *Weekly Town Talk*, August 27, 1931.

6. Williams, *Huey Long*, 504; *University Bulletin*, May 1931, 286–87.

7. Williams interview, THWP; "New L.S.U. March Honors Gov. Long," *Weekly News*, March 21, 1931; "New Louisiana State University March Honors Governor Long," *Abbeville Meridional*, April 11, 1931.

8. "'Governor Long' March Will Be Played Friday," *Reveille*, March 6, 1931; "Governor Long Will Review L.S.U. Cadets," *Morning Advocate*, March 12, 1931; "Gov. Long Was Honored at Parade Friday," *Reveille*, March 13, 1931; "L.S.U. Band Plays New Governor Long March," *Weekly Town Talk*, March 21, 1931; band story in LSU School of Music Records, box 13, LSUA.

9. Proceedings of the LSU Board of Supervisors, June 8, 1931, LSU Board of Supervisors Records, box 3, LSUA; *University Bulletin*, April 1932, 364–65; "Alumni Aid L.S.U. Land Sale Plans," *Morning Advocate*, June 9, 1931; "L.S.U. Band More Than Doubles in Size This Year," *Reveille*, November 2, 1931.

10. Williams and Hood interviews, THWP.

11. "National Defense Law, Chief Tells Reserve Officers," *Times-Picayune*, April 21, 1931; "Huey Long, L.S.U. Band Threaten to Steal Show from King of Mardi Gras," *State-Times*, February 9, 1932.

12. LSU News Bureau release, April 17, 1931, LSU School of Music Records, box 13, LSUA.

13. "Cyr Assails Long as Students Ask Him to Make Trip," *Times-Picayune*, October 2, 1931.

13. I WANT A PLAY

1. The Unofficial Observer [Carter], *American Messiahs*, 15; Bowman and Rabenhorst interviews, THWP.

2. "Educated Toe of Ben Boswell Spells Victory for T.C.U.," *Morning Advocate*, September 27, 1931; "L.S.U. Loses Foley, Bowman, Butler," *Weekly Town Talk*, October 23, 1931; Butler and Bowman interviews, THWP; Finney, *The Fighting Tigers*, 102.

3. Butler and Bowman interviews, THWP.

4. Finney, *The Fighting Tigers*, 101–2; *Spalding's Official Foot Ball Guide*, 1930, 190; "Foley Runs Wild to Lead Bengals to 35–0 Victory," *Morning Advocate*, October 4, 1931; "Arthur Foley Is Remembered," *Indian Journal*, November 2, 1967; Digby interview, THWP; "Tiger Gridders Loyal to Jones; Threaten to Quit," *New Orleans Item*, December 21, 1934; "Proposes Name for New Athletic Field," *Indian Journal*, July 9, 1936.

5. Bowman and Rabenhorst interviews, THWP.

6. Butler and Rabenhorst interviews, THWP; Oriard, *King Football*, 54–55; Mickal interview in Salvaggio, *New Orleans Charity Hospital*, 330; Williams, *Huey Long*, 509; Finney, *The Fighting Tigers*, 103; Angus Lind, "Tackling an All-American Guy," *Times-Picayune*, February 1, 1987.

7. Lautenschlaeger interview, THWP; Wirt Gammon, "Just between Us Fans," *Chattanooga Daily Times*, November 18, 1962; Mickal interview, THWP.

8. Bowman interview, THWP.

9. "Gov. Long to Show Students How to Yell at Pep Meet," *Reveille*, October 9, 1931.

10. "Tigers Use Pass Attack to Defeat Gamecocks, 19–12," *Morning Advocate*, October 11, 1931; "Neil Mixon Is Big Star for Bengals," *Time-Picayune*, October 18, 1931; "Tigers Use Pass Attack to Defeat Gamecocks, 19–12," *Morning Advocate*, October 11, 1931; "Tigers Pound Out 31-to-0 Revenge Win over Aggies," *Morning Advocate*, October 18, 1931; Bowman interview, THWP.

11. "L.S.U. Downs Arkansas by 13 to 6 Score," *Times-Picayune*, October 25, 1931; Butler interview, THWP; "Tigers Defeat Porkers 13–6 in Burning Heat," *Morning Advocate*, October 25, 1931; Keefe, "Viewing the News," *Times-Picayune*, October 28, 1931; "L.S.U. Band, Headed by Governor, Leaves Tonight on Up-State Trip," *Morning Advocate*, October 22, 1931.

12. "Gov. Long Wants 1,500 to Make Trip to New York," *Weekly Town Talk*, July 29, 1931; "See the L.S.U.–West Point Game," advertisement by Ray Mobley, LSU alumni secretary, in *Shreveport Times*, October 16, 1931; Williams, *Huey Long*, 511; quote from *Louisiana Progress*, August 18, 1931, in T. Harry Williams Papers, Research Material, box 18, LLMVC.

13. Hair, *The Kingfish and His Realm*, 152, 174–75; Williams, *Huey Long*, 336.

14. "Who Will Be Governor of State Nov. 2 to 10?" *Morning Advocate*, August 16, 1931; "Long and Cyr Agree to Leave State for Grid Game in East," *Times-Picayune*, August 16, 1931; "Official Itinerary to Tour in Canada and the U.S.A. When Louisiana Takes the 'Ole War Skule' to West Point," November 1931, brochure from private collection of Jack B. McGuire.

15. "Three Reasons Are Given by Dr. Cyr for Declining to Make West Point Trip," *Morning Advocate*, August 23, 1931; "Cyr Assails Long as Students Ask Him to Make Trip," *Times-Picayune*, October 2, 1931; "Cyr Requested to Make Journey So Long May Go," *Times-Picayune*, September 30, 1931.

16. "Mrs. Long, Children to Go to West Point," *Morning Advocate*, October 13, 1931; "L.S.U. Band Will March Skill with Army Cadets at Tiger-Mule Grid Game," *Morning Advocate*, October 30, 1931; "Nearly 300 Grid Fans Listed for N.Y. Trip," *Morning Advocate*, November 1, 1931; "17-Car Special Departs Today for L.S.U-Army Classic This Saturday," *Morning Advocate*, November 4, 1931; Hood interview, THWP; "L.S.U. Band Will Match Skill with Army Cadets at Tiger-Mule Grid Game," *Morning Advocate*, October 30, 1931; "Fighting Tigers Beaten by Better Army Club, 20–0," *Morning Advocate*, November 8, 1931.

17. "L.S.U. Tigers Begin Hard Work Today," *Times-Picayune*, November 18, 1931; "Post Mortems in Sports," *Morning Advocate*, November 18, 1931.

18. "Tulane Greenies Now Undisputed Dixie Champions," *Morning Advocate*, November 29, 1931; "The Grab-Bag," *State-Times*, November 30, 1931.

19. "Change in Athletic Department to Be Made by Dr. James Smith," *State-Times*, December 1, 1931; "Russ Cohen to Get Help in New Shift in L.S.U. Athletic Staff," *New Orleans Item*, November 30, 1931; "Rumors Rife Concerning Shake-Up in L.S.U. Athletic Department as President Smith Announces Change," *Morning Advocate*, December 1, 1931; "Report Cohen to Take Post at Vanderbilt," *Daily Advertiser*, December 8, 1931; "Cohen Resigns; Made Assistant at Vanderbilt," *Reveille*, December 22, 1931; Finney, *The Fighting Tigers*, 105.

20. Williams, *Huey Long*, 540–43; "The Kingdom of the Kingfish," *New Orleans Item*, August 27, 1939; "Capitol and Mansion Are Heavily Armed against Possible Arrival of Cyr," *State-Times*, October 14, 1931; "Paul N. Cyr Files His Suit to Oust Long as Governor," *State-Times*, October 19, 1931; "Judge Dupre Says Cyr Has Vacated," *New Orleans States*, October 21, 1931; "Supreme Court Dismisses Suit by Cyr to Oust Long as Governor of Louisiana," *Times-Picayune*, January 23, 1932.

21. "Revered Senate Traditions Tumble with Long's Antics, Says Columnist," *Morning Advocate*, February 2, 1932.

14. SELL THEM PLUGS

1. "Rumors Rife Concerning Shake-Up in L.S.U. Athletic Department as President Smith Announces Change," *Morning Advocate*, December 1, 1931; "'Biff' Jones Is Genius at West Point," *Rockford Republic*, October 31, 1928; "West Point—and Harry Wilson," *Rockford Republic*, June 2, 1928; "Jones Makes Cadets Sweat in Final Calisthenic Drill," *Jersey Journal*, November 9, 1928; "'Biff' Jones Soon to Leave West Point Coaching Post," *Charleston News and Courier*, December 21, 1929; "'Biff' Jones Transferred to Baton Rouge Where He May Coach at L.S.U.," *Times-Picayune*, January 9, 1932; Middleton interview, THWP.

2. Jones and Middleton interviews, THWP; Finney, *The Fighting Tigers*, 106–7.

3. Middleton interview, THWP; Finney, *The Fighting Tigers*, 106–7; "University Followers Now Await Coming of Coach Biff Jones and Any Further Changes in His Staff," *Morning Advocate*, January 10, 1932.

4. "No Captain Chosen; Smith Is Honored," *Times-Picayune*, February 12, 1932; Finney, *The Fighting Tigers*, 107–9.

5. "'We Did Not Come to L.S.U. to Fail,' Declares Biff Jones," *New Orleans States*, February 12, 1932; "L.S.U.'s New Coach, Jones, Given Rousing Welcome at Annual Banquet," *Times-Picayune*, February 12, 1932.

6. Davis, *Huey Long*, 150.

7. "Huey's Rag-Time Band," *Reveille*, February 12, 1932; "'Pet of the State,'" *Reveille*, February 19, 1931.

8. "Bossed Governor," *Time*, October 3, 1932, 10–11; Leche and Fisher interviews, THWP.

9. Earl Long to Huey Long, Overton Hearings, vol. 1, February 14, 1933, 840, from notes in T. Harry Williams Papers, Research Material, HPL: Notecards, box 17, LLMVC; Williams, *Huey Long*, 567; Leche interviews, THWP.

10. Field, "Louisiana and the Great Depression," 6–7; "State Faces Reductions in Expenses," *Morning Advocate*, September 21, 1932; LSU Executive Committee Proceedings, February 17, 1932, and LSU Board of Supervisors Meeting Minutes, March 11, 1932, Board of Supervisors Records, 1932–38, box 2, LSUA.

11. "Governor Allen Promises Aid to State's Schools," *Times-Picayune*, May 21, 1932; "L.S.U.

to Be Greater Says New Governor," *Reveille*, May 27, 1932; LSU Board Proclamation, August 22, 1932, Board of Supervisors Records, 1932–38, box 2, LSUA.

12. "Programs Ready for Dedicating Medical Center," *Times-Picayune*, May 8, 1932; Klein and Harkin, *A History of LSU School of Medicine New Orleans*, 5; "Last of Five Buildings Added to L.S.U. Are Now Drawing Near Completion," *Morning Advocate*, January 17, 1932; "10,000 More Seats for LSU Stadium," *New Orleans States*, July 28, 1932.

13. "Dorms in Stadium Is Now Unique Plan," *LSU Alumni News*, September 1925; Finney, *The Fighting Tigers*, 99–100; Seifried, "The Development of 'Death Valley' in Louisiana," 195–98; "L.S.U. Planning Expenditure of Additional Funds," *Times-Picayune*, June 25, 1932; "No More 'Cafeteria,'" *Reveille*, July 14, 1933.

14. Andrew Doyle, "Turning the Tide: College Football and Southern Progressivism," *Southern Cultures*, Fall 1997, 28–51; Schmidt, *Shaping College Football*, 41.

15. "Enrollment for L.S.U. Shows Gain," *Morning Advocate*, September 21, 1932; "Enrollment Exceeds All Records," *Reveille*, September 30, 1932; "Interim Report of the President to the Board of Supervisors," Louisiana State University, Spring 1933, Board of Supervisors Records, 1932–38, LSUA; "Eighty-Fourth Annual Report for the Session 1932–33," State Department of Education of Louisiana, *Bulletin* no. 266 (November 1933): 168; "Biennial Report of the President of Louisiana State University to the Governor and Members of the Legislature for 1932–34," *University Bulletin*, May 1934, 18; "College at a Corner," *Time*, September 26, 1932, 33; "Annual Report of the President to the Governor and Members of the Legislature," *University Bulletin*, October 1935, 35.

16. "Move to Declare L.S.U. Land Sale Invalid Dismissed," *Times-Picayune*, November 15, 1932; "Last of Five Buildings Added to L.S.U. Are Now Drawing Near Completion," *Morning Advocate*, January 17, 1932; "Four New L.S.U. Buildings Erected, Furnished at Expense of $2,984,302," *Times-Picayune*, July 8, 1932; "The End of a Perfect Year," *Reveille*, May 27, 1932.

17. "Irwin Says Long Offered Him State Jobs to Quit L.S.U," *Times-Picayune*, July 24, 1932; "Appointment of Dr. Maes Approved," *Weekly Town Talk*, September 21, 1932; Salvaggio, *New Orleans Charity Hospital*, 115; "Senator Long's Idea," *Time*, August 1932, 24; "Dr. M. P. Miller Resigns from L.S.U. Faculty," *Weekly Town Talk*, July 23, 1932.

18. "Dr. A. Castellani Accepts Post at Medical Center," *Morning Advocate*, January 3, 1932; "Castellani Named to L.S.U. Medical School," *Morning Advocate*, January 1, 1932; "Castellani New Medical Instructor," *Reveille*, January 19, 1934.

19. "Capital Era Passes with Smith as Grandeur of LSU Regime Fades, Speculation Begins," *New Orleans Item*, July 2, 1939; Middleton and Womack interviews, THWP; Williams, *Huey Long*, 503; Kane, *Louisiana Hayride*, 225–26.

20. Russell Long interview with author, February 2, 1989; Mann, *Legacy to Power*, 40–41; "Class Party Is Enjoyed at Bonnette Home," *State-Times*, November 4, 1931; "Allen May Urge Pay Slash of 10 Per Cent for All State Employees," *Times-Picayune*, May 9, 1932.

15. WHO IS THAT AWFUL MAN?

1. "Senator Long Will Witness T.C.U.-Tiger Game Saturday," *Morning Advocate*, September 21, 1932; "Long Pays Visit to Football Boys and L.S.U. Band," *Morning Advocate*, September 21, 1932.

2. "L.S.U. and T.C.U. Battle to 3-3 Tie," *Times-Picayune*, September 25, 1932; "Field

Goal by Torrance Gets Tigers Tie," *New Orleans Item,* September 25, 1932; Jones interview, THWP.

3. "Senator Long Will Address Crowd at L.S.U.-Rice Tilt," *New Orleans States,* September 26, 1932; "Parade Is Headed by Senator Long," *New Orleans States,* October 2, 1932; "Tom Driscoll Boots Field Goal to Give Owls Victory," *Houston Chronicle,* October 2, 1932; "Gangway! It's De Kingfish," *Houston Chronicle,* October 1, 1932; *Gumbo* yearbook, class of 1933, digital-commons.lsu.edu/gumbo/; "'Kingfish' Awards L.S.U. Band $1 Each to Last Long Time," *Houston Chronicle,* October 2, 1932; "But, Mama, Where's Amos?" *Houston Chronicle,* October 1, 1932.

4. Leuchtenburg, *Franklin D. Roosevelt and the New Deal,* 7, 96; Flynn, *You're the Boss,* 100–101; Wheeler, *Yankee from the West,* 285; Williams, *Huey Long,* 577–82.

5. Farley, *Behind the Ballots,* 170–71.

6. Williams, *Huey Long,* 602.

7. Williams, *Huey Long,* 603; "Long Greeted in Nebraska," *New Orleans Item,* October 24, 1932; "Wichita Assembly Addressed by Long," *Times-Picayune,* October 28, 1932; "Long Back, Just Wants to Rest," *New Orleans Item,* October 29, 1932; Farley, *Behind the Ballots,* 171.

8. "Long Back, Just Wants to Rest," *New Orleans Item,* October 29, 1932.

9. "15,000 Watch as Tiger Eleven Is Outplayed," *Shreveport Times,* November 13, 1932; "Gents Continue March Downing Bengals 6 to 0," *Morning Advocate,* November 13, 1932.

10. "L.S.U.-Tulane to Clash Tomorrow," *State-Times,* November 25, 1932; "More Tulane Players Are Ill," *New Orleans States,* November 25, 1932; "Tigers Realize Ambition for Perfect Conference Record," *New Orleans States,* November 28, 1932; "Tigers Win with Score of 14–0," *States Times,* November 26, 1932.

11. "Mike Mikulak Leads Coast '11' to Victory," *New Orleans Item,* December 18, 1932; "Oregon Beats Frostbitten Bengals 12–0," *Times-Picayune,* December 18, 1932; "Long Threatens Filibuster over Philippines Bill," *Times-Picayune,* December 17, 1932.

12. "Tigers Realize Ambition for Perfect Conference Record," *New Orleans States,* November 28, 1932; "Long Claims Grid Title for L.S.U.," *New Orleans States,* December 5, 1932.

16. TELL THEM THEY CAN GO TO HELL

1. "Don't Quote Me," *Morning Advocate,* January 27, 1933.

2. Williams, *Huey Long,* 619–24.

3. Schlesinger, *The Crisis of the Old Order,* 452.

4. "Long Says He Will Follow Roosevelt's Wishes on Bank Bill," *Times-Picayune,* January 20, 1933.

5. Huey Long, "How America Can Be Adjusted," March 17, 1933, speech text in *Congressional Record,* March 23, 1933, 73rd Congress, 1st Session, vol. 77, pt. 1; Long organization fliers, "The Share Our Wealth Principles" and "Share Our Wealth," Jack B. McGuire Collection of Huey P. Long Papers, box 1, LRC.

6. Brinkley, *Voices of Protest,* 57–61; Williams, *Huey Long,* 633.

7. "Sen. Long Says F.D. 'Stole My Thunder,'" *New Orleans Item,* August 23, 1933; Leighninger, *Building Louisiana,* 32; Farley, *Behind the Ballots,* 240; Boulard, *Huey Long Invades New Orleans,* 31.

8. Farley, *Behind the Ballots,* 240–43.

9. "Wants No Jobs Anyway, Says Crawfish," *New Orleans States,* August 23, 1933; "Long Declares Opponents Cause Delay in Roads," *State-Times,* October 9, 1933.

10. "Interim Report of the President to the Board of Supervisors," Louisiana State University, Spring 1933, Board of Supervisors Records, 1932–38, box 2, LSUA; "L.S.U. Enrollment Is Now Near 4,000," *Richland Beacon-News,* March 18, 1933; *Gumbo* yearbook, class of 1933, digitalcommons.lsu.edu/gumbo/37; "New Dormitory for Men Students Is Completed," *Reveille,* October 6, 1933; "Biennial Report of the President of Louisiana State University to the Governor and Members of the Legislature for 1932–34," *University Bulletin,* May 1934, 18.

11. "Work Will Begin Tomorrow on New Road to L.S.U.," *Morning Advocate,* April 2, 1933; "150 Jobless Start Making New Route to Campus," *Morning Advocate,* February 18, 1933.

12. The Federal Emergency Relief Act, enacted in May 1933, provided, among other things, funds for part-time work programs for college students; Frey interview, THWP; "400 Students to Be Aided Here by ERA," *Reveille,* July 20, 1934; "458 Students Given ERA Jobs," *Reveille,* September 21, 1934; "Interim Report of the President to the Board of Supervisors," Louisiana State University, Spring 1933, Board of Supervisors Records, 1932–38, box 2, LSUA; "First Black Undergraduate Student at the University Recounts Vile Treatment He Received on Campus," *Reveille,* February 26, 2019.

13. "Court Weighs Legality of L.S.U. Plans," *Shreveport Times,* February 5, 1933; "Loan to L.S.U. Reduced to $508,000," *Weekly Town Talk,* July 1, 1933; "Loan to L.S.U. for Buildings to Be Delayed," *Shreveport Times,* June 6, 1933; "Bills to Permit University to Borrow Passed," *Morning Advocate,* June 13, 1934; "Bills Authorizing L.S.U. to Borrow Received Approval," *Times-Picayune,* May 31, 1934.

14. Excerpt of Long speech to US Senate in February 1933, in Graham, ed., *Huey Long,* 65–67; "Clark Objection Blocks Howell's Fund Resolution," *Times-Picayune,* February 23, 1933; "L.S.U. School of Medicine Rated as 'Acceptable School,'" *Weekly Town Talk,* February 18, 1933; "L.S.U. Medical Center Filled over Capacity," *Caldwell Watchman,* September 15, 1933.

15. "Long Regime Gives Millions to L.S.U. as Schools Suffer," *Shreveport Times,* June 13, 1933.

16. "Bonds Are Sold to Cover State's Old Obligations," *Morning Advocate,* January 17, 1933; "Bonded Indebtedness Imposed by Present Regime Crushes State Taxpayers," *Monroe Morning World,* July 30, 1933.

17. "Canker Worm of Politics Bites Deep and Expensively at L.S.U.," *Monroe News-Star,* August 3, 1933; "Politicization of University Permeates Fire Insurance Issue," *Monroe Morning World,* August 6, 1933; "L.S.U. Irregularities Long Known to Leche," *Morning Advocate,* September 2, 1939; "J. Emory Adams Out on Bond in University Case," *Morning Advocate,* June 27, 1939.

18. "New Orleans Charity Hospital Cog in Long Political Machine," *Shreveport Times,* August 13, 1933.

19. "Three Caddo Men Testify," *Shreveport Times,* April 6, 1929; "Washington Is Not for Sale, Mr. Long," *Weekly Town Talk,* July 20, 1929; "Need for Investigation," *Shreveport Times,* May 15, 1930; "Murphy Sylvest Is Appointed to L.S.U. Faculty," *Morning Advocate,* September 25, 1931; "Long Branded as Enemy of Youth in Borron Rally," *Morning Advocate,* September 3, 1932.

20. "Politics Rule at University," *Monroe News-Star,* March 20, 1934; "Indicted Group All Prominent in L.S.U. or Political Circles," *State-Times,* July 15, 1939; "Edgar Jackson, Member

of Winn School Board, Now on L.S.U. Staff," *Louisiana Leader,* May 1935; Williams, *Huey Long,* 548–49.

17. A LAUGHINGSTOCK

1. "Kennedy Granted Pardon by Allen; 15 Others Freed," *Times-Picayune,* November 11, 1932; "Kennedy to Be Reinstated," *Weekly Town Talk,* June 10, 1933; "L.S.U. Law School Placed on 'Probation Status' by American Bar Association," *Times-Picayune,* May 10, 1935.

2. Raymond Moley, "Huey Long," *Today,* September 21, 1935, 12–13; Morse interview, THWP; Moley, *27 Masters of Politics,* 221–23; Terkel, *Hard Times,* 284–85; Hargrave, *LSU Law,* 67–68; "Dr. F. K. Beutel Is Named Head of Law School," *Reveille,* June 14, 1935.

3. Williams, *Huey Long,* 692–96; Hair, *The Kingfish and His Realm,* 250, 255–57.

4. Williams, *Huey Long,* 648–54; Hair, *The Kingfish and His Realm,* 257–59, 266; Huey Long statement regarding Sands Point incident, undated, Jack B. McGuire Collection of Huey P. Long Papers, box 4, LRC.

5. Williams, *Huey Long,* 654–59.

6. Williams, *Huey Long,* 661–65; Hair, *The Kingfish and His Realm,* 260–62; Roy, Hughes, and Landry interviews, THWP; "Drive in Support of Tax Plan Will Be Opened Today," *Morning Advocate,* October 15, 1933; "Long Sets Tax Talks," *New Orleans Item,* October 8, 1933.

7. Kane, *Louisiana Hayride,* 221; Hair, *The Kingfish and His Realm,* 290; Finney, *The Fighting Tigers,* 117; White, *Kingfish,* 131; "No Elephant Dips Planned Saturday," *New Orleans States,* October 11, 1950; "Ringling Circus Won't Have to Dip Any Lions and Tigers on This Occasion," *New Orleans States,* October 6, 1955; Keefe, "Viewing the News," *Times-Picayune,* October 30, 1938.

8. "Circus Will Show in City One Day, Friday, Sept. 29," *State-Times,* September 15, 1933; Ringling Bros. and Barnum & Bailey ad in *State-Times,* September 19, 1933; "Circus Will Give Four Shows Here," *Times-Picayune,* September 19, 1933; "Ringling Circus Will Show Here," *New Orleans States,* September 21, 1934; "And the Circus Is Coming to Town! Ringling Brothers Here on October 8," *State-Times,* September 24, 1934; "Ringling-Barnum Circus to Offer Rich Spectacle," *Times-Picayune,* October 6, 1934.

9. "Down the Spillway," *New Orleans Item,* October 3, 1933; "Lasting Impression Made on Grid Game Spectators by Thrill of Engagement," *Morning Advocate,* October 15, 1933; Finney, *The Fighting Tigers,* 473.

10. "Span across Red River Is Opened Here," *Shreveport Times,* October 22, 1933; "Long Rides Private Car of Executives En Route to Redistribution Talk," *Morning Advocate,* October 22, 1933; "Enthusiasm High," *State-Times,* October 21, 1933; "State Fair Days Recalled as Crowd Swelters While Seeing L.S.U. Win 20–0," *Morning Advocate,* October 22, 1933.

11. "Vandy Defense and Punter Give Commodores 7 to 7 Tie at L.S.U.'s Homecoming," *Morning Advocate,* October 29, 1933; "Same Tiger Spirit Seen Over Again," *Morning Advocate,* October 29, 1933; "Mickal Flashes Fine Form," *New Orleans Item,* November 5, 1933.

12. "30,000 Fans Flock to Game," *New Orleans Item,* December 2, 1933; "Tulane and L.S.U. Battle to 7–7 Tie before 31,000," *New Orleans Item,* December 3, 1933; "Wild Throng Kept on Toes throughout Thrilling Game," *Times-Picayune,* December 3, 1933; "Long, Flanked by Henchmen, Leads Parade of Band," *Times-Picayune,* December 3, 1933; "Wave and L.S.U. Battle to 7–7 Tie before Crowd of Over 30,000 Fans," *Times-Picayune,* December 3, 1933.

13. Fred Digby, "Looking 'Em Over," *New Orleans Item,* December 11, 1933; "Long's 'Pep' Talk Fails to Stir 'Em," *Democrat and Chronicle,* December 3, 1933.

14. Bob Murphy, "Heard on the Sportola," *Knoxville Journal,* December 12, 1933.

18. IT WAS HUEY LONG'S UNIVERSITY

1. "The Kingdom of the Kingfish," *New Orleans Item,* September 1, 1939; Hair, *The Kingfish and His Realm,* 263–64; Williams, *Huey Long,* 666–69; "Louisianans Test Huey Long's Power," *Star-Gazette,* December 21, 1933; "'No Trouble at All' Says the Kingfish," *Knoxville News-Sentinel,* December 4, 1933; "Ballots Burned by Angry Crowd," *Spokesman-Review,* December 2, 1933.

2. John Robert Moore, "The New Deal in Louisiana," in Braeman et al., eds., *The New Deal,* 137–65.

3. Williams, *Huey Long,* 793–97; Irey, *The Tax Dodgers,* 92–94; Folsom, *The Money Trail,* 61–72; "U.S. Renews Long Income Tax Inquiry," *Town Talk,* December 21, 1933; Field, "The Politics of the New Deal in Louisiana," 174–75.

4. "Huey Long's Debacle," *Bee,* December 8, 1933.

5. "Huey Long's Plan to Abolish Poverty," *Burlington Free Press,* February 6, 1934; Brinkley, *Voices of Protest,* 79; "Coughlin and Long Problem," *Evening Post,* April 18, 1935; Arthur Krock, "In Washington," *New York Times,* January 10, 1935; "121,000 Join Long's Club," *New Orleans Item,* March 11, 1934; "Louisiana's Huey and the Presidency," *Omaha World-Herald,* January 30, 1935; "Supreme Court Hurls Wrench," *Independent,* January 17, 1935.

6. "L.S.U. Building Program Likely Says Dr. Smith," *State-Times,* March 6, 1934; "University to Begin Session September 19," *State-Times,* September 5, 1934; "Annual Report of the President to the Governor and Members of the Legislature," *University Bulletin,* October 1935, 35; "Daughter of Senator Long Feels 'At Home' on Campus," *Reveille,* October 16, 1934.

7. Fred Frey oral history, T. Harry Williams Center for Oral History, LLMVC; Leighninger, *Building Louisiana,* 56–59.

8. "Decreased L.S.U. Funds Supplemented," *Louisiana Leader,* August 1934; "Bills Authorizing L.S.U. to Borrow Receive Approval," *Times-Picayune,* May 31, 1934; "Bills to Permit University to Borrow Passed," *Morning Advocate,* June 13, 1934; "L.S.U. Finances," *New Orleans States,* August 23, 1934.

9. "Charity Hospital Project Costing $8,000,000 Again Is Rejected by PWA," *Times-Picayune,* July 16, 1935; "A Necessary Loan," *Reveille,* April 20, 1934; "Dormitories Needed," *Reveille,* April 27, 1934; "Field House to Be Girls Dormitory," *Reveille,* July 13, 1934; "An Arts and Sciences Building," *Reveille,* May 4, 1934; New Construction at University to Start in January," *State-Times,* December 28, 1934; "L.S.U. to Have New Buildings," *Daily Advertiser,* December 28, 1934; "Smith Will Confer in Washington on Building Program," *State-Times,* November 8, 1934; "Additional Help to Speed Campus Building Program," *Morning Advocate,* January 15, 1935; Ruffin, *Under Stately Oaks,* 71.

10. "Busy Scenes on Old Campus as Razing of Alumni Hall Proceeds," *State-Times,* January 23, 1934; "Alumni Building to Be Completed Early in August," *Reveille,* July 13, 1934; "Building Projects Under Way or Contemplated in City Represent Expenditure of Many Thousands," *Morning Advocate,* July 21, 1934; "L.S.U. Students Are to Share in Civil Works Aid," *State-Times,* February 5, 1934; "Alumni Hall Construction Is Going On," *Reveille,* January 12, 1934; "Offices

Assigned in Alumni Hall," *Reveille*, March 2, 1934; "University Sewer System Finished by CWA Workers," *Morning Advocate*, March 11, 1934; "L.S.U. Students Are to Share in Civil Works Aid," *State-Times*, February 5, 1934; "Botanical Garden Is Being Built," *Reveille*, January 12, 1934; "Eight CWA Projects Are Under Way," *Reveille*, January 26, 1934; "Alumni Hall, Men's Dormitory Occupied," *Louisiana Leader*, September 1934; "Biennial Report of the President of Louisiana State University to the Governor and Members of the Legislature for 1932–34," *University Bulletin*, May 1934, 12; "Wooden Risers Being Built in L.S.U. Stadium," *Reveille*, January 12, 1934.

11. Quaw interview, THWP.

12. "Bill to Create L.S.U. Monroe Branch Passed," *Weekly Town Talk*, June 23, 1934; "Junior College to Become Part of Louisiana State University," *Monroe Morning World*, August 13, 1933; "Way Paved for Expansion of University as Governor Signs Three L.S.U. Bills," *Reveille*, July 13, 1934; McManus, "When It Becomes Necessary to Spank the State Administration, I Can Do It," 12–14.

13. "Junior College to Become Part of Louisiana State University," *Monroe Morning World*, August 13, 1933; "Charges L.S.U. Is 'Octopus' of the State," *Ruston Daily Leader*, September 1, 1933; "Gov. Long Vetoes Ginsberg Tick Bill and Other Measures," *Weekly Town Talk*, July 21, 1928; Harris, *We Hail Thee Now Southeastern*, 24–25.

14. "Greenville Reporter Finds Huey Long Real Kingfish in His Bailiwick in Louisiana," *Greenville News*, July 22, 1934.

15. "Mrs. Cooper Appears in Role of Dominant Figure in Rift at Louisiana Normal School," *Shreveport Journal*, March 16, 1929; "Roy Cheered by Students," *Weekly Town Talk*, March 9, 1929; Dodd interview, THWP; "Dodd Will Remain Out of College as Appeal Is Pending," *Shreveport Journal*, April 4, 1932; "Long Demands Normal Head Resign," *Weekly Town Talk*, January 20, 1934; "Fredericks Is Elected Head of State Normal," *Rayne Tribune*, July 27, 1934.

16. "Five Day Session Is Ended," *Morning Advocate*, November 17, 1934.

17. Middleton and Frey interviews, THWP; "Reminiscences of Fred C. Frey," Fred C. Frey Papers, box 1, LLMVC.

18. H. W. Stopher memo, July 10, 1942, LSU Board of Supervisors Records, box 4, LSUA.

19. Williams, *Huey Long*, 520; Don Wharton, "Louisiana State University," *Scribner's*, September 1937, 39.

20. "Development of South's Schools in Couchs' Plea," *Morning Advocate*, October 24, 1934.

21. Cutrer, *Parnassus on the Mississippi*, 26–31.

22. "Embree Will Give Fifth Talk Today," *Reveille*, March 16, 1934; Cutrer, *Parnassus on the Mississippi*, 15–16.

23. Cutrer, *Parnassus on the Mississippi*, 27–31; "Department History," Department of Political Science, Louisiana State University, www.lsu.edu/hss/polisci/about_us/department-history.php; Cutrer, *Parnassus on the Mississippi*, 31; Brooks interview, T. Harry Williams Center for Oral History; Albert J. Montesi, "Huey Long and 'The Southern Review,'" *Journal of Modern Literature*, February 1973, 65–66.

24. Robert Penn Warren, "'All the King's Men': The Matrix of Experience," *Yale Review* 53 (December 1963): 161–67; Cutrer, *Parnassus on the Mississippi*, 49; Excerpt from Proceedings of the Board of Supervisors, August 22, 1934, Board of Supervisors Records, box 2, LSUA; Harold B. McSween, "Huey Long at His Centenary," *Virginia Quarterly Review* 69 (Summer 1993), no. 3, 509–20; Winchell, *Cleanth Brooks and the Rise of Modern Criticism*, 94; "University Press

Will Be Founded," *Reveille,* September 24, 1935; Brooks interview, T. Harry Williams Center for Oral History.

25. Cleanth Brooks interview, T. Harry Williams Center for Oral History.

19. I. O. HUEY

1. "This and That," *News and Observer,* October 31, 1934; "Record Number of Lettermen on Vol Squad," *Atlanta Constitution,* August 22, 1933; "Facts and Guesses," *Daily Tar Heel,* December 13, 1933; "Huey Long and L.S.U. Boys Put on Regular Show While Train Speeds to Nashville," *Lexington Leader,* October 27, 1934; "Upon the Coast and in the South," *Evening Sun,* October 27, 1933; "G.W., Vandy Gird for Daring Duel," *Evening Star,* October 30, 1934; "Aerial Battles on Card Today," *Leaf-Chronicle,* December 9, 1933; "Picked Up on the Dead Run," *Los Angeles Times,* October 31, 1934; "Huey Long's L.S.U. Eleven Is Pointing to Rose Bowl Trip," *Standard-Speaker,* November 8, 1934; "Alabama to Get Bowl Bid, Football Fans on Coast Say," *Cincinnati Enquirer,* November 19, 1934; "West Expects Tide for Game," *Detroit Free Press,* November 19, 1934; "Stanford Chosen for Rose Bowl," *Standard-Speaker,* November 27, 1934; "The Sportlight," *Evening Star,* November 29, 1934; "Alabama and Navy Feature Final Games," *Greenville News,* December 3, 1934; "May Play in Jackson," *Knoxville Journal,* December 4, 1934; "This and That," *News and Observer,* October 21, 1934; Kane, *Louisiana Hayride,* 220.

2. "L.S.U. Battles Uphill to Get Thrilling 14–14 Tie with S.M.U. Squad," *Morning Advocate,* October 7, 1934; "Long Threatens Porter Ouster," *Morning Advocate,* October 7, 1934; "Tulane Conquers Georgia 7–6 in Hard-Fought Tilt; L.S.U. Defeats Arkansas," *Times-Picayune,* October 21, 1934; "Pair of Dazzling Touchdown Runs Mark L.S.U. Win," *Morning Advocate,* October 14, 1934; "Allen and Long Leave for Auburn-L.S.U. Game," *New Orleans Item,* October 13, 1934; "12,000 Will See Tigers Play Auburn," *Morning Advocate,* October 13, 1934.

3. "Tulane Conquers Georgia 7–6 in Hard-Fought Tilt; L.S.U. Defeats Arkansas," *Times-Picayune,* October 21, 1934.

4. Middleton interview, THWP; "Praises Deportment of L.S.U. Students," *Reveille,* October 16, 1934.

5. Williams, *Huey Long,* 768; Blinkey Horn, "From Bunker to Bleacher," *Nashville Tennessean,* October 23, 1934; Middleton and Hughes interviews, THWP; "Cadet Regiment May Be Taken to Vanderbilt Game," *State-Times,* October 15, 1934; "Plans for Cadet Trip Take Form," *Reveille,* October 19, 1934.

6. Keefe, "Viewing the News," *Times-Picayune,* October 19, 1934.

7. "Baton Rouge Will Send Huge Junket to Vandy Contest," *Morning Advocate,* October 20, 1934; "Plans for Football Specials to Nashville for Tiger-Vandy Game Are Bringing Numerous Inquiries," *State-Times,* October 22, 1934.

8. "Students Rush Huey Long for $7 Football Expense Handouts; Others Join In," *Morning Advocate,* October 24, 1934; "Long Lends Money for Students' Trip," *New York Times,* October 24, 1934; "'On to Nashville' Is General Cry All around City," *Morning Advocate,* October 25, 1934; "L.S.U. Students to Pay Back Money to Long When Dean Makes Discipline Threat," *Times-Picayune,* October 25, 1934; Corbin interview, THWP; "Students Repaying Senator Long's Loan," *Morning Advocate,* March 10, 1935.

9. "Senator Filches Baton to Lead Tiger Band in Original Fashion," *Morning Advocate,* October 25, 1934.

10. "Long Is Expected to Announce for President at Nashville," *Nashville Banner,* October 26, 1934; "'On to Nashville' Is General Cry All around City," *Morning Advocate,* October 25, 1934.

11. "3,200 Fans Leave in 'Specials' on Nashville Junket," *Morning Advocate,* October 27, 1934; "Huey Leads Song," *Morning Advocate,* October 27, 1934; "L.S.U. Football Trip Takes Five Trains," *Illinois Central Magazine,* December 1934; "Everybody Was at Depot to See Long Caravan Off for Nashville," *State-Times,* October 27, 1934; "Tempestuous Huey Makes Roman Holiday of Trip," *Nashville Banner,* October 27, 1934; "Huey Takes Show," *State-Times,* October 27, 1934.

12. "Five Special Trains from Here Arrive 30 Minutes Late," *State-Times,* October 27, 1934; "Five Trains Carrying Louisiana State Fans Leave for Nashville," *Times-Picayune,* October 27, 1934; Hawkins interview with author.

13. Hair, *The Kingfish and His Realm,* 290; "Sidelong Sidelights," *Nashville Banner,* October 27, 1934; "Tennessee Balks at Long's Troopers," *New York Times,* October 25, 1934; "Nashville Surrenders to Huey Long," *Nashville Banner,* October 27, 1934; "Long and His Team Take Nashville," *New York Times,* October 28, 1934.

14. "Saves Speech-making for Pregame Festivities at Dudley Field," *Nashville Banner,* October 27, 1934; "Long and His Team Take Nashville," *New York Times,* October 28, 1934.

15. "Long Speaks," *Morning Advocate,* October 28, 1934; "Long at Head of 5,000 Fans Puts on Big Performance for Crowds in Nashville," *Times-Picayune,* October 28, 1934; "Politician Huey Long Turns Football Fan to Give Nashville Street Show," *Austin American,* October 28, 1934; "Louisiana State Stops Vanderbilt," *New York Times,* October 28, 1934; "Mickal Leads Mates to Win before 20,000," *Knoxville Journal,* October 28, 1934.

16. "Tired Bengal Fans Return Home Happy," *Times-Picayune,* October 29, 1934; "Long and Cohorts Back in Louisiana," *New York Times,* October 29, 1934; Hawkins interview with author.

17. "3,200 Fans Leave in 'Specials' on Nashville Junket," *Morning Advocate,* October 27, 1934; "This and That," *News and Observer,* October 31, 1934; "Huey Long's Circus Thrills Nashville," *Palm Beach Post,* October 28, 1934; "Huey Long's Boys Beat Vanderbilt," *Jacksonville Daily Journal,* October 28, 1934; "Huey Long Steals Show as L.S.U. Meets Vanderbilt," *Fort Worth Star-Telegram,* October 28, 1934.

18. H. I. Phillips, "The Once Over," *St. Louis Globe-Democrat,* October 30, 1934; "Louisiana State Humbles Vanderbilt, 20 to 0," *Monroe Morning World,* October 28, 1934.

19. "Plans for Trek to Knoxville Are Given by Kingfish," *Morning Advocate,* November 11, 1934.

20. "Louisiana's Annual Classic Will Draw Throng of 33,000 When Tiger Meets Tulane in Enlarged Stadium," *Morning Advocate,* November 11, 1934.

20. SENATOR ABE MICKAL

1. "Long Declares Roads in Caddo Won't Get Help," *Morning Advocate,* November 3, 1934; "14 Amendments to Be Voted on in Tuesday Poll," *Morning Advocate,* November 4, 1934.

2. Long's foray into New Orleans is the subject of Garry Boulard's *Huey Long Invades New Orleans;* "The Kingdom of the Kingfish," *New Orleans Item,* September 11, 1939; Williams, *Huey Long,* 726; Warren M. Billings, "A Bar for Louisiana: Origins of the Louisiana State Bar Associ-

ation," *Louisiana History,* Autumn 2000, 398–400; Hair, *The Kingfish and His Realm,* 276–82; "U.S. and State Courts Overrule Dictatorship Assumed by Huey Long," *Morning Advocate,* September 8, 1934; "Long Announces Special Session of Legislature," *Morning Advocate,* November 7, 1934; "House Committee Quickly Approves 44 Bills Thrown in Special Session Hopper," *State-Times,* November 13, 1934; "44 Legislative Bills Ready for Senate Friday," *State-Times,* November 15, 1934; "Long Cracks Whip and Speeds Bills," *New York Times,* November 14, 1934; "Special Session of Legislature Is Ended Today," *State-Times,* November 16, 1934.

3. "Long Declares State Should Join Mexico," *Morning Advocate,* November 7, 1934; "Huey Long Wants Louisiana to Secede from the Union," *Chicago Daily News,* November 6, 1934.

4. "Tigers Roll Over Mississippi State for 25–3 Victory," *Morning Advocate,* November 4, 1934; "Big Star of Unbeaten Louisiana State Can Kick Goals, Run, Throw and Think," *Shreveport Times,* October 31, 1934; Angus Lind, "Tackling an All-American Guy," *Times-Picayune,* February 1, 1987; National Football Foundation, Hall of Fame, Abe Mickal, footballfoundation .org/hof_search.aspx?hof=1496.

5. "Long Promises to Make Football Stars Colonels," *Times-Picayune,* November 9, 1934; "Yesterday Was Low Point for Bengals—Huey," *Morning Advocate,* November 11, 1934; "Tigers Gain Hard 6–0 Victory over Geo. Washington," *Morning Advocate,* November 11, 1934.

6. "Here's Hope," *Cincinnati Enquirer,* November 8, 1934.

7. Williams, *Huey Long,* 666–68; *University Bulletin,* April 1930, 307; *Gumbo* yearbook, class of 1935, digitalcommons.lsu.edu/gumbo/34; "Control of L.S.U. Boasted by Long, Students Charge, Refuting Denial," *Times-Picayune,* December 5, 1934; "Ousted Students Tell Their Story at Luncheon Here," *Times-Picayune,* December 13, 1934; Juban, "Insiders"; "'Kingfish' Was Kind to Hoosier Editor," *Indianapolis Star,* September 15, 1935.

8. "Plan to Install Mickal in Senate Seat Collapses," *Times-Picayune,* November 13, 1934; "Long Ordains That Abe Mickal Shall Be Made State Senator from East Baton Rouge Parish," *State-Times,* November 10, 1934; "Mickal Chosen 'Senator' at Assembly on Campus Appears Here Nov. 19," *Morning Advocate,* November 11, 1934; "Mickal Will Flip Passes in Legislature," *New Orleans Item,* November 11, 1934; Cutrer, *Parnassus on the Mississippi,* 20.

9. "Abe Mickal Back to Take Seat as 'Senator' from East Baton Rouge," *State-Times,* November 12, 1934.

10. "Biff Jones Gives Ultimatum to Long," *New Orleans Item,* December 17, 1934; "Plan to Install Mickal in Senate Seat Collapses," *Times-Picayune,* November 13, 1934; "Mickal's Induction as 'Senator' Fails When He Refuses to Appear," *Morning Advocate,* November 13, 1934; "Seating of Abe Mickal Called Off," *Shreveport Times,* November 11, 1934; Mickal and Jones interviews, THWP.

21. THE *REVEILLE* SEVEN

1. "Reveille Letter Which Offended Long Printed," *Morning Advocate,* November 23, 1934.

2. David R. McGuire to J. D. Ratcliff of *New York Magazine,* November 23, 1934, David McGuire Papers, box 1, LRC; "Long Tirade over 'Reveille' Is Told," *Shreveport Journal,* December 4, 1934; "Control of L.S.U. Boasted by Long, Students Charge, Refuting Denial," *Times-Picayune,* December 5, 1934; Corbin and McGuire interviews, THWP; "Ousted Students Tell Their Story at Luncheon Here," *Times-Picayune,* December 13, 1934.

3. "Censure of Long Antics Deleted from 'Reveille,'" *Shreveport Journal,* November 16,

1934; "Criticism of Long by L.S.U. Soph Is Eliminated," *Town Talk*, November 16, 1934; "Sophomore's Critical Note Suppressed," *Monroe News-Star*, November 16, 1934.

4. "Control of L.S.U. Boasted by Long, Students Charge, Refuting Denial," *Times-Picayune*, December 5, 1934; "Long Tirade over 'Reveille' Is Told," *Shreveport Journal*, December 4, 1934; "Inside Story of L.S.U. Reveille Dispute Dared," *Shreveport Times*, December 2, 1934; "Report on the Events Leading to the Dismissal of Seven Students from Louisiana State University on December 5, 1934," Office of the President Records, 1934–63, box 39, LSUA.

5. "Inside Story of L.S.U. Reveille Dispute Bared," *Shreveport Times*, December 2, 1934; "Report on the Events Leading to the Dismissal of Seven Students from Louisiana State University on December 5, 1934," Office of the President Records, 1934–63, box 39, LSUA.

6. "Unworthy of a College Newspaper?" *Reveille*, February 16, 1934; "Open Forum," *Reveille*, February 16, 1934; "Faculty Profiles, Dean James F. Broussard," *Reveille*, October 2, 1934.

7. "Inside Story of L.S.U. Reveille Dispute Bared," *Shreveport Times*, December 2, 1934; "Press Freedoms," *Reveille*, May 11, 1934.

8. "Censorship of 'Reveille' Discontinued," *Shreveport Times*, November 21, 1934; "Long Censor at L.S.U. Removed," *Town Talk*, November 21, 1934; "Meet Called over Editors Quitting Work," *Daily Advertiser*, November 27, 1934; "Huey Long Defied by Student Paper," *New York Times*, November 27, 1934; "Students Back Resigned Staff of the Reveille," *State-Times*, November 27, 1934; "Staff of Reveille Resigns," *Morning Advocate*, November 27, 1934.

9. "NOTICE!" 1934 handbill "To the Students of Louisiana State University," David R. McGuire Papers, box 1, LRC; "Report on the Events Leading to the Dismissal of Seven Students from Louisiana State University on December 5, 1934," Office of the President Records, 1934–63, box 39, LSUA; "Students Back Resigned Staff of the Reveille," *State-Times*, November 27, 1934; "26 L.S.U. Students Put on Suspension," *New York Times*, November 28, 1934; "More Students May Be Suspended over 'Censorship' Issue," *Daily Advertiser*, November 28, 1934; "26 Students Who Signed Petition Are Suspended," *Morning Advocate*, November 28, 1934; "26 L.S.U. Students Suspended in Fight on Press 'Gag' Rule," *Times-Picayune*, November 28, 1934; "Wes Gallagher, 86, President and General Manager of A.P.," *New York Times*, October 13, 1997.

10. "More Students May Be Suspended over 'Censorship' Issue," *Daily Advertiser*, November 28, 1934; "'Nothing I Can Do,' Declares Huey Long," *Times-Picayune*, November 29, 1934.

11. "Students at L.S.U. in Anti-Long Strike," *New York Times*, November 29, 1934.

12. "A.A.U.P. Is Open to Hear Student Plea," *Morning Advocate*, December 1, 1934; "Offers to 'Prove' Long Brings Politics into University Control," *Daily Advertiser*, December 3, 1934; "L.S.U. Censorship Denied by Long in Wire to Editors," *Times-Picayune*, December 3, 1934; "Report on the Events Leading to the Dismissal of Seven Students from Louisiana State University on December 5, 1934," Office of the President Records, 1934–63, box 39, LSUA.

13. "L.S.U. Dismisses Cutrer, M'Guire, Leaders in Fight upon Censorship," *Times-Picayune*, December 6, 1934; "Report on the Events Leading to the Dismissal of Seven Students from Louisiana State University on December 5, 1934," Office of the President Records, 1934–63, box 39, LSUA; Troy Middleton to "The President," et al., regarding "Dismissal of Mr. David R. McGuire," December 5, 1934, David R. McGuire Papers, box 1, LRC.

14. "Reinstatement Granted for 22 of 26 Students in L.S.U. Classes," *Times-Picayune*, December 4, 1934; "Miss Williamson Reported Named Reveille Editor," *Times-Picayune*, December 1, 1934; "To the Students," *Reveille*, December 4, 1934.

15. "Charges Presented to Accrediting Body," *Times-Picayune,* December 5, 1934; "Control of L.S.U. Boasted by Long, Assert Students," *Times-Picayune,* December 5, 1934; "L.S.U. Heads Halt Student Meeting on Censor Issue," *Times-Picayune,* December 8, 1934; "L.S.U. Censorship to Be Discussed by Alumni Group," *Times-Picayune,* December 8, 1934.

16. "Publisher Answers Attack on Censorship," "Centenary Paper Flays Censorship," "Kentucky Group Commends Cutrer," and "Students Answer Long's Charges," *Times-Picayune,* December 9, 1934; "Student Editor Hits Huey" and "Daily Iowan in Row," *Morning Advocate,* December 4, 1934.

17. "College Editors Hear Roosevelt Tell of 'Scoop,'" *Evening Star,* December 28, 1934.

18. "L.S.U. Heads Halt Student Meeting on Censor Issue," *Times-Picayune,* December 8, 1934; "Student Mass Meet at L.S.U. Is Prohibited," *State-Times,* December 7, 1934; "Declare Jobs Gag Council in L.S.U. Row," *Morning Advocate,* December 7, 1934; "Student Council Backs Dr. Smith in Campus Row," *Morning Advocate,* December 6, 1934; Minutes of December 5, 1934, LSU Student Council Meeting, Student Government Records, box 10, bound vol.: Council Minutes, 1932–38, LSUA.

19. "L.S.U. President Hanged in Effigy on Campus Pole," *Times-Picayune,* December 9, 1934.

20. "L.S.U. Student Body Divided over 'Reveille' Affair," *New Orleans Item,* December 9, 1934.

21. "Expelled Student Discloses 'Inside,'" *New Orleans Item,* December 6, 1934.

22. "Publisher Answers Attack on Censorship," *Times-Picayune,* December 9, 1934.

23. "Missouri Will Accept Students Now Suspended," *State-Times,* December 5, 1934; Registrar, University of Missouri, to David R. McGuire, December 29, 1934, David R. McGuire Papers, box 1, LRC; letter to Reveille Seven students in: Office of the President Records, 1934–63, box 39, LSUA; Garay, *The Manship School,* 98; "Huey's Victims to Missouri U.," *Jefferson City Post,* January 22, 1935; "Reveille Rebels: Reveille Seven's Clash with Huey P. Long Leaves Lasting Legacy," *Reveille,* October 23, 2013; In a March 14, 1941, letter to David McGuire, LSU acting president Paul Hebert wrote,

> In attempting to express the apologies of the University over the wrong that was done to you I am mindful of the wisdom of the words of Benjamin Disraeli that "Apologies only account for what they do not alter." As young men who have suffered a grave injustice in your experience at L.S.U., it would be only natural for you to have a feeling of bitterness against this Institution which no apology could alter. And yet, somehow, I feel that as we write "finis" to this sorry episode you will accept the apologies of the University with a spirit of generosity and good will.

McGuire, who accepted the apology, did not revel in it. As his son Jack McGuire later explained, "When the [Governor Sam] Jones Legislature commissioned an investigation and made a big deal out of reinstating the seven students and clearing their records and standing, Dad felt that was just as political an act as the expulsions were" (From the personal collection of Jack B. McGuire).

24. Middleton, Cawthon, and McGuire interviews, THWP.

25. "Facts concerning Academic Freedom at Louisiana State University," David R. McGuire Papers, box 1, LRC.

26. Monroe Sweetland, "The Student Movement and Huey Long," *Student Outlook,* April 1935, 10.

27. "Dictator—American Style," *Greenwood Commonwealth,* December 1, 1934. The story also ran, among other places, in papers in Pennsylvania, Minnesota, Indiana, Ohio, and Wisconsin. "Kingfish Orders No Criticisms to Be Printed," *Greenville News,* December 5, 1934; "New Deal Placed at Top of 1934's 'Big Stories,'" *Huntsville Times,* December 26, 1934; "Huey Long, Dictator," *News-Herald,* December 27, 1934; "Long Backs Up," *Greenwood Commonwealth,* December 18, 1934; "Lester Says Long Would Be 'Dictator' of United States," *Evening Independent,* December 28, 1934; "Did You Ever Stop to Think?" *Waterloo Press,* December 13, 1934; "'Kingfish' Long's Political Reforms Amuse British," *El Paso Times,* December 16, 1934.

22. THAT BUNCH OF BUZZARDS AND VARMINTS

1. "'Too Tired' to Come Huey Tells Editor," *Enterprise-Journal,* November 16, 1934; "'Special' to Take Tiger Backers to Jackson Saturday," *Morning Advocate,* November 14, 1934; "Huey Long Coming for Ole Miss–LSU Tilt Here," *Clarion-Ledger,* November 1, 1934.

2. "Province of Mississippi Threatens Rebellion from Kingfish," *Clarion-Ledger,* November 26, 1934; "Conner Invites Long and Allen to Attend Game," *Times-Picayune,* November 7, 1934; "'Special' to Take Tiger Backers to Jackson Saturday," *Morning Advocate,* November 14, 1934; "L.S.U. Tigers Depart for Jackson," *State-Times,* November 16, 1934; "'Too Tired' to Come Huey Tells Editor," *McComb Enterprise,* November 16, 1934; Mickal interview, THWP; "California Man Sees Huey Long in Parade Here," *McComb Enterprise,* November 23, 1934.

3. "Arrive in Jackson," *State-Times,* November 17, 1934; "Huey Long Holds Field Day during Big Local Visit," *Clarion-Ledger,* November 18, 1934; "Two Touchdowns Made by Tigers Early," *State-Times,* November 17, 1934.

4. "Huey Long Holds Field Day during Big Local Visit," *Clarion-Ledger,* November 18, 1934; Jones interview, THWP; "Louisiana State Wins on Early Drive, 14–0," *New York Times,* November 18, 1934; "Many Local People See L.S.U. Win," *Enterprise-Journal,* November 23, 1934.

5. "Tigers and Tulane Will Clash Today in 32nd Contest," *Morning Advocate,* December 1, 1934; Finney, *The Fighting Tigers,* 124.

6. "Tiger Stadium Is Noisy Monster as Wave Defeats L.S.U. in Colorful Tilt," *Morning Advocate,* December 2, 1934; "Long Takes Loss in Laughing Way," *Birmingham News,* December 2, 1934; "Green Wave Beats L.S.U. 13–12 in Desperate Battle; Gloom Reigns in Tigertown," *Times-Picayune,* December 12, 1934; "Group Solicits Funds to Obtain Token for Long," *Reveille,* October 30, 1934; "Long to Receive Watch as Token from Students," *Reveille,* November 16, 1934; "Notice! Notice!" 1934 flier announcing collection for watch for Long, personal collection of Jack McGuire.

7. "L.S.U.-Tulane Tilt Stars Are Hurt in Battle," *Monroe News-Star,* December 3, 1934; Finney, *The Fighting Tigers,* 126; Tulane Triumphs on Run by Simons," *New York Times,* December 2, 1934; "Silence Reigns at Baton Rouge as Tigers Lose," *Times-Picayune,* December 2, 1934; "Huey Long's L.S.U. Eleven Is Pointing to Rose Bowl Trip," *Standard-Sentinel,* November 8, 1934.

8. "Long Takes Loss in Laughing Way," *Birmingham News,* December 2, 1934; Finney, *The Fighting Tigers,* 127.

9. Mickal interview, THWP; Pro Football Hall of Fame, "1936 National Football League Draft," www.profootballhof.com/news/2005/01/news-1936-national-football-league-draft/; National Football Foundation, Hall of Fame, Abe Mickal, footballfoundation.org/hof_search

.aspx?hof=1496; Pro Football Reference, LSU Drafted Players/Alumni, www.pro-football-refer
ence.com/schools/lsu/drafted.htm.

10. "'Coach' Huey Long Tosses Football Ethics Overboard in Toying with L.S.U. Team," *Knoxville News-Sentinel*, November 10, 1934; "Long Plans Special Train to Knoxville," *Monroe Morning World*, November 11, 1934.

11. "It's Heil Huey in Louisiana! Just Putsch-Over for Der-Kingfish," *New Orleans Item*, August 18, 1934; "Huey's Legislature Is Giving Whole State to Him," *Post-Crescent*, August 18, 1934; "Fight to Finish Seen as Long Tries Disfranchise Foes," *Evening Star*, August 20, 1934.

12. "Huey's Sore at Pegler," *Knoxville News-Sentinel*, November 13, 1934; "Huey Long Calls Off Excursion to Knoxville for Football Game," *Times-Picayune*, November 14, 1934; "West-brook Pegler's Article Saying 'Kingfish' Seeks Publicity Out of Football Brings Sudden End to Trip," *Morning Advocate*, November 14, 1934.

13. "Former Football Stars, in New York, Denounced Huey Long's 'Contemptible' Exploita-tion of Grid Team at L.S.U.," *Knoxville News-Sentinel*, November 16, 1934.

14. "C. of C. Awaits Huey's Reply to Telegram," *Knoxville News-Sentinel*, November 15, 1934; Marvin Thomson, "On the First Hop," *Knoxville News-Sentinel*, November 13, 1934; Harry P. Clark telegrams to Huey Long, November 10 and 11, 1934, and Marvin Thompson tele-gram to Huey Long, November 11, 1934, Jack B. McGuire Collection of Huey P. Long Papers, box 2, LRC.

15. "Long May Come to Watch Game," *Knoxville News-Sentinel*, December 7, 1934; Fin-ney, *The Fighting Tigers*, 127; "Senator's Dispute with Columnist Leads to Cancellation," *State-Times*, November 14, 1934; "Bad Knee O.K. after Tennessee Game," *New Orleans Item*, December 10, 1934; "Senator's Dispute with Columnist Leads to Cancellation," *State-Times*, November 14, 1934.

16. Keefe, "Viewing the News," *Times-Picayune*, December 12, 1934.

23. HOLLYWOOD'S IDEA OF A UNIVERSITY

1. "Jones Tells L.S.U. He Intends to Quit," *New York Times*, December 18, 1934; "Biff Jones Gives Ultimatum to Long," *New Orleans Item*, December 17, 1934; "'Biff' Tells His Story," *Lin-coln Star*, December 21, 1934; "Reign of Silence Blankets Flare-Up between Biff, Huey," *Morning Advocate*, December 18, 1934; Rabenhorst and Jones interviews, THWP.

2. Mickal interview, THWP.

3. "Tigers-Oregon Play by Play," *Morning Advocate*, December 16, 1934; "Seek to Smooth Long-Jones Row," *New York Times*, December 17, 1934.

4. W. I. Spencer, "Post Mortems in Sports," *Morning Advocate*, December 18, 1934; "Biff Jones Gives Ultimatum to Long," *New Orleans Item*, December 17, 1934.

5. "L.S.U. Leaders Seek to Smooth Trouble 'tween Long, Coach," *Evening Sun*, December 17, 1934.

6. "Smith Announces 'Biff' Is Relieved as Football Coach," *Morning Advocate*, December 18, 1934; National Football Foundation Hall of Fame, footballfoundation.org/hof_search.aspx ?hof=1500.

7. Finney, *The Fighting Tigers*, 128; Middleton interview, THWP; "Bernie Moore, Frack Coach, Picked as Jones's Successor at L.S.U.," *New York Times*, December 25, 1932; "No Prog-ress Reported in Selection of Successor to Capt. 'Biff' Jones," *State-Times*, December 20, 1934.

8. "Jones Took Career in His Hands When He Defied Huey Long," *Brooklyn Daily Eagle,* December 20, 1934.

9. "Tiger Gridders Loyal to Jones; Threaten to Quit," *New Orleans Item,* December 21, 1934; "Long Still Seeks New L.S.U. Coach," *New York Times,* December 20, 1934; "Long Mentions Shaughnessy as Coach at L.S.U.," *Monroe News-Star,* December 19, 1934; "Alabama Coach Says That He Knows Nothing about Report That Senator Long Wants Him to Coach at L.S.U.," *State-Times,* December 24, 1934; "Leaders of Grid Game Plot Make It Tough on L.S.U. Dictator," *Lincoln Star,* December 21, 1934; "'Biff' Tells His Story," *Lincoln Star,* December 21, 1934; "Long Transfers Grid 'Coaching' to Statehouse," *State-Times,* December 12, 1934; Jimmy Bullock, "Accent on Sports," *Shreveport Journal,* December 24, 1962; Sehrt interview, THWP; Finney, *The Fighting Tigers,* 130; Blinkey Horn, "From Bunker to Bleacher," *Tennessean,* December 21, 1934; "Huey Tapped Moore," *Birmingham Post-Herald,* April 1, 1966; "Long Handicaps L.S.U.'s Chances of Rose Bowl," *New Orleans States,* January 5, 1935.

10. "Bernie Moore, Track Coach, Picked as Jones's Successor at L.S.U.," *New York Times,* December 25, 1934; Keefe, "Viewing the News," *Times-Picayune,* December 25, 1934; "Coach Moore Has Long Experience in Many Sports," *Reveille,* January 8, 1935.

11. Keefe, "Viewing the News," *Times-Picayune,* December 30, 1934, January 8, 1935. Finney, *The Fighting Tigers,* 473–75. National Football Foundation Hall of Fame, footballfoundation.org/honors/hall-of-fame/bernie-moore/1625.

12. "Bandmaster Began His Career at Age of Six," *Morning Advocate,* April 7, 1935; Mel Washburn, "On the Merry-Go-Round," *New Orleans Item,* August 6, 1933; Boulard, *Huey Long Invades Louisiana,* 20.

13. Carazo interview, THWP; Carazo, "Huey Long"; Carazo interview, Junior League Oral History Project; Scoop Kennedy, "Down the Spillway," *New Orleans Item,* August 8, 1933.

14. Carazo interview, THWP; Norman Gamboa, "José Castro-Carazo: Every Man a King," Academia.edu, 2013, scholar.google.com/scholar?hl=en&as_sdt=0%2C19&q=castro+carazo+every+man+a+king+Norman+Gamboa&btnG=. In an interview, Carazo recalled he was heading to the hotel's Blue Room, but, as the Fountain Room was his venue, the latter was his likely destination.

15. "Castro Carazo to Be Director of L.S.U. Band," *State-Times,* December 18, 1934; Continé and Phillips, *The Golden Band from Tigerland,* 23–24; "Band Enrollment Sets New Record of 150 Members," *Reveille,* September 20, 1935; "Bennett, Col. Carazo Lead 200 Members of L.S.U. Band through Rehearsals," *Reveille,* November 24, 1936.

16. "Castro Carazo to Create Concert Band and Symphonic Dance Orchestra," *Reveille,* January 11, 1935; "Col. Carazo to Form Two Tiger Bands," *Reveille,* June 26, 1936; "New Uniforms to Be Adopted for L.S.U. Band," *Reveille,* March 1, 1935; "Castro Carazo Creates New Song," *Reveille,* April 2, 1935; "Song Contest Regulations Are Announced," *Reveille,* April 5, 1935; "Cadet Band Wins Applause at Concert," *Reveille,* April 9, 1935.

17. Quaw interview, THWP.

18. "Grid Fun Features 'Hold That Co-ed,'" *San Diego Union,* September 21, 1938; "Aging Princes of the Blood," *Dallas Morning News,* October 2, 1938; "Hold That Co-ed," 1938, ok.ru /video/248512711240.

19. Carazo and Manetta interviews, THWP; interview notes of Fats Pichon in T. Harry Williams Papers, Research Material, HPL, box 17; "School Songs Written for L.S.U. Published," *Morning Advocate,* July 3, 1935; "Huey Long's 'Miss Vandy' Just 2 Other Songs and Sig Spaeth

Finally Digs Up Its Pedigree," *Knoxville News-Sentinel,* September 5, 1935; Hunt and Davis interviews, THWP.

20. Carazo interview, THWP; National radio speech by Huey Long, ca. 1935, www.youtube .com/watch?v=Gvund-k1xw0.

21. Williams, *Huey Long,* 799n; Carazo interview, THWP; "Long Plans New York Trip for La. Students," *Shreveport Times,* March 19, 1935; "Cadet Band Wins Applause at Concert," *Reveille,* April 9, 1935; "Company Buys L.S.U. Songs," *Reveille,* October 18, 1935; "Castro Carazo, Musical King," *New Orleans States-Item,* January 20, 1978; "Farewell Is Said by Kingfish Long," *Morning Call,* January 3, 1935; "Louisiana's Vibrant New Sound," *State-Times,* September 23, 1973; Kay Long interview with author.

22. "Law School Placed on Probation," *Morning Advocate,* May 10, 1935; "K. K. Kennedy to Be Examined for Bar Admittance," *State-Times,* June 25, 1934; "K. K. Kennedy of 'Whangdoodle' Fame Gets Diploma at L.S.U.," *Shreveport Times,* June 27, 1934; "Closing Chapter of Whangdoodle Case Nears End," *Reveille,* June 22, 1934; "Decision Permits Kennedy to Take Bar Examination," *Times-Picayune,* June 25, 1934; "Kennedy among 74 Taking Bar Exam," *Shreveport Journal,* July 9, 1934; "Tullis, Law Dean at L.S.U., Retired over His Protest," *Times-Picayune,* August 23, 1934.

23. "Air L.S.U. Charges," *New Orleans Item,* December 6, 1934; "Kennedy to Be Reinstated," *Weekly Town Talk,* June 10, 1933; "Law School Placed on Probation," *Morning Advocate,* May 10, 1935; "Long Rages at American Bar," *New Orleans States,* May 10, 1935.

24. "Weiss Named in Tax Case Indictment," *Morning Advocate,* December 15, 1934; "U.S. Indicts Seymour Weiss as an Alleged Evader of Income Tax," *New Orleans States,* December 14, 1934; "Jules and Joe Fisher Indicted by U.S. for Evading Taxes on Incomes Reported at $449,017," *Morning Tribune,* December 7, 1934.

25. Hair, *The Kingfish and His Realm,* 286–87; Irey, *The Tax Dodgers,* 98–100.

26. Williams, *Huey Long,* 797–813; Terry L. Jones, "An Administration under Fire: The Long-Farley Affair of 1935," *Louisiana History,* Winter 1987, 5–17; Brinkley, *Voices of Protest,* 75.

24. MAKE THEM STEAL FOR THE SCHOOLS

1. "Long Says Cancer Cure Found," *Shreveport Times,* January 4, 1935; "WDSU Sale Price Figure Withheld," *New Orleans States,* January 1, 1935; "Oil Workers Begin Fight on Long Tax," *New York Times,* January 4, 1935; "Clinic Is Praised," *New Orleans Item,* January 6, 1935; "Long Announces He 'Understands' L.S.U. Had WDSU," *Morning Advocate,* January 4, 1935; "Long Lays Plans for Presidency," *Asbury Park Press,* December 22, 1934.

2. "Clinic Is Praised," *New Orleans Item,* January 6, 1935.

3. "L.S.U. Dental School Will Open in Fall," *Shreveport Times,* February 23, 1935; "L.S.U. Board Formally Approves Dentistry, Pharmacy Schools," *Weekly News,* February 9, 1935; "Allen to Borrow Million for L.S.U. Expansion Plans," *Times-Picayune,* December 28, 1934.

4. "Eighty-Seventh Annual Report for the Session 1935–36," State Department of Education of Louisiana, *Bulletin* no. 335 (January 1937): 222.

5. "400 Are Present at Annual Banquet for Deans of Men," *Morning Advocate,* March 1, 1935.

6. Huey Long speech, "Share Our Wealth," on National Broadcasting Company, March 7, 1935, www.americanrhetoric.com/speeches/hueyplongshare.htm.

7. "Honorary Degrees Granted to Italian Ambassador, Six Others at L.S.U. Jubilee," *Times-Picayune,* April 13, 1935.

8. "College Declines L.S.U. Invitation Because of Long," *Times-Picayune,* March 9, 1935; "French Ambassador Feted in L.S.U. Jubilee Programs, Reviews Parade of Cadets," *Times-Picayune,* April 6, 1935; "Political Control of Colleges Decried," *Shreveport Journal,* April 11, 1935.

9. *Gumbo* yearbook, class of 1935, digitalcommons.lsu.edu/gumbo/34; Cawthon interview, THWP.

10. Swing, in Graham, ed., *Huey Long,* 95–96; "The University's Progress during Depression Years," *Louisiana Leader,* March 1935.

11. Cutrer, *Parnassus on the Mississippi,* 25–26; "Chronology of the Faculty," LSU Department of Political Science, www.lsu.edu/hss/polisci/about_us/faculty-chronology.php; "New Faculty Members Begin Duties at L.S.U.," *Louisiana Leader,* October 1934; Heilman, *The Southern Connection,* 3–19; Offner, *Hubert Humphrey,* 15, 17; "Noted Opera Baritone Appointed to Faculty," *Louisiana Leader,* June 1935; "17 New Members Named on Faculty," *Louisiana Leader,* September 1935; Hargrave, *LSU Law,* 82; "Fifty-Two New Members Are Added to Faculty," *Reveille,* September 22, 1936; "Noted Concert Violinist Named to Music Faculty," *Louisiana Leader,* July 1936; "Six New Members Added to Experiment Station Staff," *Louisiana Leader,* May 1936; "26 New Members Named to Faculty," *Louisiana Leader,* September 1936; "Prominent Author Will Begin Duties This Fall," *Louisiana Leader,* September 1936; "Recent Additions of 17 to Staff Are Announced," *Louisiana Leader,* October 1936; "Noted Conductor of Opera Named to L.S.U. Staff," *Morning Advocate,* October 25, 1936; "Appointments Bring Faculty Total Near 600," *Louisiana Leader,* October 1939.

12. "New Program to Bring L.S.U. Buildings to 96," *Morning Advocate,* April 7, 1935; "Proceedings of the Board of Supervisors," May 4, 1935, LSU Board of Supervisors Records, 1932–38, box 2, LSUA.

13. "ERA Parish Projects Are Being Rapidly Completed," *Morning Advocate,* February 10, 1935; "L.S.U. Purchase of 550 Acres of Land Is Recorded," *Morning Advocate,* August 14, 1935; "University Announces Purchase of Tract to Be Used as 'Student Farm,'" *Morning Advocate,* August 13, 1935.

14. "Group Checking L.S.U. Political Control Charge," *Morning Advocate,* March 23, 1935; "Long Says He's Head of L.S.U.," *Weekly Town Talk,* March 30, 1935.

15. "L.S.U. Law School Placed on 'Probation Status' by American Bar Association," *Times-Picayune,* May 10, 1935.

16. "Student Leaders Rap 'Subserviency' of L.S.U. to Long," *Morning Advocate,* April 16, 1935; "Students of South Assail L.S.U. Policy," *Shreveport Times,* April 14, 1935.

17. "Long's Meddling at L.S.U. Scored by Theo. Green," *Morning Advocate,* June 11, 1935.

18. Albert J. Montesi, "Huey Long and 'The Southern Review,'" *Journal of Modern Literature,* February 1973, 66–73; Cutrer, *Parnassus on the Mississippi,* 60–66; "Lecture Series Ends Tonight with Speech by Norman Thomas," *Reveille,* February 9, 1934.

19. "1,777,000 RFC Loan Obtained for L.S.U. Work," *Monroe News-Star,* July 16, 1935; "L.S.U. Seeking PWA Fund for New Building," *Shreveport Times,* July 3, 1935.

20. Ickes, *The Secret Diary of Harold L. Ickes,* 399–401.

21. "Costello Is Made Public Relations Man at University," *Morning Advocate,* March 1,

1935; Keefe, "Viewing the News," *Times-Picayune,* March 1, 1935; "Ex-Hero Directs Tiger Publicity," *New Orleans Item,* February 28, 1935; Rabenhorst interview, THWP.

22. "Long Sees Tigers Drill; Says Squad Best in Country," *Shreveport Times,* March 3, 1935; "Long Plans New York Trip for La. Students," *Shreveport Times,* March 19, 1935; "Cadet Band Wins Applause at Concert," *Reveille,* April 9, 1935; Bowman interview, THWP.

25. BLOOD ON THE POLISHED MARBLE

1. "End of Dictatorship Is Vowed by Women," *Shreveport Times,* January 16, 1935.

2. Hair, *The Kingfish and His Realm,* 302.

3. "Lawmakers Hurry at Long's Bidding," *Monroe News-Star,* July 4, 1935; Hair, *The Kingfish and His Realm,* 299–301; "Long's Rule Is Based on Control over 95 Aides, Stanley Says," *Shreveport Times,* July 11, 1935; Hair, *The Kingfish and His Realm,* 304–5; Williams, *Huey Long,* 850–52.

4. Harris, *The Kingfish,* 219; Williams, *Huey Long,* 853–54.

5. Williams, *Huey Long,* 862–63; "L.S.U. Band Director Says Long Was Completing New Compositions," *State-Times,* September 11, 1935.

6. Carazo and Frey interviews, THWP.

7. Frey interview, THWP.

8. Hair, *The Kingfish and His Realm,* 321; Williams, *Huey Long,* 863–65; *University Bulletin,* May 1921, 292; *University Bulletin,* April 1923, 310.

9. "Dr. Weiss Met Wife in Paris," *New Orleans States,* September 9, 1935; "Opelousas Girl Goes to France," *Clarion-News,* June 11, 1931; Williams, *Huey Long,* 861–62; Fields, Dugas, Doucet, and Fisher interviews, THWP; Hair, *The Kingfish and His Realm,* 322.

10. Heilman, *The Southern Connection,* 5–6; Fournet, Frampton, White, and Roden interviews, THWP.

11. Frampton, Coleman, Buie, and Fournet interviews, THWP; Zinman, *The Day Huey Long Was Shot,* 129.

12. Cohn interview, THWP.

13. Williams, *Huey Long,* 874; Dent interview, THWP; Jeansonne, *Messiah of the Masses,* 174.

14. "Thousands Attend Last Weiss Rites," *Morning Advocate,* September 10, 1935.

15. W. I. Spencer, "Post Mortems in Sports," *Morning Advocate,* September 11, 1935; Dent interview, THWP; "Five Students Were to Give Blood to Long," *Morning Advocate,* September 10, 1935; "The Kingdom of the Kingfish," *New Orleans Item,* September 19, 1939; M. C. Trotter, "Huey P. Long's Last Operation: When Medicine and Politics Don't Mix." *Ochsner Journal* 12, no. 1 (2012): 9–16, www.ncbi.nlm.nih.gov/pmc/articles/PMC3307515/; Williams, *Huey Long,* 873.

16. "Funeral Plans for Long Drafted with State Shocked at His Death," *New Orleans Item,* September 10, 1935; "State Funeral for Long Planned," *New Orleans States,* September 10, 1935; "Final Hours of Long Revealed by Doctor," *New York Times,* September 11, 1935.

17. "Letters to Long Acknowledged," *New Orleans Item,* September 15, 1935; "Plans to Complete Work of Long-Allen Regime, Says Leche," *Times-Picayune,* December 3, 1935.

18. Leche and O'Connor interviews, THWP; Reed, *Requiem for a Kingfish,* 167; "Long Has New Plan on Bridge," *Morning Advocate,* September 4, 1935.

19. Carazo interview, THWP; "Thousands Join in Last Respects to Huey P. Long," *Morning Advocate,* September 13, 1935; "7-Year Political Drama Is Ended," *New Orleans States,* September 13, 1935.

20. "L.S.U. Students to Pay Respects to Senator Long," *Morning Advocate,* September 11, 1935; "Members of L.S.U. Band Form Guard of Honor at Long Bier," *Morning Advocate,* September 12, 1935; "Flower Supplies of Three Cities Taxed for Long Rites," *Times-Picayune,* September 13, 1935.

21. "L.S.U. Band Director Says Long Was Completing New Compositions," *State-Times,* September 11, 1935.

22. "L.S.U. Activities to Be Suspended All Day Thursday," *State-Times,* September 11, 1935; "L.S.U., Tulane to Curtail Grid Workouts Today," *Morning Advocate,* September 12, 1935; "Body of Senator to Lie in State until 4 O'Clock Tomorrow," *Shreveport Journal,* September 11, 1935.

23. "L.S.U. to Hold Memorial Rites for Senator Long," *Morning Advocate,* September 15, 1935; "University Will Hold Memorial Service for Long," *Reveille,* September 20, 1935; "L.S.U.'s Continued Rise Big Question Mark with Long Gone," *New Orleans Item,* September 11, 1935.

24. "About 5,000 Expected at University," *Morning Advocate,* September 15, 1935; "17 New Names Are Listed on L.S.U. Faculty," *Morning Advocate,* September 11, 1935; "L.S.U. Is Tenth in Nation among Full-Time Lists," *Reveille,* January 17, 1936.

25. "Senator Long's Family to Move to Baton Rouge," *State-Times,* September 13, 1935; "Total of 5,500 Now Enrolled on L.S.U. Campus," *Morning Advocate,* October 8, 1935; "Freshman to Be Kings November 12," *Reveille,* November 1, 1935; "Enrollment Will Reach 6,000 Mark," *Reveille,* February 4, 1936; "Russell Long and Jo Boyd Rule Frosh," *Reveille,* November 8, 1935; Mann, *Legacy to Power,* 45; Russell Long interview with author, August 8, 1989.

26. THE SECOND LOUISIANA PURCHASE

1. "Educators at Baton Rouge Are Quizzed," *Shreveport Times,* October 26, 1935.

2. "Proceedings of the Fortieth Annual Meeting of the Southern Association of Colleges and Secondary Schools," December 5–6, 1935, 35–37, SACS Archives; "L.S.U. Action Is Dropped," *New York Times,* December 6, 1935.

3. "Law School of L.S.U. Censured by Association," *Morning Advocate,* December 28, 1935.

4. "Law School of L.S.U. Censured by Association"; "Smith Hits Back at Association," *Monroe Morning World,* December 29, 1935; "Dean Calls Allen Statements Absurd," *Monroe Morning World,* December 29, 1935; "Meeting of Law Body Is Closed," *Monroe News-Star,* December 31, 1935; "Association of American Law Schools Votes Censure of L.S.U.," *Shreveport Journal,* December 27, 1935.

5. "Richard Leche Dies," *State-Times,* February 22, 1965.

6. Sindler, *Huey Long's Louisiana,* 117–23; "Governor O. K. Allen Dies Suddenly," *Alexandria Daily Town Talk,* January 28, 1936; Field, "The Politics of the New Deal in Louisiana," 206.

7. "Pratt Supported for Federal Job," *New Orleans States,* April 30, 1936; "Roosevelt Confers with Leche at White House; Breach Closed," *Shreveport Times,* April 30, 1936; "Leche Announces Progress Made in Talks at Capital," *Times-Picayune,* April 28, 1936; Leighninger, *Building Louisiana,* 45–46; Field, "The Politics of the New Deal in Louisiana," 304–6.

8. "Roosevelt Given Endorsement by Governor Leche and Legislature," *Times-Picayune,*

June 13, 1936; "'Fair Share' of U.S. Funds Will Be Allotted Louisiana, Leche Predicts after Talks," *Times-Picayune,* July 21, 1936.

9. "Stadium Addition Is Dedicated by Harry L. Hopkins," *Morning Advocate,* November 29, 1936; "Colorful Gridiron Drama Unfolded at Green Wave Bows to Ferocious Tiger," *Morning Advocate,* November 29, 1936; Seifried, "The Development of 'Death Valley' in Louisiana," 203; "Stadium Houses 1,754 Students," *Monroe News-Star,* May 5, 1938.

10. "Mrs. Roosevelt Beams," *Reveille,* March 9, 1937; "Spending a Day with the President of the United States," *New Orleans Item,* April 30, 1937; "Thousands to Line New City Park Mall to Hear Roosevelt," *New Orleans States,* April 28, 1937; "Farley Praises L.S.U. Builders in Graduation Talk," *Times-Picayune,* June 1, 1937.

11. Don Wharton, "Louisiana State University," *Scribner's,* September 1937, 38–39.

12. "The Kingdom of the Kingfish," *New Orleans Item,* September 20, 1939; "State PWA Cash Ready to Flow In," *New Orleans Item,* June 3, 1936; Desmond, *The Architecture of LSU,* 87–88; Ruffin, *Under Stately Oaks,* 77–78; "New Agricultural Building under Construction on Campus May Be Ready This Fall; Built by WPA," *State-Times,* July 23, 1937; "New Structure at L.S.U. Accepted by Dean Hebert," *State-Times,* July 23, 1937; "President Smith of LSU Discusses Growth of School," *New Orleans Item,* October 10, 1937; "Chemical Engineering 'Lab' Planned as Addition to the L.S.U. Sugar Plant," *State-Times,* August 17, 1938; "Seven Women's Dorms Now Mark Seven Years' Growth of Coed Housing Groups," *Reveille,* November 22, 1938; "Dormitory Units Soon to House 1,220 Women," *Louisiana Leader,* March 1938; "Residences for Women," *LSU Alumni News,* July 1938; "Residences for Men," *LSU Alumni News,* July 1938; "L.S.U. Begins Enrollment," *Alexandria Daily Town Talk,* September 14, 136; "New Building Started by Gov. Leche," *Reveille,* October 14, 1936; "Big Increase Shown in L.S.U. Enrollment," *Lafayette Daily Advertiser,* September 28, 1937; "L.S.U. Enrollment Greatly Increased Registrar Reports," *Shreveport Times,* September 24, 1938; "Eighty-Eighth Annual Report for the Session 1936–37," State Department of Education of Louisiana, *Bulletin* no. 367 (1938): 156; "Louisiana's New Plant for Geological Study and Research," *Louisiana Conservation Review,* Spring 1939.

27. THE LOUISIANA SCANDALS

1. Larcade and Pegues interviews, THWP; Brinkley, *Voices of Protest,* 263; Davis, *Huey Long,* 35; "Louisiana Revolution," *Saturday Evening Post,* May 11, 1940; Opotowsky, *The Longs of Louisiana,* 18.

2. Hair, *The Kingfish and His Realm,* 229; "The Camera Trapped Them," *Saturday Evening Post,* June 15, 1940; Taylor interview, T. Harry Williams Center for Oral History.

3. "Bank Moves Anew to Recover Money Borrowed by Former LSU President," *State-Times,* February 29, 1944; "Committee for Paying Banks on LSU Loans," *State-Times,* June 3, 1942; "Suit to Recover L.S.U. Loan Lost," *Times-Picayune,* September 12, 1944; "Bill Would Pay Bank Loans Made by Dr. J. M. Smith," *Times-Picayune,* May 21, 1942; "Hoarded Whisky Set Flame That Blew Top Off State Scandals," *New Orleans Item,* March 10, 1940; "Louisiana Revolution," *Saturday Evening Post,* May 11, 1940; Kane, *Louisiana Hayride,* 276–77.

4. Ryan M. Seidemann, "Did the State Win or Lose in Its Mineral Dealings with Huey Long, Oscar Allen, James Noe, and the Win or Lose Oil Company?" *Louisiana History* 59, no. 2 (2018): 196–225, www.jstor.org/stable/26475480; Kane, *Louisiana Hayride,* 145; Kurz and Peoples,

Earl K. Long, 92; Hébert, *Last of the Titans,* 109; McManus, "When It Becomes Necessary to Spank the State Administration, I Can Do It," 57; Kurtz and Peoples, *Earl K. Long,* 97–98.

5. Kane, *Louisiana Hayride,* 307–8; "Dismissed Employee Plans to Ask Federal Probe of State 'Shakedown' Policy," *Morning Advocate,* May 20, 1938; "Federal Probe Certain if Leche Is Bench Choice," *Times-Picayune,* May 24, 1938; "Senator Will Ask Probe If Leche Gets Judge Nomination," *New Orleans States,* May 23, 1938; "Leche and Morrison in Attacks," *Morning Advocate,* September 9, 1938.

6. "The Camera Trapped Them," *Saturday Evening Post,* June 15, 1940; Field, "The Louisiana Scandals," in Haas, ed., *The Age of the Longs,* 277; "Building Materials Taken to N.O. Private Property by L.S.U. Truck," *New Orleans States,* June 9, 1939; Kane, *Louisiana Hayride,* 267–68; "Evidence of WPA Scandal Bared, Say Pearson, Allen," *Minneapolis Star,* June 17, 1939; Hébert, *Last of the Titans,* 121–25.

7. "Extends Truck Investigation," *New Orleans Item,* June 14, 1939; "Smith Comments," *New Orleans States,* June 9, 1939; "$464,000 Mystery Geology Hall Rising on Campus Has L.S.U Authorities in the Dark," *Times-Picayune,* July 11, 1939.

8. "Leche to Quit Today—Long; No Trace of L.S.U. President," *Shreveport Journal,* June 26, 1939; "Fugitive President Given Checks of at Least $40,000," *New Orleans Item,* June 27, 1939; "Long Takes Over; Will Push Probe," *New Orleans Item,* June 27, 1939; "Leche Bares Smith Details," *New Orleans Item,* July 4, 1939; "Leche Tells of Plans for Future," *New Orleans Item,* June 22, 1939.

9. "Baton Rouge Stays Up Late to Get News of Smiths Return," *New Orleans Item,* July 2, 1939; "Smiths' Homecoming Is Far Cry from Triumphant Grid Returns," *New Orleans States,* July 5, 1939; "Reporter Ousted at L.S.U. Interviews Old President, Now Charged in Funds Grab," *Times-Picayune,* July 5, 1939.

10. "'There, But for the Grace of God," *New Orleans Item,* July 5, 1939; "'Won't Be Goat,' Says Dr. Smith in Baton Rouge Jail," *Times-Picayune,* July 5, 1939.

11. "The Camera Trapped Them," *Saturday Evening Post,* June 15, 1940.

12. "3 More Charged as Embezzlers," *Morning Advocate,* July 15, 1939; "Fourteen Arrested to Date in the State Investigation," *New Orleans Item,* June 23, 1939.

13. "They Sent a Letter," *Saturday Evening Post,* June 22, 1940; "Bienville Hotel Sale Included Furniture, Board Members Say," *Times-Picayune,* September 7, 1939.

14. Sindler, *Huey Long's Louisiana,* 138; "Leche Is Indicted by U.S. Jury on 'Hot Oil' Charge," *New Orleans Item,* August 7, 1939; Field, "The Louisiana Scandals," in Haas, ed., *The Age of the Longs,* 278.

15. "Poultry and Egg Dealer Taken on Charge of Fraud," *Times-Picayune,* August 4, 1939; "Barksdale Built Four New Houses in Past 2 Years," *Times-Picayune,* August 15, 1939; "Architect Gave Aid to Smith in Fraud, Charged," *Times-Picayune,* August 4, 1939; "Leche Convicted by Louisiana Jury," *New York Times,* June 2, 1940; "Leche Gets Ten Years," *New York Times,* June 12, 1940; "U.S. Scandals Indictments Name 145 Persons, 42 Firms," *Times-Picayune,* November 11, 1940; "Weiss, Two More Lose Contest to Avoid Sentence," *Times-Picayune,* October 22, 1940; "Lorio Found Guilty on One Fraud Count; Acquitted on Three," *Times-Picayune,* November 16, 1940; "They Sent a Letter," *Saturday Evening Post,* June 22, 1940; "Caldwell Gets Two Years, $1000 Fine in Tax, Fraud Charges," *Times-Picayune,* February 13, 1940; Field, "The Politics of the New Deal in Louisiana," 400; Hawkins interview with author.

16. "Smith Tries to Die in Louisiana Cell," *New York Times,* November 17, 1939; "Leche Gets

a Parole," *New York Times,* May 16, 1945; "Dr. James Monroe Smith Succumbs to Heart Attack at State Prison," *Shreveport Times,* May 28, 1949; "Leche Pardoned by Ex-President," *Times-Picayune,* January 24, 1953.

17. "Ellender Turns Fire on Rogge in Abbeville Talk," *Times-Picayune,* January 15, 1940; Kane, *Louisiana Hayride,* 288; Sindler, *Huey Long's Louisiana,* 139.

18. "Leche, Smith Coming Down," *New Orleans Item,* August 10, 1939; "Leche Plaques Stay Buried," *New Orleans Item,* August 16, 1939.

19. "Paul M. Hebert: An Outstanding Louisianian," *Shreveport Journal,* February 17, 1977.

20. Price, *Troy H. Middleton,* 129.

21. "Irregularities at L.S.U. Long Known to Leche," *Morning Advocate,* September 2, 1939; W. A. Cooper, supervisor of public funds, to Governor Richard Leche, September 28, 1938, Office of the President Records, Box 42, LSUA; "Many Changes Are Listed at L.S.U. by Auditing Firm," *Morning Advocate,* April 28, 1940; "Working Capital of $175,000 Looms at Close of Year," *Times-Picayune,* April 28, 1940; "L.S.U. Loan Is Given Approval by Lawmakers," *Daily Advertiser,* August 5, 1939.

22. "Long and LSU Board Draft Drastic Moves for University," *New Orleans Item,* July 11, 1939; "Richardson Rejects Post," *Shreveport Journal,* June 27, 1939; "Dr. P. M. Hebert, Law Dean, Picked for Smith's Job," *Times-Picayune,* June 28, 1939; "Middleton Takes Over LSU Post," *New Orleans Item,* June 30, 1939; "Better LSU Pledged by Dr. Hebert," *New Orleans Item,* August 3, 1939.

23. "19 on Staff at LSU File Protest," *New Orleans Item,* July 9, 1939; "'Resign,' Dutton Demands," *New Orleans Item,* July 18, 1939; "Reorganization Indicated for L.S.U. Board," *State-Times,* July 1, 1939; "University Board," *Times-Picayune,* July 13, 1939; "Candid and Logical," *Times-Picayune,* August 10, 1939; "Lake Charles Man Named to L.S.U. Board," *State-Times,* September 23, 1939; "Senator Peltier Quits as L.S.U. Board Member," *Times-Picayune,* September 23, 1939; "Give Us Right Men for the LSU Board," *New Orleans Item,* May 26, 1940.

24. "Football Junket Days Over, L.S.U. Assembly Told," *Times-Picayune,* October 11, 1939; "Student Aid at LSU Cut," *New Orleans Item,* July 26, 1939.

25. "$13,500,000 Spent in Nine Years at L.S.U.," *State-Times,* June 26, 1939; "Scandals Fail to Halt LSU March," *New Orleans Item,* August 23, 1939; "L.S.U. Enrollment Totals 7,796, Drop of 251 Students," *Morning Advocate,* October 10, 1939.

26. "Rose Long Elected Head of A.W.S.," *Reveille,* April 23, 1937; Mann, *Legacy to Power,* 50–52.

CONCLUSION: NEITHER SAINT NOR DEVIL

1. Thrash, "Financing Public Higher Education in Louisiana," 55–56.

2. "Some of the Morals," *New York Times,* September 11, 1935; Brinkley, *Voices of Protest,* 282. Brinkley delves deeply into the notion of Long as fascist and concludes the description is not valid. McManus, in "Sharing the Hate," explores that same question at length and concludes the term does not apply to Long's ideology. Peter H. Amann, "A 'Dog in the Nighttime' Problem: American Fascism in the 1930s," *History Teacher,* August 1986, 570.

3. Schlesinger, in Haas, ed., *The Age of the Longs,* 58; Williams, *Huey Long,* x.

4. Beals, *The Story of Huey P. Long,* 395.

5. Williams, T. Harry, "Huey Long in History," in Graham, ed., *Huey Long,* 139.

6. Harris, *The Kingfish*, 4, 159; V. O. Key, "Louisiana: The Seamy Side of Democracy," in Dethloff, ed., *Huey Long*, 62.

7. Glen Jeansonne, "Huey Long and Racism," in *The Louisiana Purchase Bicentennial Series in Louisiana History* 11: *The African American Experience in Louisiana*, Part C, Lafayette: Center for Louisiana Studies, 2002, 183–85.

8. J. B. Cade and Elsie L. Hebert, "Negro Higher and Professional Education in Louisiana," *Journal of Negro Education* 17, no. 3 (Summer 1948): 23; "Pearl and Lutrill Payne, African American Education Trailblazers since 1950," LSU College of Human Sciences & Education press release, December 18, 2015, www.lsu.edu/chse/news/pearllutrillpayne.php; Fairclough, *Race and Democracy*, 154–55.

9. "Julian White was LSU's First Black Faculty Member, and Now a Giant Mural Celebrates His Legacy," *Advocate*, September 4, 2020; "Expansion of Cafeteria to Provide Jobs," *Reveille*, June 22, 1934.

10. Campbell Gibson and Kay Jung, "Historical Census Statistics on Population Totals by Race, 1790 to 1990, and by Hispanic Origin, 1970 to 1990, for the United States, Regions, Divisions, and States," Population Division Working Paper, no. 56, U.S. Census Bureau, September 2002, www.census.gov/content/dam/Census/library/working-papers/2002/demo/POP-twps 0056.pdf; "Eighty-First Annual Report for the Session 1929–30," State Department of Education of Louisiana, *Bulletin* no. 186 (October 1930): 28–29; "Ninetieth Annual Report for the Session 1938–39," State Department of Education of Louisiana, *Bulletin* no. 432 (1940): 106.

11. "Eighty-First Annual Report for the Session 1929–30," State Department of Education of Louisiana, *Bulletin* no. 186 (October 1930): 28–29, 142–55; "Ninetieth Annual Report for the Session 1938–39," State Department of Education of Louisiana, *Bulletin* no. 432 (1940): 106, 230–36; Department of the Interior, Bureau of Education, *Educational Directory 1928, Bulletin* 1928, no. 1 (Washington, DC: US Government Printing Office, 1928), 361–94.

12. Glen Jeansonne, "Huey Long and the Historians," *History Teacher* 27, no. 2 (February 1994): 122; Sindler, *Huey Long's Louisiana*, 104; Mitchell, "Growth of State Control of Public Education in Louisiana," 437.

13. Blotner, *Robert Penn Warren*, 141; Warren, Robert Penn, "'All the King's Men': The Matrix of Experience," *Yale Review*, December 1963, 161–65.

BIBLIOGRAPHY

LIBRARIES, ARCHIVES, AND PRIVATE COLLECTIONS

Louisiana and Lower Mississippi Valley Collections, LSU Libraries, Louisiana State
    University Archives (LLMVC)
Louisiana Digital Library
Jack B. McGuire Personal Collection
Nina Carazo Snapp Personal Collection
Southern Association of Colleges and Secondary Schools Archives
Tulane University Health Sciences Center Rudolph Matas Library, History and
    Archives
Tulane University Special Collections

LOUISIANA NEWSPAPERS

Abbeville Meridional
The Advocate (Baton Rouge)
Alexandria Daily Town Talk
The Bayou Brief (New Orleans)
Bunkie Record
Caldwell Watchman (Columbia)
Clarion-Progress (Opelousas)
Clarion World (Opelousas)
The Comrade (Winnfield)
Crowley Daily Signal
Daily Advertiser (Lafayette)
Daily Advocate (Baton Rouge)
Daily State (Baton Rouge)
Daily World (Opelousas)

Monroe Morning World

Monroe News-Star

Morning Advocate (Baton Rouge)

New Orleans Item

Morning Tribune (New Orleans)

New Orleans States

Rayne Tribune

The Reveille (Baton Rouge)

Richland Beacon-News (Rayville)

Ruston Daily Leader

Ruston Leader

Shreveport Journal

Shreveport Times

St. Tammany Farmer (Covington)

State-Times (Baton Rouge)

Telegraph-Bulletin (Monroe)

Tiger Rag (Baton Rouge)

Times-Picayune (New Orleans)

Weekly News (Marksville)

Weekly Town Talk (Alexandria)

West Carroll Gazette (Oak Grove)

Winn Parish Enterprise (Winnfield)

OTHER NEWSPAPERS AND PERIODICALS

Asbury Park Press (NJ)

Atlanta Constitution

Austin American (TX)

Baltimore Sun

Bay City Times (MI)

Beaumont Journal (TX)

The Bee (Danville, VA)

Birmingham Post-Herald (AL)

Brooklyn Daily Eagle (NY)

Burlington Free Press (VT)

Charleston News and Courier (SC)

Chattanooga Daily Times (TN)

Chicago Daily News

Chicago Evening Post

Cincinnati Enquirer

Clarion-Ledger (Jackson, MS)

Daily Tar Heel (Chapel Hill, NC)

Dallas Morning News

Democrat and Chronicle (Rochester, NY)

Detroit Free Press

Evening Chronicle (DeKalb, IL)

Evening Independent (Massillon, OH)

Evening Post (Charleston, SC)

Evening Sun (Baltimore)

Evening Star (Washington, DC)

Fort Worth Star-Telegram

Greensboro Daily News (NC)

Greenville News (SC)

Greenwood Commonwealth (MS)

Houston Chronicle

Huntsville Times (AL)

Illinois Central Magazine (Chicago)

The Independent (Hawarden, IA)

Indian Journal (Eufaula, OK)

Indianapolis Star

Jacksonville Daily Journal (IL)

Jefferson City Post (MO)

Jersey Journal (Jersey City, NJ)

Knoxville Journal

Knoxville News-Sentinel

Leaf-Chronicle (Clarksville, TN)

Lexington Leader (KY)

Lincoln Star (NE)

Los Angeles Times

McComb Enterprise (MS)

Minneapolis Star

Morning Call (Paterson, NJ)

Nashville Banner

Nashville Tennessean

New York Times

News and Observer (Raleigh, NC)

News-Herald (Franklin, PA)

Northwest Oklahoman (Shattuck)

Omaha World-Herald

Orlando Evening Star

Palm Beach Post (FL)

Post-Crescent (Appleton, WI)

Rockford Republic (IL)
San Diego Union
Saturday Evening Post (New York)
Scribner's (New York)
Selma Times-Journal (AL)
Spalding's Foot Ball Guide (New York)
Spokesman-Review (Spokane, WA)
St. Louis Globe-Democrat
St. Louis Post-Dispatch
Standard-Speaker (Hazelton, PA)
Star-Gazette (Elmira, NY)
Student Outlook (New York)
The Tennessean (Nashville)
Time (New York)
Today (Dunellen, NJ)
Washington Post
Waterloo Press (IN)
Whittier News (CA)
Wilkes-Barre Times Leader (PA)
Wilmington Morning Star (NC)

INTERVIEWS

Note: Interviews by T. Harry Williams in the T. Harry Williams Papers, box 19, Louisiana and Lower Mississippi Valley Collections, LSU Libraries, are indicated by THWP.

Bowman, Sidney. February 20, 1961, THWP

Brooks, Cleanth. June 21, 1992, T. Harry Williams Center for Oral History, LSU Libraries

Buie, Jim. January 20, 1960, THWP

Butler, W. E. May 18, 1960, THWP

Carazo, Castro. March 26, 1961, THWP

Carazo, Castro. February 22, 1977, Junior League Oral History Project, East Baton Rouge Parish Library

Carriere, Oliver P. May 29 and September 19, 1961, THWP

Cawthon, Joe. May 5, 1960, THWP

Cohn, Isidore. June 18, 1963, THWP

Coleman, Elliott. January 21, 1960, THWP

Corbin, Carl. June 27, 1957, THWP

Davis, Charlotte Long. April 11, 1960, THWP

Dent, Fred. September 7, 1961, THWP

Digby, Fred. June 22, 1957, THWP

Dodd, William J. May 9, 1960, THWP

Doles, John, Sr. December 31, 1956, THWP

Doucet, D. J. "Cat." March 28, 1960, THWP

Dugas, Waldo. May 4, 1960, THWP

Dunbar, Charles E. July 18, 1957, THWP

Everett, Sara Flower (Mrs. George C.). March 23, 1960, THWP

Fields, Harvey. January 9, 1960, THWP

Fisher, Joe. July 10, 1957, THWP

Fournet, John B. July 4, 1957, THWP

Frampton, Chick. June 24, 1957, THWP

Frey, Fred. February 2, 1957, THWP

Frey, Fred. February 10, 1977, T. Harry Williams Center for Oral History, LLMVC

Gamble, Harry. July 12, 1957, THWP

Gottlieb, Lewis. July 23, 1963, THWP

Hawkins, Julia Welles. May 18, 2021, interviewed by Robert Mann

Hood, John. April 3, 1961, THWP

Hughes, H. Lester. March 18, 1960, THWP

Hunt, Lucille Long. April 11, 1960, THWP

Jones, Lawrence. December 28, 1961, THWP

Landry, Theophile. July 10, 1957, THWP

Larcade, W. V., July 29, 1958, THWP

Lautenschlaeger, Lester. July 9, 1957, THWP

Leche, Richard. January 30, 1960, THWP

Long, Kay. June 2, 2021, interviewed by Robert Mann

Long, Russell B. February 2 and August 8, 1989, interviewed by Robert Mann

Manetta, Manuel. July 1958, THWP

McGuire, David. July 11, 1957, THWP

McKeithen, John. 1982, T. Harry Williams Center for Oral History, LSU Libraries

Mickal, Abe. July 18, 1957, THWP

Middleton, Troy. September 28, 1961, THWP

Morse, Wayne. March 4, 1962, THWP

Nugent, Jesse. January 25, 1957, THWP

O'Connor, James. June 29, 1957, THWP

Pegues, W. C. January 29, 1957, THWP

Quaw, Gene. June 27, 1961, THWP

Rabenhorst, Harry. July 3, 1963, THWP

Roden, Murphy. September 25, 1961, THWP

Roy, E. P. March 20, 1961, THWP

Sanders, J. Y., Jr. November 6, 1959, THWP

Sehrt, Clem. 1957, THWP

Talbot, Edmund T. May 18, 1960, THWP

Taylor, Cecil. T. 1992, Harry Williams Center for Oral History, LSU Libraries
White, A. P. June 13, 1960, THWP
Wiegand, William. June 27, 1957, THWP
Williams, Louis. May 4, 1960, THWP
Womack, Byrne (Mrs. Frank). March 23, 1960, THWP

LSU PUBLICATIONS

Gumbo, digitalcommons.lsu.edu/gumbo/
The Louisiana Leader, Louisiana State University Archives
LSU Alumni News, Louisiana State University Archives
University Bulletin, Louisiana State University Archives

BOOKS, DISSERTATIONS, THESES, AND UNPUBLISHED MANUSCRIPTS

Bailey, Matthew. "Games That Will Pay: College Football and the Emergence of the Modern South." PhD diss., University of Mississippi, 2011.

Banta, Brady Michael. "The Regulation and Conservation of Petroleum Resources in Louisiana, 1901–1940." PhD diss., Louisiana State University, December 1981.

Beals, Carleton. *The Story of Huey P. Long.* Westport, CT: Greenwood Press, 1935.

Bledsoe V. L., and Richard, Oscar, eds. *Louisiana State University: A Pictorial Record of the First Hundred Years.* Baton Rouge: LSU Press, 1959.

Blotner, Joseph. *Robert Penn Warren: A Biography.* New York: Random House, 1997.

Boulard, Garry. *Huey Long Invades New Orleans: The Siege of a City, 1934–36.* New Orleans: Pelican Publishing, 1998.

Bowling, Lewis. *Wallace Wade: Championship Years at Alabama and Duke.* Durham, NC: Carolina Academic Press, 2010.

Braeman, John, et al., eds. *The New Deal: The State and Local Levels.* 2 vols. Columbus: Ohio State University Press, 1975.

Brinkley, Alan. *Voices of Protest: Huey Long, Father Coughlin, and the Great Depression.* New York: Vintage Books, 1983.

Brinkley, Douglas. *The Wilderness Warrior: Theodore Roosevelt and the Crusade for America.* New York: HarperCollins, 2009.

Carazo, Castro. "Huey Long: My Unforgettable Friend." Unpublished manuscript, 1982.

Carter, Hodding, ed. *The Past as Prelude: New Orleans, 1718–1968.* New Orleans: Pelican House, 1968.

[Carter, John Franklin] The Unofficial Observer. *American Messiah.* New York: Simon and Schuster, 1935.

Conrad, Glenn R., and Baker, Vaughn B., eds. *Louisiana Gothic: Recollections of the 1930s.* Lafayette: Center for Louisiana Studies, 1984.

Continé, Tom, and Phillips, Faye. *The Golden Band from Tigerland: A History of LSU's Marching Band*. Baton Rouge: LSU Press, 2016.

Cutrer, Thomas W. *Parnassus on the Mississippi: "The Southern Review" and the Baton Rouge Literary Community, 1935–1942*. Baton Rouge: LSU Press, 1984.

Dalrymple, W. H. *A Brief Sketch—Illustrated of the Louisiana State University and Agriculture and Mechanical School*. Baton Rouge: Louisiana State University, 1922.

Davis, Forrest. *Huey Long: A Candid Biography*. New York: Dodge Publishing Co., 1935.

Desmond, J. Michael. *The Architecture of LSU*. Baton Rouge: LSU Press, 2013.

Dethloff, Henry C., ed. *Huey P. Long: Southern Demagogue or American Democrat?* Boston: D. C. Heath and Co., 1967.

Dodd, William J. *Peapatch Politics: The Earl Long Era in Louisiana Politics*. Baton Rouge: Claitor's Publishing Division, 1991.

Doyle, Leo Andrew. "Causes Won, Not Lost: Football and Southern Culture, 1892–1983." PhD diss., Emory University, 1998.

Fairclough. Adam. *Race and Democracy: The Civil Rights Struggle in Louisiana, 1915–1972*. Athens: University of Georgia Press, 1995.

Farley, James. A. *Behind the Ballots: The Personal History of a Politician*. New York: Harcourt, Brace and Co., 1938.

Field, Betty Marie. "The Politics of the New Deal in Louisiana, 1933–1939." PhD diss., Tulane University, 1973.

Finney, Peter. *The Fighting Tigers: One Hundred Years of LSU Football*. Baton Rouge: LSU Press, 1993.

Flynn, Edward J. *You're the Boss*. New York: Viking Press, 1947.

Folsom, Robert G. *The Money Trail: How Elmer Irey and His T-Men Brought Down America's Criminal Elite*. Lincoln, NE: Potomac Books, 2010.

Frey, Fred. "Reminiscences of Fred C. Frey." Unpublished manuscript, 1975. Fred Frey Personal Papers, box 1, LLMVC.

Garay, Ronald. *The Manship School: A History of Journalism Education at LSU*. Baton Rouge: LSU Press, 2009.

Georgacopoulos, Christina A. "How 'Lyingnewspapers' Made Huey Long the Ruler of His State: A Model of Press-Populist Dynamics." MA thesis, Louisiana State University, 2021, digitalcommons.lsu.edu/gradschool_theses/5292.

Graham, Hugh Davis, ed. *Huey Long*. Englewood Cliffs, NJ: Prentice-Hall, 1970.

Haas, Edward F., ed. *The Age of the Longs: Louisiana, 1928–1960*. Lafayette: Center for Louisiana Studies, 2001.

Hair, William Ivy. *The Kingfish and His Realm: The Life and Times of Huey P. Long*. Baton Rouge: LSU Press, 1991.

Hargrave, W. Lee. *LSU Law: The Louisiana State University Law School from 1906 to 1977*. Baton Rouge: LSU Press, 2004.

Harrell, Kenneth Earl. "The Ku Klux Klan in Louisiana, 1920–1930." PhD diss., LSU, 1966.

Harris, Ronald. *We Hail Thee Now Southeastern: Remembering the First Seventy-five Years of Southeastern Louisiana University.* Hammond, LA: Southeastern Development Foundation, 2000.

Harris, T. H. *The Memoirs of T. H. Harris.* Baton Rouge: Louisiana State University, 1963.

Harris, Thomas O. *The Kingfish: Huey P. Long, Dictator.* Baton Rouge: Claitor's Publishing, 1968.

Hébert, F. Edward. *Last of the Titans: The Life and Times of Congressman F. Edward Hébert of Louisiana.* Lafayette: Center for Louisiana Studies, 1976.

Heilman, Robert Bechtold. *The Southern Connection.* Baton Rouge: LSU Press, 1991.

Hoffman, Paul E. *Louisiana State University and Agriculture and Mechanical College, 1860–1919: A History.* Baton Rouge: LSU Press, 2020.

Holeman, Bob. *Winn Parish.* Charleston, SC: Arcadia Publishing, 2011.

Ickes, Harold L. *The Secret Diary of Harold L. Ickes: The First Thousand Days, 1933–1936.* New York: Simon and Schuster, 1953.

Irey, Elmer L. *The Tax Dodgers: The Inside Story of the T-Man's War with America's Political and Underworld Hoodlums.* New York: Greenburg, 1948.

Jeansonne, Glen. *Messiah of the Masses: Huey P. Long and the Great Depression.* New York: Addison-Wesley Educational Publishers, 1993.

Juban, Angie Pitts. "Insiders: Louisiana Journalists Sallie Rhett Roman, Helen Grey Gilkison, Iris Turner Kelso." MA thesis, 2003, Louisiana State University.

Kane, Harnett T. *Louisiana Hayride: The American Rehearsal for Dictatorship, 1928–1940.* New York: Williams Morrow and Co., 1941.

Klein, Russell C., and Harkin, Victoria Barreto. *A History of LSU School of Medicine New Orleans.* New Orleans: LSU Medical Alumni Association, 2010.

Kurz, Michael L., and Morgan D. Peoples. *Earl K. Long: The Saga of Uncle Earl and Louisiana Politics.* Baton Rouge: LSU Press, 1990.

Lambert, F. A. *Football Officiating and Interpretation of the Rules.* Columbus, OH: R. G. Adams & Co., 1926.

Lawliss, Lucy, Caroline Loughlin, and Lauren Meier, eds. *The Master List of Design Projects of the Olmsted Firm, 1857–1979.* Washington, DC: National Association for Olmsted Parks, 2008.

Leighninger, Robert D., Jr. *Building Louisiana: The Legacy of the Public Works Administration.* Jackson: University Press of Mississippi, 2007.

Leuchtenburg, William E. *Franklin D. Roosevelt and the New Deal, 1932–1940.* New York: Harper & Row, 1963.

Long, Huey P. *Every Man a King: The Autobiography of Huey P. Long.* New Orleans: National Book Co., 1933.

MacCambridge, Michael, ed. *ESPN College Football Encyclopedia: The Complete History of the Game.* New York: ESPN Books, 2005.

Mann, Robert. *Legacy to Power: Senator Russell Long of Louisiana.* New York: Paragon House, 1992.

Martin, Michael S. *Russell Long: A Life in Politics*. Jackson: University Press of Mississippi, 2014.

Martin, Thomas. *Dynasty: The Longs of Louisiana*. New York: G. P. Putnam's Sons, 1960.

McLeod, Elizabeth. *The Original Amos 'n' Andy: Freeman Gosden, Charles Correll and the 1928–1943 Radio Serial*. Jefferson, NC: McFarland & Co., 2005.

McManus, Alex J. "Sharing the Hate: The Louisiana Establishment and Huey Long." PhD diss., Tulane University, 2016.

——. "When It Becomes Necessary to Spank the State Administration, I Can Do It: The Political Career of James A. Noe, 1932–1940." MA thesis, University of Louisiana at Monroe, 2005.

Mitchell, Guy C. "Growth of State Control of Public Education in Louisiana." PhD diss., University of Michigan, 1942.

Moley, Raymond. *27 Masters of Politics: In a Personal Perspective*. New York: Funk & Wagnalls, 1949.

——. *After Seven Years*. New York: Harper & Row, 1939.

Morgan, Chester M. *Redneck Liberal: Theodore G. Bilbo and the New Deal*. Baton Rouge: LSU Press, 1985.

Offner, Arnold A. *Hubert Humphrey: The Conscience of the Country*. New Haven, CT: Yale University Press, 2018.

Opotowsky, Stan. *The Longs of Louisiana*. New York: E. P. Dutton & Co., 1960.

Oriard, Michael. *King Football: Sport and Spectacle in the Golden Years of Radio and Newsreels, Movies and Magazines, the Weekly and Daily Press*. Chapel Hill: University of North Carolina Press, 2001.

Price, Frank James. *Troy H. Middleton: A Biography*. Baton Rouge: LSU Press, 1974.

Reed, Ed. *Requiem for a Kingfish*. Baton Rouge: Award Publications, 1986.

Ruffin, Thomas F. *Under Stately Oaks: A Pictorial History of LSU*. Baton Rouge: LSU Press, 2006.

Salvaggio, John. *New Orleans Charity Hospital: A Story of Physicians, Politics, and Poverty*. Baton Rouge: LSU Press, 1992.

Schlesinger, Arthur M., Jr. *The Crisis of the Old Order, 1919–1933*. Boston: Houghton Mifflin, 1957.

——. *The Politics of Upheaval, 1935–1936: The Age of Roosevelt*. Boston: Houghton Mifflin, 1960.

Schmidt, Raymond. *Shaping College Football: The Transformation of an American Sport, 1919–1930*. Syracuse, NY: Syracuse University Press, 2007.

Schott, Matthew James. "John M. Parker of Louisiana and the Varieties of American Progressivism." PhD diss., Vanderbilt University, 1969.

Silverman, Jerry. *New York Sings: 400 Years of the Empire State in Song*. Albany, NY: Excelsior Editions, 2009.

Sindler, Allan P. *Huey Long's Louisiana: State Politics, 1920–1952*. Baltimore: Johns Hopkins University Press, 1956.

Terkel, Studs. *Hard Times: An Oral History of the Great Depression.* New York: New Press, 2005.

Thrash, Edsel Earl. "Financing Public Higher Education in Louisiana." PhD diss., Louisiana State University, 1963.

Uhler, John Earle. *Cane Juice: A Story of Southern Louisiana.* New York: The Century Co., 1931.

Wall, Bennett H., et al. *Louisiana: A History.* 6th ed. Hoboken, NJ: Wiley-Blackwell, 2014.

Walsh, Christopher J. *Where Football Is King: A History of the SEC.* Lanham, MD: Taylor Trade Publishing, 2006.

Watterson, John Sayle. *College Football: History, Spectacle, Controversy.* Baltimore: Johns Hopkins University Press, 2000.

Wheeler, Burton. *Yankee from the West: The Candid, Turbulent Life Story of the Yankee-Born U.S. Senator from Montana.* London: Octagon Press, 1977.

White, Richard D., Jr. *Kingfish: The Reign of Huey P. Long.* New York: Random House, 2006.

Wilkerson, Marcus M. *Thomas Duckett Boyd: The Story of a Southern Educator.* Baton Rouge: LSU Press, 1935.

Williams, T. Harry. *Huey Long.* New York: Alfred A. Knopf, 1969.

Winchell, Mark Royden. *Cleanth Brooks and the Rise of Modern Criticism.* Charlottesville: University of Virginia Press, 1996.

Zinman, David. *The Day Huey Long Was Shot.* Lafayette: Center for Louisiana Studies, 1983.

INDEX

Note: Page numbers in *italics* refer to illustrations; those followed by "n" indicate endnotes; throughout the index, HPL refers to Huey P. Long.

Abraham, Cal, 197–99

academic freedom. *See* free speech and academic freedom

African Americans: anti-lynching law, federal, 266; first Black professor at LSU, 266; students, 25, 79, 147, 266–68; voters, 183, 266

Alexandria, LA, takeover of, 184

Allen, Frank, 190

Allen, Oscar K., *128;* about, 5; appointment of HPL to LSU Board, 166; building program and, 162; at ceremonies, 156; congressional election (1932) and, 159; death of, 247; federal relief funds and, 160; at football games, 136–37, 156, 170–71; Great Depression and, 128–29; as handpicked successor to HPL, 95, 107, 122–23, 127–28; Highway Commission and, 93; on HPL's death, 240; Kennedy case and, 151; loan to HPL, 13; New Orleans martial law, 184; power consolidation and, 236; signature forged by Smith, 256; Smith and, 71; Win or Lose Oil Corporation and, 253. *See also* O. K. Allen Hall (formerly Arts and Sciences Building)

Allied Associations of Southern Student Leaders and Editors, 231

Almokary, Joe, 43–44, 53, 66, 76

Alumni Hall, 163

Amann, Peter H., 264

Amato, Pasquale, 229

American Association of University Professors (AAUP), 197

American Bar Association, 223, 231

Ankeney, John Sites, 229

Arceneaux, James, 200

Arndt, Karl J. R., 229

Arts and Sciences Building (now O. K. Allen Hall), 147, 161–62, 195, 230

Association of American Law Schools (AALS), 230–31, 244–46

Atkinson, Thomas, *43;* appointed president, 41–42; campus plan and, 31; game ticket price revolt and, 54; Gartness Plantation and, 20; Long and, 37–38; office of, 1; resignation of, 70, 73; *Whangdoodle*/Kennedy case and, 59–60, 63–64

Auburn University, 74, 171

Audubon Sugar School, 17, 103

authoritarianism, 264

Bailey, B. W., 12

Bailey, Forrest, 105

Bailey, James J., 120

Baird, Pete, 171

Band, Regimental: about, 4, 110; Carazo as director of, 218–22; Guilbeau resignation, 2–6, 73; HPL's relationship with, 110–13; Jackson trip, 206; members at HPL's funeral, 242; Nashville trip, 173–80, *174, 176, 177;* parades, 4, 49–50, 112–13, 118–19, 121, 137, 140, 157, 180–81, 206; at Texas Centennial Exposition, 248; Wickboldt appointed director, 6

Barksdale, Eugene, 258

Barnhart, John D., 229

baseball, LSU, 48

Beals, Carleton, 85–86, 264–65

Bennett, Burns, 189

Bennett, W. T., 62

Beutel, Frederick K., 152, 246

Bienville Hotel scheme, 257, 258

Big Ten Editorial Association, 197

Bilbo, Theodore G., 3–4

Bird, Thomas, 238–39

Black colleges and universities, 25, 267–68

Black students, 25, 79, 147, 266–68

Black voters, 183, 266

Board of Education, 164, 165

Board of Pardons, 62, 151

Board of Supervisors, LSU: appointment of Hodges as president, 40–42; autonomy declaration, 244; Hebert appointed to, 259; HPL appointed to, 166; HPL as ex officio chair of, 37, 98, 165–66; HPL's control of, 55, 64, 71–72; mass resignation, 260–61; minutes, doctored, 252; Ransdell appointed to, 65; replacement of Atkinson with Smith, 70–73

bond debt, 148–49

Borné, Dan, xiii

Bouanchaud, Hewitt L., 30

Bowman, Sidney, 47, 114–18

Box, Alex, 250

Boyd, Annie Fuqua, 48

Boyd, Thomas D., xiv, 16–20, *32*

Bozeman, Harley, 8, 9, 12, 13, 71

Brescia, Emma, 269

Bridges, Burk A., 12–13

Brinkley, Alan, 264

Brooks, Cleanth, xiv, 167–69, 229, 231–32

Broussard, Edwin, 145, 153, 199

Broussard, James, 99–100, *116,* 125–26, 193–94, 196, 202, 230

Brumfield, Al, 228

Brunot, Harney, 24

Burden, Steele, 230

Burge, Pete, 157

Butler, W. E. "Billy," 77, 85, 99, 115, 117

Byrd High School, Shreveport, 9, 43

Cadet Corps trips, 171–72, *176–77,* 261

Caldwell, George, 162, 254, 256–58

cancer cure rumor, 225

Cane Juice (Uhler), 102–6

Carazo, Castro, 218–22, *219,* 236–37, 241–42

Carlton, Doyle E., 85

Carriere, Oliver "Ike," 31, 52–53, 79

Carriere, Theoda, 241

Carter, John Franklin, 114

Carville, James, xvi

Castellani, Aldo, 133

Cavalier Society, 63

Cawthon, Joe, 202, 208, *209,* 228, 241–42

Cayce, Frank, 191–92

Centenary College, 43–44, 140, 156, 199

Chandler, Walter "Teeter," 31

Charity Hospital, 87, 89, 149

"Choctaws" (anti-Long group), 65

Christenberry, Earle, 240

circus story, 155

Civil Works Administration (CWA), 163

Clark, Harry, 211

coeducation. *See under* women

Cohen, Henry Russell "Russ," *67;* 1930 season, 66–70; about, 44–47; attempt to dismiss, 73–78; contract renewal, 78; firing of, 121–22; HPL's interference and, 117–18; Jones and, 125; at LSU-Arkansas game, 49–50; practices and, 53; at Vanderbilt, 156

Cohn, Isidore, 88, 239

Colby, Leavenworth, 229

Coleman College, 267

Connally, Thomas, 153

Conner, Martin S. "Mike," 205–6, *207*

Constitutional League of Louisiana, 40, 52, 65

Continé, Tom, 220

Cooper, Olive Long (sister of HPL), 38

Corbin, Carl, 198, 255–56

cornpone and "potlikker" debate, 84–85

corruption allegations and investigations: Ewing papers attacks, 148–50; faculty survey on HPL's influence, 202–3; Law School investigations, 151, 223, 230–31, 244–46; mail fraud and federal charges, 257–58; Overton election (1932), 153; post-Long Smith/Leche schemes and prosecutions, 251–59; SACS investigations, 198–99, 223, 230, 244; state amendments election (1932) and, 153; tax evasion investigations, 160, 223–24

Costello, Harry, 233

Cowan, Thomas A., 229

Culpepper, A. M., 166

Currie, George, 215

Cutrer, Jesse, 187–89, 191–95, 197–99, 202, 208, 231

Cutrer, William, 192

Cyr, Paul, 65, 113, 119–20, 122–23

Dalrymple, W. H., 26–27

Daspit, Alex B., 229

Davis, Forrest, 53, 83, 251

Davis, Jimmie, xii

Day, Ben E., 208

Dean, William, 164

debating, 7–8

Digby, Fred, 66–67, 74, 77, 117, 157–58, 215–16

Dillard University (formerly New Orleans University), 267

Dinwiddie, A. B., 32, 76–77

Dodd, William, 165

Dodson, William R., 17, 31

Donahue, Mike, 30–31, 44

dormitories: F building, 146; funding and construction of, 161, 162, 226, 248; in Tiger Stadium, 129–31, 130, 248; women's, 90–91, 94, 129, 146, 147, 250, 259

Downs, M. E., 39

Doyle, Andrew, 46, 130

Dugas, Waldo, 164

Dymond, John, 23

Earley, John Joseph, 33

Edwards, Edwin, xii

Edwards, John Bel, xi

elections and campaigns: 1924 gubernatorial, 30; 1928 gubernatorial, 36; 1930 senatorial, 64–65, 84; 1932 congressional, 159–60; 1932 presidential, 137–40; 1934 congressional, 187; 1936 gubernatorial, 246; "election" of Mickal to state senate, 187–91; state constitutional amendments, 153, 183

Ellender, Allen, 248

Elliott, William Yandell, 232

Embree, Edwin P., 168, 169

English Department, 229

Enis, Ben, 44

Evans, Morton, 8

Everett, George, 71, 73, 95, 134

"Every Man a King" (campaign song), 222

Ewing, John, 148–50

Ezekiel, Mordecai, 144

Farley, James, 139–40, 144–45, 224, 227, 249–50

fascism, 264

Fatherree, Jesse, 189, 205, 214

"F building," 146

Federal Emergency Relief Act (FERA), 146, 160, 291n12

Fenner & Beane, 252

Fernandez, Claude, 59

Field House (Huey P. Long Field House), 94–95, 132, 133, 146, 262

Fields, Harvey G., 62

Finney, Peter, 116

Fisher, E. H., 164

Fisher, Joe, 223

Fisher, Jules, 223

Flory, Ira S., 151

Foley, Arthur, 115–17

Fontenot, Rufus W., 252–53
football games: Alabama, 49, 70; Arkansas
  (annual State Fair game), 30–31, 47, 49–50,
  53, 69–70, 156, 171; Auburn, 74, 171; Centenary, 140, 156; George Washington, 186;
  Georgia, 74; Louisiana Polytechnic, 66;
  Millsaps, 156; Mississippi State, 67, 74,
  114–15, 118, 183; Ole Miss, 70, 121, *177*, 182,
  205–7; Oregon, 140–41, 207, 213–14; Rice,
  137, 154–56, 244; Sewanee, 68, 140; South
  Carolina, 67, 117, 118, 156; Southern Methodist, 155, 170; Southwestern Industrial
  Institute, 66; Spring Hill College, 101, 116;
  Tennessee, 157, 182, 209–12; Texas Christian, 111, 114, 116, 136–37; Thanksgiving
  Day (1924), 35; Tulane, 35, 50–51, 53, 74–
  78, 121–22, 140, 157, *157*, 207–9, 234, 248,
  249; Vanderbilt, 156, 171–82, *177;* West
  Point, 112–13, 119–21
football program, LSU: Cohen as coach, 44–
  47; Costello as publicity hire, 233; end of
  "long jaunts," 261; funding increases, 78;
  Fuqua and, 48–49; HPL as creator of plays,
  117–18; HPL's behavior at games, 30–31,
  136; HPL's interest in, 82–83, 85–86, 114–
  15; HPL traveling with the team, 49–50,
  112, 119–21, 137, *138;* injuries, 67, 114–15,
  186; night games, lighting for, 101; practices, 44, 48, 53, 136–37, 234; recruitment
  of players, 43–44, 46, 53. *See also* Tiger
  Stadium; *and specific coaches and players
  by name*
Fournet, John B., 156, 170, 247
Frank, Glenn, 228
free speech and academic freedom: autonomy declarations, 244–45; HPL's
  non-meddling, 167; post-Long reforms,
  260–61; prohibition against public criticism of HPL, 167; *Reveille* censorship and
  the "Reveille Seven," 191–204, 231; Uhler
  case, 102–7. *See also* corruption allegations
  and investigations
French House, 161, 162, 230
Frey, Fred, xiv, 2–5, *3,* 39, 80–81, 99–100, 146,
  166, 236–37

Fuqua, Henry L., 29–30, 35, 45, 48–49, 80
Fuqua, James, 48

Gallagher, Wes, 195
Gamble, Harry, 84
Gartness Plantation, 20
Gassler, F. Leon, *32,* 102–6, 239
Gay, Edward, 31, *32*
George Washington University, 186
Gilkison, Helen, 187, 192–94, 239
Glass, Carter, 142, 143
Godbold, L. Rea, 198
Gormley, Francis Thomas "Tad," 73
Gottlieb, Lewis, 47, 52
"The Governor Long March" (song), 111
Grady, Henry W., 7
Grambling State University (formerly Loui-
  siana Negro Normal and Industrial Insti-
  tute), 267
Great Depression, 108–9, 128–29, 142–44,
  146
Green, Theodore Francis, 231
Gregory, Kenneth, 182
Grouchy, Alex, 20
Guilbeau, Frank T. "Pop," 2–6, 49–50, 73, 110

Hair, William Ivy, 109, 224
Hall, Jerome, 229
Hall, Luther, 42
Harris, Julian L., 84
Harris, Mary Elizabeth, 8–9
Harris, Thomas H., 8, 20, *32,* 42, 100, 268
Harris, Thomas O., 236
Hasselmans, Louis, 229
Hawkins, Julia Welles, 258
Headden, Damon, 179
Heard, Thomas "Skipper," xiii, 101, 115–16,
  116, 129, 215–16
Hébert, F. Edward, 253–54
Hebert, Paul, 99–100, 259–62, 299n23
Heilman, Robert B., 229, 237–38
Heilman, Ruth, 237–38
Herman, Dave, 241–42
Highland Hall, 162
High School Rally debating contest, 7–8

highway construction, 64, 109

Highway Department, 24–25, 91–94

Himes, Robert L. "Tighty," 1, 58, 60, 62, 150

Hodges, Campbell B., *40,* 40–42, 51, 165

Hodges, W. H. "Will," 40–41

Holcombe, Charles A., *32*

"Hold That Co-ed" (film), 221

Hood, John T., 110, 112, 121

Hoover, Herbert, 42, 160

Hope Estate Plantation, 230

Hopkins, Harry, 160, 248, *249*

Howse, Hilary, 180

Humphrey, Hubert H., 229

Hyneman, Charles S., 229

Ickes, Harold, 144–45, 224, 232–33, 248

impeachment, 38–39

Ireland, Gordon, 229

Irey, Elmer, 160, 224

Irwin, Emmett, 133

Jackson, Edgar N., 150, 192, 199, 255, 256–58

Jeansonne, Glen, 268

Jindal, Bobby, xi–xii

Johnson, Hugh, 144, 227

Johnston, Alva, 251

Jones, Lawrence "Biff," *210;* final game and
    resignation of, 213–15; hired as coach,
    124–26; HPL's noninterference and, 136–
    37, 181, 212; Law School investigation and,
    245–46; Mickal "election" and, 189–90; in
    Nashville, 206–7; press on, 157–58, 182

Jones, Llewellyn, 106–7

Jones, Sam, 2, 65

Journal of Southern History, 169

Kane, Harnett T., 86, 154, 170, 253–54

Keefe, William McG., 119, 172, 212

Kemp, Bolivar, 73, 187

Kemp, Lallie, 159–60

Kennedy, John N., xi, 82

Kennedy, Kemble K., *61;* corruption inves-
    tigations and, 223, 230–31, 245; criminal
    libel conviction, 62–63, 105; expulsion
    and refused diploma, 64; HPL and, 165,

184, 197; pardon, reinstatement, and spe-
    cial diploma, 151, 223; reporting to HPL
    on Tullis, 54–56; the *Whangdoodle* and,
    59–64, 102

Key, V. O., Jr., 80, 265

Khoury, Ed, 114–15, 189

King, Alvin O., 120, 123

Krock, Arthur, 161

Kron, Harry, 241–42

Ku Klux Klan, 49, 266

Landry, Theo S., 261

Lautenschlaeger, Lester, 117

Law Club, LSU, 54, 59–60

Law School, LSU: corruption investigations,
    151, 223, 230–31, 244–46; growth of, 229;
    Tullis as dean, 53–56; the *Whangdoodle*
    scandal and Kennedy, 57–60, 151, 223

Leake, William, 22–23, 87

LeBlanc, Dudley, 108–9

LeBreton, Edmond, 200

Leche, Richard, xiv, 99, 128, 240–41, 246–50,
    247, 253–58, 262

Leuchtenburg, William E., 83–84, 139

Link, Theodore C., 31–32, 275n12

loans to students, 173, 261

Lobdell, William, 187, 200

Long, Earl (brother of HPL), xii, 127–28, 247,
    253, 255, 258–59

Long, George (uncle of HPL), 12

Long, Huey P.: assassination of, xiv–xv,
    236–41; assault at Sands Point club, 153;
    as attorney, 12; childhood, youth, and edu-
    cation, 7–10; circus myth, 154–55; consoli-
    dation of absolute power, 235–36; defense
    of education agenda, 52; defense of inter-
    ference in LSU, 227–28; dictator image of,
    160, 182, 193, 203–4; early career, 10–12;
    funeral of, 241–42; hanged in effigy, 160;
    impeachment of, 38–39; "Kingfish" nick-
    name, 85; legacy and assessment of, 262,
    263–70; legislature, relationship with, 38–
    39; libel trial (1921), 23–24; national prom-
    inence, 83–84; NBC radio address, 226–27;
    personality of, 52–53; presidential cam-

Long, Huey P. (*continued*)
paign, expected, 174, 178; press coverage and, 82–83; on Railroad Commission, 12–14; songs composed with Carazo, 221–22; as traveling salesman, 10–12; in US Senate, 126, 140–44, 224. *See also specific topics, such as* elections and campaigns
—photos of: with Allen, *128;* with band in Houston, *138;* with Gov. Conner, *207;* with Jones, *210;* at LSU-Tulane game, *157;* Nashville trip, *175–77;* with Smith, *72;* in Tiger Stadium, *69;* as traveling salesman, *11*
Long, Julius (brother of HPL), 12, 39
Long, Katherine (granddaughter of HPL), 222
Long, Pamela (granddaughter of HPL), 222
Long, Rose (daughter of HPL), 161, 262
Long, Rose McConnell (wife of HPL), 10–12, 120–21, 134, 178, 240
Long, Russell B. "Bucky" (son of HPL), xvi, 50, 134, *135,* 152, 178, 229, 231, 243, 262
Lorio, Cecil, 239
Lorio, Clarence, 137, 186, 239, 245, 257–58
Louisiana Negro Normal and Industrial Institute (now Grambling State University), 267
Louisiana Polytechnic Institute, 66, 268
Louisiana State Agricultural Federation, 17
Louisiana State Bar Association, 151, 184. *See also* State Bar of Louisiana
Louisiana State Normal College (now Northwestern State University), 165, 268
LSU (Louisiana State University): 75th anniversary ceremonies, 227; audit and Hebert–Middleton reforms, 259–62; Audubon Sugar School, 17, 103; budgets, 80–81, 149, 264, 267; building programs and construction, 90–93, 100–101, 129–31, 146–47, 161–63, 226, 230, 248, 263; campus design and opening ceremony, 31–34, *32, 33;* College of Agriculture, 17; criticism of finances of, 148–49; death of HPL, impact of, 244–50; enrollment numbers, 80, 131, 146–47, 161–62, 226, 242, 250, 261, 275n30;

faculty expansion, 167–69, 229; faculty survey on HPL's influence, 202–3; founding of, 17; HPL bragging about, 148, 164–65; HPL's defense of interference in, 227–28; Northeast Center, 163–64; old campus in north Baton Rouge, *18,* 19, 38, 74, 91–94, 163; Parker's "Greater Agricultural College" expansion, 16–20, 25–30; post-Long scandals and corruption, 251–59; reputation of, 98, 168–69, 190, 215, 231–32, 261, 266; School of Journalism, 195–99; School of Library Science, 100; School of Music, 166, 229; Soldiers' and Sailors' Memorial Tower ("Campanile"), 34; student costs, 81; tension between academics and athletics, xii–xiii; US Army, relationship with, 17. *See also* Band, Regimental; Board of Supervisors, LSU; football program, LSU; Law School, LSU; Medical School/Medical Center, LSU
LSU Alumni Association of North Louisiana, 41
LSU Alumni Federation, 94, 96
LSU Board of Supervisors. *See* Board of Supervisors, LSU

MacArthur, Douglas, 125–26, 139
Maes, Urban, 133
Maestri, Robert, 5
Martin, Frank, 201
Martinez, Harry, 66–67
McCann, M. G., 69
McClendon, Charles, xii
McCracken, Harlan L., 229
McGugin, Dan, 45–46, 117, 122, 180, 216, 240
McGugin, Lucy Ann, 221
McGuire, David, 96, 192, 194, 197, 202, 255–56, 299n23
McKeithen, John, xii
McKevlin, Anthony J., 181
McLachlan, James, 254
Medical School/Medical Center, LSU: cancer cure rumor, 225; construction of, 93; graduate Schools of Medicine and of Nursing, 226; HPL's boasts about, 148; HPL's

control of, 133; opening of, 96, 129; planning for, 86–89, 91; schools of dentistry and pharmacy, 163, 225–26, 232–33

Meehan, Chick, 216

Messina, Joe, 50, 180, 189

Mickal, Ibrahim Khalil "Abe," 118, 157, 181, 185–91, *188*, 205–9, 212, 214, 217, 241

Middleton, Troy, *104, 177;* band directors and, 4–6, 220; on impact of HPL, 96; Jones and, 124–25; as president, 100; recollections of, 95, 166, 171; reforms by, 260–62; on *Reveille* affair, 202; *Reveille* censorship incident and, 197–98

Mikulak, "Mighty" Mike, 141

Miles, Les, xi–xii

Millsaps College, 156

Mississippi State University, 67, 74, 114–15, 118, 183

Moley, Raymond, 152

Montague, Sam, 195, 198, 200–201

Moody, Dan, 224

Moore, Bernie, 136, 216–18, *217,* 234, 242

Morgenthau, Henry, Jr., 160

Morrison, James H., 254

Morse, Wayne, 152, 165, 245

Murphy, Bob, 158

Music and Dramatic Arts (Fine Arts) Building, 91, *92,* 94, 133, 146, 163

Nashville trip with Cadet Corps and band, 171–82, *174–77*

National Association of Deans and Advisers of Men, 226

National Guard, 184, 236

National Guard Band, 241–42

NBC radio address, 226–27

New Orleans, HPL's conflict with, 183–84, 236

New Orleans University (now Dillard University), 267

Neyland, Robert, 124

Noe, James A., 163, 240, 247–48, 253–54, 258

Norman, Duyane R., 191–92

Northeast Center of LSU (now the University of Louisiana at Monroe), 163–64

Northwestern State University (formerly Louisiana State Normal College), 165, 268

Nugent, J. M. "Jess," 93

O. K. Allen Hall (formerly Arts and Sciences Building), 147, 161–62, 195, 230

Ober, Granville, 1–2

Ochsner, Alton, 87

O'Connor, James, 241

Odom, John Fred, 63, 239

Old Regulars, 236

Olmsted, Frederick Law, Jr., 26, 31

Opotowsky, Stan, 251

Orgeron, Ed, xi

Ouachita Parish Junior College, 163–64

Overton, John H., 145, 148, 153

Palmer, John, 167

Parker, Cecile, 35

Parker, John M., *18, 32;* at campus dedication, 33; Coliseum named after, 250; compared to HPL, 268–69; conflict between HPL and, 21–24, 52, 65; federal patronage and, 144; "Greater Agricultural College" expansion of LSU, 16–20, 25–30; Harris and, 42; highway construction, 21–22, 109; Hodges on, 41; modest ambitions for LSU, 79–80; at Thanksgiving Day football game, 35; at Weiss's funeral, 239

patronage appointments, federal, 144–45, 160

Pavy, Benjamin, 238

Pearson, Drew, 254–55

Pegler, Westbrook, 210–12

Peltier, Harvey, 73, 190

Percy, Elena Carter, 131, *131*

Phillips, Faye, 220

Phillips, H. I., 182

Pipkin, Charles, 168–69, 231–32

Pleasant, Ruffin, 14–15, 19–21, 35. *See also* Ruffin G. Pleasant Hall (formerly Smith Hall)

Political Science (Government) Department, 229

Porterie, Gaston, 184

Prescott, Arthur, 80–81
press freedom. *See* free speech and academic freedom
Public Works Administration (PWA), 232–33, 248

Quaw, Gene, 163, 221

Rabenhorst, Harry, 44, *45,* 47, 53, 114, 117, 136, 233
race, 266–68
Railroad Commission, 12–14, 21
Ransdell, Joseph E., 64–65
Reconstruction Finance Corporation (RFC), 162
Red River bridge ceremony, 156
Reeves, Dobie, 68
Regimental Band, LSU. *See* Band, Regimental
Reveille, 199; Carazo and, 220; end of censorship of, 260–61; on football, 78; Mickal incident, censorship, and the "Reveille Seven," 187, 191–204, 231; on student jobs, 81; Uhler and, 102, 107; on the *Whangdoodle,* 58–59
Reynolds, Hal, 216
Rice University, 137, 154–56, 244
Richardson, E. S., 259
riding school, 134
Ringling Brothers, Barnum & Bailey Circus, 155
Robinson, E. B., 164
Robinson, Joe, 143
Robinson, W. C., 9
Roden, Murphy, 255
Rogge, John, 257–58
Roosevelt, Eleanor (wife of Franklin), 248–49
Roosevelt, Eleanor (wife of Ted), 35
Roosevelt, Franklin D., 42, 84–85, 137–40, 142–45, 160–61, 199, 224, 232, 246, 248–50
Roosevelt, Theodore, 16, 19, 21
Roosevelt, Theodore "Ted," III, 35
Roy, Victor L., 39, 165

Ruffin G. Pleasant Hall (formerly Smith Hall), 90–91, 94, 129, 146, *147,* 259

Salvaggio, John, 87
Sanders, Jared "J. Y.," 48, 144–45
Sanders, Jared Y., Jr., 159–60, 187, 239
Sanderson, E. L., 240
Sands Point Country Club, 153
Sanson, Jerry P., 79
Schlesinger, Arthur M., Jr., 84, 264
scholarships, 71–73, 81, 112, 201
school funding in Louisiana, 79–80, 109. *See also* Black students
School of Journalism, 195–99
School of Library Science, 100
School of Music, 166, 229
Schott, Matthew J., 26, 282n2
Scott, Charlie, 179
secession, talk of, 185
Senate, US: corruption hearings, 153; HPL in, 126, 140–44, 224; HPL's 1930 run for, 64–65; Russell Long in, 152
Sewanee, 68, 140
Sexton, George, 43–44
Share Our Wealth plan, 161, 226, 232
Shaughnessy, Clark, 216
Sherman, William Tecumseh, 17
"Shine On, Harvest Moon" (song), 112, 136, 137, 156, 174, 179, 206
Shlosman, Stanley, 198
Simons, Monk, 208
Sindler, Allan P., 65, 259, 268
Smith, Al, 50
Smith, James B., 54–55, 59
Smith, James Monroe, *72, 175;* on AALS report, 246; appointed president, 70–73; autonomy declaration, 244; brass choir and, 166; building program, 90–93, 100–101; at ceremonies, 156; Cohen and, 78, 122; corruption and, 149, 251–59; effectiveness and reputation of, 99–100; Great Depression and, 108, 128–29; on growth, 146–47; hanged in effigy, 200; HPL, relationship with, 96–99; inauguration of, 100; "Biff" Jones and, 124–26; Jones resignation and,

215, 216; Kennedy case and, 151; lasting accomplishments of, 265; Medical School and, 226; name erased from buildings, 259, 262; PWA and, 232–33; resignation and arrest of, 255; *Reveille* censorship affair, 192–202; sentencing and suicide attempt, 258; stadium construction and, 130–31; Uhler firing and, 105–7; West Point trip and, 120–21

Smith, Jimmie, 134

Smith, Thelma, 133–34, 251, 255–57

Smith, Tom, 68

Smith Hall (women's dormitory, now Ruffin G. Pleasant Hall), 90–91, 94, 129, 146, *147,* 259

Socialist Party of America, 203, 232

Sopkin, Stefan, 229

Southeastern Louisiana College (now Southeastern Louisiana University), 164

Southern Association of Colleges and Secondary Schools (SACS), 198–99, 223, 230, 244

Southern Historical Association, 169

Southern Methodist University, 155, 170

Southern Review, 169, 231–32

Southern/Southeastern Conference, 34, 66, 122, 141, 190, 194, 218

Southern University, 25, 267

Southwestern Industrial Institute (SLI, now University of Louisiana at Lafayette), 42, 66, 70

Spencer, Mason, 235

Spencer, W. I., 70, 74–75, 118, 121, 182, 208, 214–15

Spring Hill College, 101, 116

Square Deal Association women's auxiliary, 235

Standard Oil of Louisiana, 14–15, 21–24, 38–39, 184–85

Stanley, Eugene, 236

State Bar of Louisiana, 184, 223. *See also* Louisiana State Bar Association

State Board of Education, 39, 42–43

Stephens, Edwin L., 42

Stoke, Harold, xiii

Stopher, Henry, 163

Stovall, Jerry, xii

Stovall, J. J., 61

Stovall, Lloyd, 186

Straight College, 267

Strenzke, King A., 58

Stubbs, Frank, 21

student center construction, 73–74

Student Council, LSU, 54, 200

student jobs, 81, 261

Student Outlook, 203

Sullivan, Walter, 205

Swing, Raymond Gram, 228–29

Sylvest, Murphy J., 149–50

taxes: 1933 plan, 154; poll tax, 183, 266; severance taxes, 21–22, 25, 38

Tax Reform Commission, 154

Texas Centennial Exposition, 248

Texas Christian University, 111, 114, 116, 136–37

Theta Nu Epsilon (TNE), 57–58, 60–63, 133

Thomas, Frank, 216

Thomas, Norman, 232

Thompson, Marvin, 211

Tiger Stadium: construction and opening of, 34–36; expansion and dormitories, 129–31, *130,* 163, 248; Long and referees in, *69;* night-game lighting and stadium expansions, 101

Tiner, Stanley, xiii

Tison, W. W., 39, 165

Touchdown Club of New York, 211

"Tribute to Senator Huey P. Long" (*Gumbo*), 228

Truman, Harry, 258

Tulane University: football games, 35, 50–51, 53, 74–78, 121–22, 140, 157, *157,* 207–9, 234, 248, *249;* Julius Long at, 12; School of Medicine, 86–88; Theta Nu journalism fraternity, 199

Tullis, Robert Lee, 53–56, *55,* 58, 62, 149, 151, 165, 223, 239, 245

Tureaud, A. P., Jr., *147,* 266

Uhler, John Earle, 59, 61, 102–7, *104*, 149, 165, 256
uniforms, band and football, 110–11
University Graduate Club, 167
University of Alabama, 44–46
University of Arkansas, 30–31, 47, 49–50, 53, 69–70, 156, 171
University of Georgia, 74
University of Louisiana at Lafayette (formerly Southwestern Industrial Institute), 42, 66, 70
University of Louisiana at Monroe (formerly Northeast Center of LSU), 163–64
University of Mississippi, 3–4, 70, 121, *177*, 182, 205–7
University of Missouri School of Journalism, 201–2
University of Oklahoma, 10
University of Oregon, 140–41, 207, 213–14
University of South Carolina, 67, 117, 118, 156
University of Tennessee, 157, 182, 209–12
University of Virginia, 201–2
US Military Academy, West Point, 112–13, 119–21

Vanderbilt University, 156, 171–82, *177*
Vidrine, Arthur, 87, *88*, 89, 225, 239

Wade, Wallace, 44–47, 70
Walker, Ed, 207
Walmsley, T. Semmes, 145, 183–84, 236
Warren, Robert Penn, xiv, 168–69, 229, 231–32, 269–70
Watterson, John Sayle, 46
WDSU radio station, 225
Weiss, Carl Austin, xv, 237–40
Weiss, Seymour, 223, 240, 257–58

Weiss, Yvonne Pavy, 238
Western Conference College Editors, 197
West Point US Military Academy, 112–13, 119–21
Whangdoodle broadsheet, 57–64, 102
Wharton, Don, 79, 98, 250
Wheatley, Ralph, 203
White, H. H., 164
White, Julian T., 266
White, Richard D., Jr., 38
Wickboldt, Alfred W., 6, 111–12, 121, 173–74, *176*, 178, 180, 220
Wilkerson, Marcus, 194
Wilkinson, Horace, 20
Williams, Louis "Lew," 111, 137
Williams, T. Harry, xiii–xiv, 10, 12, 16, 23–24, 37, 52, 70–71, 80, 82, 85, 98–99, 111, 119, 139, 167, 184, 202, 222, 236, 239, 264–65
Williamson, Grace, 192–93, 198
Wilson, Harry D., 160
Wilson, Riley J., 40
Winnfield High School, 9
Win or Lose Oil Corporation, 224, 253
women: coeducation, 32, 98–99; debate on women's suffrage, 8; Highland Hall, 162
women's dormitories, 90–91, 94, 129, 146, *147*, 250
Woodin, William, 144
Works Progress Administration (WPA), 248–49, 250, 254, 257

Xavier College, 267

Yates, Bert, 118
Young, Roy O., 41–42

Zimmerman, Don, 53, 76, 281n22